ORGANIZATIONAL CHANGE AND DEVELOPMENT

We work with leading authors to develop
the strongest educational materials in business,
bringing cutting-edge thinking and best learning
practice to a global market.

Under a range of well-known imprints, including
Financial Times Prentice Hall, we craft high-quality
print and electronic publications which help
readers to understand and apply their content,
whether studying or at work.

To find out more about the complete range of our
publishing please visit us on the World Wide Web at:
www.pearsoneduc.com

ORGANIZATIONAL CHANGE AND DEVELOPMENT

A Reflective Guide for Managers, Trainers and Developers

BOB HAMLIN · JANE KEEP · KEN ASH

FINANCIAL TIMES
Prentice Hall

An imprint of Pearson Education

Harlow, England · London · New York · Reading, Massachusetts · San Francisco · Toronto · Don Mills, Ontario · Sydney
Tokyo · Singapore · Hong Kong · Seoul · Taipei · Cape Town · Madrid · Mexico City · Amsterdam · Munich · Paris · Milan

Pearson Education Ltd

Edinburgh Gate
Harlow
Essex CM20 2JE
England

and Associated Companies around the World.

Visit us on the World Wide Web at:
www.pearsoneduc.com

_____

First published 2001

ISBN 0–273–63886–6

British Library Cataloguing-in-Publication Data
A catalogue record for this book can be obtained from the British Library

Library of Congress Cataloging-in-Publication Data
Organizational change and development : a reflective guide for managers, trainers and
developers / Bob Hamlin, Jane Keep, Ken Ash, [editors].
     p. cm.
   Includes bibliographical references (p.) and index.
   ISBN 0-273-63886-6 (alk. paper)
    1. Organizational change. 2. Personnel management. 3. Management. I. Hamlin, Bob.
II. Keep, Jane. III. Ash, Ken.

   HD58.8 .O72896 2000
   658.4'06- -dc21

                                                                00-057293

10 9 8 7 6 5 4 3 2 1
05 04 03 02 01 00

Typeset by 30
Produced by Pearson Education Malaysia Sdn Bhd,
Printed in Malaysia, KVP

Contents

Preface

The multi-dimensional process required to bring about sustained change is too often oversimplified to cope with the complexity.

However, as I reminded my co-editors during our many meetings leading to the publication of this book, I am a 'simple man'. By that, I mean I understand and act upon problems and situations through simple processes. Throughout the preparation of this publication we have tried to 'get to grips with' and be mindful of the paradox, complexity and simplicity that concerns itself with 'change'.

Even the term used to describe and identify the contributors' work had to be clarified (simplified). If we had expressed their work as 'case studies', this could be misinterpreted that there was an amount of work for the reader to do with the text. It was thought that in the context of this type of publication one can usually expect to use such 'case studies' as a means of 'in-depth' analysis. As you read through the book you will find that this is not the purpose of this publication.

A more suitable and appropriate heading for the contributors' writings has been used and it is that of 'Reflections on Practice'. The reasoning behind this heading is that most of our contributors have 'reflected on practice' in small to medium-sized organizations, subsidiaries and business units, as well as in large conglomerates and multinationals. This in itself reflects the reality of the employment situation of most practising managers, trainers and developers. The main emphasis and tone of the book is high on 'insights' gained from reflective practice and low on 'prescriptions'.

It should also be made clear at this point that the 'reflections on practice' are personal views expressed by the contributors and that the reader may have taken a different view of the same situation. Also, that each published reflection is a personal sense-making exercise which then allows you, the reader, to make of it 'what you will'.

'Those who cannot remember the past are condemned to repeat it' (funnily enough, I can't remember who said that). One of the primary aims of this book is to focus on the lessons learned from change management practitioners with whom readers can relate by way of the organizational settings, cited in the reflections, being similar to their own.

As will be further explained in the coming chapters, this book was put together by the co-editors largely because of their dissatisfaction with the available advice on change implementation, as well as the fact that there is scarce literature on approaches to evaluating the effectiveness of change.

It is all well and good having people with vision (which could be another word for theory), which invariably requires some degree of change to take place. But without the skill and expertise of the practitioner to put that vision/theory into practice effectively, the 'organization' can lose sight of the reasons and focus for the change, thus the whole initiative falls into disrepute and is seen as a failure.

I believe as we enter the new millennium that a good many organizations may have too many 'visionaries' (theorists) and too few 'finishers' (practitioners). This book sets out to recognize the contribution that managers, trainers and developers can make towards the successful and beneficial management of change through reflection and honest critical review.

Ken Ash

Contributors

Ken Ash MSc, Dip.TM, MIPD, MiMgt is a personnel and training development manager for a global organization with over 2500 employees. His involvement with people development started in 1985, when he was a full-time quality circle co-ordinator. Since 1994 he has been in the forefront of his company's challenge to 'unlock' the potential of its employees, with particular focus on team development and the management of change. Acting as an 'internal consultant' he has promoted the services of HRD with the objective of integrating them more fully into the mainstream management of the business.

A graduate in human resource development with a production/manufacturing background, he has progressed to successfully take charge of a training and development role in this large, well-respected organization.

His 15 years experience has helped him guide a multi-site, market leader company to improve continuously through progressive HR policies. He is a great advocate of the approach that HR should be at the formulation of business decisions rather than just at the implementation stage.

Fiona Katherine Campbell BSc Ph.D is a researcher in the Management Resource Centre at the University of Wolverhampton Business School. She is engaged in both research and consultancy projects looking at organizational change, downsizing and managerial effectiveness. She recently completed her doctorate in human resources management through Bristol University, looking specifically at the implications of redundancy on those remaining in an organization, the survivors.

Prudence A. Clarke MSc has continuously developed her company, Prudence Clarke Resource, during the past eight years, supporting its ever-growing national and international client base, focusing upon people during ongoing organizational change.

The company philosophy is based upon promoting all aspects of 'best' employment practices, inextricably linking the client's business strategy with the needs of the employee. Her company's particular success is in developing training and development programmes, researching and matching appropriate training consultants to encompass clients' business and individual needs, in much the same way as matching people to organizations during recruitment assignments.

Professor Cary Cooper is the world's foremost authority on occupational and workplace stress. He has published extensively on organizational psychology and management and achieved a pre-eminent role in both the American and British Academies of Management. Currently he is a BUPA Professor of Organizational Psychology and Health at the Manchester School of Management at UMIST, where he is also pro-vice chancellor of the university. Additionally, he is a visiting professor at three UK universities and is a Fellow of the Royal Society of Arts, the Royal Society of Medicine and the Royal Society of Health.

Gron Davies BSc (Hons), MEd, MSc, PhD, C Psychol is a chartered psychologist who is a product of the ERSC Conversion Fellowship Scheme, through which he developed his consulting skills in organizational change. He has had extensive experience of teaching psychology and organizational behaviour to undergraduates and postgraduates, though currently his teaching as a principal lecturer in the Wolverhampton Business School is mainly concerned with research skills and strategic leadership skills development for MBA students. His main research interest relates to cross-cultural management issues, with particular reference to forced organizational change in Britain and Eastern Europe.

Jaap Germans Dr. Ir is an independent consultant who works mainly in the Netherlands and Germany as an OCD specialist helping both public and private sector organizations manage complex organizational change and development programmes. Until recently, he has been working concurrently as Director of Studies of the Masters in Learning and Development programme at the TIAS Business School, which is attached to the University of Tilburg, and as a visiting professor at several other Dutch universities. Additionally Jaap is on the supervisory boards of a number of large household-name organizations in the Netherlands. Prior to becoming an independent consultant, he spent 25 years with Phillips Industries in a variety of senior management roles, including that of head of internal training and consultancy. Jaap obtained his doctoral degree in organizational theory and social psychology from the University of Tilburg.

Nadine Green MIPD, Dip.TM, BSc, MSc works as a consultant and lecturer in management and organizational development. She teaches on a number of postgraduate courses at Leicester De Montfort University and the Institute of Healthcare Management. Her professional background includes a number of personnel, training and organizational development roles in the National Health Service. She is now consulting to both public and private sector organizations, is undertaking doctoral research into action learning as a model for managerial development and working towards chartered status as an occupational psychologist.

Peter A Grice MCs is the general manager of the Man-made Fibres Training Trust and a co-director of a training and development consultancy. He has worked during the last ten years within the man-made fibres sector on organizational change programmes, linked to competence-based learning and development, and in recent times with companies implementing 'high-performance work' models. He also advises national training organizations in the process, manufacturing and scientific sectors on strategy implementation and infrastructure issues.

Bob Hamlin BSc (Hons), MPhil, FIPD, MIMgt is a principal lecturer at the University of Wolverhampton Business School currently responsible for its HR programmes, including the MSc in human resource development, for which he is the course director. Prior to joining WBS in 1984 he spent over 20 years in the chemicals, plastics and engineering industries as a senior manager and professional trainer. As a business academic his teaching has been focused mainly on management and organization development and trainer training. He is research-active in the field of managerial and leadership effectiveness, management behavioural competencies and management culture change within both private and public sector organizations. The results of his research have been published widely. Additionally he is active as a management and training consultant working mainly with local companies but also internationally. For over nine years he was a divisional manager within WBS, responsible for the HR subject area. He is external examiner at London Guildhall University for the MA in Human Strategies degrees, and is on the Advisory Board of Human Resource Development International.

Alf Hatton BA (Hons), DMS, MBA, MSc, MPhil, MIPD, AIMC, MHSM, MTS, FMA, Certified NLP practitioner is an independent management consultant. His consultancy work specializes in change management, strategic reviews and strategy building, as well as the more usual business planning, feasibility studies, and organizational and management development projects with (among other public, voluntary and non-profit organizations) a wide range of museum and heritage attractions.

Jane Hatton MSc, Dip.TM, Dip. Business Excellence, FIPD has 12 years experience in the public sector, in roles including service delivery, management and staff development. Since 1990, she has worked as an independent human resource development consultant, specializing in management development and equality. Her company, People Working in Partnership, has a wide range of clients from public, private and voluntary sectors. Her main interest is helping organizations harness and maximize the diverse talents of their people.

Jane Keep MPhil, MSc, FIPD, MiMgt has 20 years experience of working in and around the NHS, including extensive work as a senior OD and change practitioner. This has included leading on organizational change projects as an internal and external consultant, and working as a national HR policy adviser within the NHS.

During the last five years she has coupled this with teaching, writing and researching in OD, HR and change as a Fellow at the Health Services Management Centre, University of Birmingham, nationally and internationally.

Her specialist interests include developing evidence and reflective-based change and OD practice, ethical and moral OD and change within the public sector, and evaluating organizational change, using for example action research as a continuous cycle of evaluation.

Nick Kemp MSc, Dip.TM, MIPD is a consultant in organizational change and development, specializing in strategic HR leadership and management development and HR consultancy. Initially focusing on training and development, he has managed a number of significant cultural and operational changes in HRD in a major high street financial services organization. He is currently working on developing a holistic, integrated HR framework and a model that delivers a closer alignment between performance management and measures of business performance.

Julie Knowles MSc has ten years management and HR experience in both the public and private sector. She consults widely on quality issues and change management and is currently a lecturer working in further and higher education.

Chris Luty MSc, MIPD is a specialist in the areas of vocational management and trainer development. Working for the Training Suppliers Network, he provides consultancy support for a variety of large and small service sector and manufacturing sector organizations. Having completed an MSc at the University of Wolverhampton, he is now undertaking extended PhD research, examining the differing approaches to vocational management development compared with traditional academic techniques. He has published several papers giving a practitioner's perspective of current trends in vocational management development.

Vince McGregor BA, DPA, MSc, MIPD has over 20 years experience in learning and development in both the public and private sectors. He has spoken at conferences on the use of learning and development in cutting down stress at work and also Investors in People and its contribution to business.

Vince is currently employed by the Civil and Aerostructures arm of British Aerospace as a learning and development adviser. This involves influencing a budget of over £2 million, ensuring it meets the personal and organizational needs of the 2000 people employed in this area of the business. His role also includes ensuring that actions reflect the corporate learning and development strategy.

Peter Mayes MSc, MIPD is a consultant who specializes in enabling organizations to implement change in a way that develops the potential of people. He has operated as both an internal and an independent consultant for a variety of manufacturing and service organizations, drawing upon his prior experience as a senior functional manager in production and design disciplines. His work and interests are mainly in the action learning and strategic team development.

Margaret A. Reidy Dip. Fine Art is a research officer with HM Customs & Excise. She was brought up in Ireland and moved to Suffolk shortly after graduating from art college in Waterford. She is currently studying for her MPhil/PhD with Nottingham Trent University. Her longitudinal research has focused on organizational culture and behaviour and strategic change. She has co-written articles with Bob Hamlin and Jim Stewart for journals such as *Journal of Applied Management Studies*, *Strategic Change*, *Human Resource Development International* and *Management Development Forum* and has also co-presented their joint research findings at several prestigious conferences in the UK and Ireland. In conjunction with Bob and Jim she is currently engaged in further research on organizational behaviour and change looking at self-analytical/self-assessment tools which utilize the findings of their research to date.

Peter A. Shields is a graduate of University College Dublin and the University of Leicester. He is currently studying for an MSc in human resource development at the University of Wolverhampton. He is the HR director with a multinational pharmaceutical company in Ireland. Earlier career experience was in university teaching, management consultancy and commercial management in the brewing industry.

Graham Smith MSc, MIPD is a local government training and development manager. He has a wide range of HRD experience in both the public and private sector. In recent years he has specialized in organizational development aimed at achieving quality improvements in service delivery.

His specialist research interest is in the field of organizational behaviour analysis at the time of change.

Alison Thomas PGCE, MA has been a freelance journalist since she left teaching in 1995. The scope of her work is broad and she has written for a diverse range of publications, including national broadsheets. Her specialist fields are education and business, and she is a regular contributor to the *Times Educational Supplement* and *Training* (sister publication of *Personnel Today*). Her work includes features in the business sections of the *Herald* (formerly *Glasgow Herald*) and *The Sunday Times*, as well as an article on trading overseas for *Director* and two chapters in the 1998 *Director Publications' Guide to Understanding Global Business*.

Paul Turner PhD, BA (Hons), FIPD is the group HR business director for Lloyds TSB. During his ten years with the Lloyds TSB Group, Paul has held a number of HR directorships and is a member of the group HR executive.

Paul is a member of the CBI's Education and Training Affairs Committee and is a visiting professor at Nottingham Business School. He has published articles in books and international journals and has spoken at conferences in the United States and Europe.

Before working at Lloyds TSB, Paul held a variety of career roles, including that of a director of British Telecom and general manager at Plessey, as well as a period in Hong Kong as the regional manager responsible for Plessey's Far East operations.

Professor Les Worrall BA (Hons), MCD, PhD, MRTPI, FSS, FRSA has degrees from the University of Hull (BA Hons) and from the University of Liverpool (MCD and PhD). He is a Fellow of the Royal Statistical Society and was elected a Fellow of the Royal Society of Arts in 1997. He was also elected as a council member for the British Academy of Management in 1999.

Professor Worrall is currently associate dean (research and consultancy) at Wolverhampton Business School and is also a senior research fellow in the Manchester School of Management at UMIST.

He is co-researcher, with Professor Cary Cooper, of the Quality of Working Life Project funded by the Post Office in conjunction with the Institute of Management and the Manchester School of Management at UMIST. This five-year project, running from 1997 to 2002, is examining the changing nature of managerial work and the dimensions and impact of organizational change in the UK.

Acknowledgements

We would like to acknowledge the main sources of inspiration for this book, who are the MSc students in human resource development (HRD) at the University of Wolverhampton, as without their insights and struggles to close the theory–practice gap throughout the past few years we would not have seen the benefit of reflective practice for organizational change and development (OCD). We particularly thank those who have contributed their own 'reflections on practice' for providing honest and insightful sound bites, and their organizations for letting us include their names to ensure the reality around each case.

There are many other people who have helped inform and inspire this book, from the many organizational change and development theorists in universities around the globe (many of whom are quoted in the text of the following chapters), to practitioners whom the editors have had the privilege of working with during our organizational change and development and human resource development consultancy projects. Specifically, we should like to thank Gron Davies, Alf Hatton, Les Worrall, Cary Cooper and Fiona Campbell for their valuable contributions.

We would also like to thank each other, the helpful folk at Pearson Education, and our friends and families through what has been a learning process for us all.

Ken Ash, Jane Keep and Bob Hamlin

The publishers wish to thank the following for permission to reproduce the material:

The Times and *Financial Times* for use of their headlines in connection with the Lloyds TSB merger in 1995 and *The Independent* for the extract from Hamish McRae's report of 12th October 1995.

Figure 9.5 from Higgins, James M. and Vincze, Julian W., *Strategic Management: Text and Cases, Fifth Edition* (1992) The Dryden Press.

Table 3.1 from Johnson, 'Managing strategic change: the role of symbolic action', *British Journal of Management*, V1 (1990) 1 Table (British Academy of Management, Blackwell Publishers).

ORGANIZATIONAL CHANGE AND DEVELOPMENT PRACTICE IN CONTEXT

Introduction

1

Ken Ash, Bob Hamlin and Jane Keep

HOW THIS BOOK CAME INTO BEING

The first seeds of an idea for this book were germinated independently by the three of us at different times and in different ways. Our meeting of minds came about through serendipity when we were brought together by chance through the MSc in human resource development programme at the University of Wolverhampton, UK. It was there that we decided to join forces to co-author and co-edit a book on organizational change and development. Between us we have over 80 years experience as practising managers, trainers, developers and business academics. Each of us at various times of our careers has been an internal and/or external change agent working with, for or through colleague line managers or top organizational leaders of both private and public sector organizations. In these roles and in our own respective ways we have made significant and at times pivotal contributions towards the better understanding and resolution of managerial problems and dilemmas concerned with effecting beneficial organizational change and improving organizational performance. From our collective observations and experiences it is our view that organizational leaders who direct and manage business enterprises and public organizations in today's world are facing an unprecedented set of demands and dilemmas relating to the management of change. Yet many managers and organizations are ill-equipped for the task. This can be inferred from the high proportion of organizational change and development programmes that fail to deliver the intended benefits expected but instead end up with the accrual of unintended and undesired damaging consequences.

For one of us, currently a business academic in the University of Wolverhampton Business School, the idea of writing a book such as this arose through various discussions with successive cohorts of managers, trainers and developers attending the university's MSc in human resource development programme, for which he is the Director of Studies. In various ways these students had expressed degrees of dissatisfaction with much of the British and American literature on change management.

Their concerns were mainly two-fold. First, the literature appeared to be focused predominantly on big businesses, global enterprises and large-scale organizations, with few case study examples drawn from organizational settings similar to their own. Second, most books on the subject appeared to be written by internationally renowned experts such as leading-edge consultants, top-flight business academics and management gurus whose professional and practical experiences were far removed from their own and who, therefore, were difficult to relate to. In particular there appeared to be few evaluation studies of long-term change initiatives, and certainly very few discussions based on candid, personal reflections on personal experiences. While undoubtedly these students had benefited from reading the rich source of received wisdom contained in the wide array of literature, they felt they wanted additional guidance from examples of change agency practice carried out by change agents more like themselves – in other words, experienced practitioners who had grappled with the same sort of key issues and critical factors associated with bringing about beneficial change in organizations of comparable size and complexity, and with whom they could identify readily.

A second co-author of this chapter has worked most of his life in manufacturing industry, and for him the first tentative ideas for the book arose out of his personal experience as a Training Facilitator operating in the role of internal change agent while studying for his MSc in HRD at the University of Wolverhampton in 1996 and 1997. At that time he was in particular need of support and guidance for an organizational change programme involving the introduction of team-working. Being a proponent of research-informed professional practice in the field of HRM and HRD, he initiated a programme of internal research designed to help inform and shape the required change initiatives.

However, his ongoing, comprehensive and painstaking review of the available literature proved to be both frustrating and disappointing. This was due to a number of reasons. One of these was centred on the fact that the majority of publications concerning change, in particular those concerning team-working, were based on large American companies. The citations of success were just as difficult to ignore, because they seemed far removed from his own company's experiences in the UK. More often than not, the organizations featured in the literature were multinational giants such as AT&T and Federal Express. In practical terms, the strategy, planning, operational problems and solutions revealed and discussed by the respective authors appeared to bear little relevance or help to a privately owned, small to medium-sized manufacturing company located in England.

Although the wide array of literature dealing with the key issues of implementing team-working included, for example, 'how teams work' and 'how they are different', and emphasized such things as 'the four stages of building strong teams' through to 'the development of a training plan', they failed to answer in a satisfactory way his questions concerning the particular change process he was engaged with in his organization. There seemed to be no guidance on how to ascertain the knowledge required to determine in departmental terms whether a team approach was right or not.

In one well-known book the authors, when discussing the broad issues of team-working, suggested to readers that they should 'determine if the organisation's vision (mission) and values are sufficiently clear and compatible to enable empowered teams to operate', but then (in parentheses) they added the non-helpful, non-committal afterthought that '(if not, appropriate actions must be taken)'. They gave no further advice or guidance as to what those actions might be. Nor was this crucial piece of sought-after help forthcoming from the other management literature that he could find. It appeared that most authors failed to answer the critical question of 'how does an organization actually move towards successfully implementing teams and team-working in the sure knowledge that the operatives (the front-line employees) are able to work in the prescribed systems?' Many omitted to mention that embedding team-working so as to comply or fit in with an organizational mission is not enough to prevent resistance to or eventual failure of the organizational change programme. Hence he had to find this out for himself the hard way, at times agonizingly so.

What he had been looking for in the literature was a clearly identified relationship between the problems he encountered and possible ways of arriving at 'solutions' that would work. In particular, he wanted access to 'tools' that he could realistically use to facilitate the process of team-building and team-working within his own particular organizational setting. In reality, what he actually encountered were principles and theories that appeared sound but, in practical terms, were no more than very broad pointers to the 'do's and don'ts'.

The third co-author of this introductory chapter has worked as both an internal and an external OCD practitioner/change agent in public sector organizations for 20 years. During the latter five years as a portfolio worker, she has combined these roles with that of being a part-time public policy (NHS) academic in the Health Services Management Centre of a 'red-brick' university in the UK. While working in this dual role, it became apparent that the 'theory–practice' gap was wide. She found straddling the two roles to be difficult. Moreover, it was even more apparent that both academics and practitioners were fairly isolated in their respective worlds of work, even though they were often dealing with the same problems and tackling the same issues. It was from frustration with the lack of recognition and importance being placed on the need for practitioners to become research/evidence-based in their practice, to develop theory through their own research and professional practice, and the opportunity to do so, that her first ideas for this book emerged. To her, reflective practice seemed to draw the two worlds closer together. It seemed to have the power and potential for learning to take place between the practitioner and academic using each other's media for disseminating and sharing insights. Reflective practice appeared to be of paramount importance for learning and growth. As change is about learning and growth, the two seemed to go hand in hand.

With the increase in technological change, and more and more evidence available at the fingertips of practitioners, she felt it is becoming increasingly important to use available evidence from empirical research to inform practice. Equally, evaluation as a continuous process within this enables new and emerging theory to be built, current theory to be evaluated, and learning from the outset to be greater. Thus, for her, reflective change management practice forms an important part of this evaluative loop.

As a result of us meeting and sharing our respective tentative ideas we jointly perceived a potential market niche for a book on organizational change management, but one with a difference. As you will find, our book has been written primarily 'by practitioners for practitioners'. It attempts to demonstrate 'best practice' and the 'value of applying theory and research as part of everyday change agency practice' through examples drawn from the candid and insightful reflections and perspectives of a diverse range of seasoned reflective change practitioners.

THE AIMS OF THIS BOOK

Organizational Change and Development: A Reflective Guide for Managers, Trainers and Developers is an attempt to fill the perceived gap in the literature on change management as discussed in the foregoing. We hope it will help readers to appreciate more fully the complexities of bringing about organizational change and development, not least the cultural factors in the change process, and the value of using theory and rigorous internal research in a very conscious and focused way to inform, shape and measure their own change agency practice. Hence the main theme of the book is concerned with the process issues of change as experienced and reflected upon by a wide range of practising managers, trainers and developers.

Its specific aim is to bring to the attention of readers practical insights and perspectives on 'what helps or hinders' the effectiveness of organizational change and development programmes. A further aim is to illustrate an array of successful, and in some cases not so successful, organizational change initiatives drawn from a wide cross-section of organizational settings from which lessons can be learned. Additionally, we hope to identify the extent to which theoretical perspectives have helped to inform practice, but also where reflective research-informed practice has shed light on possible new theory. In particular, we hope you will glean from the various cases the thought and decision-making processes the change practitioners went through, and thereby gain further insight.

As you will by now have inferred, the book is predominantly a reflective and practical guide based around a series of 'reflections on practice' written by practitioners for other practitioners. However, in each case, the contributors of these reflective pieces have been invited to draw attention to the 'theory and model' they used specifically to inform, shape or measure the formulation and implementation of their change strategies, the lessons they learned from reflecting on their own change agency practice, and the insights gained (if any) concerning emergent 'new theory' arising from their practice.

Our aim has been to draw the attention of readers to lessons that can be learned from 'reflective' practitioners similar to themselves, practitioners whose organizational settings are similar to those of their own and with whom most can relate and identify with readily. As explained in the Introduction to Part III of the book, the 'lessons' are focused on a series of questions concerning the particular processes of change actually carried out by the respective change agents/reflective practitioners.

These 'reflections on practice' are encapsulated in a number of ways, ranging from 'cameos' and 'caselettes' of minor change initiatives, through to substantial 'case history' expositions of major transformational change programmes that have been successfully implemented to a greater or lesser extent. They have been drawn from a wide range of organizational settings spanning the private, public, voluntary and not-for-profit sectors. It is our hope that there will be something here of particular relevance and direct interest to all readers.

WHO THIS BOOK IS FOR

The primary audience for this book is two-fold, namely senior and middle managers who have particular responsibilities for project-managing organizational change programmes within their own organizational settings, and professional HRD practitioners, OD consultants, trainers and developers who operate as either internal or external change agents as part of their regular professional practice. In addition, the book is for directors and all other managers and HR professionals who have an interest in or involvement with the process issues of managing organizational change and development. In the realization of the editors' wishes to produce a practical source of relevant guidance written for and by reflective practitioners similar to themselves, they hope it will be a useful addition to the literature base.

THE STRUCTURE OF THE BOOK

As stated in the foregoing, the overriding purpose of the book is to help you enhance your change agency practice in the field of organizational change and development. To this end it has been our intention for it to have both a practical and an academic focus. Some of you will relate more to one aspect than the other, depending upon your current needs and tasks. Hence we have endeavoured to offer readers valuable insights from the personal reflections not only of managers, trainers and developers but also of business academics.

Part I of the book is aimed primarily at providing a 'foundation' of underpinning knowledge and understanding and a 'theoretical anchor' for the 'practical focus' of Part II and the 'reflections on practice' revealed in Part III. The aim of Part IV has been to draw things together by reflecting upon the 'reflections on practice', highlighting where 'generalized insights' appear to have emerged from the 'practice' of our respective contributors, and by giving some pointers for 'moving practice forward' into the 21st century.

AN OUTLINE OF THE CHAPTERS

Chapters 2, 3 and 4 have been written from an 'academic' perspective by business academics. Chapter 2 provides a 'theoretical introduction' to the book through a review and synthesis of the current context and practice of organizational change and development as revealed in British, European and American management literature. The author makes the case for managers, trainers and developers to become more 'expert' as change agents. The chapter provides a rationale for all of the following chapters.

Chapter 3 is also 'theoretically' focused. It provides a critical overview of the espoused 'best practice' approaches to organizational change and development as paraded in the management literature base, draws attention to some of the latest insights about successful change management based on more recent practice, and discusses the increasing complexities of modern-day organizational life, which challenge the role of the change agent.

Chapter 4 is 'research' focused, reporting as it does on the findings of the UMIST–Institute of Management baseline research study into the impact of the substantial changes that have taken place in most UK private and public sector organizations in recent years, and the effects on the 'quality of working life' of corporate Britain. This pathological perspective on organizational change provides valuable insights into how change is being managed in the UK, and highlights issues which give considerable cause for concern.

The content of these three chapters should provide readers who have studied or are studying for academic qualifications in management or HR-related subjects a useful reminder and reinforcement of their 'learning of theory' in the area of organizational change and development. For those readers who are practising managers but have no formal academic or professional qualifications, it will provide them with a valuable overview of relevant 'theory and practice' and a useful source of reference when reading the other parts of the book. Additionally, it provides pointers to a range of management literature that they might also wish to access.

As already mentioned, the two chapters comprising Part II have a predominantly 'practical' focus. They have been written by two seasoned practitioners who between them have gained a wealth of experience as change agents during their past careers as senior line managers/executives and developers in public sector organizations, and recently as independent OCD consultants. Based upon in-depth reflections on their own professional practice, including both their successes and failures, they each provide a distinctive insight into the realities of 'as it is' change agency in practice 'on the ground'.

Chapter 5 is based mainly on the personal perspectives of the author derived partly from her knowledge and understanding of the literature but also from the many dilemmas and challenges she has experienced as a senior-level change agent from both the inside and outside of a number of major organizations, particularly in the health sector.

Chapter 6, in contrast, is a piece of reflective writing on what the author calls the 'complexity–clarity paradox' confronting managers, trainers and developers when acting as change agents. The author has held senior executive positions in a variety of organizations, notably in the heritage sector, has worked as an independent consultant and is currently director of the Hunterian Museum and Art Gallery, University of Glasgow. The chapter focuses on his own ideas of how best change agents might 'get to grips' with the 'paradox' described.

Part III comprises Chapters 7, 8, 9 and 10, which are aimed at providing additional insights into effective and ineffective change agency in practice as told through the personal stories of practising managers, trainers and developers reflecting critically on the things that have gone well for them and things that have gone not so well or even badly. These stories, which can be viewed as critical studies of organizational change and development programmes, will, we hope, provide knowledge and insights that readers can use to inform their own professional practice as change agents. They are similar in purpose to what Professor Tony Watson (1999) refers to as 'negotiated narratives' in the field of 'critical management education and learning'. He argues that such stories, which 'tell the story behind the story', can be among the most powerful and effective means through which managers learn deeply about the actual realities of managerial work and how best to act within their own organizational settings.

For our purposes we have chosen to refer to these stories or narratives as critical 'reflections on practice', which is in keeping with the over-arching theme of the book. These 'reflections on practice' are intended to give you the opportunity to benefit from the learning of other managers, trainers and developers who have reflected deeply on their own observations and practical experiences of managing and facilitating organizational change and development, either in their own or in host organizations. As already mentioned, we have chosen a wide range of organizational settings from very small to very large, drawn from all sectors including two from other countries, so that you can find some 'reflections on practice' that are particularly relevant and helpful to you in your unique organizational environment. The 'reflections' have been allocated to one of each of the four chapters and focus on a particular theme of organizational change and development, namely 'transformational and cultural change', 'quality initiatives', 'OD processes' and 'training and development'. These chapters are preceded by a short introduction including an explanation of a common structure that the various contributors of the 'reflections on practice' were invited to follow. It is our hope that the rich and diverse range of 'reflections' will provoke thought and discussion, and cause readers to want to reflect deeply and critically upon their own change agency in practice, as well as gain fresh insights.

Part IV comprises three chapters, which are aimed at 'pulling things together' and providing pointers for the future. Chapter 11 focuses on the 'theoretical' implications and considerations arising out of the earlier parts of the book. It concentrates upon a critical review of 'theories in practice' as revealed through the perspectives and reflections contained in the preceding chapters, and draws attention to where 'practice has clearly challenged or informed theory'. Additionally, an academic commentary is provided which highlights the even greater beneficial outcomes that could be accrued through the further application of what the research content in some of the reflective pieces tells us. Particular discussion is given to the problems of scientific, cause–effect, rational–linear and 'quick-fix' models of change management as evidenced in the chapters in Parts I and II. Furthermore, the author offers and discusses a conceptual framework that illustrates the linkage between 'relevant, robust and rigorous internal research' and 'organizational change consultancy', and the processes of 'bridging the research–practice gap' to enhance the effectiveness of change agency practice. These ideas, concepts and arguments are supported not only by the recent calls for more research and evidence-based practice in the field of management and organization development as reported in British and American management literature but also by the various lessons that have emerged from the 'reflections on practice' of the various contributors to this book. The chapter closes with a number of speculations about the future direction of 'theory and practice' in the field of managing and facilitating organizational change and development, and the implications for managers, trainers and developers including those who educate, train and develop them.

In contrast, Chapter 12 is wholly 'practitioner' focused. The authors pull together the various threads of learning, insight and guidance to be gained from the book regarding 'how to bring about organizational change effectively and beneficially'. They do this in summary form from the particular perspective and practical standpoint of practitioners.

Chapter 13, which is the final chapter, comprises a number of reflections and conclusions that do not naturally fit elsewhere, plus a few closing comments from the editors.

HOW TO USE THE BOOK

The book is written with a progressive logic. It starts with a range of contextual and theoretical perspectives, critical arguments and research findings as contributed by business academics, which act as a platform of underpinning knowledge to enable readers to more fully understand and appreciate the personal perspectives, in-depth general reflections and specific 'reflections on practice' of practitioners that make up the chapters in Part II and Part III. The chapters in Part IV offer even further insights into the process issues of change management by way of the authors reflecting on the various 'perspectives' and 'reflections' in the earlier chapters. One implication of this logical structure is that it is sensible for you to start at the beginning and read through to the end of the book. However, that approach may not necessarily be your preference, as you may wish to dip into particular sections of the book in a different sequence. This is perfectly possible, as each section in terms of the respective parts and chapters of the book is reasonably self-contained and can be read in isolation.

References

Watson, T.J. (1999) Beyond Managism: Negotiated Narratives and Critical Management Education in Practice. Paper for the First International Conference on Critical Management Studies, University of Manchester, 14–16 July 1999.

A review and synthesis of context and practice

2

Bob Hamlin

INTRODUCTION

For the past decade or so, organizations both large and small, whether in the private, public or voluntary sectors, have been subjected to enormous environmental pressures and forces of change, which have led to major transformations in organizational structures and the contexts in which management has had to operate and succeed. Such changes are increasing in frequency, pace, complexity and turbulence, and there appears to be no sign of abatement. Hence one of the major challenges facing managers and also trainers and developers is how to help people through the transitions of change, and how to survive in working environments that are in a constant state of flux. As will be discussed later in the chapter, all too often organizational change programmes fail because management fails to rise to the challenge which change brings. However, for organizations that do manage change effectively, change itself becomes the driving force that perpetuates future success and growth. In these organizations, every change becomes welcomed as an opportunity for increasing efficiency and for building new organizational success.

With the above in mind, the purpose of this chapter is first to draw your attention to the drivers of change currently impacting upon organizations, then to discuss the reasons why so many organizational change and development programmes fail, and finally to highlight the implications for managers, trainers and developers in their role as change agents. It is hoped this will provide you with an increased understanding of the rationale for the subsequent chapters of the book.

CURRENT ORGANIZATIONAL TRENDS OF CHANGE

Based on a study of leading-edge European industrial organizations, Barnham *et al.* (1988) reveal how corporate environments have become more growth- and customer-oriented, faster-moving and increasingly international, and how these trends demand greater responsibility, initiative and leadership from managers at all levels of the organization.

More recently, Champy and Nohria (1996) in the USA claim that the three major drivers stirring organizational change faster than ever before are as follows:

1 *Technology*: particularly IT, which is transforming businesses in dramatic ways.
2 *Government*: rethinking its role in business, with all governments on a worldwide basis initiating deregulation, privatization and increasing free trade.
3 *Globalization*: where companies from all parts of the globe are competing to deliver the same product or service, anytime, anywhere at increasingly competitive prices, which is causing organizations and companies to organize themselves in radically different ways.

Drawing on a wide range of management literature, but also upon his own extensive experience of consulting and facilitating management development for organizations worldwide, Hussey (1996) identifies 'competition', 'more demanding customers', 'accelerating pace of technological obsolescence' and 'pressure to deliver shareholder value' as the major long-running forces of change.

Based on a series of studies conducted with managers, trainers and developers attending postgraduate management programmes over the past six years, the author's own findings at grass-roots level in both private and public sector organizations support the findings of the above commentators, as illustrated in Table 2.1.

Table 2.1 Comparison of the trends of change perceived and felt at grass-roots level in private and public sector organizations in the UK

Private Sector Organizations	Public Sector Organizations
Increased flexibility and multi-skilling the workforce	Flexible working patterns and shifting of skills/professional boundaries
Focus on quality and value for money	Focus and drive on quality
Flatter structures	Flatter structures
Decentralization	Devolution
Increased competition	Compulsory competitive tendering/best value
Mergers and acquisitions	Unification and amalgamations
Downsizing	Downsizing
Greater customer orientation	Emphasis on 'customer' care
Globalization of businesses, the economy and society	EU influences on shifting populations Greater mobility and transferability of skills
More contracting out of functions	Privatization of services
Increasing impact of IT and other technological advances	Rapid advancement in the application of information technology
Greater diversity in gender and ethnicity and fair and ethical practice	Increasing emphasis in equal opportunities
More periphery, temporary and home workers	More short-time and part-time contracts
Citizens' Charter initiative	Patients' Charter initiative
Increased stress at work	Increased stress at work

From the comparison, it is evident that most of the forces stirring change in private sector organizations are the same as, or similar to, those impacting upon organizations in the public sector. Inevitably these trends of change are changing the characteristics of both business enterprises and public bodies.

According to Champy and Nohria (1996), the business organization of the future, 'twisted into a new shape by fierce global competition, changing markets and technological breakthroughs, is emerging with distinct characteristics. It will be:

- information-based,
- decentralized, yet densely linked through technology,
- rapidly adaptable and extremely agile,
- creative and collaborative, with a team-based structure,
- staffed by a wide variety of knowledge workers, and
- self-controlling,

which is possible only in an environment of clear, strong and shared operating principles and of real trust'. It will also become 'a fluid network where connections form and reform almost organically, like the branches of the human nervous system. There will be authority and some hierarchy, but the archaic organisational shape – the pyramid – will be gone for ever'.

The implications for management are profound, particularly regarding the way people will need to be managed in these 'fluid' organizations. Barnham *et al.* (1988) argue that managers should let go of the 'command and control' styles of management typically associated with traditional hierarchy and bureaucratic structures. Instead they need, for example, to be more sensitive to the external forces and influences; to give more attention to lateral as opposed to vertical relationships; to exercise leadership that mobilizes and energizes others; to be more committed to achieving high performance; to be more forward-looking and more prepared to anticipate, initiate and respond to change. Furthermore, they need the awareness and abilities to harness IT effectively, to relate to the external economic, social and political environment, and to manage in the complex organizational structures and fluid networks as predicted by Champy and Nohria.

The need for these managerial skills and abilities has been further demonstrated by the author of this chapter through his research into managerial effectiveness in various UK organizations (see, for example, Hamlin 1990, Hamlin and Reidy 1997). Of particular note from this research is the fact that 'managing change and innovation' featured strongly as one of the identified criteria of managerial effectiveness in each of the organizations studied. Interestingly, Yeung *et al.* (1996) identify 'the capacity to facilitate and implement change' as one of three critical competencies required of senior HR generalists.

THE FAILURE OF ORGANIZATIONAL CHANGE AND DEVELOPMENT PROGRAMMES

It is of crucial importance to all that have a stake in the success of an organization, not least the workforce, that organizational change and development processes are managed effectively and beneficially. Hussey (1996) claims 'organizational success depends on the soundness of the strategic decisions taken by management, and the ability of the organization to implement these'. As he rightly warns, 'an organization can sink from having a poor strategy' and also sink 'if (even with a good strategy) it does not implement strategy effectively'. The management literature reports many examples of managerial failure in both the formulation and implementation of strategy, particularly strategies involving significant organizational change and development. Evidence suggests that the majority of 'downsizing' and 'delayering' exercises are unsuccessful. Few ever achieve the aimed-for goals of increased competitiveness and profitability, and many end up with lower profit margins and poorer returns on assets and equity than are achieved by equivalent firms that have not downsized (see Howard 1996; Wyatt & Co. 1994; de Meuse *et al.* 1994; Hussey 1997).

A majority of TQM and BPR programmes are purported to fail. For example, Schaffer and Thompson (1992), who surveyed 300 electronics companies in the USA, found that of the 229 reported as having implemented some form of TQM programme, 63 per cent failed to yield improvements in quality and only 10 per cent of these programmes were successful. This finding is supported by Hammer and Champney (1993), who reveal the failure rate of BPR initiatives in the United States to be in the region of 50–70 per cent. With regard to TQM strategies, Kearney (1994) reports they have not produced the benefits claimed, and according to Hamel and Prahalad (1994) this situation also applies to BPR programmes.

The picture is much the same in Europe. Although over two-thirds of the top 500 companies in Britain have introduced TQM, only 8 per cent of managers (in these companies) believe it has been successful (Wilkinson *et al.* 1993). Most BPR initiatives undertaken by European companies have been shown to be process simplification exercises rather than re-engineering (Coulson-Thomas 1996), while in the UK there is real uncertainty as to whether organizations reporting BPR activity really do apply BPR principles (Hussey 1997). Hussey considers it unlikely that BPR success rates in Britain are any higher than those reported for the USA, a view supported by the findings of Nelson and Coxhead (1997). Of the companies they surveyed only 10 per cent achieved major breakthroughs from applying BPR principles, and they estimate that over 50 per cent of BPR change initiatives fail to achieve the results intended. With regard to culture change, research by the Industrial Relations Service (IRS 1997) suggests that as many as 80 per cent of this type of organizational change programme fails. A similar failure rate is also reported for IT-related change. According to a study conducted by OASIG in 1996, 80–90 per cent of investments in new IT fails to meet their performance goals (see Holland and Aitken 1999).

It is the case that many organizational change initiatives fail badly, with unintended and damaging consequences. Although recognizing that organizations have to change and restructure in order to maintain or enhance competitiveness in the face of fierce global competition, changing markets or technological breakthroughs, Marks (1994) argues that the rapid pace and massive scope of organizational change in recent years have increasingly taken a psychological toll, not least on those employees who emerge as 'survivors' of the turmoil of change, irrespective of whether it is caused by mergers, acquisitions, corporate rationalizations, delayering, TQM, BPR or downsizing. In particular, he refers to the unintended human consequences, which he identifies as:

1 The 'wrenching experiences', which are often poorly or even badly handled by top management, who tend not to get involved. Instead they leave the handling to middle managers and supervisors, who are invariably ill-equipped to cope with the situation.

2 The 'psychological reactions to the transitions', which lead to the survivors of the change programme feeling guilty for still being in a job. They lose confidence in management, become fearful, suspicious, cynical and demoralized; they also feel less loyal to the organization because the old psychological contract, which embraced 'job security' as one of its components, has been broken by the company.

3 The 'behavioural reactions' of the remaining workforce in the post-transition organization, where workloads are generally bigger and working hours extended; where people suffer a lack of direction, tend to work at a 'frantic' pace and struggle to 'keep their heads above water'; and where risk taking plummets, political games increase, role ambiguity abounds and high stress levels become endemic. All of these unintended consequences can lead to employee alienation and possible psychological withdrawal from the organization.

Marks also discusses the unintended 'business consequences' resulting from organizational change and development failures, such as the 'increased costs in retraining the remaining workforce', the 'increased use of temporary consultants and overtime', the 'loss of the wrong people' and the (enforced) 'contracting out of entire functions'.

A similar situation of unintended 'human consequences' arising from mergers applies in the UK, as reported by Devine and Hirsch (1998), who claim:

> the danger of badly handled mergers is that people employers want to keep become disaffected and leave. Also failure to manage the people dimension risks disruption, mistrust, political infighting, a legacy of bad feeling, the loss of key employees and a negative impact on business performance.

Reporting a major baseline study on the 'Quality of Working Life in Corporate Britain', Worrall and Cooper (1997) have exposed a number of unintended human and business consequences which ask questions about corporate governance and the effective management of change. Their research revealed that the majority of change initiatives had been driven by cost reduction, delayering, headcount reduction and performance improvement; that where change had taken place there was evidence that the objectives which had driven the change process had not always been achieved, and that there was clear evidence that many change management programmes had had strongly negative effects on employee loyalty, motivation, morale and sense of job security.

Furthermore, there was strong evidence that in larger organizations (those employing over 500 people) a 'schism has emerged in the UK management between directors and above, and senior managers and below which pose some intriguing questions about the continuation of the large, corporate structures which have traditionally dominated the organizational landscape'. Other key findings from this research project provide evidence of unintended human consequences similar to those reported by Marks, such as 'not having enough time to get work done, the organization not learning from its mistakes, the lack of resources to get work done effectively and the organization being left with the wrong mix of skills'. Additionally, in many instances, there has been 'too much change which had stripped out much of the organizations' knowledge base and had replaced it with cheaper, but less effective agency staff to a point where it was no longer possible to deliver quality services'. Subsequent research by Worrall and Cooper (1998) has reinforced their earlier findings:

> In the 1997 survey, we were led to conclude that the impact of the considerable amount of restructuring that had taken place in UK business organizations over the 12 months prior to the survey had had a considerable negative effect on employee loyalty, morale, motivation and, particularly, perceptions of job security. In the 1998 survey, these results have been replicated very closely. Our research has revealed that organizational restructuring has imposed considerable human and social costs on the recipients of that change.

However, it should be noted that their 1998 findings also confirmed that the effects of restructuring on loyalty, motivation, morale and sense of job security were 'much less pronounced in family-owned businesses and private limited companies than in Plc's and the public sector'. With regard to downsizing and/or delayering, Worrall *et al.* (1999) have also exposed a number of findings which challenge the core assumptions that many senior managers hold about the use of various methods of organizational restructuring – particularly redundancy. Their research demonstrates that redundancy and the way it is handled 'has a huge negative impact on the victims, on the people who survive it, and on the organizations within which they work. The attitudes of the surviving managers are substantially modified, they become more risk averse, their loyalty tends to switch from the organization to themselves, and decision making becomes slower as their spans of control widen and they become subject to increased task overload and reduced role clarity'.

Furthermore, as already outlined above, organizational knowledge and skills bases are also perceived to be eroded as expensive 'lifers' are replaced by temporary and contract workers. While organizational change is inevitable, their research indicates that companies have a long way to go in learning how to manage change effectively and to prevent the downward spirals that can result from uncritical use of the blunt instrument of redundancy. Undoubtedly their findings have posed serious questions about how well organizational change is being managed in the UK. It also reinforces the concerns expressed by Micklethwait and Wooldridge (1996) in America, who draw attention to the negative effects of (top) management 'trying to change organizations or using the management flavour of the month to disguise Weberian methods to bring about drastic or draconian change. Management gets the idea that it owns the organization and that the employees are merely resources for their command. They often forget that they are organization employees too'.

In discussing the issue of downsizing and the management of change, Thornhill *et al.* (2000) support the view of Shaw and Barrett-Power (1997) that the hard num-bers-based corporate measures typically used to assess the effectiveness of downsizing are inadequate as a means for understanding and managing the impact of the process on stakeholders such as work groups and individuals who survive the event. However, as these writers argue, although such measures may indicate that downsizing has had a negative impact on those who survive as employees, they 'can only serve to highlight the presence of psychological and behavioural conse-quences for [the] survivors'. Drawing on the work of Tomasko (1992), Cameron (1994) and Mishra and Mishra (1994), Thornhill *et al.* draw attention to the fact that only 20–50 per cent of organizations engaging in downsizing achieve their objectives of improved productivity, higher investment returns, reduced costs and increased profits.

From the weight of evidence one must conclude that the process issues associ-ated with organizational change and development are far more complex and difficult to manage successfully than is often supposed, and that managers are gen-erally insufficiently skilled in change agency.

WHY ORGANIZATIONAL CHANGE AND DEVELOPMENT PROGRAMMES FAIL

That such a high proportion of organizational change programmes fail is somewhat surprising, bearing in mind the plethora of 'best practice' advice and guidance on the 'how to' of change management available in the management literature. These range from straightforward, plainly written 'practical guides' and 'handbooks' writ-ten by consultants from their everyday practical experiences as practitioners, through to textbooks written by academics mainly for the education market. Some of the former can be criticized for being too pragmatic and 'feet on the ground' to the point of being no more than prescriptive recipes bordering on the simplistic. In contrast, some of the latter can be so theoretical and philosophical as to appeal only to academics and students of particular specialisms within the field of organi-zational change and development (OCD). Even so, to a greater or lesser extent, the range of literature can be of some value in helping to inform, shape and challenge a change agent's thinking about managing change.

Many authors in the field have offered their readers 'a planned change manage-ment model'. Although these have tended to differ one from the other in varying respects, all have incorporated a common systematic 'step-by-step' approach to the management of change. This usually comprises some or all of the 'phases' or 'stages' that make up the 'generic model for managing planned organizational change', as illustrated in Figure 2.1. This model is a 'composite' based on those offered by, among others, Bullock and Batten (1985), Cummings and Huse (1989), Carnall (1990, 1991), Beckhard and Pritchard (1992), Goss *et al.* (1993), Warrick (1994), Burnes (1996) and Stewart (1996).

Stage 1   Diagnose/explore the present state and identify the required future state

Stage 2   Create a strategic vision

Stage 3   Plan the change strategy

Stage 4   Secure ownership, commitment and involvement, including top management support

Stage 5   Project-manage the implementation of the change strategy and sustain momentum

Stage 6   Stabilize, integrate and consolidate to ensure perpetuation of the change

---

Figure 2.1 A generic model for managing planned organizational change

An easy-to-remember model originating in the UK is that of Hussey (1996), who uses the mnemonic 'EASIER' to memorize his six-stage approach to managing change, as follows:-

Envisioning:	the process developing a coherent view of the future (a vision) in order to form an over-arching objective for the organization.
Activating:	the task of ensuring that others in the organization understand, support and eventually share the vision.
Supporting:	the helping of others to play a key part in the implementation process.
Implementation:	the process of developing detailed plans to enable the (change) strategy to be implemented and controlled.
Ensuring:	the process of checking that existing monitoring and controlling processes are adequate and establishing supplementary controls as required.
Recognizing:	the giving of recognition, either positive or negative, to those involved in the (organizational change) process.

A well-known managing change model originating from the USA is one developed by W. Warner Burke (see Siegal 1996). The 'change process' part of this model comprises four sequential dimensions, as follows:

1 *Planning change*: concerning the causes of change in organizations, articulation of the vision, how to get from the present to the future, and barriers to effective transitions.

2 *Managing the people side of change*: concerning how, when and how much to communicate change within the organization, and psychological issues related to transition.

3 *Managing the organizational side of change*: concerning the design and structural issues of systemic and long-term change efforts.

4 *Evaluating the change effort*: concerning indicators of a change effort's effectiveness.

Besides having the knowledge to apply the 'change process' dimensions, Warner Burke also argues that managers need to have knowledge of the 'fundamental aspects of change' relating to two additional dimensions, namely:

1 *Individual response to change*: concerning the nature, prevalence and utility of resistance to change.

2 *The general nature of change*: concerning whether effective large-system change is evolutionary or revolutionary in nature and the characteristic patterns that typify change efforts in organizations.

Implicit in this and other change management models is the expectation that managers possess the 'knowledge base', and by inference the 'expertise', to manage change effectively. But the failure rates of organizational change programmes, as discussed in the preceding sections of this chapter, suggest the majority do not. Evidence also suggests that in organizations where organizational change programmes fail, these failures follow a predictable pattern (see Bulletpoint 1997). Typically this starts with the senior management announcing a new corporate change initiative, quickly followed by a series of short, company-wide training events to bring everybody 'up to speed', the setting up of cross-functional committees to discuss 'the way forward' and then the subsequent re-allocation and re-arrangement of resources. However, through this process, the organization and its management lose sight of the reasons and focus for the change, which leads to a loss of momentum and resources. The change then fails. Causes of failure can be many and varied, but the vast majority come from within the organization. They include, for example:

- people viewing change as a destination rather than as a process needing good planning, preparation, project managing and constant attention;
- a lack of clear vision about both the short- and long-term goals;
- the legacy of previous organizational change programmes that have been handled badly or have failed, which produces a sceptical risk-averse culture, middle management inertia and general employee resistance to change;
- failure to provide the necessary encouragement, training and skills that enable employees to adapt and adjust to organizational change;
- inadequate communication about the change including, for example, giving information to employees too gradually, which then risks the 'grapevine' getting to them first;

■ focusing the change effort too narrowly on one aspect of the organizational 'equation' and ignoring the 'inter-connectedness' of organizational life. For example, investing in management training to bring about changes in managerial style but failing to adjust the reward systems to support the required changes in managerial behaviour.

These failures are examples of weaknesses or omissions in the application of what might be termed 'best practice' approaches to the effective management of planned change. Although most if not all managing planned change models promoted in the management literature are basically sound and have high face validity, in many cases the simplified diagrammatic/summary formats of the models can appear overly simplistic and just plain common sense. Herein lies what the author considers to be a potential weakness of change management 'models' and 'prescriptions', namely that they are subject to over-simplification. This can then lead to the 'skipping of important steps' and a lack of rigour in the application of the change management model. It is suggested that these weaknesses come about most likely as a result of a lack of change agency expertise of various kinds on the part of managers, trainers and developers. Furthermore, these may be exacerbated by one or more of a number of underlying root causes or 'failings' in facilitating and managing organizational change, as follows:

Failing 1: Managers not knowing the fundamental principles of change management

Some organizational change programmes fail because the managers responsible for initiating and implementing change are either totally unaware, or insufficiently aware, of the fundamental principles and 'best practice' approaches in the field of organizational change and development. Through 'ignorance' they blindly launch into change programmes that are therefore doomed to failure. In the case of BPR, the overwhelming majority of failures can be attributed to a small number of root causes. Hammer, who is regarded as the 'high priest of re-engineering' in the USA, together with Stanton, has demonstrated that the single most significant contribution to BPR failure is the fact that '... people engaged in the re-engineering effort don't know what they are doing; they misconstrue or fail to comprehend the fundamental nature of re-engineering; their techniques are improvised or random, not based on practical experience' (Hammer and Stanton 1995). Causes of BPR failures in UK and European organizations are probably much the same as those identified by Hammer. It certainly is the case in the UK that 'complacency and ignorance remains a strong inhibitor of change and improved performance' (RSA 1995) and that the 'biggest barrier to implementing change happens to be managers themselves' (Gamblin 1997).

The situation regarding change management failures begs the question as to why managers are 'complacent' or 'don't know what they are doing'. For those managers who received no formal management education as part of their career progression as a manager, the reason may be clear and understandable. However, for those managers who possess management qualifications such as an MBA or diploma in management, the reasons are less clear and understandable, because the theory and practice of change management usually features strongly in the syllabuses of these qualification programmes. It may be the case that insufficient attention is given to the 'behavioural issues' of change management or to developing the 'soft skills' required to manage change effectively.

Clearly, whatever the cause of this lack of knowledge and expertise, it behoves all managers to take responsibility for educating themselves fully in the whole area of change management, particularly the process issues of organizational change and development.

Failing 2: Managers succumbing to the temptations of the 'quick fix' and 'simple solutions'

Even when managers are sufficiently aware of the 'theory and practice' of organizational change and development, too often they succumb to the temptation of the 'quick fix' or 'simple solution'. The temptation may be induced by the urgency of the change, or by managers themselves oversubscribing to the KISS (keep it simple, stupid) approach to managing. Gamblin (1997) argues that one factor above all seems to drive managers for 'quick fix' solutions, and that is 'short-termism'. Another is waiting for the 'big idea' that will transform the organization. Using the analogy of the 'wind surfer who waits for the next big wave to come along, finds the ride exhilarating but ends up back in the same place', he claims that 'the truth about real lasting change is that it is rather more difficult and complex to manage than managers first imagine', and that 'they need to start looking at the problems associated with change with a little more depth of understanding, rather than simply waiting to be carried forward by the next big wave'.

Various commentators warn against 'quick fixes' and 'simple solutions', including, for example, Kilman (1989) and Hussey (1996). After observing at close range the organizational change programmes of over 100 major organizations, including Ford, General Motors, British Airways, Eastern Airlines and Bristol Myers Squibb, Kotter (1996) concluded that 'the change process goes through a series of phases that usually requires a considerable length of time; that skipping steps creates only the illusion of speed and never produces satisfying results', and that 'critical mistakes (or omissions) in any of the phases can have devastating impact, slow momentum and negate hard won gains'. Clearly managers need to guard themselves against succumbing to the attractions of the 'quick fix' or 'simple solution'.

Failing 3: Managers not fully appreciating the significance of the leadership and cultural aspects of change

Many managers fail to appreciate the full significance of the 'leadership' and 'cultural' aspects of change and give insufficient attention to these critically important issues. Beckhard and Pritchard (1992) discuss in some detail the interdependence of what many expert commentators regard as being the three most important factors in a fully functioning organization, namely the 'leadership', the 'culture' and the 'management of change'. They argue the case for managers to take these into account in an integrated way when managing fundamental organizational change.

From their studies of organizational re-engineering programmes Hammer and Stanton (1995) identify '… proceeding without strong executive leadership' and '… adopting a wrong style of implementation' as two of the top ten mistakes made by managers responsible for initiating and facilitating change. The latter mistake has much to do with leadership style, which is an aspect of the management culture. Warrick (1995) contends that 'competitive advantage can best be achieved when organizational leaders lead, champion change and adopt a sound change process. When leaders fail to lead, efforts to improve the organization will under-achieve the desired results or, as is often the case, make things worse and add more chaos to an already chaotic situation'. He goes on to claim that the reasons why leadership is so important in today's intensely competitive and rapidly changing corporate environment is that leaders are the single most important factor in determining the success and effectiveness of organizations. They are the main shapers of organization culture and can make or break organizations by the way they manage. Managers can create or destroy trust, which is the ingredient that makes change possible and accelerates the change process. If they are good leaders, they can provide the focus, direction and continuity necessary to keep perspective during times of rapid growth and change, and momentum and hope during difficult times.

From their study of the barriers to technical and organizational innovation within a finance clearing house of the Bank Giro Centrale in the Netherlands, Boonstra and Vink (1996) identified the autocratic style and quality of leadership as a major impediment to change. This led to a lack of employee involvement and acknowledgement by senior management of the experience they could contribute to the change process, and also to a lack of openness by management about the objectives and the methodologies to be used. Furthermore, other barriers observed within the social system of the organization that limited people's ability to change included the norms and values, the existing power configuration, and poor inter-functional teamwork.

In explaining how and why transformation efforts fail, Kotter (1996) identifies eight mistakes typically made by managers when leading change, as follows:

1 Not establishing a great enough sense of urgency.

2 Not creating a powerful enough guiding coalition of key people who can work together as a team (of change agents) and lead the change effort.

3 Not having a vision to help direct the change effort and failing to develop the strategies required for achieving it.

4 Under-communicating the new vision and not setting a good example by exhibiting the required new behaviours themselves.

5 Not removing obstacles to the new vision (whether things or people).

6 Not systematically planning and creating short-term wins visible as performance improvements, or recognizing and rewarding those employees involved.

7 Declaring victory too soon, which can lead to momentum being killed, change coming to a halt and tradition creeping back in.

8 Not anchoring changes in the corporation's culture.

Clearly all eight mistakes relate to the 'leadership' and 'cultural' aspects of the 'change management' process.

A UK example of a major transformational change programme failing because of insufficient attention being given to the 'cultural' issues has been well documented by Brooks and Bate (1994). It relates to the government-led Next Steps Initiative launched in 1988 to bring about transformational change in the British civil service, which failed to 'spark off the required cultural revolution at the local level that was necessary for the initiative to fully succeed'. Brooks and Bate reveal how this major change initiative, which had been imposed top-down, had been frustrated by a strong, resilient, yet 'non-relevant' cultural infrastructure applying at the grass-roots level of the organization. This had acted in a way as to neutralize the desired changes. In a later article, Bate (1996) uses the term 'cultural lag' to describe the condition when a culture remains unchanged, becomes no longer relevant to the needs of the organization undergoing change and acts as an impediment. The importance of addressing the cultural issues associated with transformational change programmes will be found in the Industrial Relations Service (1997) management review on cultural change.

From their 1998 research findings into the 'quality of working life' referred to earlier in this chapter, Worrall and Cooper (1998) conclude that 'the achievement of significant (organizational) change requires sustained top management commitment which has to be evident and consistent throughout the process'. For organizational change and development programmes to succeed it is evident from the above that adequate attention must be given to the 'cultural' issues and to the quality of the 'leadership'.

Failing 4: Managers not appreciating sufficiently the significance of the people issues

In many instances, neither the top management team initiating the change programme nor the coalitions of managers, trainers and developers leading the change process give sufficient attention to the people issues. This can be inferred from the range of unintended and undesired human consequences resulting from many organizational change programmes, as reported by Marks (1994) and Worrall and Cooper (1997, 1998). Hammer and Stanton (1995) claim that failure to attend to the concerns of the people 'is one of the top ten mistakes in re-engineering'. Drawing upon and interpreting the research work of Alexander (1991) in particular, but also other writers, Hussey (1996) identifies a range of problems concerned with the management of change. These relate to the mishandling of the HR elements of strategic management, which typically leads to strategy implementation failures. Skilling (1996) claims that 'the most often neglected and misunderstood dimension of change effort is the human side'. As he argues, effectively managing the human side of change means paying attention to the psychological processes that people experience in dealing with change, whether planned or unplanned. It is 'not so much the change itself that causes difficulties but rather the transition process which generates confusion and disrupts lives. Change occurs when something (new) starts or something (old) stops and it takes place at a particular point in time. Transition is the gradual psychological process through which people reorient themselves so they can function and act appropriately in the changed situation'. Drawing on the ideas of Bill Bridges, a transition management author, he cautions us to remember that it is a three-phase psychological process. People have to be enabled first to let go the old ways of the past and its memories (endings) while holding on to some aspects as necessary, second to re-invest in the new way of doing things (in-between time), and third to become fully committed to the 'new' direction and organization (new beginning). Hence, he argues, if organizational leaders (and managers) who are managing change are to achieve success, it is critically important they understand the distinction between change and transition and pay sufficient attention to the human side of change.

Failing 5: Managers not knowing the critical contribution that the human resource development function can make to the management of change

Of all the omissions and failings on the part of managers in addressing and attending to the people component of change management, perhaps of greatest concern is their failure to use human resource development (HRD) to best effect as a tool for managing change. The understanding of HRD which the author has in mind here is close to the definitions offered by McLagan (1989) and Swanson (1995) in the USA, and the even 'more inclusive' concept of HRD in the UK as offered by the University Forum for HRD (1998) and more recently demonstrated from evidence by Walton (1999). These define HRD as a strategic, dynamic, business-driven and/or individual-driven function which embraces both 'training and development', 'organization development' , 'career development' and ' vocational learning', which may or may not be organizationally focused. This interpretation and understanding of modern-day HRD contrasts sharply with what can be argued are the outdated understandings of many managers and HR people. For example, some view HRD as one of many sub-sets of administrative activities comprising the personnel management function, with the training specialism responsive only to immediate knowledge and skill deficits. Even though personnel management is increasingly being referred to as human resource management (HRM), which many claim is strategic in focus, evidence suggests the concept of strategic HRM still remains more rhetoric than reality (see Guest 1990 or Armstong and Lang 1994). As Hussey (1996) observes, 'until recently HRM has been associated (primarily) with administrative functions and procedures', a view also echoed by Herriot (1998), and as recent research by West and Patterson (1998) reveals, 'too many organizations have only a nominal commitment to HR practices'. Grundy (1993) also observes that 'Human Resources is considered to be one of the key ways of gaining competitive advantage which is hard to imitate. Yet human resources strategies offer little concrete guidance to practising managers on the process of human resources – and in the context of a strategic plan'.

However, it has long been the case that some HRD practitioners have practised at a strategic level, have made pivotal contributions towards the achievement of organizational effectiveness and success, and have helped create the critical capabilities required for the organization to adapt, change and transform itself.

Unfortunately, many managers have 'blind spots' regarding HRD, seeing it only in terms of high-cost external training courses, or long-term development/qualification programmes for young and new employees. Too often they see training and development as an undesirable drain on the organization's resources, an expenditure that can only be afforded when profit or funding is plentiful, rather than as an essential investment the organization can ill afford not to make even in the toughest of times, especially during periods of organizational change. Hence, in the everyday situation of managing, managers tend not to turn naturally to trainers and developers for help or support, or proactively to use HRD as a tool for managing change. Yet in all change there are HRD implications, whether the change is as large as a major shift in corporate direction or as small as a minor modification to the working practices of an operator required to perform a new task or procedure. For every change, both large and small, either 'new' knowledge, attitudes, skills and habits (KASH) have to be acquired, as in the case, for example, when new products, services, technologies, structures or systems are introduced; or alternatively 'existing' knowledge, attitudes, skills and habits must be redistributed, as in the case of downsizing or when mergers or acquisitions take place. Unless the KASH gaps flowing inevitably from organizational change initiatives are bridged efficiently and effectively, whether at the organizational, group or individual level, the organization will not develop the critical capabilities required to make a successful transition from the present state to the new desired future state. If people lack the requisite KASH to perform to the expected standards, organizations are bound to risk failure or partial success only. The scale and nature of the HRD effort built into an organizational change and development programme will determine whether or not the planned change is a success. Change can either be brought about beneficially with the organization reaching its desired future state, or detrimentally with the organization suffering unintended, damaging consequences and ending up in an unwanted state, as illustrated in Figure 2.2.

Hence, for managers to be in control of change, they must ensure they are in control of the KASH issues associated with change itself. This means giving sufficient time and attention to the 'soft' HRD (and HRM) aspects of managing the change process, as Stewart and Hamlin (1990) and Stewart (1993, 1996) have been advocating for over ten years. This stance is supported by Bennett and O'Brien

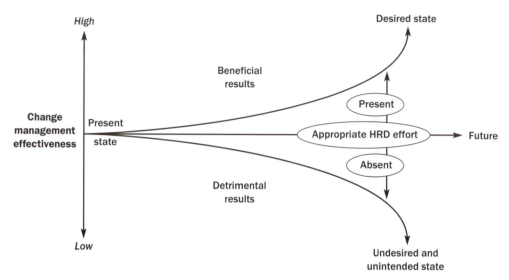

Figure 2.2 The critical contribution of appropriate HRD effort to change management effectiveness
Adapted from: Stewart and Hamlin (1990)

(1994), who argue that 'training and education efforts play a key role in transforming an organization's practices. Training is an integral, complementary component of change and growth'.

Similarly, in discussing the use of action training and research (AT&R) for changing organizations, Bruce and Wyman (1998) state that 'AT&R practitioners need to direct considerable attention to the development of the skill and methods among the people of the organization so that they can constantly change as needs and the environmental situation shift. Indeed, if the organization is to become a changing organization, it must be able to transform itself in anticipation of the changing needs of the people that its products and services support'.

More recent writers, including Thornhill *et al.* (2000), have claimed that HRD lies at the very heart of managing change through people because the consequences of any change process is that people will need to think and/or behave differently. However, they comment that 'its central status is not always reflected in practice'. Walton (1999), in discussing the management of transformational change from an HRD perspective, argues that 'by positioning HRD as a linchpin between the individual and organization dynamics of the process, it draws attention to the central role that HRD can play by mediating between those two elements'. Building on the work of Burack (1991), he describes a five-stage model for effectively managing transformational change and how HRD can contribute at every stage of the process, from recognizing the need and diagnosing the capacity for change through to initiating the change process, managing the transition and sustaining momentum.

Interestingly, from a recent seven-year study of 100 medium-sized manufacturing firms in the UK, West and Patterson (1998) reveal that 'investment in people management accounted for 19 per cent of the variation in profitability and 18 per cent of the variation in productivity of these firms'. In contrast, while 'emphasis on

R&D investment accounted for a respectable 8 per cent, emphasis on quality, new technology and competitive strategy barely crept above 1 per cent in terms of contribution'. Hence they argue that senior managers need to become 'convinced about the use of effective people management for creating an organization that views investment in people as the source of competitive advantage'. This requires managers 'managing creatively and effectively the whole person, skills acquisition and development, the community of their organization and the well of innovation from which they must draw to survive'.

The research findings of Hamlin and Reidy (1997) also reinforce the notion that to be effective, particularly during times of major organizational change, managers need to give time and attention to the HRD issues. Six criteria of managerial effectiveness were identified as applying in HM Customs & Excise, each of which comprised a cluster of managerial behaviours strategic to success. Besides those relating specifically to the 'managing change' criterion, most of the managerial behaviours underpinning the other five criteria related to the expertise required to manage change effectively. For example, the research revealed that managers needed to adopt a more participative and supportive style of leadership; to be team oriented; to be good team leaders and team members; to be effective at delegation; to empower their people; to act proactively in situations; and also to invest time and effort to the training, coaching and mentoring of staff.

Grundy (1993) also draws attention to the crucial link between HRD and strategic change. Specifically, he argues the case that strategic human resource planning and development (HRPD), which entails the close integration of thinking about future HR needs with thinking about competitive strategy, organizational strategy and the business environment, can and should play a key role in the evolution of specific competitive strategies. It should also be instrumental in implementing major changes, developing future competencies and in more tactical implementation.

In conclusion, for managers to manage change effectively and beneficially they need consciously to incorporate training and development into the very 'fabric' of their everyday management practice. They also need to use HRD as a tool of management, particularly in the area of managing organizational change and development. The ultimate would be for managers to embed HRD into the 'blood stream' of the organization, thereby increasing its potential of becoming a 'learning organization': in other words, an organization that has the capability to adapt readily and transform itself efficiently and effectively in the face of endemic change, and thereby to survive and thrive.

Failing 6: Trainers and developers lacking credibility in the eyes of line managers

Historically, many trainers and developers have been in roles perceived as being of lower status than those of professionals in other functional areas such as finance or marketing. Generally they have lacked 'credibility' in the eyes of line managers, which has not been helped by being part of personnel departments that have also lacked credibility due to the dominant focus of many HRM professionals on administration. As Ulrich (1997) points out, for too long the HR function 'has been plagued by old myths that have kept it from being a profession' and which has resulted in 'line managers placing uniformly low expectations upon the function' and hence on HRM and HRD practitioners. Consequently, comparatively few in-company personnel and training practitioners have gained access to top management, or have been in positions of strategic influence. Drawing on for example Sisson (1994), Thornhill *et al.* (2000) comment that 'the lack of status of the personnel function in the UK has long been noted as an impediment to HR specialists playing a strategic role through influencing business strategy'.

Exceptionally, some professional trainers and developers have reported directly to a chief executive officer, managing director, personnel director or other main board director who has had an enlightened understanding of HRD. Current trends suggest that more people are entering HRD after having had a successful professional career in other functional specialisms, including line management. They also find themselves in HRD roles that are strategic in orientation and structured into the senior management team. However, too many trainers and developers still remain in relatively 'low status' positions, lack credibility in the eyes of line managers, and do not have access to or opportunities for influencing top management. Some of these constraints are determined by the limited role expectations placed upon them by the organization or by particular managers. This can be due largely to the managers' lack of recognition or understanding of the critical contributions that modern-day HRD professionals can make towards business efficiency, organizational effectiveness and strategic change. However, the constraints can be self-induced, either in part or wholly, as a result of the limited role expectations of trainers and developers themselves (for further elaboration, see Reid and Barrington 1997; Harrison 1997). Some choose to interpret HRD solely as the provision of training and development programmes to meet needs identified and predetermined by others in the organization. They choose to see themselves primarily as direct trainers, instructors, training providers or administrators of training, not as strategic organizational facilitators, change agents and internal OD consultants. Hence the roles performed by many trainers and developers are narrow, prescribed and often limited to the safety/comfort zone of the training room.

Until recent times the majority of trainers employed by large private and public sector organizations spent most of their time within centralized training departments running prescribed, standardized courses for large populations of employees, often on a 'conveyer belt' basis. Their contact with the organization outside the training department was generally limited or even non-existent. Consequently, training in many organizations has been seen by line managers as a 'divorced' activity far removed from the realities of the mainstream activities of the business, often 'irrelevant', 'out of touch' and 'expendable'. In their report on the attitudes of British management to investment in vocational education and training commissioned by the then Manpower Services Commission and National Economic Development Office, Coopers and Lybrand (1985) revealed that 'Training Managers tended not to view their activities at the cutting edge of the competition of their firms, and nor do senior executives. In consequence training managers and departments tend to have a relatively low status within firms'. In light of this it should be no surprise that when times became tough for business organizations in the late 1980s and early 1990s, many organizations got rid of their training departments and staff.

It was around this time that Phillips and Shaw (1989) advocated that trainers should be developing a consulting approach to training. They proposed three development paths leading to the trainer roles of 'training consultant', 'learning consultant' and 'organization change consultant'. Barnham *et al.* (1988) also anticipated that 'training departments will [need to] more and more act as facilitator and advisor to line managers and individuals' and 'trainers will [need to] increasingly see themselves as change agents'.

Furthermore, Stewart and Hamlin (1990) strongly argued the case for trainers to face the challenge of ensuring training is relevant to management and the organization by

> concerning themselves primarily with the mainstream business of the organization and with live operational issues both at the level where the organization 'mission' is determined and where the knowledge and skills required for effective performance of the simplest task needs to be developed. The management of change presents this challenge in its clearest form. It provides trainers with the opportunity of making their most significant contributions, through facilitating the ability to confront the need for change: developing the ability of managers and others to cope with change and utilize change processes; and through developing the necessary knowledge, skills and attitudes to meet the consequences of change. Such contributions ensure trainers remain relevant to organizational performance and effectiveness. If achieved, change is more likely to lead to beneficial rather than detrimental outcomes.

More recently, Rosemary Harrison (1997) has argued that human resource development should 'no longer be seen as a specialism within HRM responsive only to immediate skill deficits' but that 'developing people must be a dynamic and strategic-led function which enables people to cope with unstable environments and drives the capability of the organization towards long-term innovation, profit-ability and growth'. Furthermore, as the management of change is a major theme in today's businesses, 'HRD practitioners must be able to advise on appropriate change strategies and on the learning experiences that can support them'. Similarly, HRD practice in the USA has only recently entered a state of transition, moving from learning to a performance paradigm (Bassi *et al.* 1996). As Holton *et al.* (1998) observe, 'if HRD is to be respected it needs to position itself as a strategic partner with line managers and achieve the same level of importance as traditional core organizational processes such as finance, production and marketing'. They argue that 'a performance improvement approach' will enable HRD to become a strategic partner, and this is best accomplished through consulting partnerships with line managers of the kind advocated by Robinson and Robinson (1995). Additionally, Ulrich (1997), in the light of the new competitive realities, believes HR professionals in general 'must focus more on the deliverables of their work than on doing it better if they are to face up effectively to the next agenda for competitiveness'. To this end, they need 'to become a strategic partner with line managers, an administrative expert, an employee champion and a change agent'.

However, the majority of trainers, developers and other HR professionals will continue to find themselves operating at the margins of organizational life unless, that is, they improve their 'credibility' in the eyes of line managers. But this may be dependent upon the five OCD 'omissions' and 'failings' of managers, as outlined above, being overcome. Unfortunately, traditional approaches to manager and management training and development do not adequately address these 'failings'. As Hamlin and Stewart (1998) claim, much of the management training and development that UK organizations invest in, whether off the job or on the job, is not that effective or beneficial, because it lacks a sound and sufficient empirical base. Drawing on the views of a wide range of expert commentators, they highlight the relative dearth of empirical research into the everyday 'practical realities of managerial life' and 'particularities' of effective and ineffective management applying in British organizations, not least in the area of bringing about beneficial organizational change. In contrast, evidence-based practice in the fields of medicine and healthcare is firmly established as an everyday reality. Hamlin and Stewart suggest that most management development in both Britain and the USA relies too heavily on the views of the classical theorists and modern-day 'gurus'. Hence the management approach and climate in many organizations is not conducive for trainers or developers to operate strategically as internal change agents, OD consultants or research-based HRD practitioners. This precludes the development of appropriate management development initiatives that could help managers to overcome their 'failings' and 'blind spots' concerning the management of change. A 'vicious circle' appears to be in play where the five OCD 'failings' of managers contribute to the creation of the 'credibility' problems of HRD/OD practitioners. These in turn lead to a lack of 'appropriate' HRD/OD effort incorporated into OCD programmes, which then fail to question the 'appropriateness' of the management development programmes offered to managers. Such programmes then fail to address and overcome the five particular OCD 'failings' of the managers and so the 'vicious circle' goes on *ad infinitum*, as illustrated in Figure 2.3. At the heart of this is a perceived lack of sufficient evidence and research-informed professional practice on the part of line managers, trainers, developers and other HR professionals.

It is clear from the above that the role and direction of HRD need to be strategically focused towards organizational change and development. This has significant implications regarding the future role of trainers, developers and other HR professionals. Potentially, HRD practitioners can make very significant contributions to organizational effectiveness and performance when given the chance to do so, as previously argued. Furthermore, when acting in a consulting capacity, whether as internal or external change agents, they can perform key roles in helping line managers achieve success in bringing about organizational change effectively and beneficially. Performing in an OD capacity they can perhaps have, as Warrick

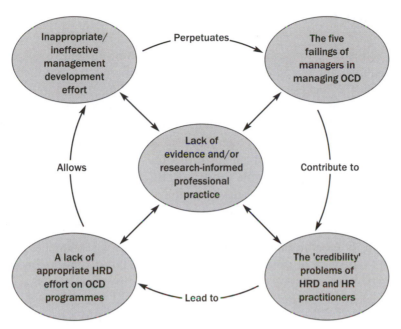

Figure 2.3 Management and organization development 'vicious circle'

(1995) claims, 'the greatest impact by helping organization leaders lead, champion change, and adopt a sound change process that is practised throughout the organization'. However, it is incumbent upon them to 'sell' to line managers the services they can offer and the critical contributions they can make. But it behoves managers to update themselves on modern-day HRD theory and practice, and to consider more seriously using the services of HRD professionals, integrating them more fully into the mainstream management of the organization. With regard to managing an organizational change and development programme, line managers are urged to include HRD and HRM professionals as members of the 'coalition' of key players who have responsibility for leading the change. Unfortunately, all too often they exclude them, as the research of Holland and Aitken (1999) suggests. Their study into 'Getting the best from IT-related change' revealed that 'at most, only a third of the IT-related change projects we looked at had significant HR involvement. There was little evidence of HR executives as business partners of their line colleagues'.

However, for collaborative business partnerships to come about, it is suggested that HR professionals, particularly trainers and developers, should engage proactively with managers in the processes of instigating and managing strategically led organizational change and development initiatives. Managers, trainers and developers, as well as their other HR colleagues, should be striving harder to work together professionally in strategic partnership for the purpose of ensuring maximum success in managing the process issues of organizational change and development.

CONCLUSIONS

The conclusions to be drawn from the above discussion of context and practice are clear. Managers, trainers and developers all need to become more skilled in managing effectively the process issues of organizational change and development. This means becoming more expert as change agents. It also means becoming more cognizant of the critical and interdependent contributions each could and should make towards the successful and beneficial management of change; and of the benefits of working collaboratively in professional partnership from the original conception of a change programme through to its completion.

An implicit assumption contained within the aims of this book is that most readers will identify strongly with the notion that evidence-based practice, namely the conscientious, explicit and judicious use of current best evidence derived from good research in decision making, should be a commonplace characteristic of management. It is the view of this author that for beneficial outcomes to be assured and maximized, evidence-based or at least research-informed practice will need to become an essential feature of managing organizational change and development. Hence, managers, trainers and developers should consider using research regularly to inform, shape and measure their effectiveness as change agents. As Quirke (1995) observes, 'the use of internal research as an instrument on the corporate dashboard' provides 'continual feedback that allows greater responsiveness' and helps 'to speed up the changing behaviour within organizations'. Several other UK writers have similarly argued the case for research-based approaches to management development, HRD and organizational change (see Jacobs and Vyakarnam 1994; Hamlin and Davies 1996; Hamlin and Reidy 1997). Similar arguments have been made in the USA. For example, Swanson (1997) exhorts HRD professionals to advance their professional practice by becoming truly expert practitioners through what he calls 'back yard' research; while Jacobs (1997) calls for collaborative partnerships between HRD practitioners and HRD scholars to integrate research and practice. More recently, Holton *et al.* (1998) have demonstrated how HRD research and theory, integrated into practice through a university–organization partnership, can enable an organization to advance and enhance its HRD practice significantly. A telling argument for research-based HRD practice in the post-industrial information economy has been put forward by Russ-Eft *et al.* (1997), who draw attention to the fact that it is human intellect, creativity and innovation which provide the basis for a successful organization. As a result, they argue that executives must manage this human capital to improve organizational performance and bring about organizational change, and to deploy HRD professionals who can provide the tools and methods in their roles as 'chief knowledge officer' or 'chief learning officer'. However, these HRD professionals must be aware of the relationships between individual learning and performance, team learning and performance, and organizational learning and performance. Hence Russ-Eft *et al.* strongly support Holton *et al.* in encouraging HRD practitioners to use current HRD research in these fields in order to enhance their professional practice.

It is a strongly held view of this author that reflective research-informed HRD practice, and active collaborative partnerships between managers, trainers and developers on the one hand and business academics on the other in conducting good internal research, will become increasingly important in the drive for excellence and expert practice in the change management field. From his own personal experience operating as one of two business academic partners in a recent collaborative HRD practitioner/scholar partnership within HM Customs and Excise (Anglia Region), the application of research-based OD was particularly powerful and effective in bringing about change in the management culture. It should be noted that the benefits and value of these particular OD interventions carried out under the visionary leadership of the regional head centred on the academic rigour and credentials of the internal research, its relevancy as perceived by the employees of the organization with whom the findings 'struck a chord', and the ensuing sense of ownership of the data (see Hamlin *et al.* 1997, 1999b).

In conclusion, managers, trainers and developers should recognize the complexities, contradictions and paradoxes associated with the change process and develop the skills required to manage change successfully: first the ability to diagnose and make sense of the organization; second to formulate appropriate change strategies; third to implement these strategies effectively and beneficially; fourth to critically evaluate the effectiveness of their contributions; and finally to draw lessons by reflecting upon their own good practice. These aspects of change agency are discussed in some depth in the following chapter. This provides an overview of 'best practice' approaches to organizational change and development, draws attention to some of the latest insights and provokes thought on the increasing complexities, contradictions and paradoxes of modern-day organizational life which challenge the role of the change agent.

As a final observation and comment arising from the review and synthesis of context and practice provided by this chapter, it is not unreasonable to contend that organizational change and development devoid of operating principles, theories and research to guide the OCD effort will tend to lead to poor practice and undermine the credibility of the change agent. Hence internal research should be considered an essential counterpart to OCD practice. This contention is explored further in the next chapter and is also illustrated by the numerous 'reflections on practice' discussed in Part III of the book.

References

Alexander, L.D. (1991), Strategy implementation: nature of the problem. In Hussey, D.E. (ed.), *International Review of Strategic Management.* Chichester: John Wiley.

Armstrong, M. and Lang, P. (1994), *The Reality of Strategic HRM.* London: Institute of Personnel and Development.

Barnham, K.A., Fraser, J. and Heath, L. (1988), *Management for the Future.* Ashridge Management College/Foundation for Management Development.

Bassi, L., Benson, G. and Cheney, S. (1996), The top ten trends. *Training and Development*, 50(11), 28–42.

Bate, S.P. (1996), Towards a strategic framework for changing corporate culture. *Journal of Strategic Change*, 5, 27–42.

Beckhard, R. and Pritchard, W. (1992), *Changing the Essence: The Art of Creating and Leading Fundamental Change in Organisations.* San Francisco: Jossey Bass.

Bennett, J.K. and O'Brien, M.J. (1994), The 12 building blocks of the learning organisation. *Training*, 31, 41–48.

Boonstra, J.J. and Vink, M.J. (1996), Technological and organisational innovation: A dilemma of fundamental change and participation. *The European Journal of Work and Organisational Psychology* 5(3).

Brooks, I. (1996), Leadership of a cultural change process. *Leadership and Organisation Development Journal*, 17(5), 31–37.

Brooks, I. and Bate, P.S. (1994), The problem of effecting change within the British Civil Service: a cultural perspective. *British Journal of Management*, 5, 177–190.

Bruce, R. and Wyman, S. (1998), *Changing Organizations: Practising Action Training and Research*. Thousand Oaks, Calif.: Sage.

Bulletpoint (1997) Why change fails: the enemies within. *Bulletpoint* sample issue, January. Redhill, UK: Bulletpoint Communications Ltd.

Bullock R.J. and Batten, D. (1985), It's just a phase we're going through: a review and synthesis of OD phase analysis. *Group and Organisation Studies*, 10, December, 383–412.

Burack, E.H. (1991), Changing the company culture – the role of human resource development. *Long Range Planning*, 24(1), 88–95.

Burnes, B. (1996), *Managing Change: A Strategic Approach to Organisational Dynamics*, 2nd edn. London: Pitman.

Cameron, K.S. (1994), Investigating organisational downsizing – fundamental issues. *Human Resource Management*, 33(2), 183–188.

Carnall, C. (1990), M*anaging Change in Organisations*. London: Prentice Hall.

Carnall, C. (1991), *Managing Change*. London: Routledge.

Champy, J. (1995), *Re-engineering Management*. New York: Harper Business.

Champy, J. and Nohria, N. (eds) (1996), *Fast Forward: The Best Ideas on Managing Business Change*. Boston: Harvard Business School Press.

Coopers and Lybrand Associates (1985), *A Challenge to Complacency: Changing Attitudes to Training*. A Report to the Manpower Services Commission and the National Economic Development Office. Sheffield: Manpower Services Commission.

Coulson-Thomas, C. (1996), Business process re-engineering and strategic change, *Strategic Change Journal*, 5(3), 165–178.

Cummings, T.G. and Huse, E.F. (1989), *Organisation Development and Change*. West.

Davies, G. (1996), Research methods and HRD. In Stewart, J. and McGoldrick, J. (eds), *Human Resource Development: Perspectives, Strategies and Practice*. London: Pitman Publishing.

de Meuse, K., Vanderheiden, P. and Bergamann, T. (1994), Announcing layoffs: their effect on corporate financial performance. *Human Resource Management*, 33(4).

Devine, M. and Hirsch, W. (1998), *Mergers and Acquisitions: Getting the People Bit Right*. Roffey Park Research Report.

Gamblin, C. (1997), Why the paradigm shift approach rarely works: in search of the magic bullet. *Organisation and People – The Quarterly Journal of AMED*, 4(4), 18–20.

Goss, T., Pascale, R. and Athoss, A. (1993), The re-invention roller coaster: risking the present for a powerful future. *Harvard Business Review*, November–December, 97–108.

Grundy, T. (1993), *Implementing Strategic Change: A Practical Guide for Business*. London: Kogan Page.

Guest, D. (1990), Human resource management and the American dream. *Journal of Management Studies*, 27(4), 377–397.

Hamel, G. and Prahalad, C. (1994), *Competing for the Future*. Boston: Harvard Business School Press.

Hamlin, R.G. (1990), The competent manager in secondary schools. *Educational Management and Administration*, 18(3), 3–10.

Hamlin, R.G. and Davies, G. (1996), The trainer as change agent: issues for practice. In Stewart, J. and McGoldrick, J. (eds), *Human Resource Development: Perspectives, Strategies and Practice*. London: Pitman Publishing, pp. 199–219.

Hamlin, R.G. and Reidy, M. (1997), Effecting change in management culture. *Strategic Change Journal*, special edition, December.

Hamlin, R.G., Reidy, M. and Stewart, J. (1997), Changing the management culture in one part of the British civil service through visionary leadership and strategically led research-based OD interventions. *Journal Of Applied Management Studies*, 6(2), 233–251.

Hamlin, R.G. and Stewart, J. (1998) In support of evidence-based human resource development practice. Lancaster–Leeds Collaborative Conference: Emergent Fields in Management–Connecting Learning and Critique. Leeds University.

Hamlin, R.G., Campbell, F., Reidy, M. and Stewart, J. (1999a), In support of research-based organisation change and development through professional partnerships. Occasional Paper Series 1999 No. OP002/99, University of Wolverhampton Business School.

Hamlin, R.G., Reidy, M. and Stewart, J. (1999b), Effecting management culture change through research-based management development. *Management Development Forum*, Empire State College, State University of New York, 2(1), 21–47.

Hammer, M. and Champney, J. (1993, 1996), *Re-engineering the Corporation*: *A Manifesto for Business Revolution*. London: Nicholas Brearley.

Hammer, M. and Stanton, S. (1995), *The Re-Engineering Revolution*: *A Handbook*. New York: HarperCollins.

Harrison, R. (1997) *Employee Development*. London: Institute of Personnel and Development.

Herriot, P. (1998), *Trust and Transition: Managing the Employment Relationship*. Chichester: John Wiley.

Holland, N. and Aitken, A. (1999), HR, line & IS as business partners in IT-related change; Will you, won't you, join the dance? *AMED News*, April/May, 10.

Holton III, E.F., Redmann, D.H., Edwards, M.A. and Fairchild, M.E. (1998), Planning for the transition to performance consulting in municipal government. *Human Resource Development International*, 1(1), 35–55.

Howard, C. (1996), The stress on managers. *The Globe and Mail*, 30 January.

Hussey, D. (1996), *Business Driven Human Resource Management*. Chichester: John Wiley.

Hussey, D. (1997), Strategic management past experiences and future directions: Part 1 – Why do so many organisations suffer strategic failure despite their processes of strategic management? *Strategic Change Journal*, 6(5), 261–271.

Industrial Relations Service (1997), Cultural change. *IRS Management Review*, 11(4).

Jacobs, R.C. and Vyakarnam, S. (1994). The need for a more strategically led research-based approach in management development. BPS Occupational Psychology Conference, Birmingham, UK.

Jacobs, R.L. (1997), HRD partnerships for integrating HRD research and practice. In Swanson, R. and Holton III, E.F. (eds), *Human Resource Development Research Handbook*: *Linking Research and Practice*. San Francisco: Berrett-Koehler.

Kearney, P. (1994), Business process reengineering. *Training and Development*, March, 14–17.

Kilman, R.H. (1989), *Managing Beyond the Quick Fix*. San Francisco: Jossey Bass.

Kotter, J.P. (1996), Leading change: why transformation efforts fail. In Champy, J. and Nohria, N. (eds), *Fast Forward*: *The Best Ideas on Managing Business Change*. Boston: Harvard Business School Press.

Kotter, J.P. and Heskett, J.L. (1992), *Corporate Culture and Performance*. New York: The Free Press.

Marks, M.L. (1994) *From Turmoil to Triumph*: *New Life After Mergers, Acquisitions and Downsizing*. New York: Lexington.

McLagan, P. (1989), *Models for HRD Practice*. Alexandria, Va.: ASTD Press.

Micklethwait, J. and Wooldridge, A. (1996), *The Witch Doctors*: *Making Sense of the Management Gurus*. New York: Times Books, Random House.

Mishra, A.K. and Mishra, K.E. (1994), The role of mutual trust in effective downsizing strategies. *Human Resource Management*, 33(2), 261–279.

Nelson, T. and Coxhead, H. (1997), Increasing the probability of reengineering/culture change success through effective internal communication. *Strategic Change Journal*, 6(1), 29–48.

Phillips, K. and Shaw, P. (1989), *A Consultancy Approach for Trainers*. Aldershot: Gower.

Quirke, W. (1995), *Communicating Change*. Maidenhead: McGraw-Hill.

RSA (1995), *RSA Inquiry Tomorrow's Company*: *The Role of Business in a Changing World*. London: Royal Society of Arts.

Reid, M.A. and Barrington, H. (1997), *Training Interventions: Managing Employee Development*. London: Institute of Personnel and Development

Robinson, D.G. and Robinson, J.C. (1995), *Performance Consulting*: *Moving Beyond Training*. San Francisco: Jossey Bass.

Russ-Eft, D., Preskill, H. and Sleezer, C. (1997), *Human Resource Development Review*: *Research and Implications*. Thousand Oaks, Calif.: Sage.

Shaw, J.B. and Barrett-Power, E. (1997), A conceptual framework for assessing organisations, work groups and individual effectiveness during and after downsizing. *Human Relations*, 50(2), 109–127.

Schaffer, R. and Thompson, H. (1992), Successful change programs begin with results. *Harvard Business Review*, 70, (1), 80–89.

Siegal, W. (1996), Understanding the management of change: an overview of managers' perspectives and assumptions in the 1990s. *Journal of Organisational Change Management*, 9(6), 54–80.

Sisson, K. (ed.) (1994), *Personnel Management: A Comprehensive Guide to Theory and Practice in Britain*. Oxford: Blackwell.

Skilling, D. (1996), Beyond the quick fix: how to manage more effectively in the heart of change. *Industrial and Commercial Training*, 28(4), 3–7.

Stewart, J. (1993, 1996), *Managing Change Through Training and Development*, 1st and 2nd edn. London: Kogan Page.

Stewart, J. and Hamlin, R.G. (1990), The management of change: what contribution can training make? *Training and Development*, August, 11–13.

Swanson, R.A. (1995), Performance is the key. *Human Resource Development Quarterly*, 6(2), 207–213.

Swanson, R.A. (1997), HRD research: don't go to work without it! In Swanson, R.A. and Holton III, E.F. (eds), *Human Resource Development Research Handbook*: *Linking Research and Practice*. San Francisco: Berrett-Koehler.

Thornhill, A., Lewis, P., Millmore, M. and Saunders, M. (2000), *Managing Change*. Harlow: Financial Times Prentice Hall, p. 253.

Tomasco, R.M. (1992), Restructuring: getting it right. *Management Review*, 81(4), 10–15.

Ulrich, D. (1997), *Human Resource Champions*. Boston: Harvard Business School Press.

University Forum for HRD (1998), Draft Report from the Standing Committee for Professionally Focused University Postgraduate Programmes in HRD. Unpublished.

Walton, J. (1999), *Strategic Human Resource Development*. Harlow: Financial Times Prentice Hall.

Warrick, D.D. (1994), What executives, managers and HR professionals need to know about change. In French, W.L., Bell Jr, C.H. and Zawacki, R.A. (eds) *Organisation Development and Transformation*: *Managing Effective Change*. Burr Ridge Il: Irwin.

Warrick, D.D. (1995), Best practices occur when leaders lead, champion change, and adopt a sound change process. *Organisation Development Journal*, 13(4), Winter, 91–101.

West, M. and Patterson, M. (1998), Profitable personnel. *People Management*, January.

Whetton, D., Cameron, K. and Woods, M. (1994), *Developing Management Skills for Europe*. London: HarperCollins.

Wilkinson, A., Allen, S. and Snape, E. (1993), *Quality and the Manager*, Institute of Management Report. London: Institute of Management.

Worrall, L. and Cooper, C.L. (1997), *The Quality of Working Life: 1997 Survey of Managers' Changing Experiences*. London: Institute of Management.

Worrall, L. and Cooper, C.L. (1998), *The Quality of Working Life: 1998 Survey of Managers' Changing Experiences*. London: Institute of Management.

Worrall, L., Cooper, C. and Campbell, F. (1999), False economy. *Human Resources FT Mastering Management Review*, March, 36–38.

Wyatt & Co. (1994), *Best Practices in Corporate Re-structuring*. Toronto, Ontario.

Yeung, A., Woolcock, P. and Sullivan, J. (1996), Identifying and developing competencies for the Future. *Human Resource Planning*, 19(4), 48–59.

Managers, trainers and developers as change agents

3

Bob Hamlin and Gron Davies

INTRODUCTION

As concluded in the previous chapter, managers, trainers and developers with responsibilities for bringing about organizational change effectively and beneficially, whether separately or in collaborative partnership, need to be appropriately skilled as change agents and reflective practitioners. The purpose of this chapter is first to provide an overview of what might be termed 'best practice' approaches to and 'received wisdom' on organizational change and development, as has been reported in the management literature over the past decade or so; second, to draw attention to some of the latest insights concerning how to bring about change successfully based on examples of more recent theory and practice; and finally to discuss the realities of modern-day organizational life which are not fully reflected in the literature, but which challenge the role of the change agent.

The tasks of the change agent are complicated by virtue of the increasing complexities, contradictions and paradoxes of organizations, as can be gauged from the personal reflections on practice revealed by Alf Hatton in Chapter 6 and from reading Ralph Stacey's book *Complexity and Creativity in Organizations* (Stacey 1996a). These tasks are, invariably, first to understand and make sense of the organization and what is going on; second to formulate appropriate change strategies; third to implement these strategies; and fourth to evaluate their effectiveness. Change agents should also make a conscious effort to reflect upon their own professional practice in order to draw lessons for the future. We acknowledge that organizations and the people employed in them are more complex than is often implied by much of the management literature, and that 'solutions' to organizational change 'problems' are also more difficult to grasp than many 'experts' imply. Therefore, we stress here that change agents need not only to be very selective in the theoretical approaches they use to inform and shape their practice but also that they need to build into their organizational change and development programmes sufficient time for review and reflection. From such reflection new theoretical insights can be gained as to why particular aspects of change programmes either succeed or fail. Also, new ways of approaching the problems of change will emerge through the development of new 'theories' informed by the change agent's own professional practice. Furthermore, because organizational change settings are far more complex than is often supposed, we argue the case for change agents to incorporate research activities into their professional practice for the purpose of better informing, shaping and evaluating what it is they do. The practical importance of internal/in-company research cannot be over-estimated. Conducting internal research itself is a process which can help make change occur. It can, when conducted with appropriate academic rigour, lead to deep-seated fundamental issues concerning the effective functioning of the organization being brought to the surface and being confronted: for example, those aspects of managerial behaviour and management culture which impede or block organizational change and innovation. In-company research that is recognized and accepted by people within the organization as being relevant, rigorous and of a high ethical standard is likely to 'strike a chord'. As a result, they are more likely to admit in public both the effective and ineffective features of organizational life, including their own individual performance or behaviour deficiencies (see Hamlin *et al.* 1997, 1999). Also, they are more likely to advance personal 'theories', reactions and opinions, which otherwise would not be revealed. Such research gives HRD/OD practitioners the evidence required to 'hold a mirror up to the organization' that will 'reflect accurately' the truth and realities of organizational life. This view is supported by Bruce and Wyman (1998). In discussing 'action training and research' as a method for developing changing organizations, they suggest that 'practitioners can help people address organization taboos they may have about discussing certain organizationally sensitive issues' by acting as 'an organizational mirror [that] can reflect such issues into the action research arena that otherwise may not be addressed'.

Being able to think and act like an academic researcher gives the practitioner, whether manager, trainer or developer, the additional skills and disciplines required to be a true expert in their own field of change agency practice. This implies having the capability to obtain consistently the results required by the organization, rather than regularly getting lost in the processes of organizational change and development as advocated or prescribed in the literature. As mentioned in Chapter 2, evidence and research-informed practice should become an essential feature of managing organizational change and development.

Reflecting on the 'emerging waves and challenges of change' that confront organizations, and the 'need for new competencies and mind sets', Morgan (1988) suggests that one of the challenges for managers is to create semi-permanent order out of turbulence. Handy (1989) indicates that the major problem in the future will be dealing with what he calls discontinuities in organizational environments. Whether we like it or not, this future is the present reality for many, if not most, organizations. Hence the need to develop a deeper understanding of the challenges to be met as organizations change and develop.

THE ORGANIZATIONAL CHALLENGE

From speculations developed in the late 1980s, various management consultants, 'gurus' and business academics have advocated the need to develop different forms of organization (Peters 1988; Drucker 1988; Handy 1990; Champy and Nohria 1996, among others) and these have led practitioners to develop a more robust orientation to strategic management. One of the implications of this type of management thinking has led to greater emphasis on the development of strategies for changing organizations. The focus for change through the 1980s to the present has shifted progressively from that of stressing values of efficiency to one where efficiency, quality, flexibility and innovation as managerial value imperatives have become the common experience of those currently in work. Employees, as a collective in the working environment, are being exhorted to become more efficient, more quality-oriented, more flexible and more innovative – in order to keep costs down and so ensure organizational survival and dynamism. Commonly, people at work are being forced or encouraged to adapt the ways they work and behave, and to accept different ways of being organized and managed in order for the organization to gain a competitive advantage. This transformation of working practice, and of organizational and managerial thinking, has implications for people at work, especially those involved in training, development and/or management.

The implications for trainers, developers, OD consultants and other HR professionals are particularly potent. In the past there has been much practical confusion about the role of the trainer and of the training department, as indicated in the previous chapter. Often the function has been located and subordinated within a more amorphous personnel department, or has found itself separated and peripheral to the main activities of the business. As such this functional subordination and separation has frequently affected the way that the deliverer of training has been involved in the change management process or in the development of people and of the organization. At best, the trainer may have been involved in dealing with human resource issues and policies, with training being delivered within that involvement. At worst, the trainer will have mechanistically delivered training within some policy vacuum – where training has been seen by the organization as an end, not as a means of realizing a part of a coherent organizational strategy.

This quasi-debate about the relative role, value and importance of the training function as opposed to the more generalized, policy-driven personnel function has been overtaken by the practical implications of organizations actively pursuing change. The continual pursuit of organizational change, which has become a common phenomenon for most organizations, calls for training, development and HR in general to be everyday line management tasks, as Hamlin argues in Chapter 2. Managers, not just HR specialists, need to be actively engaged with the human resource development (HRD) aspects of change in particular, as well as being active as change agents and reflective change practitioners. There is an increasing recognition by trainers, developers and managers that HRD must be a dynamic, strategic, business-led, values-driven function which meets the needs of the organization in its drive for competitive advantage, survival and long-term success, whether selling products in the commercial world or providing value-for-money services to the community.

Organizations, most of which are in a state of permanent change, need HR specialists who can think and act strategically. It is within this different orientation that the role of people within the HRD function is changing such that trainers and developers need to adopt a different set of expectations concerning new and different roles. A full discussion on and exploration of the emerging concept of HRD/strategic HRD (SHRD), and the implications for trainers, developers, managers and staff with regard to the changing expectations and demands on their respective roles and relationships in HRD/SHRD, can be found in Walton (1999). Similarly, the HR function generally is having to focus increasingly on organizational change issues. This means more personnel and HRM generalists are also having to take on the consultancy role of the internal change agent (see Wallace and Ridgeway 1996; Ulrich 1997). As change consultants, HR professionals are becoming more involved with top management in formulating and implementing organizational change strategies.

As already implied, this chapter aims to make clear to managers, trainers, developers and other HR professionals that the quality of their decisions concerning the effective management of change will be of crucial importance within the context of rapidly changing organizations. We believe that a fuller understanding of these newer consultancy roles involves them in taking a stance which can be best understood as that of the 'reflective practitioner'.

For the purposes of this chapter, our ideas concerning the reflective practitioner refer particularly to managers and HR professionals who are given the scope and have the expertise to operate strategically, who have a practical involvement in the formulation, implementation and evaluation of change strategies, who have the skills to develop people to meet the strategic objectives of the organization, *but who are mindful of the need to reflect on their respective contributions to the change process.* This raises a number of issues, the immediate one being that in order for them to transform and transcend their previous roles they must be conversant with current theory and practice concerning strategic thinking, organizational change and the role of the change agent. This means they need to understand theory in order to apply and evaluate it in practice – the traditional argument being that theory informs practice, where the extent to which this is a useful and practical conjunction is dependent on the quality of different kinds of reflection concerning the change process or problem. Furthermore, they need to evaluate their own effectiveness as change agents. Reddin (1985) defines managerial effectiveness as 'the extent to which a manager achieves the output requirements of the position'. Similarly, change agency effectiveness could be defined as 'the extent to which a change agent achieves the required outcome requirements of his or her respective role' in the organizational change process. As already implied in the preceding paragraphs, to be effective as a manager or facilitator of change, the change agent needs to be able to understand the particular organization, to devise or be involved in the formulation and implementation of an appropriate strategy for change, and also to evaluate the effectiveness of that strategy. In what follows, we deal with these as discrete categories but with the understanding that the change agent needs to think processually. The categories, therefore, make up phases in a process of change within which any one organizational change programme has been 'rationalized'.

ORGANIZATIONAL UNDERSTANDING

Organizational understanding, or making sense of an organization, is regarded as being of crucial importance because structure, function and their relationship to the core activity of the organization (the culture) need to be analysed in depth before effective strategies for change can be devised. Crucially, such analyses create a 'set of critical/analytical spectacles' through which the organization can be 'looked at', where the method of 'looking at' the organization will affect the way in which change agents should act to initiate and manage change subsequently. Theoretical models and conceptual frameworks provide the change agent with the 'practical tools' for creating suitable 'spectacles' through which to understand and make sense of the organization. Incorporating rigour into practice similar to that of the academic researcher also enables the change agent to use these 'spectacles' expertly.

Historically, academic analysis of organizations has embraced the theories of social scientists, psychologists, biologists, information theorists and anthropologists. In attempting to understand organizations, the field of study has moved from an original industrial/business focus to a wider application, including analyses of private, public and voluntary sector organizations. The theory, which is designed to inform thinking about organizational practice, has become the study of organizational behaviour, which is now theoretically eclectic and diverse. The main problem confronting the change agent is that, as often as not, there is a conflict between the 'implicit' theories of the individual based on practice and the different requirements needed to develop rigorous analytical, strategic thinking, which by its nature is more abstract and difficult to apply. This tension between the 'practical 'and the 'academic' may be real because in our experience there tends to be a gap between theory and practice. The HR professional or manager is being asked to 'fill the gap' when taking on the role of change agent.

In what follows, we give very brief descriptions of the assumptions behind the main theoretical perspectives of organizational behaviour as a field of study, and state how these can provide a focus for the study of organizations. We then state what the change advocated by the theory implies for change strategies in an organization when 'looked at' through these particular sets of 'critical/analytical spectacles'.

Mainstream theoretical perspectives

- **'Structural functionalism' perspective**
  - Organization: A set of structures within which people are directed to function.
  - Analysis: Analyse both the formal and informal structures of the organization and focus on conflict, particularly between managers and workers.
  - Change: Change the structures and hence the functions in order to reduce conflict in the organization.

- **'Human relationships' perspective**
  - Organization: A network of patterned relationships, where the pattern is determined by the organization.
  - Analysis: Analyse the needs and motives of individuals in order to understand the conflict between organizational goals and individual needs.
  - Change: Facilitate change so that organizational structures and functions more readily meet the needs of the individual.

- **'Psychodynamic' perspective**
  - Organization: A psychodynamic defence against anxiety.
  - Analysis: Analyse the individual's projections, rationalizations, dependence and counter-dependence behaviours.
  - Change: Facilitate the individual to realize the implications of defensive behaviour and then implement these realizations for behaviour by creating different structures and functions in the organization.

- **'Systems theory' perspective**
  - Organization: A hard system of variables (within and across functions) interacting with soft variables (people) in organizations.
  - Analysis: Analyse the organizational systems but understand that any part of the system analysed will be affected by the other parts, systematically.
  - Change: Change parts of the system but understand that this change will have systematic effects on the other parts of the organization making up the whole.

- **'Contingency theory' perspective**
  - Organization: A set of systems and subsystems, which are dependent on the particular contingencies of the system or subsystem.
  - Analysis: Analyse the organizational systems of management and attempt to understand how these systematic features of the organization are contingent upon the nature of the organizational tasks and the organizational environment.
  - Change: Change the contingencies within the system to develop the most appropriate management system and structure.

■ 'Action frame of reference' perspective

- Organization: A network of actively constructed meanings.

- Analysis: Analyse the interactions within organizations to establish the meaning of the interactions from the participants' point of view, in order to understand the rules which govern organizational behaviour.

- Change: Change the rules which inform behaviour so as to change and transform the meaning of the organization for the individual.

■ **'Cultural, ethnographic and metaphorical' perspectives**

- Organization: Interpreted as a constructed, distinctive, symbolic culture.

- Analysis: Interpret the symbolic significance of the actively negotiated, shared symbols and meanings in the organization by understanding the emergent pattern of interactions and meanings from the point of view of the members of the organization.

- Change: Change the meaning of the symbols within the culture of the organization.

Other perspectives

There is a view that many of the theoretical perspectives identified above are mechanistic in terms of the way the analytical approaches based upon them are applied. This has been contrasted with an organic approach to understanding features of organizations. Buchanan and Boddy (1992) differentiate between 'crisp' rules of authority as features of mechanistic organizations, and 'fuzzy' rules associated with organic authority structures. Another distinction that is being drawn by academics is between the modern, mechanistic organization and a post-modern critique, which develops ideas concerning the post-modern organization (Hassard and Parker 1993). These analyses tend to be academic in nature, but the mechanistic/organic distinction is part of recent organizational analyses and studies of change management processes.

In using different approaches for understanding organizations, Hallworth (1994) argues a case for combining the best of the 'hard' systems perspectives – through understanding organizational structures and systems – with the best of the 'soft' systems perspectives – through understanding motivation, team development and HR as utilized in the concept of re-engineering learning processes. This approach focuses on those key processes that are dynamically interlinked and which have a significant influence on organizational change, namely business strategy, organizational culture and organizational learning. Further, the idea of understanding organizational learning is also gaining currency. Handy (1989) suggests that new knowledge-based organizational structures will and must evolve as practical tools for facilitating organizational change. Pedler *et al.* (1991) and Swieringa and Weirdsma (1992) have developed concepts concerning the need to understand organizations as learning environments. Walton (1999) explores in depth a full

range of organization-wide issues embracing the organizational learning implications of TQM and various notions of the 'learning organization', 'corporate
university' and 'virtual organization' among others. Hence, the idea of an organization actually learning to create opportunities for its employees to learn how to
adapt to change has clear implications regarding what is meant by learning, and
who the learning is for.

More pragmatic approaches to organizational analysis and understanding have
been developed from a business strategy perspective. This has tended to frame or
map the organization in relation to practical, managerial understandings of particular organizational functions, which need to be understood practically. The
understanding gained then acts, drives or guides subsequent pragmatic strategies
for change. Good examples of this are Galbraith's organization design variables (see
Robinson 1992) and the McKinsey 7S's conceptual model, which strongly advocates the need to understand strategy, structure, systems, style, staff, skills and
shared values. Another is that advocated by Harrison (1988), who suggests that an
analysis should include reference to the organizational environment, organizational goals and tasks, structure, technology, workforce and political system.
Similarly, Trahant and Burke (1996) suggest the analysis of the external environment, mission, strategy, leaders, culture, structure, management practices, systems,
policies and procedures, work climate, skills and job match, motivation, individual
needs, values and performance. Reddin (1985) advocates as an important first step
the analysis of the organizational philosophy and the influences shaping that organizational philosophy.

These pragmatic approaches to organizational analysis, which appear much
favoured and advocated by consultants and academics alike, are based on the
assumption held by most managers that successful change is primarily concerned
with establishing a new order, of moving the organization from a comparatively
'unhealthy' to a more 'healthy state', and of maintaining a degree of 'fit' between
the configuration of the strategy, structure and systems of the organization and the
external environment. Furthermore, such approaches are based on a mechanistic
perspective, which views change as an incremental process of adjustment comprising a series of logical, interrelated sequential steps from a present 'undesired' stable
state to a future 'desired' stable state. Another assumption is that the destination
for the change is clear. In comparatively stable environments such incremental
changes are possible. However, in rapidly changing environments the value of the
mechanistic approach to organizational change is less certain, and for organizations adapting to turbulent and volatile environments it can be inappropriate.

Based on the findings of empirical research, Miller (1990) and Pascale (1990)
argue that whereas outstandingly successful organizations exhibit strong tendencies
to develop configurations of strategy, structure, systems, style, culture and other
aspects of organizational design in order to achieve consistency, harmony and
internal 'fit' leading to integration, stability and a 'state of stable equilibrium',
these strengths are at one and the same time the cause of their downfall. At first,
such configurations may be a source of success but, as Miller's research revealed,

organizations tend to give way to the forces for integration ('fit') by continuing to develop such configurations to excess. This then leads to organizations failing by becoming ossified and incapable of changing easily. Pascale reached similar conclusions. He argues that successful organizations have to strive to achieve 'fit' between the 7S's of the organization, but at the same time they must also be ready to break apart, differentiate, decentralize, innovate and develop new perspectives to prevent ossification. Such simultaneous displays of 'fit' and 'split' create tensions which creatively provoke inquiry and questioning, and produce, through organizational learning, new organizational configurations better suited to the changed environment. However, Pascale also revealed that some organizations pursue differentiation with such persistence to the point of instability and a 'state of unstable equilibrium'. This results in disintegration and failure. Hence, he argues, organizations which strive to maintain a 'state of equilibrium', whether of the stable or unstable kind, will inevitably fail. Organizational success is thought by Pascale to be strongly related to maintaining the contradiction between 'stability and integration' on the one hand, and 'instability and disintegration' on the other. This sense of organizational chaos with which organizations need to contend is fully discussed by Stacey (1996a, 1996b), who has applied chaos theory and the 'science of complexity' to organizations. He invites members of organizations to work at developing a whole new frame of reference (or set of critical/analytical 'spectacles' as we would call it) for seeing, analysing, understanding and making sense of organizational life.

Morgan (1993), drawing on theory emerging from the study of termite behaviour, provides metaphors for rethinking managerial behaviour in organizations. The 'termite' theory suggests that termite mounds are created from the random chaotic activities of termites guided by what seems to be an overall sense of purpose and direction, but in an open-ended manner. Using this as a metaphor, Morgan suggests that managers who operate as 'strategic termites' have clear aspirations about what they would like to achieve but, rather than trying to 'force fit' their vision, or direct and control a situation, instead they manage in a much more open-ended way, encouraging and allowing durable initiatives to emerge from the evolving situations being faced. They exhibit incremental and opportunistic approaches to change management. Such managers are strategic in the sense that while their activity is open to the influence of random opportunity in a chaotic environment, decisions and actions are always informed by a strong sense of what they ultimately want to achieve.

Clearly, the difficulty the change agent encounters is that of making a decision concerning the appropriate form of analysis when faced with such a diverse body of pragmatic and theoretical forms of knowledge. The problem becomes more acute when there is conflict between locating the analysis in theoretical terms as applied in the different theoretical perspectives, models and conceptual frameworks identified above, and adopting a more grounded approach. A grounded approach is eclectic, rooted in current experience and has direct functional consequences for the type of change strategies to be adopted. Consultants, 'gurus' and academics influencing practice tend to agree that the analysis of the organization must take place as the important first step. The understanding gained from the analysis acts as the ground stone for the development and implementation of appropriate strategies for change. It can be likened to that of front-end evaluation, or the first and starting point in an integrated evaluative framework. Within this traditional understanding of the first practical step to be taken, decisions made regarding the formulation of appropriate change strategies need to be a function of the reflections of the practitioner. Reflective practitioners make a habit of using theory to inform and shape their practice as the means of consistently obtaining high-quality results.

STRATEGIES FOR CHANGE

Currently, strategic management is undergoing a re-examination in terms of its assumptions and implications. As referred to earlier, Stacey (1996a, 1996b) applies chaos theory and the science of complexity in trying to develop an alternative form of thinking about strategy. He is convinced that other methods do not work, because of the rational, predictive assumptions that strategic managers have made in the past. Johnson (1987), however, suggests the strategic approach has developed different perspectives which have been applied to different organizations in the past. He distinguishes between rationalist, adaptive and interpretative views. A rationalist view is seen as the outcome of a sequential, planned search for an optimum solution to predefined problems, with implementation following on from the decisions made about such problems; an adaptive view is one which is incremental, and the problem solution evolves as a result of the monitoring of an incremental additive pattern; and an interpretative view is one in which strategy is seen as the product of individual or collective sense-making.

Buchanan and Boddy (1992) suggest that any devised plan for action must take into account an appropriate time span into the future; must see change as a process and not an event; and must make reference to the internal and external context of the organization. They advocate the use of rational strategies for planning and implementing change within the organization, yet they also suggest that change agents need to recognize rationally that change is chaotic. They characterize the chaos of the internal, organizational environment in terms of continuously changing organizational agendas and priorities, the discontinuity of the management task, and the occurrence of unexpected organizational events.

Unfortunately, the organizations that people experience at work do not fit into ideal types. If they did, it would be easier for the management 'myth makers' to be more prescriptive about what is necessary in the planning of organizational change. However, our experience and knowledge of the world indicates that organizations have been devised for different purposes to meet different kinds of objectives and therefore they do not constitute an ideal type. Consequently, the change strategists, when developing their particular strategies, are having to recognize that the possibilities for change are dependent on whether:

1 The change is incremental over time and involves changing the core objectives of the organization.

2 The change is incremental over time and involves changing the peripheral objectives of the organization.

3 The change is radical/major over time and involves changing the core objectives of the organization.

4 The change is radical/major over time and involves changing the peripheral objectives of the organization (after Buchanan and Boddy 1992).

Clearly, the type of change being considered and how the change is going to be implemented will have different consequences for the people in the organization and for their patterns of work. For instance, both private and public sector organizations are currently applying 'off-the-shelf' strategies for change to meet quality and efficiency objectives. ISO 9000 has been adopted by a large number of organizations as part of a drive towards total quality management (TQM). Furthermore, in manufacturing, many organizations have attempted to develop *kaizen* strategies of continuous improvement in order to change working practices, cut costs and increase the quality and competitiveness of their products, whereas other organizations have implemented change strategies based on the principles of business process re-engineering (BPR). However, as discussed in Chapter 2, a very high proportion of these change programmes have failed and have led to unintended and unwanted consequences.

To counter such failures, a recent feature of organizational change programmes has been the emphasis given to developing a strategic focus of change based on ideas concerning the learning organization. For instance, Swieringa and Weirdsma (1992), as well as identifying features of learning and the learning organization, suggest that change comes about according to the 'trekker model'. This can be parodied as '... even though we do not know precisely where we are heading and certainly not where we will finish up, we choose a direction and off we go'. They suggest that 'change will take place in a common, collective learning process in which thought, action, reflections and decisions interchange with each other'. West (1994) echoes this by suggesting that organizational effectiveness 'is increasingly dependent on developing an environment which fosters learning and the sharing of information as a foundation to deal with uncertainty'. This kind of approach, which is concerned with the development of managers and rests heavily on the long-term commitment of organizational leaders, is increasingly being adopted in different kinds of organization. Franklin (1996), who strongly criticizes the formulaic 'right approach' to strategy, shows how the empirical and practical efficacy of different forms of strategic thinking are fatally flawed. However, he suggests that strategic practice involving planning provides managers with a basis for organizational learning.

It seems to us that a number of underlying problems exist concerning ideas about strategy, strategic direction and the future of organizations. What appears to be held in common is that most of the reported approaches for bringing about strategic change, whether formally prescribed or advocated in academic texts, or the result of the practical experience of managers and consultants, tend to indicate that either the planning of change or the change process itself is problematic. Clearly there are implications for the reflective practitioner. Bearing this in mind, we will now consider a number of these perceived problems concerning the effective management of change.

STRATEGY IMPLEMENTATION

Appropriate organizational analysis and knowledge of the characteristics of a proposed change strategy are crucial for ensuring that the strategy becomes successfully implemented. This belief is one that is increasingly being shared by organizational change consultants, academics and researchers and has gained currency to counter the common managerial practice of picking a change strategy 'off the shelf' and then implementing the strategy as by a recipe. A recognition is growing that the discontinuities of organizational life are continuous, that the change advocated will be likely to increase the discontinuities, and that the change processes implemented need to be constant and continuing over long periods of time. Organizational change cannot be a formulaic 'quick fix' if it is to be implemented successfully. Advocates of the 'quick fix' have developed recipe implementation formulae, which have frequently had unfortunate implications. For example, early developments in the field of organizational change and development rested heavily on the work of Lewin (1958). He suggested a three-stage model, which was applied originally to explain change in small groups. Lewin argued that implementation should proceed in three stages: the first involves unfreezing the existing 'undesired' organizational state as reflected in the attitudes and behaviours expressed in the organization; the second involves changing these attitudes and behaviours in the desired direction; and the third stage involves re-freezing these changed attitudes and behaviours so that the new 'desired' organizational state will be maintained, permanently.

This model has been refined by Johnson (1990), who argues that the implementation strategy can be regarded as a series of symbolic acts to be utilized by the change agent. These are shown in Table 3.1.

These models imply that organizations are not in a state of flux and implicitly assume that the change process is discrete rather than continuous. Therefore, their applicability seems dubious, particularly as they assume, metaphorically at least, that people in organizations 'can be taken out of refrigerators, changed, and then put back to be frozen permanently'. Furthermore, Johnson's model is not clear as to what is being symbolized, although the symbols may signify a particular type of 'totalitarian' leadership. Both models lack an ability to be generalized because they may not apply in all circumstances. They reflect the psychology of small group behaviour in the case of Lewin, and the imperatives of the privatized utilities in the case of Johnson.

Table 3.1 Implementation strategies

Change agent acts	Change agent behaviour
Unfreezing	Challenge current ways of doing things, close down parts of the organization, move people around
Flux	Foster conflict and dissent through open argument
Information building	Set up task forces, use consultants reports, commission special reports
Experimentation	Devise management development training programmes, signal change with new product displays, services and other departures from the previous ways of doing things
Refreezing	Send signals of irreversible and permanent change, through celebrations and new key appointments

Another form of strategy implementation is to apply conventional organizational development (OD) models to realize the strategy for change. However, Harrison (1994) suggests there is a need for change agents to move beyond the traditional OD model because it is based on a narrow view of organizational effectiveness. He identifies how training and small group interventions of the kind favoured by OD practitioners have often failed to come to terms with organizational politics and culture. He also indicates that where OD interventions have been appropriate, they have only yielded minor, incremental improvements in organizational effectiveness, as opposed to the sometimes radical transformations required to recover from crisis and decline (Dunphy and Stace 1988). However, based on extensive research Heracleous and DeVoge (1998) have demonstrated that an 'integrated organizational model' based on an action research paradigm, which integrates OD into strategic management and the strategic change process, is 'a powerful tool for diagnosis, action planning and implementation of strategies'.

Stacey (1996b) claims that the basic OD model and mainstream models of change strategy implementation, with their emphasis on the concept of linear and negative feedback systems, do not take adequate account of the complex dynamics of organizations caused by the effects of positive feedback and non-linearity. Hence, he argues, OD interventions designed to bring about, for example, large-scale culture change often fail, the main reasons being:

- OD effort provokes and reinforces powerful organizational defence routines that are difficult to identify and deal with.

- OD education and training programmes which try to get people to expose and question the values of the existing systems, upset people and arouse management fears of losing control. This leads to reduced commitment.

- OD programmes that do succeed in dispersing power, weakening central authority and spreading participation and teamwork can set off positive amplifying feedback loops, which lead to greater peer rivalry or passive loyalty, both of which block or undermine creativity and decision-making ability.

■ OD programmes, by being what they are, inevitably raise anxiety levels. This is because they are about major organization-wide change, which alters people's power positions and jobs. Higher uncertainty levels and higher anxiety levels inevitably provoke positive feedback loops of unconscious behaviour which blocks effective functioning. This results in organizational defence routines and unconscious defence mechanisms against anxiety.

Another problem appears to be one of implementing strategy in particular contexts 'made up' by the power and the politics of the organization. Buchanan and Boddy (1992) suggest that change agents need to develop 'backstage' political skills to manage the process. They should constantly analyse and monitor the politics in a change situation, develop the political strategies necessary to counter the political moves of others in the organization, and gain support for the change. As will be understood, the change agent would need to become skilled at dealing with the managerial and other barriers to change. We will not deal with the problem of overcoming the barriers to change, except to indicate that Carnall (1990) identifies what the personal, group and organizational 'blocks' to change are. In many instances the biggest problem of implementation involves the politics of people in organizations, the cultural issues and the differences between people. As a result, there are a number of change models in the management literature which emphasize these different aspects of the change process.

From our experience and research we conclude that there is no one best way for all change contexts. Different strategies need to be implemented to satisfy different change criteria dependent on specific organizational situations. However, specific to healthcare, Edmonstone (1995) suggests there is an emerging consensus with regard to effective strategy implementation. He states that the knowledge and skills of individuals are reinforced by recurring work activity; that the primary focus for change should be behaviour within a network of roles, relationships and responsibilities at work; and that effective change usually starts 'bottom-up' not 'top-down'. On the other hand, Gould (1996) claims that for businesses in general it much depends on the wish of organizational leaders acting as change agents when making choices with the intention of navigating change. He suggests that depending on particular strategically defined situations change agents can act in a number of alternative ways. Furthermore, they can act to conserve and continue present practice, preserve and build on current practice, revolutionize and brutalize practice in times of crisis, or innovate through transformation.

It appears there are issues here concerning the efficacy of different forms of strategy, and debates in practice as to whether 'top-down' as opposed to 'bottom-up' implementation strategies are more appropriate. However, neither Edmonstone nor Gould give consideration to the very significant impact that organizational leaders have on change processes. (We discuss this in the next section.)

Another issue, which has been much discussed in the management and professional literature with regard to implementation strategies, concerns changing the organizational culture. Clearly, if culture is defined as employee attitudes and behaviours (Drennan 1992), there are implications that the reflective practitioner may need to understand. Azjen and Fishbein (1980) make a convincing case demonstrating that there is little relationship between attitudes as measured and subsequent behaviour. As a result, it may be important for change agents to focus on changing behaviour and beliefs about behaviour as an outcome for change implementation strategies, rather than attitudes, values and other associated internal states which are referred to in the management literature. Clearly, behaviour change is the major outcome intended in most change strategies; changes in the culture may follow.

This view is supported by the work of Schneider *et al.* (1996), who draw attention to the fact that organizations often go through cycles of attempting to bring about change without achieving success. They suggest that the reason for the failure is a possible relationship between organizational culture and climate. However, in creating a climate and culture for sustainable organizational change they advocate that culture can best be changed through a focus on the organizational climate.

As implied by the foregoing, it is important to recognize that issues concerning strategy implementation are complex. The agent for change must have a clear idea of the type and time scale for the change to be implemented, the importance of the change within the overall objectives of the organization, and how much the change to be adopted will be disruptive of behaviour and of beliefs about behaviour. The change agent needs to develop the skills of leadership, of managing 'up', 'across' and 'downwards' depending on the organizational structure, and of developing organizational and political 'nous' in order to manage the process in terms of the power and politics of the organization. Furthermore, the change agent must constantly analyse, reflect and monitor the politics of the situation to develop appropriate political strategies which enable the change to take place within the political support system. This includes the leadership of the organization. We believe that if these highly specific contextual issues are identified, reflected upon and managed, one set of managerial barriers to change will have been removed, more or less.

We suggest the change agent should think strategically about how to implement a change strategy, bearing in mind the specific characteristics of the organizational environment. The classification of the type of strategy to be utilized is important, but he or she needs to work practically within the boundaries of what the organization is, and then reflect on that constantly. The whole process of implementation must be managed effectively – all of the time. This implies the need to 'perform' across the different levels of the organization in order to facilitate the change process at the individual, group and organizational level. This also implies that the change agent needs constant support from the leadership of the organization – otherwise, if this is not forthcoming and is not continuous from the start of strategy formulation through to strategy implementation and evaluation, the change strategy will fail. However, to prevent failure being contemplated spuriously the change agent needs to be able to evaluate the effectiveness of the change strategy that has been implemented.

EVALUATION OF CHANGE EFFECTIVENESS

There appears to be a lack of literature concerning the problem of evaluation, which Jane Keep explores in Chapter 5, yet paradoxically change is still advocated as a 'good thing'. Carnall (1991) has reported the reasons for the failure of change implementation strategies in 93 organizations, which appear to relate to different types of organizational feature. They are:

■ Implementation took more time than originally allocated.

■ Major problems surfaced during implementation which had not been identified beforehand.

■ Co-ordination of implementation activities was not effective enough.

■ Competing activities and other crises distracted management from implementing the change decision.

■ The capabilities of employees involved were not sufficient.

■ Training and instruction given to lower-level employees was inadequate.

■ Uncontrollable factors in the external environment had an adverse impact on implementation.

Carnall goes on to suggest that the effectiveness of change strategies can be evaluated if appropriate questions are asked concerning the people, finance, marketing, operations and business development over time. However, the analysis reported above is of necessity de-contextualized. It may be that identifying contextual reasons for the failure of strategy implementation would be more powerful in developing the management ideology. Dunphy and Stace (1988) argue that the effectiveness of the change may depend on whether the change strategy is participative or forced, and whether the transformation involved will be charismatic or dictatorial in terms of the authority, power and leadership characteristics shown by the management involved in the changes advocated.

We believe that if HR professionals and line managers are going to take on the mantle of change agents, they must be placed in a position of being able to contribute to the process of strategic decision making concerning the effectiveness of the organization into the future. This is a different way of saying that those responsible for the formulation of mission statements and business plans should involve those who will have to implement such decisions. However, as Ulrich (1997) argues, it is incumbent upon HR professionals to position themselves as 'strategic partners' with top managers so they do become involved as members of the senior management coalitions held responsible for the formulation of business strategy and its translation into action. To do so requires them to learn to perform disciplined organizational analyses and diagnoses, and to conduct these collaboratively with top managers to turn strategy into action. The use and value of a 'deep' analysis as advocated in this chapter is the derivation of a series of effectiveness/ineffectiveness statements concerning individuals, groups and the organization itself. These will enable the change agent, whether manager, trainer, developer or other HR professional, to monitor and reflect upon the effect of the change strategy envisioned in discussions of organizational strategy. In the process of business planning, the organizational analysis made will act to enable appropriate effectiveness criteria to be tested out in practice, once the change is in process. We believe the change agent must adopt the stance of evaluation at the beginning of the planning process.

The problem of evaluating strategies for change needs to be recognized as one of the most under-reported issues in the British management literature. There are plenty of exhortations on the need to change organizations and, as indicated in the preceding chapter, considerable literature on how to change organizations. But there are only a few longitudinal studies effectively evaluating change processes in different organizational contexts. This may be because the problem is seen as a research issue. However, the implication for managers, trainers and developers operating as change agents is that they have a need to address the problem using appropriate evaluative and research skills to validate claims that could be made in relation to the success or otherwise of a change strategy. (See Davies 1996 for an introduction to research skills specifically for HRD specialists, and Swanson and Holton 1997 for a broader-ranging introduction from an American perspective.) Interestingly, in their discussion on using 'action research' in the study of organization and management, Bruce and Wyman (1998) advocate that 'rather than simply bringing in professional behavioural scientists and industrial engineers to study the people working, action research also seeks to provide the people involved in the action being researched with the tools they need to participate in researching the action themselves'.

There has been recently an increased emphasis in the management literature on the effectiveness of different types of leadership and its influence on the effectiveness of organizational change and development programmes. This implicitly assumes that the failure of change strategy implementation and evaluation is a failure in leadership. Hence there have been efforts to examine effective leadership in the context of change innovations. For instance, Binney and Williams (1995) explore the myth of managing change by contrasting mechanistic views with organic views of the process, and locate the problem of effectiveness within the ambit of organizational leadership. They claim that organizational change will only be achieved when successful leaders face up to the paradox of giving away power in order to become more powerful, and of listening to become more forthright. This view is developed within the context of internal and external analysis of the leaders' particular environment and the development of a clear, practical vision based on the internal and external realities. In stressing the importance of learning by doing, Binney and Williams construct a view of changing organizations by 'leaning into the future'. With regard to using 'action training and research' (AT&R) for changing organizations, Bruce and Wyman (1998), draw on the experiences of a wide range of key people who practised action training and research in developing their respective changing organizations to argue that:

> leadership of the AT&R project must always remain with the people in the organization. One of the major pitfalls for AT&R practitioners is to assume a leadership role, just to get the project started. If the practitioner is unsuccessful in transferring leadership to the organization, the commitment to the change program will probably leave when the practitioner leaves ... AT&R can be useful in organizations with any variety of management styles and cultures. Clearly, less participative leadership styles and authoritative values are not conducive to supporting change, least of all from the bottom up. However, that is the challenge of the AT&R method. (p. 77)

Essentially, the views of both Binney and Williams (1995) and Bruce and Wyman (1998), based as they are on reflections concerning the experiences of consultants and practitioners, could be dismissed as mere exhortation. However, more empirically based studies are also indicating the importance of the organizational leader.

Jones and Gross (1996) contrast the effectiveness of leadership styles in two Australian public sector organizations. They show how the different leadership styles of the two chief executives were reflected in the particular change strategies adopted, the one being a 'top-down' and the other a 'bottom-up' approach. In both cases, effective organizational change was achieved. Evaluating these changes, Jones and Gross conclude that the differences between the achievements in the two organizations were reflected in how the leadership in the one case was prepared to force change to a timetable, and in the other to facilitate change through time. However, it appears that the type of change strategies advocated by the two organizational leaders were not particularly relevant in defining the effectiveness of the change achieved. Rather, it was the constant expression of their personal commitment to change. Similarly, Hamlin and Reidy (1997) show that the commitment and continued support of an executive head to a longitudinal research study into organizational culture, which he commissioned as part of an ongoing organizational change programme, created the climate for effecting significant changes in what had become a maladaptive management culture.

From this it is apparent that in order for principles of change and change management to be formulated in a particular organization, managers, trainers and developers need to be prepared to evaluate constantly their change agency practice against change effectiveness criteria. These need to be negotiated with organizational leaders, whose active interest, involvement and support are important. Visionary leadership from the top is often the key factor for success. To conclude, we look at the implications in the foregoing for the role of the change agent.

IMPLICATIONS FOR THE ROLE OF THE CHANGE AGENT

What has been said in the previous sections will give cause for reflection and reappraisal, particularly for those whose function is currently that of trainer, developer or training manager. Recent changes in their respective roles have been fuelled over the past decade by the important realization of the need for modern-day HRD practitioners to be specialists not only in training and development focused on resolving immediate organizational and individual skill deficits but also in the disciplines of organizational behaviour, organization development and strategic human resource development focused on the creation of long-term competitive organizational capabilities. Organizations need the services of HRD (and HRM) professionals who can operate effectively as change agents in collaboration with line managers, and who are capable of taking appropriate action reflectively. As has been implied, the changing roles of managers, trainers and developers have clear implications for the development of new sets of skills and abilities in the area of change management. These are discussed in some detail in Chapter 4. However, we wish to draw particular attention here to the work of Buchanan and Boddy (1992) and Carnall (1990), which identifies a range of competencies considered necessary in order to develop expertise as a change agent. We suggest that the emphasis placed by these authors on role expectations will be helpful to anyone wishing to acquire the necessary skills. We would add, however, that they underplay the role of the change agent as an internal consultant, in which capacity he or she must clearly work in order to initiate, modify and maintain the change process. Burgoyne (1990) identifies features of the successful client–consultant relationship in a practical fashion, stressing that the client needs to be helped to take responsibility for the change. The consultant as change agent should also support and confront the internal client about the appropriateness of the action being advocated. Rose and Kennedy (1996) suggest there is an ethical dimension to this activity whereby consultants need to be aware of the confidentiality involved in such a relationship. Other ethical dilemmas confronting change agents are explored by Jane Keep in Chapter 5. On becoming 'strategic partners' with line managers helping organizations respond to change initiatives, process changes and culture change, Ulrich (1997) stresses the need for HR professionals to 'provide leadership in improvement practices' within the organization, and sets out what they and managers need to do in mastering both the theory and practice of change management. Wallace and Ridgeway (1996) also provide valuable insights into the leadership of strategic change through a number of 'change leadership concepts' derived from their research findings. In addition, they present a range of 'best practice' case studies and self-assessment instruments to help managers and HR professionals develop their capacity to lead change successfully in what is a chaotic world. They have identified eight types of 'change leader', each requiring a different sets of skills and expertise, namely the 'Visionary Leader'; the 'Influential Leader'; the 'Facilitative Leader'; the 'Leading Change in a Crisis Leader'; the 'Leading Change in a Developmental-Participative Way Leader;' the 'Leading Change Where the Organization Needs New Vision Leader'; the 'Leading Change in a Flexible Manner Leader'; and the 'HR Manager as a Strategic Change Influence Partner'.

As already mentioned in Chapter 2, Quirke (1995) advocates the use of internal research as a potent tool for change, while Ormerod (1996) argues the need for consultancy to be supported by research. Furthermore, Jacobs and Vyakarnam (1994) call for strategically led research-based approaches to management development, while Hamlin *et al.* (1997) argue the case for strategically led research-based organizational change and development.

A further consideration is that change agents ought to recognize that there is a psychodynamic associated with the change process (see Neumann *et al.* 1997, who consider in some depth psychodynamic approaches to organizational consultancy in rapidly changing conditions). Any change creates stress and anxiety; this is because as human beings we deal individually with uncertainty in different ways. It is important that HR professionals and managers alike develop support networks in order to cope with the stress that can be created by the differing pressures associated with the change agent role. Carnall (1991) is helpful in identifying a psychological process which accounts for different behavioural and performance variations through the change process. He suggests that individuals and groups in the organization will experience differential effects on performance because of the effect that the change process will have on role expectations. New systems, new procedures, new processes and new ways of behaving will have to be learned, which will take time and will reflect a learning curve. When these new behaviours are being learned the effects of 'progression' will need to be anticipated. What this means is that modifications will have to be developed to deal with 'snags' as they arise in the change process. Carnall suggests that significant organizational change will have differential organizational effects on the self-esteem of different individuals in the organization as they become affected by the implications of the change.

The change agent must be aware of these implications in terms of the significance for behaviour of direct change processes, and also of the associated psychological processes. Carnall describes these processes in relation to stages; the first being denial of the need to change, successively followed by stages of defence of the old ways of doing things, a discarding of these old behaviours by the majority before adaptation to the new changes, followed by a stage of internalization of the change behaviours. Therefore, change agents need to understand, and get their organizational leaders to understand, that whatever the strategy of change being advocated happens to be, the change process needs time: time for planning, time for implementation, time for evaluation, and also time for reflection in order to take account of the vagaries of the psychological processes that organizational members and change agents will inevitably experience. The points made here are reinforced and further illuminated by the reflections on actual change agency practice from the various reflective practitioners who have contributed to Part III of this book.

References

Ajzen, I. and Fishbein, M. (1980), *Understanding Attitudes and Predicting Behaviour*. Englewood Cliffs, NJ: Prentice Hall.

Binney, G. and Williams, C. (1995), *Leaning into the Future: Changing the Way People Change Organizations*. London: Nicholas Brearley.

Blyton, P. and Turnbull, P. (1992), *Reassessing Human Resource Management*. London: Sage.

Buchanan, D. and Boddy, D. (1992), *The Expertise of the Change Agent*. London: Prentice Hall.

Burgoyne, J. (1990), A behavioural science perspective on operational research practice. In Wilson, D. and Rosenfeld, R., (eds) *Managing Organizations*. London: McGraw-Hill.

Burns, T. and Stalker, G. (1966), *The Management of Innovation*. London: Tavistock.

Bruce, R. and Wyman, S. (1998), *Changing Organizations. Practicing Action Training and Research*. Thousand Oaks, Calif.: Sage.

Carnall, C. (1990), *Managing Change in Organizations*. London: Prentice Hall.

Carnall, C. (1991), *Managing Change*. London: Routledge.

Champy, J. and Nohria, N. (eds) (1996), *Fast Forward: The Best Ideas on Managing Business Change*. Boston: Harvard Business School Press.

Davies, G. (1996), Research methods and human

resource development. In Stewart, J. and McGoldrick, J. (eds), *Human Resource Development, Perspectives, Strategies, and Practice*. London: Pitman.

Drennan, D. (1992), *Transforming Company Culture*. London: McGraw-Hill.

Drucker, P. (1988), The coming of the new organization. *Harvard Business Review*, February, 43–53.

Dunphy, D. and Stace, D. (1988), Transformational and coercive strategies for planned organizational change. *Organization Studies*, 9(3), 317–334.

Edmonstone, J. (1995), Managing change: an emerging new consensus. *Health Service Management*, 21(1), 16–19.

Franklin, P. (1996), Dialogues in strategy. *Strategic Change*, 5, 211–221.

Gould, R.M. (1996), Getting from strategy to action: processes for continuous change. *Long Range Planning*, 29(3), 278–289.

Hallworth, M. (1994), 'Re-engineering learning processes'. *Training and Development*, October, 36–37.

Hamel, G. and Prahalad, C. (1994) *Competing for the Future*, Boston: Harvard Business School Press.

Hamlin, R.G. and Reidy, M. (1997), Effecting change in management culture. *Strategic Change*, special edition, December.

Hamlin, R.G., Reidy, M. and Stewart, J. (1997), Changing the management culture in one part of the British civil service through visionary leadership and strategically led research-based OD interventions. *Journal of Applied Management Studies*, 6(2), 233–251.

Hamlin, R.G., Reidy, M. and Stewart, J. (1999), Effecting management culture change through research-based management development. *Management Development Forum*, State University of New York, 2(1), 21–47.

Handy, C. (1989), *The Age of Unreason*. London: Random Century.

Handy, C. (1990), *Inside Organizations*. London: BBC Books.

Harrison, R. (1988), *Training and Development*, London: IPM.

Harrison, M. (1994), *Diagnosing Organizations*: *Methods, Models and Processes*. London: Sage.

Hassard, J. and Parker, C. (eds) (1993), *Postmodernism and Organizations*. London: Sage.

Heracleous, L. and DeVoge, S. (1998), Bridging the gap of relevance: strategic management and organizational development. *Long Range Planning*, 31(5), 742–754.

Jacobs, R. and Vyakarnam, S. (1994), The need for a more strategically led research based approach in management development. British Psychological Society Occupational Psychology Division Conference, Birmingham.

Johnson, G. (1987), *Strategic Change and Management Process*. Oxford: Blackwell.

Johnson, G. (1990), Managing strategic change: the role of symbolic action. *British Journal of Management*, 1, 183–200.

Jones, R. and Gross, M. (1996), A tale of two councils: strategic change in Australian local government. *Strategic Change*, 5, 123–139.

Kearney, P. (1994), Business process re-engineering. *Training and Development*, March, 14–17.

Lewin, C. (1958), Group decision and social change. In Maccoby, E., Newcomb,T. and Hartley, E. (eds), *Readings in Social Psychology*. London: Holt, Rinehart & Winston.

Miller, D. (1990), *The Icarus Paradox*: *How Excellent Organizations Can Bring About Their Own Downfall*. New York: Harper Business.

Morgan, G. (1988), Emerging waves and challenges: the need for new competencies and mindsets. In Henry, J. (ed.), *Creative Management*. London: Sage.

Morgan, G. (1993), *Imaginisation*: *The Art of Creative Management*. London: Sage.

Mullins, L. (1993), *Management and Organizational Behaviour*, 3rd edn. London: Pitman.

Nelson, T. and Coxhead, H. (1997), Increasing the probability of re-engineering/culture change success through effective internal communication. *Strategic Change*, 6(1), 29–48.

Neumann, J.E., Kellner, K. and Dawson-Shepherd, A. (1997), *Developing Organizational Consultancy*. London: Routledge.

Ormerod, R.J. (1996), Combining management consultancy and research, Omega. *International Journal of Management Science*, 24(1), 1–12.

Pascale, R.T. (1990), *Managing on the Edge – How Successful Companies Manage Conflict to Stay Ahead*. London: Viking Penguin.

Pedler, M., Burgoyne, J. and Boydell, T. (1991), *The Learning Company*. London: McGraw-Hill.

Peters, T. (1988), *Restoring American Competitiveness*: *Looking for New Models of Organizations*. The Academy of Management Executive.

Peters, T. and Waterman, R. (1982), *In Search of Excellence*. New York: Harper & Row.

Quirke, B. (1995), *Communicating Change*. London: McGraw-Hill.

Reddin,W. (1985), *The Best of Bill Reddin*, 2nd edn. Trowbridge: IPM.

Robinson, G.M. (1992), *Managing after the Superlatives – Effective Senior Management Development for the 1990's*. London: Tudor.

Rose, A. and Kennedy, E. (1996), Ethical dilemmas of the HR consultant. Unpublished paper, University of Westminster.

Schneider, B., Brief, A. and Guzzo, R. (1996), Creating a climate and culture for sustainable organizational change. *Organizational Dynamics*, Spring, 24(4), 7–19.

Stacey, R. (1996a), *Complexity and Creativity in Organizations*. San Francisco: Berrett-Koehler.

Stacey, R. (1996b), *Strategic Management and Organizational Dynamics*. London: Pitman.

Swanson, R.A. and Holton III, E.F. (1997), *Human Resource Development Research Handbook*: *Linking Research and Practice*. San Francisco: Berrett-Koehler.

Swieringa, J. and Weirdsma, A. (1992), *Becoming a Learning Organization, Beyond the Learning Curve*. New York: Addison-Wesley.

Trahant, W. and Burke, W.W. (1996), Travelling through transitions. *Training and Development*, February.

Ulrich, D. (1997), *Human Resource Champions*. Boston: Harvard Business School Press.

Wallace, B. and Ridgeway, C. (1996) *Leadership for Strategic Change*. London: IPD.

Walton, J. (1999), *Strategic Human Resource Development*. Harlow: Financial Times Prentice Hall.

West, P. (1994), The concept of the learning organization. *Journal of European Industrial Training*, 18(1), pp. 15–21.

The pathology of organizational change: a study of UK managers' experiences

Les Worrall, Cary Cooper and Fiona Campbell

INTRODUCTION

As suggested in the previous chapters, the implications and effects of change on the future of organizations are far-reaching. HRD and OD professionals are having to cope with frequent and often cyclical change. As outlined by Hamlin and Davies in Chapter 3, those involved in change management – managers, trainers and developers – will require a new set of skills and abilities to implement change effectively and successfully in the future. The purpose of this chapter is first to illustrate the effects of continuous and often unsuccessful downsizing and change on organizations in the UK and the perceptions of UK managers. Results are drawn from recent research conducted by UMIST–Institute of Management on the 'Quality of Working Life' project and show both the extent of organizational change and its implications for business performance. Second, to explore the impact of organizational change as a basis for advising on the development of more informed human resource development strategies and on the development of better-informed approaches to the management of change.

THE REDEFINITION OF WORK AND CHANGING ORGANIZATIONS

In a recent report by the Royal Society of Arts into the redefinition of work (RSA 1998), the author of the report, Valerie Bayliss, said that 'Work is redefining itself: the patterns of people's working lives are changing fundamentally. This will affect everything linked to work – pensions and social insurance, education and training, how employers manage their workforce. Most people are learning to handle change but too many decision takers are behind the game'. Not only is work being redefined, so too is the nature of organizations and organizational life (Cooper 1998a, 1998b). In the last five years, the scale of organizational change has been considerable.

Delayering, outsourcing, out-placement, right-sizing, business process re-engineering, broad-banding, market testing, compulsory competitive tendering, TQM and focusing on core competencies, coupled with the emergence of more competitive pressures in the global economy, have had considerable impact on organizational structures and, perhaps most importantly, on career structures, employee expectations and the quality of working life, particularly for middle and senior managers, who form the focus of our research. Recently, levels of job insecurity and the decrease in traditional career paths have been a significant worry to employees across both public and private sectors. Downsizing and redundancy have caused violations to the psychological employment contract and left HRD professionals to redefine and realign the career expectations of the surviving workforce towards more non-traditional rewards and development (Holbeche 1997).

While there have been a number of studies which have sought to explore the nature of organizational change (Morgan 1997), there are relatively few cross-sectional studies which have sought to assess how well these change management processes have been managed and what the impact of the (mis)management of these changes has been on managers in different industrial sectors and different types of organization and, more importantly, what the differential impacts have been on managers at differing levels in the organizational hierarchy. The results shown will address these issues.

This chapter is based on the preliminary findings of a five-year research programme (Worrall and Cooper 1997, 1998a,b) designed to paint a picture of the impact of organizational change on managers' experiences. In turn, this provides a more socially complete view of the changes in organizational structures and working patterns that have affected corporate Britain (Lees 1997). The essence of our research is to explore how well human resources are being managed within organizations; to assess the impacts of organizational change on managers; to assess how well change management processes are being managed; and to assess whether the human resource base of UK organizations is being wasted, whether it is being worn out, how well it is being motivated, how well it is being developed and how well it is being managed as an asset through active and well-informed investment.

In the natural environment, there has been much concern with developing environmentally friendly policies and with the concept of 'sustainability'. Sustainability requires us to move to a level of growth and a pattern of change which will not cause the long-term destruction or depletion of the world's natural resources. Perhaps there is a need to develop a more 'manager-friendly' approach to human resource management geared less to making 'the assets sweat' than to 'keeping them fit' and not wearing out managers physically and/or mentally. Previous research (Campbell 1999; Thornhill *et al.* 1997) suggests that the trap of cyclical decline has an increasingly negative effect on managers/employees over time and that organizations continue to concern themselves with internal structures and lose sight of the external market, the customer and the competition. The challenge, therefore, is to relocate the focus of HRD and OD professionals towards replenishing the depleted organizational human resources to help regain sight of organizational objectives.

THE RESEARCH DESIGN

This chapter is based on a UMIST–Institute of Management research programme labelled the 'Quality of Working Life', which is conducted annually using the Institute of Management's membership database as a sampling frame. A questionnaire was designed based on our extensive prior research (Worrall and Cooper 1995; Liff *et al.* 1997; Cooper and Lewis 1994; Institute of Management 1996a, 1996b; Charlesworth 1996). The questionnaire was sent to a panel of 5000 members of the Institute of Management. The exercise generated 1362 valid responses in 1997 and 1313 in 1998, which represented response rates of 27 and 26 per cent, respectively. A detailed profile of the panel of respondents is contained in Worrall and Cooper (1997, 1998a).

It is important to emphasize here that the sample reflects the structure of the membership of the Institute of Management, particularly when exploring the distribution of respondents by management level. The profile of respondents by managerial level for 1998 is presented in Table 4.1.

Table 4.1 The structure of the sample by managerial level

Management level	Number	Percentage
Chair	20	1.5
CEO/MD	152	11.6
Director	204	15.5
Senior manager	390	29.7
Middle manager	316	24.1
Junior manager	131	10.0
Other	65	5.0

The distribution by managerial level must be borne in mind when examining figures related to the total panel of respondents, as the responses will reflect the profile of membership of the Institute of Management rather than the status profile of managers in UK businesses. The panel tends to over-represent managers at more senior levels, and, as we shall see later on, there are significant differences in attitudes, behaviours and experiences in relation to respondents' positions in the organizational hierarchy.

THE EXTENT OF ORGANIZATIONAL CHANGE AND THE DIMENSIONS OF RESTRUCTURING

The extent of organizational change in 1997 and 1998

Our baseline report in 1997 highlighted the extent of organizational change in UK business organizations. In 1997, we reported that 59 per cent of respondents had experienced some form of organizational change over the last year. In 1998, the rate increased to 62 per cent. This reveals not only a considerable degree of dynamism but also an increasing pace of change and, perhaps, an increasing level of employment instability and insecurity. While there has been an overall increase in the number of managers affected by restructuring, there has not been an across-the-board change by either type of organization or by size of organization. Charity and not-for-profit organizations appear to have had a significant increase in the amount of restructuring. The extent of restructuring remains substantially higher in public limited companies (Plc's) (particularly the former public utilities) and public sector organizations than in any other type of organization. While the extent has remained roughly constant in the public sector, there has been a 4-percentage-point increase among public limited companies. An analysis by firm size also revealed that there was a systematic relationship between size and the likelihood of restructuring having taken place (see Table 4.2). While 33 per cent of respondents in organizations employing under 51 people had undergone some form of restructuring, this increased to 76 per cent in organizations employing over 500 people.

Table 4.2 The changing extent of organizational change by type of organization

Has your organization carried out a restructuring in the last 12 months? 1997 Base 1361 1998 Base 1312	% Yes 1997	% Yes 1998
Charity/not for profit	44	62
Family-owned business	38	36
Partnership	38	30
Private limited company	58	61
Public limited company	71	75
Public sector	73	72
Sole trader	20	10
All	59	62

As discussed by Hamlin in Chapter 2, different sectors have been affected by different pressures causing different forms of organizational adaptation. The almost wholesale privatization of the former public utilities, the fragmentation of the NHS into a myriad of health trusts, attempts to drive down local and national government costs through market testing and compulsory competitive tendering, the application of IT in the financial services sector and the implications of global competition on manufacturing have all caused massive changes in these sectors. Elsewhere (Worrall, Cooper and Campbell 2000), we have commented in detail on the significant differences in the extent of restructuring and the form it has taken, particularly in the public sector and among managers in the former public utilities. As can be seen in Table 4.3, the extent of change experienced by different industrial sectors varies considerably, from a high of 88 per cent in the utilities sector to a low of 32 per cent among consultancies.

Table 4.3 The extent of organizational restructuring by industrial sector

Base 1311	Respondents	Yes %	No %
All	1311	62	36
Construction/engineering	113	54	45
Consultancy	130	32	68
Manufacturing/production	229	72	28
Distribution/transport	34	56	41
Retail/wholesale	36	53	42
Banking/insurance/finance	47	74	26
Utilities	49	88	12
Public administration/government	132	72	27
Education/training	146	64	34
Health services	78	69	31
Uniformed services/emergency	60	75	25
Business services	63	44	56

It is clear that the extent of organizational restructuring tends to be highest in the public sector and the former public sector (the utilities, public administration, education, health and the emergency services all have rates over 64 per cent) with manufacturing (72 per cent) and the financial services sector (banking, insurance and finance at 74 per cent) being the only private sector groups to have levels over the 62 per cent average.

Having established that there are significant differences in the extent of restructuring between industrial sectors, it is important to identify the extent to which these changes have been manifested in different ways across the sectors (see Table 4.4). Subsequent tables relate only to those 818 (62 per cent of) managers in 1998 who reported that their organization had experienced some form of restructuring over the last year.

The utilities sector stands out as having been most heavily affected by a wide range of forms of organizational restructuring. Over 60 per cent of respondents from the utilities sector report that the restructuring which had affected their organizations had involved the use of contract staff, culture change programmes, redundancies and cost reduction programmes. The health, public administration, utilities and distribution sectors appear to have been among the most affected by cost reduction programmes and redundancies and by the increased use of temporary staff. In the manufacturing sector, given the impact of increasing global competition, it is not surprising that the main emphasis has been on cost reduction and redundancies.

In this chapter, we have quantified the scale of the impact of organizational change and restructuring in the UK. In our surveys, we have shown that around 60 per cent of managers have been affected by organizational restructuring in the

Table 4.4 The nature of organizational restructuring by industrial sector (%)

	Closure of sites	Cost reduction	Culture change	Delayering	Outsourcing	Redundancies	Use of contract staff	Use of temporary staff
All	27	57	49	32	18	45	28	31
Construction/engineering	23	39	44	23	15	43	23	26
Consultancy	20	32	24	15	15	22	29	27
Manufacturing/production	27	62	55	34	21	48	29	33
Distribution/transport	21	68	37	32	11	58	16	32
Retail/wholesale	32	32	63	21	11	53	26	21
Banking/insurance/finance	29	57	43	26	23	40	29	34
Utilities	56	74	65	56	37	70	61	51
Public administration/government	28	66	49	44	23	54	26	40
Education/training	17	51	48	29	7	37	19	33
Health services	26	74	41	35	6	57	30	35
Uniformed services/emergency	38	58	49	24	20	27	42	20
Business services	21	57	25	11	11	29	21	18

last year, and that appears to have increased over the two years of our research. We have demonstrated that the scale of change and the forms of change are variable across UK organizations. They have been shown to vary by type of organization, by industrial sector and by size of business. Perhaps more importantly, we have shown that the form that organizational change has taken varies at the sectoral level. Having quantified the extent of change and analysed the differing forms that organization change and restructuring have taken, it now remains to assess the impact of this change on managers' working experiences.

THE PERCEIVED IMPACT OF RESTRUCTURING ON ORGANIZATIONAL PERFORMANCE AND EMPLOYEE ATTITUDES

The impact of organizational change on business performance

Organizational change, according to the textbooks, is implemented to solve some organization problem and to yield business benefits. Kets de Vries and Balazs (1997) suggest factors such as lower overheads, decreased bureaucracy, organizational efficiency, faster decision making and smoother communication as the expected benefits. Whether or not these benefits materialize is another question. We are of the opinion that the change management programmes are often not evaluated rigorously and often have unintended outcomes. Consequently, in our research programme, we set out to explore managers' views of the effects of their organizational change on organizational performance measures in terms of accountability, speed of decision making, the skills mix, productivity and profitability. The analysis presented here relates only to those respondents (814 in 1998) who reported that they had experienced organization restructuring in the last year. In Table 4.5, a 'net agree' score has been used, which is the percentage 'agreeing' with the proposition minus the percentage 'disagreeing' with the proposition.

Table 4.5 shows that evidence of winning positive benefits from the significant amount of restructuring is mixed. When all respondents are analysed together, it

Table 4.5 The effects of recent organizational change on perceived business performance (net agree)

Performance factor	All	Chair/ CE/MD	Director	Senior manager	Middle manager	Junior manager
Accountability has increased	53	80	67	50	52	37
Decision making is faster	−1	48	24	−5	−7	−25
Participation has increased	11	60	34	6	4	−3
Flexibility has increased	18	65	35	11	15	−8
Key skills have been lost	24	−24	2	24	43	27
Productivity has increased	21	70	47	16	12	−1
Profitability has increased	26	48	47	24	15	22

would appear that some of the harder benefits of restructuring may have been won in the form of increased accountability, profitability and productivity. However, it is noticeable, at the aggregate level, that the gains in some of the softer factors are less clear-cut. For example, there appears not to have been any improvement in the speed of decision making as a result of organizational change, and, while participation and flexibility have been perceived to have increased, the improvement of these factors following restructuring is below that of the harder factors listed earlier.

There is a clear view that restructuring has left organizations lacking the right mix of skills. This measure increased from a net agree score of 14 in 1997 to 24 in 1998. While there is a degree of stability in the other measures used, the increase on the 'now lacking skills factor' is significant and is linked to our concern that the forms of occupational restructuring being used – such as outsourcing, delayering and the use of temporary and contract staff – are having a major effect on the skills bases of organizations, further evidence that the core workforce is shrinking and there is a greater willingness by organizations to buy in skills from a contingent workforce.

The main body of Table 4.5 explores the extent to which respondents from different levels in the management hierarchy have differing views about the effects of organizational restructuring; this is shown graphically as Figure 4.1. The scale of differences between the highest and lowest levels of the hierarchy is staggering and it is clear that perceptions of the business benefits of change and the impact of change are viewed very differently depending on where one sits in the managerial

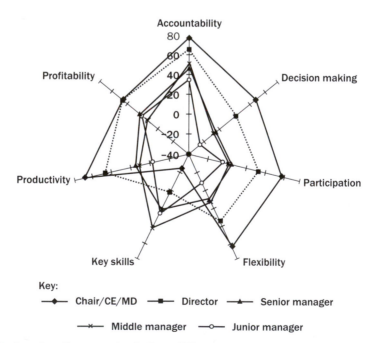

Figure 4.1 A radar diagram depicting different perceptions of the impact of change by managerial level in the organization

hierarchy. Those who inflict change from the top of the organization have very different views of the impact of change to the recipients of change. Chairmen, CEs and MDs are the only group that thinks that key skills have not been lost and, with Directors, are the only group to think that decision making has become faster as a result of organizational restructuring and change.

While it is perhaps not surprising that junior managers have the least favourable impression of the impact of change, the dissonance between their views and those at the top managerial levels in organizations is considerable. Middle and junior managers are much less likely to consider that the hard and soft objectives which underpinned organizational restructuring have been achieved. For example, while chairman, CEs and MDs have net scores of 70 and 60 for increased productivity and participation, junior managers recorded net scores of –1 and –3, respectively.

A more detailed analysis of two of the measures is shown in Figure 4.2 (participation has increased) and Figure 4.3 (key skills and experience have been lost). For the most senior level of managers, the percentage agreeing with the proposition was in excess of 65 per cent, declining to around 35 per cent for both middle and junior managers. While 50 per cent of chairmen, chief executives and managing directors disagree that key skills and experience have been lost, this declines to 25 per cent of junior managers.

Table 4.6 reveals that the perceived impact of organizational restructuring on both hard and soft measures of business performance is highly variable across different types of organization. It is noticeable, however, that in one aspect, there is a degree of consensus across different organizational types in that restructuring is viewed as having focused managerial accountability. Managers in all types of organization now appear to be much more aware of their own accountability. The broad similarity of views found on the accountability factor is not replicated

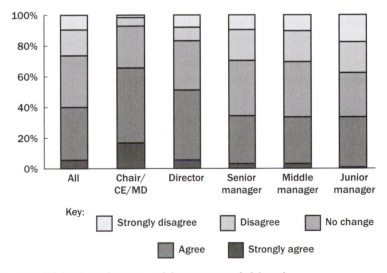

Figure 4.2 Flexibility has increased by managerial level

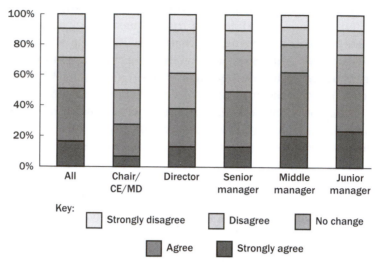

Key:
Strongly disagree   Disagree   No change
Agree   Strongly agree

Figure 4.3 Key skills and experience have been lost by managerial level

elsewhere. Respondents from Plc's and the public sector were much more likely to feel that the impact of restructuring had been to reduce the skills and experience base of their organizations. In several instances, the public sector revealed sharp differences from other types of organization (see Worrall and Cooper 1998a for a fuller discussion). For example, the public sector had relatively low scores on both the increased participation and flexibility measures. Respondents from the public sector are least likely to think that restructuring has increased the speed of decision making than those in any other type of organization.

The analysis has revealed a number of issues of how the management of change in organizations is perceived by managers. First, the evidence that organizational change has brought about the hard benefits on which it was justified is less than conclusive and varies considerably with the respondent's position in the

Table 4.6 The effects of recent organizational change on perceived business performance by type of organization (net agree score)

Performance factor	All	Charity/ not-for- profit	Family- owned business	Partnerships	Private limited company	Plc's	Public sector
Accountability has increased	53	58	53	46	60	54	47
Decision making is faster	2	13	−7	−7	11	6	−11
Participation has increased	12	22	17	40	29	10	−3
Flexibility has increased	19	28	38	53	24	17	9
Key skills have been lost	23	2	−10	−40	-3	30	50
Productivity has increased	23	33	52	34	37	23	5
Profitability has increased	27	21	52	39	34	43	2

organizational hierarchy. Second, there appears to be a view that while accountability has increased and been brought into sharper focus, there is much less of a consensus that productivity and profitability have been improved. Third, in the soft benefits arena, there is even less evidence that the impact of organizational change has had positive benefits in terms of increasing the speed of decision making, flexibility and participation. Finally, what is most noticeable is that many managers, particularly those at the lower levels of the management hierarchy, feel that the main impact of change has been to leave their organizations lacking people with the right mix of skills. In order to assess further the impact of organizational change on managers, we now turn to exploring the impact of change on managers' perceptions of loyalty, motivation, morale and their sense of job security.

The impact of organizational change on employees

After exploring the impact of change on organizational performance, attention was then focused on examining how managers' perceptions of their loyalty to the organization, their morale, their motivation and their sense of job security had been affected by recent organizational change. Again, the analysis relates to the 814 respondents in the 1998 survey who had experienced some form of restructuring in the year prior to the survey. In both the 1997 and 1998 survey reports (Worrall and Cooper 1997; 1998a), we were led to conclude that the majority of restructuring on UK business organizations had a considerable negative effect on employee loyalty, morale, motivation and, particularly, perception of job security. Our research demonstrates clearly that organizational restructuring has imposed considerable human and social costs on the recipients of that change. In this section, we examine how the impact of organizational change affects managers' perceptions by their level in the organization, by the type of organization they work in and by the size of organization in which they are located.

An analysis of the data by the respondent's level in the managerial hierarchy reveals massive differences in the perceived impact of restructuring on the individual. It is clear that for three of our measures – loyalty, motivation and morale – there are huge differences by level in the organization, with a substantial proportion of chairmen, CEs and MDs feeling that restructuring increased their morale, motivation and to a lesser extent their loyalty (see Figures 4.4a, 4.4b and 4.4c). The effects have been perceived much more negatively by senior, junior and, particularly, middle managers. While responses for senior, middle and junior managers were significantly negative for the loyalty, motivation and morale measures, it is noticeable that the greatest negative impact has been on morale.

An examination of the perception of job security measure shows that the majority view for all levels of management is that restructuring has significantly reduced their sense of job security. This finding provides clear evidence of the strength of the impact of organizational change on the nature of work and managers' perceptions of their own security of continuing employment.

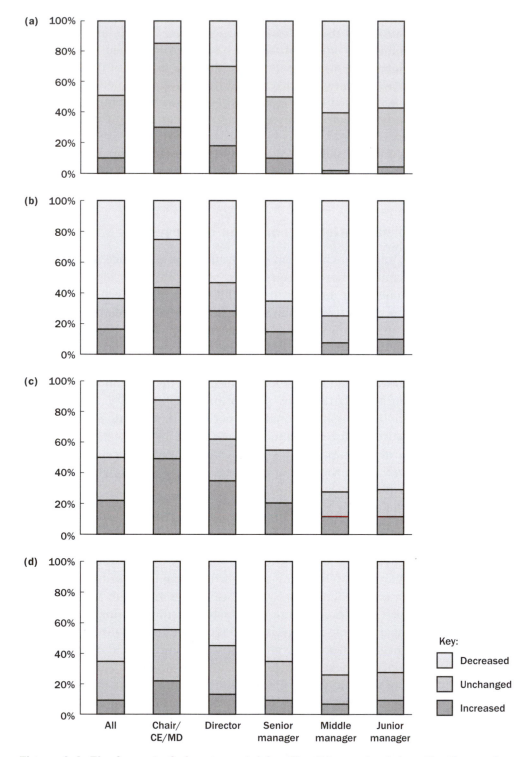

Figure 4.4 The impact of change on (a) loyalty, (b) morale, (c) motivation and (d) sense of job security by managerial level

Elsewhere (Worrall, Cooper and Campbell 2000), we identified that the impact of organizational change on our four measures varied considerably by industrial sector, with respondents in the public sector and the former public utilities (now Plc's) recording much stronger levels of disaffection than respondents from, for example, private limited companies and family-run businesses. In the 1997 report, we were led to hypothesize that there was a relationship between the governance style of an organization and the probability that organizational change would occur, and also that when organizational change did occur, the perceived effect of that change by managers would also vary. Some of the analysis which led us to make that assertion is presented below.

Table 4.7 contains an analysis of the impact of organizational change on managers' sense of loyalty, morale, motivation and job security by type of organization. The impact of change has generally been most detrimental in Plc's (particularly the former public utilities) and the public sector. Respondents from the public sector show the highest negative scores (labelled decreased in Table 4.7) on all of the four factors listed. Restructuring had reduced the respondents' sense of job security and their morale in 79 and 76 per cent of cases in the public sector, respectively, compared with 54 and 36 per cent among managers in family-run businesses and 51 and 50 per cent in managers from private limited companies.

Table 4.7 The impact of change on loyalty, morale, motivation and sense of job security by type of business

	All	Charity/ not-for- profit	Family- owned business	Partnerships	Private limited company	Plc's	Public sector
Effect on loyalty							
Increased	10	14	21	14	15	7	6
Unchanged	44	45	52	57	52	42	36
Decreased	46	42	28	29	33	51	59
Effect on morale							
Increased	17	20	36	40	26	15	8
Unchanged	21	20	29	7	23	26	13
Decreased	62	60	36	53	50	59	79
Effect on motivation							
Increased	22	28	25	33	30	21	14
Unchanged	30	23	39	20	37	34	23
Decreased	48	49	36	47	34	45	63
Effect on perceived job security							
Increased	11	9	14	13	19	10	5
Unchanged	26	29	32	40	30	25	19
Decreased	64	62	54	47	51	65	76

It is also noticeable that the perceived negative impacts of restructuring are generally lower in family-run businesses, indicating, perhaps, the existence of different management styles in different organizational settings. This supports our assertions (Worrall and Cooper 1997) that the impact and effect of restructuring vary with the prevailing managerial and governance styles in organizations and with the way that change is planned, communicated and implemented in different types of organization and differing cultural settings.

In the 1997 report, we identified a strong relationship between the perceived negative impact of organizational restructuring and the size of organization, with managers in large (5000+ employees) organizations reporting higher levels of disaffection with the impact of change than those in smaller organizations. Table 4.8 shows that the percentage of respondents noting that restructuring has had a negative impact on their sense of loyalty, morale, motivation and job security increases with the size of the organization. For example, while 24 per cent of respondents in firms employing under 50 people think that change decreased their sense of loyalty, 56 per cent of respondents in very large firms (5000+) felt their loyalty had been undermined by organizational restructuring.

Our analysis has revealed that the volume of organizational change was considerable but highly variable by type and size of business and that it increased between 1997 and 1998. The analysis presented here reinforces our view that

Table 4.8 The impact of change on loyalty, morale, motivation and sense of job security by firm size

	All	Under 50	51–500	501–5000	5000+
Effect on loyalty					
Increased	10	28	8	6	8
Unchanged	43	48	51	43	36
Decreased	46	24	41	51	56
Effect on morale					
Increased	17	36	19	14	12
Unchanged	20	26	25	16	18
Decreased	62	37	57	70	70
Effect on motivation					
Increased	22	38	23	21	15
Unchanged	30	36	36	24	30
Decreased	48	27	42	55	54
Effect on perceived job security					
Increased	10	17	12	9	7
Unchanged	26	40	28	21	23
Decreased	64	43	60	70	70

change has had differential impacts on managers in different types of organization, in different sizes of firm and, particularly, at different levels of the organizational hierarchy. The differences in perceptions of the business and human impacts of organizational change vary massively with the respondent's location in the management hierarchy, with the 'inflictors' of change having hugely different impressions of its impact from the recipients of that change.

We have identified some important outcomes of the processes of restructuring affecting UK-based organizations. First, there is a clear view that restructuring is leaving many UK organizations – particularly very large organizations, Plc's and those in the public sector – with a depleted skills and experience base. Second, we have found that while there is wide variation on three of our measures (loyalty, morale and motivation), all levels of management tend to consider that the impact of restructuring has been to make their jobs less secure. The main outcomes of organizational change would appear to be a sharpening of accountability, but at the cost of decreased employee loyalty, reduced motivation, undermined morale and a reduced sense of job security, particularly for middle and junior managers, those in the public sector and former public utilities and those in organizations employing over 5000 workers.

Perhaps most important, we have identified that the extent of change and its negative impact varies with type of organization, the negative effects of restructuring being much less pronounced in family-run firms and private limited companies than in Plc's and the public sector. A key finding is that there are strong concerns that organizational change is depleting the skills and experience base of organizations, with this view having sharpened between the 1997 and 1998 surveys. This finding indicates, perhaps, a misalignment between organizations' human resource management strategies and their change management agendas. Senior managers appear to have an insufficient understanding of the likely impacts of their change agendas on their managerial workforce. This finding indicates strong support for the assertion made by the RSA quoted in our introduction that 'most people are learning to handle change but too many decision takers are behind the game' (RSA 1998).

The extent to which the views of top managers and those at the lower levels of the organizational hierarchy conflict is a key finding and poses major questions about how well change is being managed, about the mix of stakeholder interests being reflected in the nature of the restructuring decisions made and about the effectiveness of organizational consultation and communications strategies. While a degree of change is inevitable, our findings pose questions about the need for such a high and quickening pace of change and about the way change is managed.

MANAGERS' VIEWS ON HOW TO IMPROVE THE QUALITY OF WORKING LIFE

All questionnaire surveys are to some extent restrictive and do not give respondents the opportunity to express their views. Consequently, in order to obtain insights into respondents' experiences, they were asked to make suggestions about how they thought the quality of working life in their organization could be improved. The largest single category of the comments received related to the vitally important and clearly neglected or badly managed issue of corporate communications. Here comments like 'communicate and involve', 'improve two-way communications', 'listen to your employees', 'share information to manage change', 'more transparency, more consultation, more open management', and 'talk to us' were commonplace. A clear message from the research is that there is a need for increased and better communication from the most senior levels of management. There were many exhortations to senior managers to 'trust people, communicate and delegate', to 'listen and talk and then make decisions', and that senior management should 'listen and learn from their mistakes'.

Perhaps more important were the views that senior management should always try to 'explain why change is necessary' and 'listen to staff, where there is a lot of sound knowledge and advice available'. In addition, managers were concerned about honesty in communications: 'let's have fair and honest feedback' and 'let's have honesty in relationships' were comments which supported this assertion. There was also a strong realization that 'continuously maintained, two-way communications is vital' and that management should 'communicate positively and not use the grapevine'. The need for change management programmes to be supported by an effective communications strategy was also commented upon, and the view was expressed that managers should 'communicate clearly and promptly at times during periods of organizational change'. In essence, it was felt that managers should 'think strategically, then communicate clearly'. These findings support previous research, which suggests that communication greatly influences managers' perceptions of fairness and hence their reactions to organizational change (Campbell 1999).

A second major theme was that many respondents gave the distinct impression that they felt under-valued, with a view being expressed that managers should 'think about people in organizations as human beings not pegs in holes', that they should see 'people are assets not costs', see staff as 'individuals with needs' and see 'workers as people who deserve respect'. Several respondents also noted the existence of 'blame cultures', as a counter to which it was suggested that managers should 'look for solutions to problems not someone to blame' as 'staff will come up with solutions when they are given ownership and are kept informed'. A related concern was that managers thought that they needed 'a more structured approach to career progression to avoid frustration and good people leaving'.

Other respondents raised a series of issues about the implications of business strategy and continuous organizational change on their working lives. It was suggested that 'aggressive growth is not sustainable in the long term', that companies should 'stop downsizing every year', 'stop replacing core staff with agency staff just to save money as it does not work' and 'slow the pace of change' as there is 'initiative fatigue' in many organizations. Views were also expressed that staff 'should participate more in setting the strategy' and in 'setting realistic targets' and that management should 'set clear priorities and let staff know what is essential and what is only desirable'.

Views were expressed that cost-saving initiatives had gone too far, as one respondent observed that 'the way to increase group profitability is to increase income not to keep trying to reduce costs to the point where it is not possible to provide an adequate level of service'. Other respondents stated that employers should 'not abuse people's work ethic', that they should 'be realistic and have fewer targets' and realize that 'perfection is not possible and should stop trying to achieve it'. Related concerns were that 'senior management should just not make assumptions' but should try to 'understand the people at the sharp end better' and 'give people sufficient resources to allow them to lead a more balanced life between home and work'.

Comments were also expressed that management 'should practise what they preach'; that management should 'concentrate on results not procedures' and that 'top management needs to adopt a new, more informed leadership style'. However, there was a view from the top that argued that 'we need to be aware of the stress and isolation experienced by senior managers and put in place a variety of support mechanisms'. A number of people commented on the 'lack of fun' and that management should try to 'put fun and enjoyment back into work'. And finally, the quotation that encapsulates the main theme of our five-year research programme: 'Remember that managers have families and lives. If they are not allowed a good quality family life, work, and ultimately the organization, will suffer'.

CONCLUSIONS

The results shown here suggest that managers in UK organizations are having to cope with 'doing more with less', having to remain competitive in a fast-changing work environment, dealing with low organizational morale, demotivated employees and new working contracts. The hard measures of change may be being achieved in terms of increased accountability, yet the softer measures of faster decision making, greater flexibility and participation are not being realized. Perhaps more important are the managerial perceptions of how change affects the organization's skills and knowledge base. Senior management appears to be 'out of touch' with the skill and knowledge requirements of the restructured organization. In the age of knowledge management this highlights the lack of strategic workforce planning and development. An organization should anticipate the need for certain combinations of skills and knowledge to achieve its mission, and must learn to integrate this effort into the overall planning process. These results also reflect the need for new leadership values in terms of developing individual employees, supporting their career and leadership development and managing by the new organizational values.

The infrastructure of work values, compensation, incentives, training, employee and career development and supervision must shift from the traditional perspective to enhance and support the newly expanded work roles. If change or restructuring is not reinforced and supported by changes in policies and cultural elements, then the initial positive changes (i.e. in increased accountability) will decay over time and morale could drop even lower. For example, it makes little sense to celebrate employees' tenure in an organization which attempts to be temporary and flexible in the way it employs people; rather, the organization should begin to reward achievements and recognize the accomplishments of the individual. Further, employees require the support of training and a chance to practise new skills and ways of working together.

In terms of the effects of change on employees' morale, motivation, loyalty and security, organizations should enable workers to express their feelings and understand where they will stand in the new order of things. The results suggest that current change management practices are ignoring the 'human element' of change; in particular, the 'inflictors' of change are unaware of the implications of restructuring on the individual, especially in large organizations (over 5000 employees). Research (Campbell 1999) suggests that involving employees in the decision-making aspects of change programmes increases survivors' perceptions of fairness and level of acceptance, thereby supporting the notion that future change programmes need to engage in participative management prior to and not just following change. Second, to increase perceptions of fairness and hence reduce the negative effects of change, organizations must embrace open and honest communication systems. The organization should provide timely, accurate and full information which outlines new expectations, the reasons for them and what options and choices are available to employees. This in turn will engender trust in employees and help to maintain allegiance to the firm and its renewed objectives.

Change is increasingly becoming a major component of everyday managerial life. All organizations must adapt to change if they are to survive and to deliver high-quality services and products to their customers. If change is endemic, then the ability to manage change effectively to achieve business objectives but also to at least maintain, if not enhance, the quality of life is a core managerial competence. Yet we are reminded that many implementers of change are 'behind the game' (RSA 1998) and that much of the managerial rhetoric about 'people being our most important assets' is often insincere and lacks substance. Our research has shown that in any one year, over 60 per cent of managers can be expected to be affected by organizational restructuring and that this rate is increasing.

Our analysis has also revealed that there is no clear consensus that the hard business benefits which must justify much change are actually being won, apart from a sharpened sense of accountability. What limited business benefits would appear to have been gained are being won at the cost of dramatic decreases in managers' loyalty, motivation, morale and sense of job security, particularly at middle and junior management levels, in the public sector and the former public utilities and in large organizations. We have also identified a clear view that continuous organizational change often leads to replacement of experienced but inflexible workers with more flexible contract and temporary staff. This has particular implications for the residual knowledge base of downsized organizations. Perhaps our main finding is that the view from the top of the organization, and particularly from behind the boardroom door, on the business impact and human impact of change is radically different from that derived from the experiences of those at the base of the managerial hierarchy.

In this chapter, we have attempted to take a pathological perspective on organizational change, how it is managed in different organizational settings and how it is perceived to be managed from different vantage points in the managerial hierarchy. It is our view that our findings give considerable cause for concern about how change is being managed, indicating that many senior managers are 'behind the game', lacking the ability to implement change management initiatives, and, most importantly, are taking too bounded a view of the impact of change. There is more to managing a business than ruthlessly cutting costs in an attempt to maximize the figure at the bottom of the profitability spreadsheet.

References

Campbell, F.K. (1999), Survivors of redundancy: a justice perspective. Paper presented at Plant Closures and Downsizing in Europe Conference, 28–30 January, Leuven, Belgium.

Charlesworth, K. (1996), *Are Managers under Stress?* London: Institute of Management.

Cooper, C.L. (1998a), The psychological implications of the changing patterns of work. *Royal Society of Arts Journal*, 1(4), 74–81.

Cooper, C.L. (1998b), The 1998 Crystal Lecture: 'The future of work: a strategy for managing the pressures'. *Journal of Applied Management Studies*, Vol 7 No 2, 275–281.

Cooper, C.L. and Lewis, S. (1994), *Managing the New Work Force: the Challenge of Dual Income Families*. San Diego: Pfeiffer.

Holbeche, L. (1997), *Career Development: The Impact of Flatter Structures on Careers*. Roffey Park Management Institute. Oxford: Butterworth-Heinemann.

Institute of Management (1996a) *Survival of the Fittest*. London: Institute of Management.

Institute of Management (1996b) *A Question of Balance*. London: Institute of Management.

Kets de Vries, M.F. and Balazs, K. (1997), The downside of downsizing. *Human Relations*, 50(1), 11–50.

Lees, Sir D. (1997), The management of strategy. *Journal of Applied Management Studies*, 6(2), 253–260.

Liff, S., Worrall, L. and Cooper, C.L. (1997), Attitudes to women in management: an analysis of West Midlands businesses. *Personnel Review*, 26(3), 152–173.

Morgan, G. (1997), *Images of Organization*. London: Sage.

OECD (1996), *OECD Economic Surveys. The UK 1996*. Paris: OECD.

Royal Society of Arts (1998), *Redefining Work*. London: Royal Society of Arts.

Thornhill, A., Saunders, M. and Stead, J. (1997), Downsizing, delayering – but where's the commitment? Development of a diagnostic tool to help manage survivors. *Personnel Review*, 26(1/2), 81–98.

Worrall, L. and Cooper, C.L. (1995), Executive stress in different industrial sectors, structures and sizes of business. *Personnel Review*, 24(7), 3–12.

Worrall, L. and Cooper, C.L. (1997), The quality of working life: the 1997 survey of managers' experiences. Institute of Management Research Report. London: Institute of Management.

Worrall, L. and Cooper, C.L. (1998a), The quality of working life: the 1998 survey of managers' experiences. Institute of Management Research Report. London: Institute of Management.

Worrall, L. and Cooper, C.L. (1998b), Managers' perceptions of their organisation: an application of correspondence analysis. Working Paper WP019/98, Management Research Centre, University Wolverhampton.

Worrall, L., and Cooper, C.L. (1999) Working hours and their impact on managers. *Leadership and Organisation Development*. Vol 20(1), 6–10.

Worrall, L., Cooper, C.L. and Campbell, F. (2000). The impact of organisational change on the attitudes and behaviours of public sector managers. *Personnel Review* (forthcoming).

PRACTITIONER PERSPECTIVES ON ORGANIZATIONAL CHANGE AND DEVELOPMENT PRACTICE

The change practitioner: perspectives on role, effectiveness, dilemmas and challenges

Jane Keep

Everything flows and nothing stays.
Heraclitus: Cratylus (Plato), 402a

INTRODUCTION

A personal view on change practitioners

You may by now have read in previous chapters an overview of the need for more managers, trainers and developers to take on the role of the change practitioner and the need for enhanced change management practice. At this point in the book, it feels important to explore the change practitioner from a number of personal reflective perspectives, and this chapter sets out to offer some thoughts relating to this.

Many aspects of change agency practice have been explored extensively by academics worldwide, it being a well-covered subject. You can even find change management books in petrol stations and airports! Equally, through their work in organizations, and their continuing professional development, much has been experienced by the organization-based change practitioners themselves, although little has been written about their views. Each of these perspectives builds up a wider picture, adding new insights, and these need linking with each other, practice to theory, theory to practice, as change practitioners have as many if not more insights to offer, thus aiding their own growth towards reflective and evidence-based change management. My own hunger to make sense of this led me to study two master's degrees, one in human resource development and one in philosophy. Additionally, working part-time in a university as an academic fellow while working as a change practitioner in a busy NHS hospital enabled me to have one foot in each camp. During this time I worked hard to close the 'theory–practice' gap and to use evidence for practice and practice to build evidence.

Influences impacting on change management

With the widely accepted notion that change is constant, and indeed the only thing we can be sure of in each and every one of our lives, there is much that influences the work carried out by those actually working to enable, enact and evaluate change. Paradoxically, change practitioners are often both facilitating and evaluating change while undergoing great change themselves, living in what may seem at times a world like that encountered by Alice in Lewis Carroll's *Alice in Wonderland*. Feeling sometimes big, sometimes small, sometimes having a key to 'unlock' a door in the journey forward, sometimes searching, meeting many different characters and challenges along the way, sometimes wondering what the new reality is, or even the present reality – particularly when so much rhetoric exists.

There is paradox, ambiguity and dichotomy (as further discussed by Alf Hatton in Chapter 6). These come with rationality and irrationality both at the same time. There are many global environmental influences, all having an effect on the role and outcomes of the change practitioner, as illustrated by Hamlin in Chapter 2. Economies, politics and even the weather have an impact on us all with a frequency of disasters and freak weather conditions. With advancing technology and cheaper global telecommunications opening many pathways to the wider world, and with the enthusiasm of the media to report and share much of the world's news, we see change on an hourly or even more frequent basis. So much can be learned or understood about the environment in which we find ourselves, whether in the context of organizational transformation or personal change around the world. Access to many networks, information and experiences from organizational mergers, reconfigurations, partnerships and alliances, from the Internet, professional associations and journals and many international conferences or seminars influences the shape of organizations, the types of relationship between them, within them, and the work of change practitioners themselves. Common themes are those of organizational and individual resilience, flexibility, culture and diversity, performance, productivity and effectiveness, welfare, moral virtues and values, often requiring continuous reframing in this complex world of work, and all of this has had major effects on people in the workplace and the way people are managed and resourced.

There are also ongoing changes around the role of traditional organizational and individual functions such as human resources, finance, marketing and production, as boundaries between roles disappear and generalism or specialism changes to suit the climate and context. There is a continued need to take stock of functional specialists such as human resource professionals, who strive to work at the leading edge of change practice, although many other functional specialists are equally placed and indeed working to do so. Change practitioners may be from many functions, professions or disciplines, or change may form part or all of these specialist or generalist roles. For example, in some cases a change practitioner may spend all his or her working hours promoting and enabling change, or a 'portfolio' worker may have a 30 per cent role in one organization as a change practitioner and 70 per cent in another as a hands-on, front-line service delivery practitioner or technician. External change management consultants may spend 100 per cent of their time on change agency but only a small percentage in any one organization. Certainly in service-based organizations this is often the case, with a split between direct service delivery and generic managing, whereby the practitioner also changes the function to meet service needs. These roles are at best challenging and satisfying but at worst often difficult to pull together, with many stakeholders to please, working to maintain high levels of service, while planning, implementing and monitoring change at the end of very busy days. The change practitioner is of generic importance to all organizations and workplaces in all parts of the world, and change practitioners work in all guises and in all types of ways. Having personally experienced a vast range of change practitioner roles and contracts, it can be a multifaceted, multi-skilled, yet ambiguous and challenging role.

The role is not for the faint-hearted, or for the less resilient, or for those unable to work autonomously, analytically and often bravely in the face of adversity. Chameleon-like, change practitioners find themselves dealing with strategic problems and operational puzzles in the same breath, relating to a myriad of wider issues, communicating and liaising with a wide range of managers and staff at any one time. The role has many plus points, as well as the everyday stresses, challenges and strains found in all walks of organizational life. However, it seems at times to have more than its fair share of stressors. Changing long-standing practice or approaches and challenging the 'norm', diagnosing difficult organizational and individual problems is often not palatable to those concerned. It can also be extremely isolating.

From a personal standpoint, this chapter outlines only some aspects of the change practitioner's role, its tasks, skills or competencies, dilemmas and ethical issues, and there are far too many to mention in one reflective chapter. While change practitioners reading this may not relate to all the aspects discussed, much of what is expressed will mirror a wide range of experiences for those working as change practitioners.

THE ROLE OF THE CHANGE PRACTITIONER

Why should we have change practitioners? Exploring the role

The role of the change practitioner takes a number of forms, but at the most basic level it requires the holder of the role (whose exact title may be one of a myriad such as facilitator, coach, supervisor, manager, trainer, developer, adviser, etc.) to be involved in organizational and/or personal change and development, analysing, diagnosing, researching, advising, implementing or evaluating changing circumstances. Change can be across the whole organization, departmental, inter-team or team, or about coaching one individual in a particular aspect of service delivery or personal behaviour. It can be short-, medium- or long-term, and it can require association with others in similar roles or be carried out in isolation.

Equally, there are many reasons why organizations and individuals require and seek 'consultation' or 'facilitation' support in dealing with change management or development issues. Organizations and individuals may choose an internal or external change practitioner for a range of 'reasons', of which the following list is by no means exhaustive:

- bafflement
- uneasy feelings
- check-ups or reviews
- standards of performance excellence
- change motivations
- conflict
- behavioural science issues/knowledge requirement
- morale and cohesion
- competence deficiency
- specific professional or technical expertise
- 'saving face'
- snubbing competitors (internal or external)
- 'keeping up with the Joneses'
- objectivity
- taking the 'heat' out of an issue
- beating the 'Peter principle'
- disposing of funds

Often these reasons are not apparent at the outset or upon the first meeting with the 'client', and sometimes they are never truly apparent, remaining opaque; however, the more the change practitioner can appreciate the reason for consultation, the more chance the intervention has of success. Getting clients to admit the reason for seeking consultant help is, however, a delicate task as some will be very reluctant to 'come clean' about their own or the organizational state of affairs. This is the first part of the change management project albeit it might be outside the formal contract, but it is an important milestone to pass.

Equally, these reasons for seeking change management 'support' lead us to the realization that many different skills, behaviours, competencies and past experiences are required by the change practitioner, and that a number of specific role interventions can be undertaken. Broadly these can be highlighted by separating to one end of a 'spectrum' the more directive approaches such as being an advocate, a technical specialist or an educator, to neither being directive nor non-directive looking at collaboration in solving problems, or seeking alternatives, to a more non-directive approach, which may be around process facilitation, or acting as a reflector (and at the opposite end of the spectrum). This 'spectrum' has been used in the context of management consultancy but, arguably, these categories could be equally relevant for all change practitioners working from any perspective or role, and at any one time the change practitioner may find him or herself working from one end of the spectrum to the other. Thus each time the change practitioner is tasked with a particular 'project', it is imperative at the 'contracting' or initial stages of this work to reflect with the 'client' or 'stakeholder' which of these approaches is appropriate, or perceived to be required. Confusion often occurs when stakeholders presume change practitioners are operating in one mode when the latter have assumed they are working in another. Of course, life is not often so neatly fragmented or divided, and one role or approach may overlap with another. But there is quite a difference when the range is spread from one end of the spectrum to the other.

Many managers and organizations want answers – quick-fix, practical solutions to move them on – and 'consultants' or change practitioners seemed to provide this during the 1970s and 1980s with many off-the-shelf so-called solutions. However, sustaining the change in these circumstances becomes difficult as the clients themselves have not been enabled to 'solve' the problem or make their own diagnosis; thus change practitioners, unless they are technical specialists, are best placed to work along the spectrum, enabling the client, working as either an educator, fact finder or even reflector, so that the client too can work along the spectrum, gaining or enhancing the skills for future problem diagnosis and solution.

Tasks and interventions for the change practitioner – using OD as a framework

Within the spectrum of roles, it appears the focus of a change practitioner is composed of many intricate and specialized tasks and, dependent upon the way you work, there are different ways of categorizing these tasks. One particularly useful way I have found these can be categorized is to look at them as organization development interventions. For example, French and Bell (1990) give a useful definition of organization development (OD) as

> A long range effort to improve an organization's problem solving and renewal processes, particularly through a more effective and collaborative.management of organizational culture ... with the assistance of a change practitioner, or catalyst, and the use of theory and technology of applied behavioural science, including action research.

If we accept this as a general definition of organization development, and that organization development is fundamentally about emergent change, we can tap into a range of OD techniques and interventions, which can be based on individual issues such as performance, role and job design, personal development and behaviour modification; group and team issues such as inter- and intra-group work, conflict resolution, team building and cultural issues; or process issues such as process facilitation, education and training, structure and systems reviews.

In accepting this framework as an example, we can track through a process of change as the change practitioner might do, recognizing that not all of these techniques might be useful at one time, but a combination of a few may be more suitable – there is no one best way. With this in mind, French and Bell (1990) also usefully provide an iterative sequential model to guide change practitioners through OD interventions as:

1 Initial exploration of organizational change focus with clients and involving stakeholders.
2 Design of a data-gathering approach.
3 Collection and feedback of data to the client group.
4 Discussion of the data.
5 Action planning.
6 Action taking.

This sequence could apply to many other processes or interventions relating to change, thus becoming a useful generic model to be adapted by the change practitioner to a given situation or context. What is missing from this model, however, is the evaluative loop, which would form the link between point 6 and point 1, before going back through the six stages, and also the notion that the process is iterative, open, and can also be non-linear.

Much of the skill of the change practitioner is in the ability to adapt and transfer between contexts and environments each generic change management model, which is therefore locally tailored. Testing and developing, or extending models in 'safe' environments or with certain projects, and piloting different approaches leads to the continuing development and familiarization of models or frameworks and the broadening of the change practitioner's skills. This benefits both change practitioners themselves and the organizations within which these approaches are undertaken. Models or guides are thus useful, although they benefit from piloting, and transferring to ensure environmental specificity. Action research (Lewin 1946; Elden and Chisholme 1993, for example) is equally a useful process to work through as it is completely generic so can be adapted to all change situations, integrating action, reflection and evaluation, and linking theory to practice.

Competencies and skills of the change practitioner

As already highlighted, change practitioners come from a wide range of backgrounds and professions, each having core and peripheral sets of skills and competencies. People with professional and educational disciplines from social science, such as sociologists, organizational psychologists and organizational behaviourists, bring a range of relevant skills, knowledge and competence in a wide variety of tasks such as analysis, diagnosis and implementation. Economists can offer support to human labour accounting activities, while philosophers can add ethical or moral dimensions. Human resource management professionals can offer support, particularly in the field of employment legislation or employee relations, and employee resourcing, whereas trainers, developers and educators as HRD specialists offer coaching, training, facilitating and personal development, as well as OD consulting. Thus in any number of academic, professional or practitioner backgrounds there are many tools and approaches essential for managing change in organizations. A combination may be found in one person or in a team of people acting as a project team of 'change practitioners'. One of the advantages of this is the avoidance of a fragmented approach to change, which may lead to some 'stones unturned' in a particular change project. So, multi-professional approaches aid the move away from fragmentation and working with other professions, just as learning other perspectives can shed light or help in the overall sense-making process of change.

Looking specifically at competencies, Boddy and Buchanan (1992) and Carnall (1990) suggest a range, as do O'Driscoll and Eubanks (1993), who in addition look at OD practitioner effectiveness, adding a qualitative dimension. Again, specific sets of general competencies can be clustered in a variety of ways, with each area having a number of specific skills or behaviours supporting these 'cluster competencies'. From my own experience, examples of these could be as shown in Table 5.1.

Table 5.1 Cluster competencies

Cluster	Skill/competence
Project management	Planning, resource allocation, etc.
Contracting (with 'clients')	Defining the task, establishing relationships
Team building	Such as defining roles, maintaining good working relationships
Analysis and diagnosis	Data collection, problem solving
Data utilization	Qualitative or quantitative data, paper-based reviews, or survey techniques
Interpersonal skills	Communication, time management
Communication skills	Listening, written presentations
Political awareness	Sensitivity, influencing
Intervention implementation	Participation, involvement
Monitoring and evaluation	Criteria setting and reviewing, measuring effectiveness
Technical skills	Financial interpretation, psychometrics
Process skills	Facilitation, systems thinking
Self-awareness and insight	Reflection, critical thinking, intuition

Each cluster will have a range of supporting behaviours to capture the whole range of skills.

For the individual to enhance or develop in these areas, some of these will require training and development support, others personal reflection or coaching, and real project situations can provide an excellent training ground for practice. Personally speaking, I always have a mentor for at least one aspect of my work, if not more. Mentoring provides external support, a safe ear, a place to bounce ideas off, and either professional or technical support. In addition, mentors can open doors or make introductions to new forums and individuals. Equally, setting up networking forums or learning sets of OD and change practitioners, either from one industry or across a range of industries, provides professional support. The Internet can also offer 'discussion pages' for cross-exchange of ideas and new theories or case studies. Change practitioners can usefully review themselves at regular intervals, or gain 360° feedback on a range of competencies required for their role as they develop or progress in different organizations or projects. All of these and many more options (some discussed later in this chapter) provide professional and personal support for the change practitioner, which is fundamental, particularly in a role that is constantly changing and can be isolating and challenging too.

PERSPECTIVES ON EFFECTIVENESS

Internal or external change agency – is there a difference?

Change practitioners may operate as internal or external practitioners, and experience suggests that there are positive and negative aspects of working in either of these roles. When looking specifically at the differences cited between internal and external change agents, they could probably be reversed in certain organizations or situations, dependent upon the individual and their relationship with the work they are undertaking. Many of the skills and competencies required to undertake change management projects will be the same although the context in which they practise these will shift to form a strong influence on inputs, outputs and outcomes and effectiveness, and whereas selection processes for external change practitioners may be fairly rigorous, such as a formal tendering procedure, internal change practitioners may be 'in the right place at the right time' and thus require no real selection as such (outside the initial selection for the permanent role). Change practitioners can gain much from acting in internal and external capacities where this is possible, learning to transfer useful approaches from one project to another and from one side of the 'fence' to the other.

Internal change practitioners have an advantage in that they have an in-depth understanding of the culture of the organization, enabling them to understand where people are 'coming from' when they are involved in any aspects of change. They may therefore be fairly socialized into the organization norms and beliefs, thus being more sensitive to local politics and behaviours. However, they may also hold a level of subjectivity, perhaps unbeknown to them as they become 'socialized' into their work environment. They have the ability to maintain longer-term relationships and interactions with all those involved in change, although experiences can be likened to 'walking on eggshells' at difficult times so as to preserve relationships. It is assumed that one can monitor quite closely the changes in relation to evaluating effects, although the socialized eye may not notice a difference on a day-to-day basis, or may be influenced by knowing the organization too well. There may also be other disadvantages as internal change practitioners are perceived by the organization and its members in a certain way or are stereotyped as having certain traits or behaviours. Additionally, they may also face positional issues whereby their ability to influence certain factions may be less than that of an external change practitioner, or be seen to be fairly threatening in relation to openness and trust, and thus integrity and credibility require extensive attention. Building personal resilience, including some element of 'healthy detachment' from the organization, offers the ability to maintain objectivity in many of these circumstances.

External change practitioners are more often independent of the organization, less 'socialized', and their association with the organization in question is often seen as 'fleeting'. The value systems of external change practitioners may be more in line with traditionally acknowledged generic OD values, and they may not base their decisions so much on specific organizational imperatives. A number of other perceived differences can also be highlighted. These relate to external change practitioners having a more 'purist' view untainted by local politics or norms, and thus their ability to think critically and be more focused will prove beneficial. The downside to this relates to the ability of the change practitioner to undertake an extensive ongoing evaluation following completion of the programme or change, as they may leave the organization upon completion of a specific task or project. From experience, commitment but detachment plays an important role for the change practitioner, whether internal or external. The ability to translate between local contexts and environments, transferring lessons from one to the other, developing 'tailor-made' solutions designed with each client in mind, requires the external change practitioner to reflect, network, keep up to date, and gain a 'portfolio' of experience, skills and knowledge.

Skilled or competent? What is an 'effective' change practitioner and how do you evaluate change?

Experience tells us that measuring any aspect of effectiveness is a difficult issue. What measures do you use? How can you separate cause and effect? Effective is one of the 'x' factor words and it requires defining before using, and worse still, defining within the context and surroundings it is used. Becoming 'better' or 'improved', or indeed 'more effective', means nothing without defining to what extent and how much each of these words signifies in any given situation. Therefore, when looking to measure your own effectiveness, or that of other change practitioners, take time to consider and define what constitutes effectiveness in the situation you find yourself in. Separating cause and effect in any change situation is difficult enough without having ill-defined success criteria or standards. The same goes for measuring the overall effect of any change management or organization development interventions or initiatives.

In looking at the effectiveness of the change practitioner one might ask what the gold standard of being an effective change practitioner is. What does this consist of and how do you become one? We have probably all had experience as clients or have observed change practitioners working around us in our organizations in addition to reviewing our own performance as a change practitioner. From this, each of us will have developed our own view of 'effective' practice.

From my own experience and literature searching, ineffective change practitioners can be shown to adopt certain attitudes or behaviours such as superiority or impatience. They may propose instant 'pre-packed' solutions and be more interested in their own views than those of the client. In addition to this, not only might they fail to deliver the agreed outputs but they may also blame or criticize other colleagues or the client for their own failures.

Effective change practitioners are likely to show an ability to listen, summarize and accept data from the organization without criticizing or showing judgement. Time will be taken to assess problems, thus giving confidence to the 'client' not only through their interpersonal skills and general behaviour but also through delivering outputs, to time scales, within budget. Adopting a positive approach, working to facilitate rather than direct, they will wish to impart skills and knowledge to those they are working with, thus leaving a self-sustaining unit or individual once the task is completed, providing a longer-term approach as part of the solution itself. Integrity will be built through acting confidentially, openly and reliably, and keeping promises made. As self-awareness is a key 'competence' in itself, the change practitioner will continue to learn and grow personally through reflection and self-awareness, gaining feedback where appropriate while working at projects and tasks. Clients overall will feel a sense of direction, and full involvement in all that is taking place to undertake the change in question.

Other 'gold standard' behaviours might include:

- resilience, and maintaining focus and a sense of priority;
- pride, wishing to be associated with high standards (Bott and Hill 1994);
- charisma and passion, showing a contagious energy which instigates good feelings;
- having the ability to communicate ideas in a clear, concise and persuasive manner;
- showing positivity and optimism about the future, noticing positive behaviours by others;
- conflict resolving, looking to use conflict positively, resolving constructively;
- recognition of where working as a team member is more useful than working as an individual, and *vice versa*;
- having the capacity to enable ideas to be turned into action, involving key stakeholders along the way;
- being resourceful, coming up with possible ways of dealing with problems;
- thinking clearly and logically, dealing with ambiguity, complexity and confusion;
- being dependable, staying at the task and doing 'what is expected'.

There is much to learn from times when things don't go exactly to plan, and process reviews and evaluations help identify the learning from these. Goss *et al.* (1993) looked at the top 20 reasons for 'why new executives fail'. Such failings could equally apply to the change practitioner, whether internal or external. These are listed as:

- being unclear or confused over one's deliverables;
- failing to identify stakeholders and build key partnerships;

- learning the job too slowly;
- poor diagnosis – dealing with symptoms and not real problems;
- doing what comes naturally – staying in one's existing comfort zone;
- being unable to adapt to differences (organizational and people);
- becoming overwhelmed/lack of composure;
- being unable or unwilling to make tough decisions;
- lacking cross-functional and work process perspective;
- failing to staff or build a team effectively;
- interpersonal problems;
- key skill deficiencies;
- difficulty in making strategic transitions;
- over or micro-'managing';
- performance problems;
- political problems;
- lack of balance between work and personal life;
- strengths that used to matter becoming less important;
- new untested skills required.

Considering the change practitioner's behaviour when evaluating change is thus one important aspect of evaluation.

Looking at evaluation more broadly, setting up some form of data collection can give the change practitioner an opportunity to start to evaluate change, but this cannot be exhaustive as often there can be too much information and seldom the time to undertake an extensive data-collection exercise. One suggested approach to evaluation is outlined below using the 'manager' as the change practitioner (Spurgeon and Flanagan 1996):

Evaluating approaches to organizational change:

1 Adequacy of organizational diagnosis
   - Has the manager selected and adequately defined an appropriate organizational problem?
   - Has the manager obtained appropriate and sufficient evidence to evaluate the nature of the problem?
   - Has the manager drawn reasonable conclusions from his evidence?
   - Has the manager fully evaluated the ramifications of the relationships in his or her diagnosis?

2 Value of expected outcomes
   - Are the expected outcomes realistically attainable?
   - Are the expected outcomes worth pursuing?
   - Do the expected outcomes have little or no appeal to any of the organizational interest groups?
   - Has the manager considered the possibility of negative as well as positive outcomes?

3 Appropriateness of change strategy

- Has the manager considered the alternative change strategies?
- Does the selected change strategy seem appropriate?
- Is the selected change strategy practical?
- Does the process of implementation have little or no appeal to any of the organizational interest groups?

4 Compatibility of organizational diagnosis and change strategy

- Has the change strategy been specifically derived from the organizational diagnosis?
- Is the change strategy compatible with the organizational diagnosis?
- Are the justifications for the links between diagnosis and strategy reasonable and even apparent?
- Is the change strategy directly or indirectly linked to the organizational diagnosis?

5 Compatibility of change strategy and expected outcomes

- Are the expected outcomes specifically seen to result from the change strategy?
- Are the expected outcomes compatible with the change strategy adopted?
- Are the justifications for the links between strategy and expected outcomes reasonable or even apparent?
- Are the expected outcomes directly or indirectly linked to the change strategy adopted?

6 Explicit and implicit justifications

- Are the explicit justifications sensible?
- Does the model suggest underlying 'real' reasons rather than the 'good' reasons suggested?
- To what extent is the model a rationalization?
- Is the model distorted because of inappropriate justifications?

Certainly, these questions are worth asking at some time before, during and/or after any change programmes or interventions.

There are two other further types of evaluation that should be mentioned here. These do not specifically relate to the effectiveness of the change practitioner but to the combination of the change management or organizational development approach overall, including the change practitioner's inputs. They are particularly useful, as evaluating organizational change and development is complex and the process is deemed more successful when it links to the learning and growth of the organization and its individuals. Often working in a more 'scientific' manner to evaluate outcomes can be extremely complicated, and not entirely appropriate. Hence, more recent advocates of change evaluation suggest incorporating two other features:

Firstly, there is a 'learning-based evaluation' approach, whereby in any OD process 'the main purpose of any evaluation is to maximize learning. Effective organizations are those which provide frequent opportunities for their people to learn, develop and grow ... by reviewing how the change was managed by all concerned it is possible to:

- identify ways in which changes in the client system might be handled better in the future

- examine human process issues that are affecting the client system

- clarify related problems which haven't yet been addressed

- help the consultant examine areas for improvement when handling future projects'. (Cockman *et al.* 1999: 229)

Second, an equally valuable perspective when looking at evaluation as a total systems approach is that 'Evaluation is necessary ... to draw lessons from experience gained (second order learning). The creation of learning moments during and after the change process can offer the insight needed to boost the success of future change initiatives. Thus evaluation is not a one-time only management task, but rather a continual task' (Koster and Bouman 1999).

Thus the integration of evaluation into organization development and change allows the design and development of the evaluation frameworks to be part of the overall change process. This usefully links us back to an earlier suggestion in this chapter as to the use of the action research (Lewin 1946; Elden and Chisholme 1993) model as this does exactly that, combining learning and research, closing the gap between theory and practice and forming a learning process in itself (Bate *et al.* (forthcoming); Goldstein 1992).

Further understanding your own influence as a change practitioner

> I feel I am more effective when I can listen acceptantly to myself, and can be myself ... who by no means functions at all times in the way I would like to function. (Rogers 1967)

Following on from the discussion of effective change management above, there are a number of things change practitioners can do to understand further their own effectiveness and development. These may include keeping reflective diaries and journals, which will aid effectiveness. Often the passing of time distorts memory and the view of the world in the past. Reviewing the past from the present is in itself a subjective process, based on interpretation. Keeping records of an organizational change journey can ensure every aspect is covered. The change practitioners themselves can see how far they have travelled, as well as how successfully they made the journey.

Other forms of personal evaluation can be via peer review, 360° appraisal, and of organizational evaluation via observation, or time series analysis against a series of questions or problems, with a form of analysis and diagnosis carried out at periods during the change project itself, and post-project completion.

As stated above, there are many combinations of perceived behaviours and competencies for change practitioners, one of the most important aspects being contextually or environmentally specific, almost chameleon-like. This obviously has an effect upon the individual as a change practitioner, as the continual need to change to suit or mirror your environment is challenging and taxing. Success in relation to effectiveness in each task requires the change practitioner to think critically, forecasting measurable outcomes from the outset, in both task and process terms. Success in measuring effectiveness requires clearly defined, achievable outcome measures or standards. Time to reflect is invaluable: 'Better than a hundred years lived in ignorance without contemplation is one single day of life lived in wisdom and deep contemplation' (the Buddha's teachings).

DILEMMAS FACED BY CHANGE PRACTITIONERS

Individuality and the change practitioner – what about you as a person?

'Life at its best is a flowing, changing process in which nothing is fixed ... I find that when life is richest and most rewarding it is a flowing process' (Rogers 1967). As already stated, life often feels frenetic, fragmented, lacking integration within the now seemingly complex and diverse world we live in. There are often feelings of scepticism or cynicism when undertaking tasks or projects that seem to be so much more complex, with no obvious answers. Personally speaking, in previous decades it used to feel as though there were answers; for example, one could use many models and frameworks directly 'off the shelf' to support organizational change. This approach now seems to have little validity in today's rapidly changing and diverse world of work, and consequently there may often be no clear answer or solution. Thus the change practitioner may feel as though he or she is working in isolation, alone in the pursuit of excellence in facilitating and achieving change.

'Turning things in the light, seeing different impressions as I do so, sometimes glimpsing many layers underpinning one surface representation. No one image is the only truth, or the only plausible account although some may feel more authentic, consistent with a person's values being more chosen than imposed' (Marshall 1995). Your own perspectives on problems are important when thinking about the many perspectives and views understood by all of the other people in the organization. Indeed, they are often your only and best guides. With personally different backgrounds, ethnicity, gender and socialization, no one can expect all individuals to view one event in the same way. As a change practitioner, you may find yourself 'turning things in the light', viewing them from one perspective while others are seeing things in a different way. As part of the continuous journey of 'becoming a person' and the constantly changing environment we work in, our own reflections and understandings of our own personal change, in addition to organizational change, are fundamental aspects upon which to build the future of our work and personal lives. Intuition is important and learning to use it, letting it guide you while you decide amongst a myriad of solutions, is a fine art in itself, particularly when you need to relate it to 'evidence'.

How do you maintain resilience and calmness in tough and challenging times? Running when the 'orange light is flickering', to use a car/petrol analogy, is not healthy; at some stage everything will grind to a halt until new resources and fuel are provided, or the 'system' (person) is maintained or serviced. Many change practitioners find they are close to 'burnout', having endured many months or even years of difficult times that have had to be faced and worked through. Respect for self, and understanding when enough is enough is important.

As previously mentioned in the discussion on personal development and competencies, networking offers not only support but also ideas and forums for sharing views and information, enabling access across a wider selection of industry or organizations. In these disparate and fragmented times many change practitioners rely heavily on networking. Networking is a useful part of the 'resource investigation' aspect of the change practitioner's role, and a useful way of 'testing' ideas or perspectives. Again, mentors here can provide much-needed objectivity, critical thinking and thoughtfulness. A little time invested in finding a mentor, preferably from outside your workplace, will pay major dividends.

Where are the ethical minefields?

There will be factors that impede the process or progress of the change practitioner. These may be from the environment, the organization, specific individuals or they may even be self-imposed (knowingly or unknowingly) by the change practitioner. Change programmes or projects often commence among a myriad of uncertain and complex issues providing a somewhat transient foundation. The frenetic nature of the organization, pressures or drivers for and against the change itself, lack of resources, lack of systematic work processes, limited data, and very often limited opportunity to test and retest actions provide a challenge. Understanding as much as you can about both the approaches to the project and the task itself provides a good starting point. However, the reality in organizations is that change projects or programmes are evolutionary by nature, often becoming clearer while the project is actually under way.

Organizational politics can be overbearing at times, and cultural issues relating to power and the psychological contract between one manager to another, or one director to another, can affect the change practitioner's ability to pursue or complete a piece of work. Very often the change practitioner is seen as the devil's advocate or as a challenger to previous behaviour – and perceived to be threatening or undermining the roles of managers or directors. Issues arising from the particular role of the change practitioner and his or her chosen type of intervention cause misunderstandings or confusion, as does the change practitioner's attempts to gain trust and be seen to be credible, possessing integrity. Open explanations and discussions about the change practitioner's role and the possible types of intervention are useful here. Using an example, the dentist tells patients what he/she is doing as he/she is treating them, so as to cause no unnecessary alarm. In the same way, change practitioners should tell their colleagues or clients what they are planning to do and why. Sometimes this process alone can serve to rectify problems or clarify organizational issues that were perceived to be more problematic than they actually were.

Often change practitioners are asked to feed back into 'the system' their findings or work to date. Unfortunately, this is an ethical dilemma in itself. Change practitioners find themselves asking 'do I tell them how it really is? Or do I tell them what they want to hear?' How open you think you can be is a huge issue. Many change practitioners have found difficulty in striking the right balance here. Do you want repeat business from this client? If so, do you feel pressured to tell them what they want to hear? Or will your conscience tell you to do otherwise? For this and other reasons given in this chapter, the role of the change practitioner is often lonely and isolated. You can find yourself used as a political tool by others in the organization, or you can find yourself isolated by those threatened by your presence. Openness about your intentions or your approach will help here. Stakeholder analysis for each project or programme entered will provide you with a better under-standing of who has a stake in what you are doing, and give you a chance to think about the relationship you may wish to build with them, such as building alliances or support. Undertaking stakeholder analysis (see Beckhard and Harris 1987) with other colleagues or managers involved in the projects you are undertaking will also provide you with other perspectives on power and relationship issues.

At times, internal change practitioners find themselves wrongly placed within an organizational structure. For those working as external consultants, they can find their 'client' is wrongly placed within their organization. Both of these scenarios can cause problems with access to data/information, legitimacy to undertake the task, responsiveness of the client or staff or respect for the expert skills and knowledge the change practitioner may have. Careful thought about the organizational 'map' and where you are placed within this may help to identify where else on the 'map' you should be, in addition to allowing you to read the 'moral ethos' of the organization.

Is your practice ethical? Ethics are complex. There are many themes and many perspectives, thus creating contradictions at times in terms of both ethical living and ethics within the workplace. 'Corporations have the potential to create a large amount of benefit and harm both directly and indirectly to human beings' (Ostapski et al. 1996). The nature of work is multifarious; people and their behaviour in the workplace are often perplexing. Ethics can be described as referring to sets of rules or principles that may guide (or claim to guide) actions of individuals and groups, and can also be described as 'the systematic study of reasoning about how we ought to act' (Singer 1994). Ethics can thus be the science of morals, concerned with character or disposition or with the distinction between right and wrong. Many organizations contain a multiplicity of values, from the different professions or work roles, from the different functions, and also from each individual's background, beliefs and ideals. Many organizations in my experience have tried to set corporate values, but these are often only rhetoric, while the reality is a different story. These can also be cold and inhuman, as behaviourally they have never actually been realized by the organization – in other words, no one has stopped to consider what exactly the behaviours might look like if they all followed value 'x' or 'y'. Additionally, in orga-nizations values have to be part of a pragmatic approach to ethics, as purist ethics are difficult to fulfil in a changeable world of unique individuals.

There is also a more specific point about ethics related directly to organizational change programmes or interventions. Wilson and Rosenfeld (1990) cite 'within crit-ics of behaviour modification ... there are ethical issues raised when managers are provided with the tools designed to control subordinates. Managers themselves can often feel uncomfortable with the thought of having control over someone else's behaviour. There is a large amount of authoritarianism built into behaviour modification. It presumes that the controllers of behaviour all have unquestioned control and authority'. It thus leaves us with questions such as what are the rights or wrongs in organizational change? Does the change practitioner 'have the right' to modify others' behaviour?

Anthony (1996) brings to the forefront issues around morality and management, asking whether managers are the 'makers of morality' in the workplace. The very nature of organizational development and change can impinge on any number of individuals, groups or teams of employees. And again, a number of questions require answering. Whose benefit is this change for? What will be the outcomes? What gain or pain will there be for those affected? How will the change programme or project affect clients or those in the wider social community? Thus there are ethical or moral considerations when looking at change management.

Helpfully, however, French and Bell (1990) highlight an example of the need for minimum OD ethical standards as:

■ Interventions must be selected that have a high probability of being helpful in the particular situation.

■ The consultant should not use interventions that exceed his or her expertise.

■ The client system should be as informed as is practical about the nature of the process.

■ The consultant must not be working any personal hidden agendas that obtrude into high-quality service for the client.

■ Commitments to confidentiality must be kept.

■ Individuals must not be coerced into divulging information about themselves or others.

■ The client must not be promised unrealistic outcomes.

So when considering ethics and morals, where do change practitioners go from here? Woodall (1996) suggests that 'at the very least we could identify the process of reasoning by which ... decisions and acts are justified'. Ovretveit (1996) suggests an 'ethical approach means deciding which principle is the most important in the situation, and goes on to suggest steps for an ethical analysis such as looking at choices or alternatives; looking at the ethics of each; looking at the importance of each and why; making an ethical choice – which alternative best upholds this principle and why; thinking about the consequences; looking at the self-interest bias; justification; and time – is it likely that spending time on the decision will help you make an ethical decision?

All of these challenges are worthy of thought and practice.

CONCLUSIONS

Change agency is complex, yet challenging. This chapter has used the personal reflections and theories of a change practitioner in order to look at a range of perspectives, from the environment, the role and competencies, understanding effectiveness to some of the dilemmas faced. A change practitioner's role is strongly related to the effects and influences of the environment, and the personal skills and characteristics of the individuals themselves. What may at first appear to be a difficult yet achievable task is not always what it seems. Further reflective perspectives are drawn out in the next chapter relating more specifically to the complexity of the environment, and indeed the notion that there are 'recipes' for success.

References

Anthony, P. (1996), Morality, reality and management. Paper for teaching on MPhil in critical management, Lancaster University.

Bate, S.P., Khan, R. and Pye, A. J. (forthcoming), Culturally sensitive restructuring: where organization design meets organization development. *Organization Science*.

Beckhard, R. and Harris, R.T. (1987), *Organizational Transitions Managing Complex Change*, 2nd edn, OD series. Reading, Mass: Addison-Wesley.

Bott, K. and Hill, J. (1994), Change agents lead the way. *Personnel Management*, August.

Boddy, D. and Buchanan, D. (1992), *The Expertise of the Change Agent*. Englewood Cliffs, NJ: Prentice Hall.

Carnall, C. (1990), *Managing Change in Organizations*. London: Prentice Hall.

Cockman, P., Evans, B. and Reynolds, P. (1999), *Consulting for Real People. A Client-centred Approach for Change Agents and Leaders*. Maidenhead: McGraw-Hill.

Elden, M. and Chisholme, R.F. (1993), Emergent varieties of action research: introduction to the special issue. *Human Relations*, 46, 121–142.

French, W. and Bell, J.R. (1990), *Organization Development: Behavioural Science Interventions for Organization Improvement*, 4th edn. Englewood Cliffs, NJ: Prentice Hall.

Goldstein, J. (1992), Beyond planning and prediction: bringing back action research to OD. *Organization Development Journal*, 10, 2, 1–7.

Goss, T., Pascale, R. and Athos, A. (1993), The reinvention roller coaster: risking the present for a powerful future. *Harvard Business Review*, 71(6), 97–108.

Koster, E. and Bouman, W. (1999), The balanced change card: a framework for designing and assessing organizational change processes. Paper presented to Academy of Management, Chicago, August 1999.

Lewin, K. (1946), Action research and minority problems. *Journal of Social Issues*, 2, 34–46.

Marshall, J. (1995), *Women Managers Moving On*. Routledge.

O'Driscoll, M.P. and Eubanks, J. (1993), Behavioural competencies, goal setting and OD practitioner effectiveness. *Group and Organization Management*, 18(3) September, 308–327.

Ostapski, A.S., Oliver, J. and Gonzales, G.T. (1996), The legal and ethical components of executive decision making: a course for business managers. *Journal of Business Ethics*, 15, 571–579.

Ovretveit, J. (1996), Ethics: counsel or perfection. *The IHSM Network*, 3(13).

Rogers, C. (1967), *On Becoming a Person*. Constable.

Singer, P. (1994), *Ethics*. Oxford Readers, Oxford University Press.

Spurgeon, P. and Flanagan, H. (1996), *Public Sector Managerial Effectiveness: Theory and Practice in the NHS*. Buckingham: Open University Press.

Wilson, D.C. and Rosenfeld, R.H. (1990), *Managing Organizations: Text, Readings and Cases*. Maidenhead: McGraw-Hill.

Woodall, J. (1996), Managing culture change: can it ever be ethical? *Personnel Review*, 25(6), 26–40.

The complexity–clarity paradox

Alf Hatton

INTRODUCTION

The main thrust of this chapter is that organizations and people are more complex than much organizational change practice and research imply, and thus 'solutions' to 'problems' are also more difficult to grasp than implied. Together, organizations and people, and people in organizations, are so complex that frequently recipes for the management of change and/or organizational development can offer little satisfaction, with change agents and managers pragmatically settling for what they can achieve, step by step. This directly contradicts the optimizing, idealistic, near-utopian perfection that much of the literature of change management seems to imply. If manager A in organization B simply does the following, all will be all right with the world. Well, if not the world, certainly with that organization, that manager, and his/her subordinates until well into the future.

Underlying such an apparently simple, easy-to-use 'quick-fix' organizational development toolkit is an unfulfillable wish for an uncomplicated organizational life. Organizational life is not just not uncomplicated, it is highly complex, in environments where stability apparently used to exist, but which feel ever increasingly fragmented and volatile. I say apparently, because there must now be a generation of managers (if not two) who have never experienced 'organizational stability'. Just as some new voters in Britain had known nothing but a Conservative government until 1997, and so had no benchmark by which to compare either party's track record, those young managers who will lead organizations in the 21st century also have no benchmark of organizational stability.

Even the new managerialism offers idealistic forms and recipes, e.g. faster, friendlier, more focused, nearer to the customer, and so on (see Burnes 1992: 56 *et seq.*), as the new set of management beliefs, a sort of neo-Taylorism (there is one best way, and it is management's job to find it). Yet since evidence for the increasing rate of change and increasing complexity of life actually exists in abundance (see Toffler 1970; Gleick 1987), that is, if life in general is getting more complicated, why do we expect organizational life to be simple?

I will attempt to provide a personal perspective on this complexity, from which managers and OD practitioners can more readily assimilate the multiple viewpoints generated in organizational change practice. I will attempt to do this by discussing the implications of six subthemes to my main one of complexity: the subject matter itself – what we know about management; sector and size – the type of organization we are working with or studying; organizational focus and level – the level at which we set up subjects for action or study, their scope and span; language, metaphor and meaning – what do our words and actions as change agents mean to others and what 'language(s)' are others using; identity – senses of identity, both individual and group; and finally, the problem of science – how we know what we think we know about organizations we have interacted with, whether as change agents or researchers, and whether we should even attempt to separate cause(s) and effect(s) in some linear sequence, if, indeed, we can.

A PERSONAL EXPERIENCE IN A PUBLIC SECTOR ORGANIZATION

In the contracting and analysis stages of a project as an internal change agent in an urban museum and art gallery, an overly simple analysis (and hence in this case, an overly simple proposed solution) identified high spending as the problem. In UK public sector organizations in the early 1990s, this was an accusation of some seriousness.

It had not been stated by what benchmark or comparator this view had been established. Indeed, no benchmark was in use, although the gut feeling of the top management team that all was not well indeed proved accurate on further analysis. What had been happening was that intuitive 'data' (perfectly valid as data if analysed appropriately) had been shoe-horned, pseudo-scientifically, into a classic, managerialist, accountancy-based analysis. This analysis itself was flawed, although it seemed to the top management team that they had found the 'right' answer. In fact, it was a case of the wrong data, the wrong kind of analysis, quasi-objectivity, starting with the answer and then finding the evidence to support it. In this case, a valid reason was being sought to cut the museum and gallery's budget.

The accuracy of this analysis appeared to be supported by the fact that the museum and art gallery was at that time clearly in the higher spending bands when calculated against a performance indicator of net expenditure/visitor. This was introduced by the Audit Commission (1991: 20) and equates with average cost or subsidy per user, though it had not been used by the organization in establishing its view.

The frequent restatement of this 'fact' by other insiders within the organization's management clearly reflected an intention to cut budgets, and seemed to indicate that organizational members (other than those working in the museum and gallery itself), did not seem to mind how severe such cuts would be. Indeed, potentially, the more severe the cuts proposed, the more kudos the change agent/manager would gain, and incidentally the less serious the scrutiny other parts of the department would face at that time.

However, another 'reality' was discovered, ironically after some fairly straight-forward financial analysis. The museum and gallery was found to be:

- a low earner – it did not earn the kind of average income recovery for its category (Audit Commission 1991: 21);
- it was centrally carrying staff overheads of five other cost centres; and
- it was maintaining, free of charge, as well as carrying overheads for, offices/office services for other parts of the multi-functional department of which it was a member.

Indeed, analysis of its overheads also revealed an ongoing payment for a number of previous internal organization and methods studies, tasked to sort the 'problem' out, which they had clearly failed to do!

The point of this example here is to illustrate, at the outset, that simple analysis can produce simple solutions, and that these may or may not deal with the problem. In fact, the simple analysis in this example failed any test of rigour as analysis, since it failed to identify any problems that might be lying behind the surface 'problem'.

One answer to this is to adopt a research-based organizational analysis (Hamlin and Reidy 1996: 20). Another is to accept that multiple perspectives on issues, process and outcomes in management of change both can be and are the norm. No matter how open, humane and sensitive the process is, ultimately one probable outcome in terms of end perspectives will be that there are winners and losers. The research-based organizational analysis mode is the most likely process to guarantee development of such a multiple-perspective position.

Although in the case of the museum and art gallery a significant part of the problem clearly was financial, the causes of the malaise which led to under-performance on income were simply not even identified, let alone addressed. Finance had been identified as a problem when in fact it was a symptom.

If this is true for classical approaches to the management of change, how much truer must it be for the 'softer', more complex issues involved in approaches dealing with human resources? Sadly, the sort of surface-level analysis referred to above has not prevented managers and OD practitioners taking action based on such superficial views.

Watson (1994: 25) presents evidence for such multiple explanations of phenomena based on his strategic exchange perspective. He states that simply labelling the actions of others is taking a moral position, whereas accepting the 'essential two-sidedness of social life' (*ibid*.: 24) dispels the view that managers' actions are short-term, self-interested and for personal convenience.

His evidence is that while managers could be seen to resist change agendas which they regarded as short-termist (where their own interest was potentially threatened), their objections were also based on values and moral objections (*ibid*.: 210). Thus he rejects 'crude "either-or" judgements' of actions as self-interested or altruistic.

Had the museum and gallery example referred to above been the subject of rigorous analysis, a view might have formed that high spending and low earning were both feasible hypotheses, and that further analysis was needed to identify which was nearer to fact. Potentially, the view formed by the management team could be read as taking a moral stance on the museum and art gallery's lack of performance in income earning, whereas later analysis showed that the infrastructure for income generation simply did not exist.

It occurs to me that, as change agent practitioners and management researchers, we often fail the test of rigour. We seem to require simple explanations and recipes for all manner of organizational issues, yet experience and research tells us that the world is complex and opaque.

Our very yearning for simplicity may indeed be obscuring salient data which, once revealed, may complicate our picture of organizations and of people but will also actually enrich it in such a way that clarity then becomes possible. In other words, out of complexity we can find clarity, but we do have to go through complexity first. Parodying sport, in the field of management of change and organizational development, if you find it easy, you are probably not doing it right: where there is no pain (in this case, intellectual pain), there is no gain!

SOME COMPONENT PARTS OF COMPLEXITY

There are six subthemes to this, but I will not pretend to provide answers to any of them. Merely raising them, I hope, will instil some nagging doubts about any management of change processes. These doubts, I hope, will engender a healthy and sceptical view that will invigorate analysis and enrich practice.

They are:

- *The subject matter itself* – management is not one cohesive field, and thus offers its own complexity:
  - What do we know about management as theory or practice?
  - Where does it derive its concepts?
  - If it derives one concept from one field, e.g. psychology, how can we integrate this with concepts from other fields, e.g. economics?
- *Sector and size* – how organizations 'are' is highly dependent on context, and this creates its own complexity:
  - What type of organization are we working with or studying?
  - Is it for-profit, public sector, voluntary, or non-profit, and what difference, if any, will this make?
  - Is it a large organization, an SME (small to medium-sized enterprise), a small business, a professional practice, a shop or a manufacturer, and what differences, if any, will these factors make?

- *Organizational level* – organizations are not smooth, cohesive 'wholes' with 'seamless joins'; they have constituent parts with different functions, maybe different geographical locations; these different parts, e.g. head office and branches, may have different cultures; these factors create some complexity in terms of (1) where action programmes start and are focused, and (2) how intervention effects or findings impact on other parts:

  – At what level do we, as change agents, set up programmes of action?
  – What is the scope and span of our programmes?
  – Are we ignoring perfectly legitimate perspectives from top management in favour of a group dynamic perspective, or *vice versa*?
  – Are we offering analysis from one level which might have little or no meaning at another level in the organization?
  – Can our change programmes and research methodologies take account of the systemic whole?

- *Language, meaning* – communication can be likened to a 'black art' in the sense that it is easy to flag up on an overhead projector but notoriously difficult to get a grip on: 'The greatest problem with communication is the illusion it has been accomplished' (George Bernard Shaw). In a workshop, we may all use the same words, attach radically different meanings to them (through gender differences alone), and leave feeling a lot was achieved; workshops may raise questions of behavioural change, but what makes the change happen?

  – What do our words and actions as change agents mean to others?
  – What 'language(s)' are others using?
  – Do we note non-verbal messages, gender differences in meaning; just what does 'an open system of communication' mean to those not included in it?
  – How do we ensure we read others correctly?
  – When we get the language 'right', what does this mean, if anything, in terms of action?

- *Identity* – national, cultural, social, class, familial and personal identities all play a part in 'who we are'; OD programmes may (almost certainly will?) flag up issues of personal development which are either driving or restraining forces (Lewin 1951) for the OD programme; where is the ethical code for dealing with identity issues?

  – Are we dealing with the senses of identity of those affected by the change programme, both as individuals and in groups?
  – Do our programmes take account of multiple layers of identity – professional manager, father, brother, husband, son, team-mate – or lifestyle and life-stage differences which will affect our interaction?
  – How much do our own senses of identity and values affect how we deal with process and those affected by it?

■ And finally, *the problem of science* – not all research fits the narrow confines of 'science' or 'scientific method'; one difficulty in this field would be that the programme (of action or research) could not be repeated exactly, because organizations are all different and hence might not be seen as 'scientific'; while there are satisfactory rebuttals to this (Eden and Huxham 1996), it does further complicate our work:

  – How do we know what we think we know about the organizations we have interacted with, whether as change agents or researchers?
  – Should we even attempt to separate cause(s) and effect(s), if, indeed, we can?
  – How do we describe organizational phenomena in processual terms, to avoid simplistic, linear, and entitative 'cause-and-effect' interpretation?
  – How do we deal with intuitive knowledge in a world hooked on 'facts'?

Any one of these considerably complicates our work. Together, they complicate our analyses of the problems presented to us for action in such a way that the whole is more likely to be a picture that is complex and opaque rather than simple and clear.

This in fact conflicts with what both managers and students are looking for: simplicity and clarity. It may be beyond the power of management and OD as a field of study to give students and managers simplicity, since the world, from any perspective, is understood to be increasingly complex. Clarity, however, does seem to be an achievable goal.

UNDERSTANDING THE SUBJECT MATTER

The first point is that theories of management, organizational change and organizational development are all extremely complex subjects. They draw their concepts and models from a wide and diverse range of other academic disciplines, sometimes from areas not even cognate, or linked in any way other than that they all seem to have some relevance to management and, indeed, not necessarily interlinked relevance.

There could also be said to be two general but divergent views about how to do research in the social sciences, to which management and OD belong (Hollis 1994: 5):

> One attempts to account for the action by reference to movement in an encompassing social structure and thus proceeds, so to speak, 'top down'. The other takes the actions of individuals to be the stuff of history and regards structures as the outcome of previous actions. Here the direction is 'bottom up'.

Since OD must start from a position of analysis, the issue of divergent approaches is very germane. Do we accept framing of the problem as 'a given', especially when management has framed it and is also the client? Or do we negotiate some independent access to data, maybe missed (or not looked for) by the client, in order to (1) check the framing of the problem is accurate and (2) help the client reframe it if we find it is not accurate, or at any rate incomplete?

Indeed, these debates and intellectual controversies still bubble away and are distant echoes of debates during the last years of the 19th century and the years immediately preceding the First World War. The debate then was about the nature of being and knowing (see Lichtheim 1970: 14 *et seq.*). It amounted to a revolt against rationalism, borne ultimately of the Romantic movement, and is crucial to an understanding of the social sciences on which much (but not all) management theory rests. It allowed for an understanding of events not dependent on causal explanations. It allowed for holistic interpretations as against the linear interpretations of science.

The underpinning concepts and logic in the early 20th-century polarization between scientific-rational management on the one hand, and the human relations school on the other, can clearly be seen as a direct descendant of this dichotomy. Hence, practice and study drawing on these different schools of thought, and those developed since (e.g. contingency – see Burnes 1992: 39 *et seq.*; for the different schools of strategic thought, see Whittington 1993: 10–41; McKiernan 1997), may unwittingly run foul of the underlying intellectual contradictions.

For instance, classical or scientific-rational management draws essentially on administrative science and economics, i.e. 'top-down', whereas the various forms of human resources management draw more generally on the social sciences, 'bottom-up' (see, for instance, Burnes 1992; Thomas 1993; Whittington 1993; Wilson 1992). Research in these areas uses different methodologies so, consequently, there is unlikely to be common understanding in the sense that the concepts in use have differing bases.

Finally, these differing approaches often fail abysmally to specify clearly what the focus of the study really is. That is, studies jump alarmingly from individuals (e.g. motivation at work, job satisfaction), to groups (e.g. dynamics, organizational culture), to organizations (e.g. organizational theory, strategy and marketing), and even to nations (as in the continuing debate over the management of public services). They often even weave many of these together within one text without clarifying that a jump has been made.

As Valentine states (1992: 3):

> A general assumption held in varying degrees of strength by scientists concerns the relation between different sciences. Many would agree that sciences can be arranged in a hierarchical order according to the size of unit or level of analysis; for example, it might be said roughly that sociology deals at the levels of groups, psychology at the level of individuals, physiology with parts of individuals, biochemistry at the intra-cellular level and physics at the molecular.

This is clearly of some importance in management of change: blending concepts, which may not be blendable, will lead to confusion. Equally, assembling data at one level of analysis (or organization), and using it to draw conclusions in another, is simply nonsensical.

The problem starts because a lot of what is written about management is derivative, first from American experience, and second, predominantly from manufacturing experience. For example, the preponderance of texts in the British management literature during the 1980s was on multinational and transnational organizations, and so on, with only a few of these not being American. Even in specialized parts of the management literature, e.g. organizational behaviour, a rigorous literature review revealed that 80 per cent of all the studies (11,000) were American (Adler 1983).

Management as a subject in fact spans a number of broad composite fields of knowledge: it is not a deep, unitary body of knowledge. Its several different composite fields each draws on parts of several different bodies of knowledge. Examples would be non-verbal language and behaviour (see, for instance, Bull 1987; Bull and Frederikson 1995), which draw largely on social psychology, and decision making, which draws largely on experimental psychology. Both of these bodies of knowledge, alongside sociology and social anthropology, contribute significantly to the fields of human resource management and development, organizational behaviour, organizational change and organizational development.

They all use different methodologies to build up their respective bodies of knowledge. For example, social psychology has been criticized for relying on students for its experiments. Students as a group are not typical of the whole population, so the results may be distorted and general observations may thus be flawed (Radford and Govier 1991: 40–41). Hence, lifting elements of this body of knowledge into an OD programme without some awareness of both its intrinsic value and its intrinsic limitations may undermine the programme's effectiveness. One wonders, sometimes, just how many unintended outcomes of OD programmes might be attributable to this sort of factor.

I believe that internal and external change agents need to know more about many more of the concepts engaged in such debates, and also more about the historical context in which these concepts were born, since they differ enormously from the present-day context(s) in which we use them as practitioners and/ or researchers.

Without this understanding, OD risks a continued existence on the margins of strategic change work, while the managers who contract OD and change programmes will retain control of overall change strategies, seeing practitioners more as jobbing contractors for parts of programmes than as equals in the change management process (see, for example, Coles 1997). Conversely, dealing in the ideas of management directly with managers will start to alter subtly this perception of practitioners, moving them towards a more central and strategic role. At this level, OD can and should be tied effectively into all the organization's other strategies: finance, marketing, and so on.

SECTOR AND SIZE

The vast majority of those of us who call ourselves 'management' or 'managers' operate in small to medium-sized organizations, i.e. not multinationals or indeed manufacturing organizations. Many of us also operate within identifiably discrete subdivisions of larger organizations. Hence, surely, few serious researchers or managers would expect to find a large organizational workforce which on close and rigorous examination actually 'identified as one'.

Figure 6.1 attempts to set out graphically the improbability of significant congruence of views about organizational issues and dilemmas. Living in such different places in an organization must mean perspectives differ, if only in terms of our human need to make sense of our world. When brought down to any group of specifics (pay, hours of work, working conditions, changes in process, etc.), these differing perspectives will immediately become evident.

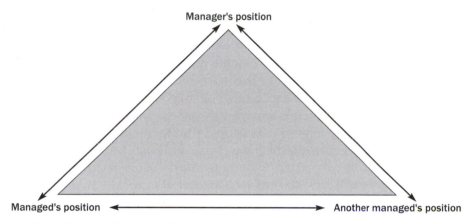

Figure 6.1　Shared viewpoints?

Figure 6.2 uses a representation of larger organizations typical of the management literature. It shows an even more complex 'multiple-reality' situation for many, if not all, organizations. It shows that managers and the managed exist at many points in an organization. It also shows that being a manager and being managed are at the very least parallel and simultaneous activities at many positions

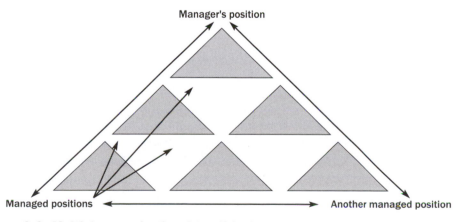

Figure 6.2　Multiple organizational 'realities'

in an organization. They cannot and should not be separated as if they were some-how unrelated and totally distinct, the one from the other, the way much of the literature and, indeed, much practice implies.

In fact, the virtual silence of the academic management and OD literature on the experience of being managed is to be very much regretted, since it presents a one-sided picture of 'management'. There is the thought that the utopian theme running through much of them (how to do it better), may be surrogate inverse evidence of how well management is not being done.

How likely is it, given the differing personalities, lifestyles, interests and work motivations of employees, that one viewpoint will be held by an entire group in an organization, let alone an entire organization? Even given what we know about group dynamics and consensus making, it seems more realistic for us, as change agents, to plan for the complication that some or many in the workforce will disagree, and diverge in opinion. They will quite possibly, more or less quietly, subvert our best efforts. The impediments of such counter-cultures are increasingly being written about in the organizational culture literature (see Hamlin and Reidy 1996). After all, is it not quite reasonable to expect this resistance to change? One pillar of the human resources ideology is that people should be 'in charge' of their own futures, and that in negotiated settlements, small and large, both parties should get something in return for giving up something. Maybe more attention needs to be paid to Watson's symbolic and abstract exchanges (1994: 26).

Claims to such unity of purpose in the literature can best be described as part of corporate rhetoric, top management's wish list, or part of the corporate culture (Anthony 1994: 3), as opposed to a clearly recognizable feature of a cohesive organizational culture (*ibid.*) which represents common ways of thinking, doing and even being.

Many of us, in fact, live, act, think and 'manage' mainly in one sector (or possibly a cross-section or hybrid of more than one): for-profit, public, non-profit voluntary. Each of these not only has differing economic bases but also has different operating assumptions. One set of managerial and organizational development concepts may or may not serve them all.

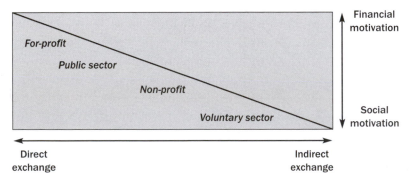

Figure 6.3 The four sectors' differing economic bases and operating values

Figure 6.3 attempts to show that the sector in which an organization operates as its principal medium or operating environment will fundamentally alter the characteristics of that organization as these two principal axes – economic exchange and motivation – interact. Where any organization sits along these two axes will determine much of its collective value system and thus much of its decision making.

I have attempted to show a sliding scale for economic exchange, as more and more public, non-profit and voluntary sector organizations move towards quasi-trading operating styles. Organizations from these three sectors, however, still seem to cluster principally towards a social motivation. In terms of the conceptual distance shown between these three sectors and for-profit, one is bound to pose the question of the wisdom of managerial paradigms drawn almost exclusively from one end of this spectrum of management experience.

At the level of exchange economics, for-profit organizations deal in direct economic exchange (i.e. exchange of cash for goods or services), with motivation driven purely by financial gain, although a debate exists about precisely whose financial gain that is (see Higson 1986: 19).

A public sector organization more frequently, but not exclusively, deals in indirect economic exchange (i.e. use of taxes to fund goods and services equitably for all), in some sense, regardless of the ability to pay, and thus operates with a motivation aimed primarily towards social objectives.

Non-profit, a sector which has grown enormously throughout the 1980s and 1990s in the UK and elsewhere, is similar to the public and voluntary sectors in giving primacy to social objectives rather than financial ones. They tend more often to employ professionals to carry out their roles, one source of some of the criticism of their seemingly high overheads as compared with other voluntary organizations with similar social objectives.

Voluntary organizations do similar things to public and non-profit sector organizations but rely more on grants from taxation and, among other things, altruism through donations (see Butler and Wilson 1990: 1 *et seq.*) than any form of trading or exchange.

It is difficult to be exact in the broad-ranging definitions represented in Figure 6.3, partly because the definitions themselves are elusive (see McCarthy *et al.* 1992), and partly because of global changes in the distribution of governmental and social functions since the Second World War (e.g. in the UK privatization of water, gas and electricity; contracting out; compulsory competitive tendering (CCT) and best value; the purchaser–provider split in the NHS). The distinctions between the four sectors can thus be seen to be breaking down rapidly, and it is worth noting that this process of reconstruction is not unique to the UK (see Bryson 1988: 4).

Many non-profit and voluntary organizations do trade in the literal sense, without it being their main stream of income. Many public sector organizations also have considerable trading operations (e.g. in leisure), but financial gain is not their main motive. Equally, many for-profit organizations can be seen to be actively engaged in what is charitable activity (e.g. sponsorship) because it achieves some social objective, such as enhancing their reputation, which it is presumed assists in maintaining or achieving some financial goal. Many also actively and deliberately engage in 'corporate citizenship', i.e. taking an active part in the communities in which they are situated. They are not, however, established for this social purpose.

The economic bases by themselves do not necessarily cause huge problems within change management, except when proposed changes appear to (or actually do) conflict with the value systems which drive the actions of the organization's members. For instance, in one sense, it should not matter whether a local authority provides a service itself or 'buys it in' from some other organization, so long as its community receives the particular service, or the improved service.

Many of the recent changes in the management of the UK public sector have in fact conflicted with the public service ethic (Flynn 1990: 172). In local authorities, they actually mean a complete reversal of roles (Clarke and Stewart 1990: 4). Added to this, the new model of service provision generates a wide range of pragmatic worries for public sector workers as to quality, reliability, equitable access, and so on. This conflict and the concerns it engenders are themselves hugely problematic. Seen as an attempt at radical and transformational change, its top-down, coercive nature does beg the question as to who the government's OD advisers have been.

Yet the prevailing value system, in many cases, will militate against successful introduction of these new models, and not just in the sense of staff self-interest being threatened. It challenges the moral bases upon which managers and staff build part of their identity (Watson 1994: 210).

This has profound implications for management of change programmes, where 'changing the way we do things' to some future state (1) affects existing, if unexplored, value sets and (2) brings in unfamiliar, maybe even unwelcome, new ones. Simply using 'business-speak' in some public sector bodies implies acceptance of the values that are embedded in and accompany that language.

> The psychological price of loyalty towards one's own group can be antipathy toward another, especially when there is a long history of enmity between the groups. (Goleman 1996: 156)

The actual model used, for instance 'customer orientation', may be perfectly reasonable (if not neutral) in that it seeks closer awareness of and attention to user needs. The implied relationship change (from service provider/service user to service seller/service purchaser or customer), even where the actual form of exchange and core organizational motivation do not change, may be chipping away at senses of identity (see below), some of which are in a dynamic relationship between people and their choice of organization and sector of employment.

In some sense, people actively choose their type of employment because it suits their values, and in turn, they reinforce the values found in that type of employment. Surely, this is one of the principal mechanisms – socialization or acculturation – that helps novices in any group to acquire membership and then binds that group together. This is no different for fully fledged professions and trades than it is for joining, remaining in and becoming successful (as a member) in any other group or organization.

If we do not actually work in organizations which to some degree are hybrids of one or more of these sectors, our lives are most certainly affected by organizations which are. Our private leisure (and many of our most basic public services) may be delivered within a facility administered by a public sector agency but which 'trades' as a quasi-commercial organization (QCO). Our worship may be undertaken in a building owned by a non-profit organization, a registered charity or a voluntary association.

So why do many of us think it acceptable to buy some goods and services from profit-making companies, but not education or health? Values and views of right and wrong underlie resistance to this sort of change, with clear implications for practice and research. There are even tremendous objections to the shorthand definitions of the various sectors (Figure 6.3) on the grounds, for instance, that:

- They polarize both thought and experience, minimizing opportunities for the passing on of best practice and even research findings.

- They ignore huge complexities in terms of value systems, frameworks, scripts, cognitive maps and other psychologically or socially derived factors affecting the practice of management and the experience of being managed.

- These definitions are in the main both economics-based and entitatively derived, i.e. they come from classical-rational approaches to management, organizations and people, which, in the main, treat organizations and people as 'things' that can be studied.

- They even treat people and groups of people in organizations as 'things' which can be studied but, rather perniciously, as 'sub-things', i.e. subsets of the 'main things', organizations.

As Hosking and Morley state (1991: ix): 'Many texts speak of person and organization, usually to emphasize one at the expense of the other'. Uniqueness of organizational problems is an often-stated cause of 'difficulty' and is best understood perhaps as a euphemism for unwillingness to engage (a 'management' interpretation), or an example of the externalizing of some incongruence, or cognitive dissonance, within the individual (a 'human resources' interpretation). It may on occasion reflect that a language and/or value conflict exists between the sector the change model is drawn from and the sector in which it is being applied.

Therefore, the issue of being absolutely specific about the nature of the organization in question, and hence its main operating assumptions, seems to me to be crucial. Although sector is likely to be neither especially significant nor unique in practitioner diagnostics or research findings for OD (other than perhaps where the trigger for change comes from), it will be significant in terms of the value sets of the organization's members. Organizational size in the sense of its shape and structure, its command and communication systems, and thus, its organizational culture, must also be significant, if not critical.

ORGANIZATIONAL FOCUS AND LEVELS

There is another sense in which the simplification of what 'management' is, and what 'managers' do is ever-present in the literature: it is the sense in which managers 'do' and 'the managed' are 'done to'. As a typology, it implies that managers are:

- powerful,
- thinking,
- capable,
- reflective of their actions and the consequences,
- reflective of both expected and unexpected outcomes,
- use feedback from their environment to make careful adjustments to their plans,
- are neutral, ethical and moral, except of course in relation to organizational goals, which have all been *a priori* participatively set and agreed on.

Whereas, the 'managed' on the other hand are:

- unempowered,
- non-thinking,
- incapable (at any rate of thought, or contributing from experience, especially of the job they actually do),
- don't reflect on their actions or the consequences (especially the unintended outcomes),
- don't know what feedback is, since they see such feedback as managers give them as 'criticism',
- are overtly (and frequently also covertly) partisan and self-interested in undermining perfectly reasonable targets, thus jeopardizing not only the organization's goals but even its very survival.

This polarization can best be debunked by restating that there is only one thing that 'managers' and 'managed' can (and do) agree on: both want more for less. Though this may seem cynical, is it really sensible to expect people who are likely to differ potentially on so many grounds to agree on very much?

For instance, managers and managed, except in the so-called knowledge-based industries, are likely to differ in some or all of the following potential areas:

- educational achievements
- training and acquisition of skills
- economic and social status and power
- organizational power
- possibly, religious, ethnic, class and other social memberships
- political affiliations
- lifestyles
- life goals and expectations, both material and more esoteric ones.

So why pretend that shared meanings and understandings are possible, when it is clear viewpoints must differ? It is also clear that action has to be taken, and so presumably must be based on one viewpoint, at least in the opening phase of some process of change.

One explanation of this over-simplification is in the way our minds work. As Hosking and Morley point out (1991: 21):

> there is a very large literature about moves we make to keep our cognitions simple, stable and consistent:
>
> ■ seeking self-serving analogies
>
> ■ engaging in various forms of wishful thinking
>
> ■ the use of negative logic
>
> ■ relying on a small number of highly salient clues
>
> ■ seeking out evidence to strengthen our beliefs
>
> ■ overweighting evidence which is consistent with our beliefs
>
> ■ underweighting evidence which is not consistent with our beliefs
>
> ■ polarizing judgements (especially if different alternatives are championed by members of competing groups).

As they state:

> The net effect is that people see too much order and certainty in their social worlds; have too much confidence that their initial diagnoses are correct; and prefer explanations which are simple to explanations which are complex. (*ibid.*)

The polarization above is an example of organizational focus and can be seen in terms of McGregor's theory X/theory Y (1960) in that its simplicity, like theory X/theory Y, disguises the spectrum of beliefs we all hold, varying at times and over time, in relation to differing situations, and dependent on a multitude of factors. For example, people in general decry theft of private property, yet some see no contradiction in supplying themselves with office stationery: beliefs seem to be context-specific. Once again, Watson's 'either-or' judgements (1994: 210) can be seen in action.

This is not an attempt to retake the high ground for classical-rational managers and good old 'command and control', because managers are likely to be 'better off' in most of these categories and should therefore have primacy in shaping strategies for change. Nor is it just an implicit restatement of McGregror's theory X and theory Y proposition implying that managers are on one side of the scale and the managed are on the other. The theory X/theory Y proposition and other such polarizations, at their most essential – good guys and bad guys – are so basic to human society everywhere and over all time that they run the danger of being as useful (or useless) as horoscope predictions.

A second type of effect of organizational over-simplification is to do with the lack of definition of the level at which the wisdom, prescription or advice is aimed. For instance, the only Chinese philosopher most Westerners can quote (at least in jokes) is Confucius (551–479 BC) (see Waley 1964: 21 *et seq.*). If the anachronism can be forgiven (after all, he stated the proposition a couple of millennia before McGregor), Confucius was a theory Y man. His most able disciple, Mencius (372–289 BC) (see Waley 1963: 115 *et seq.*; Ware 1960), over a century later, rewrote and reinterpreted the canons of Confucianism in the light of his own experience of China at that time and no doubt within his own ideological understanding of the master's thought, but also as a theory Y man.

But another disciple, Hs'üan K'uang (315?–238? BC) (Ware 1960: 8), though still 'Confucian', actually upended a basic tenet to propound the idea that Man was basically born evil and needed to be rectified by education. Confucius and Mencius believed just the opposite, that Man was born good, and it was the vicissitudes of life that wrought his downfall.

So in not defining the context from which advice is drawn and the level at which it is aimed, management literatures are generalizing from one context to another. This is indeed the aim of much management research, but it ignores the question of what happens during the decontextualization and recontextualization process:

> ... prophets, poets, and philosophers have gleaned important truths in the past, truths that are essential for our continued survival. But these have been expressed in the conceptual vocabulary of their time, so that to be useful, their meaning has to be rediscovered and reinterpreted every generation. (Czikszentmihalyi 1997: 2)

The important word here is 'rediscovered', i.e. that such 'truths' cannot simply be left to interpret themselves: they need careful reinterpretation in order to find relevance in any new context. Also, advice may be pitched at a number of different levels:

- societal and, in these days of 'international management', global;
- sector by principal means of economic exchange or industry;
- organizational (in for-profit terms – group vs division vs factory or production unit; in public sector terms – corporate body vs department vs division vs actual unit of service delivery);
- group, as sub-units of larger legally corporate entities;
- group, as defined by organizational culture; individual.

Is particular advice transferable to a new context? This is important because, pursuing my example, Confucius was a political philosopher. He did not actually manage anything. He made his living, rather precariously as it happens, advising the different sovereign nation states in what we now call China on how to effect good government (China was not unified until 221 BC – see Bodde 1967: 1). Clarke (1997) deals at length with these issues of de/recontextualization in terms of oriental philosophical ideas finding their way into Western thought, some of which, later, find their way into the HR aspects of management through psychology:

> ... deep philosophical differences, involving fundamental divergences in how people conceptualise nature, human actions, and values, may be encountered as we move from one linguistic/cultural tradition to another. (*ibid.*: 184)

Thus using Confucius' advice now, it is entirely possible to derive, interpretatively, reasonable prescriptions of 'good' (or effective?) behaviour, either for kings, as he did, or other 'rulers', leaders or managers, however defined.

This seems scarcely less positive or less effective than any other prescriptive advice (management of change, organizational development, interpersonal skills training, etc.) on offer to managers, which is similarly decontextualized, i.e. lifted from its original context (science, psychology, social psychology or sociology, political science, administration, organizational theory, politics, philosophy, and their multiple hybrids in the management literature), and then recontextualized elsewhere without attending to what may be transferable or not.

It also seems clear to me that any such prescriptions, from whichever 'science' they are drawn, embody values, and that the values may or may not carry over to the new context. For example, a manager describing the 'leaner, fitter, healthier organization', which will provide a better experience of work after his/her changes have been implemented, may or may not subscribe to those values. The workforce affected may or may not subscribe to them. The values may be context-specific, i.e. to the manager's own context of being managed by a new boss espousing that model.

Indeed, values will almost certainly not carry over unless they are overtly explored and engaged as part of any organizational change process. For the reflective practitioner or researcher, the dangers of this process of decontextualization/recontextualization lie in creating yet more opportunity for misunderstanding, misinterpretation and confused communication. However, the alternative of being precise, relevant and appropriate to the particular focus, unit or level of the organization in question, and addressing the nature of the sector to which it belongs, will lessen the confusion by bounding the discussion. That is, by avoiding generalizations and universalizations, specifics like 'What does it mean for us?' can be addressed.

Being more clear-cut and specific about the outcomes our clients or ourselves as change agents want, and about whether they are achievable in part or in total, will to some extent overcome a marked tendency in the literature to speak in generalized terms such that embedded and implicit values are overlooked, or worse from the standpoint of ethical practice, disguised within concepts of 'progress', 'survival', 'changes for the better', and so on.

Perhaps an ethical stance is needed in OD practice and research that admits that no prescription, model or change instrument is value-free. Leaving the implicit values unexplored is unlikely to be a force for change. Since OD practice and research are committed to successful change initiatives, identifying restraining forces and dealing with them would seem to be a critical and useful early part of any OD process.

LANGUAGE, METAPHOR AND MEANING

Hosking and Morley (1991: ix) visualize both organizational behaviour and human resources management literature as metamorphosing both people and organizations into 'Russian dolls': how many organizational development practitioners, teachers and researchers have used the metaphor of 'peeling back the layers of an onion' in their work or 'digging into even deeper strata'? It seems to me to be of some significance that one of the most influential (though not undisputed) psychological writers of the 20th century, Freud, also used 'layers', as in archaeological excavation, strata by strata, as it were, as one of his principal metaphors (Nye 1996: 8). The point here is that the use of metaphor (mechanistic, organic-biological, etc.) identifies our individual starting points for dealing with management and the managed (Oswick and Grant 1996). How we think about organizations and people must determine to an extent how we deal with them.

An example is that organizations are often characterized in the management literature as 'context independent of the human actor' (Hosking and Morley 1991: ix), i.e. the concept of rational economic man is still extant. Rational economic man makes rational choices out of multiple options available, each option having been thoroughly examined. This is referred to as subjective expected utility theory (Table 6.1).

> The theory has been heavily criticized because it represents an ideal of rationality which is quite impossible for people to attain. (Hosking and Morley 1991: 36)

Table 6.1 Subjective expected utility theory summarized

Main features	Main criticisms
To define rational choice between alternative policies	Represents an ideal of rationality which is quite impossible for people to attain
Each policy may lead to different states of the world	Says nothing at all about a number of important psychological processes
Some states are more likely than others	Nothing to say about the construction of alternatives
Each state of the world has advantages and disadvantages	Nothing to say about the way values are organized and aggregated so that the actor is able consistently to apply a well-defined utility function
A single cardinal number is assigned to each state of the world designating its net worth (or value)	
The utility of each possible state of the world is then weighted according to its likelihood (forming a product: probability times value)	Nothing to say about the ways in which we ascertain what is happening now, and what is likely to happen in the future
The policy which maximizes expected utility (the sum of the products of probability and value across each state of the world is then chosen)	

That is, these literatures tend to ignore what might be seen from this perspective as the idiosyncratic effects of individuals:

> There are a number of features of the behaviour of organisms that have raised doubts about the appropriateness of the mechanistic model [as in science]. One is purposiveness ... the issue of consciousness ...' (Valentine 1992: 2–3)

The literature even ignores the effects that groups of individuals in organizations have on their own contexts, both at the organizational level and, indeed, at the macro-societal level. That is, relying on only one mental model about organizations and people, we limit our potential behavioural flexibility. Our language reveals our thinking, and our thinking tends to predetermine to some extent the nature of our behaviour.

As an example, it is not too far-fetched to see some of Margaret Thatcher's reforms of the public sector and unions as her own (and many others') reactions to what came to be known, in the Conservative ideology of the 1980s, as the ineffectiveness and extravagant expenditure of the public sector on the one hand, and overuse, and indeed abuse, of economic power by unions on the other. That is not to say that I either agree or disagree with that 1980s ideological interpretation of the then socio-economic position of the UK, or indeed that interpretation of what was the best 'cure' for it. Indeed, there is some evidence that first, the linchpin of that ideological position (public sector profligacy) was not in fact the case (Flynn 1990: 24 *et seq*.), and second, that it was a position adopted by many Western governments of both left and right political persuasions during that same period (Taylor and Lansley 1990: 219).

The example serves merely as a useful illustration that groups of people (in this case, public sector workers and trades unions) clearly affected their own context, if only through others' perceptions of their effects on that context. These, in turn, with Thatcherism as the dominant political ideology of the 1980s, clearly affected them back, as governmental reactions began to take effect, restricting public sector finance and union power (see Figure 6.4).

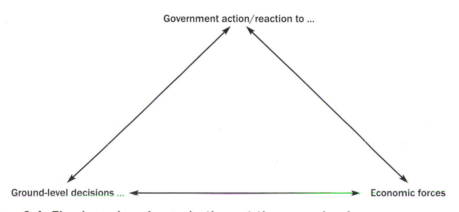

Figure 6.4 The dynamics of organizations at the macro level

As Wilson states (1992: 119):

> At the national and international levels of analysis, it seems that the socio-economic context in which all organizations operate really sets the strategic agenda for change. Of course, this revisits the paradox of incrementalism. Whilst we may argue that the wider context determines everything we also have to consider how the prevailing strategies of the state came about. They, too, may have been the product of many smaller, more operational decisions which, when taken together, give the appearance of a large, global strategy.

While it is impossible to say that, had public sector workers and trades unionists taken account of the potential effects of their activities prior to Margaret Thatcher's premiership, her policies would have been less stringent, it is possible to state that a greater awareness of the potential effects might have led to some modification of those very activities. A different iteration would have occurred. We can only surmise, however, that it may have been less confrontational, with possibly less dramatic effects on the public sector and the unions.

The same question arises at various levels in the organization. Ignoring the iterative effects of any organizational intervention leads, in old management-speak, to a situation where you 'solve one problem and create another'. Maybe a code of practice ought to include a quality standard that reflective time-outs be built into any intervention:

- to check for over-simple analysis;
- to brainstorm all the possible effects of the intervention (i.e. more than just the desired one), avoiding tunnel vision;
- to undertake some risk estimation and contingency planning.

In line with my worries about simple analysis, quick fixes should be avoided, most especially those that offer simple solutions to problems which have probably not been rigorously analysed in the first place. To quote Wilson again (*ibid.*: 129):

> The danger lies in assuming change to be a simple phenomenon, attached as a sub-theme to organizational behaviour and manageable through a finite list of behavioural recipes and managerial competencies.

Maybe also, the use of the word 'problem' is at odds with good practice, in the sense that it is likely to be negatively interpreted. So analysis should start out with 'what is right with what we are doing' first, in order to start from a position of balance and perspective. It will certainly set the 'problem' into a rounder picture of the organizational whole.

As Hosking and Morley put it:

> An entitative approach fails to represent what it means to be human, misrepresents the qualities of relational processes and, more generally, grossly distorts the relationships between person and organization. (1991: ix)

They proffer a thesis which aims at developing ideas on a psychologically adequate picture of people interacting dynamically with organizations while interacting with other people, who are interacting with organizations, and so on.

All this leads to what might be termed the excluded management agenda, including such key areas as:

- motivation
- formal and informal systems of order in groups and organizations
- collective action
- leadership
- relational processes
- sense making
- political processes
- negotiation.

Hosking and Morley characterize much of this complexity thus:

> ... politics simply is seen as a naughty self-serving activity. This view is grounded in an entitative perspective of person and organization. A psychologically adequate picture of persons and their relationships with their contexts – relations of mutual creation – leads to the view that political processes are endemic to organizing. (1991: xii)

Though I am a little unhappy with their term 'endemic', since it makes politics sound like a disease (this is another popular metaphor in use: the 'sick organization', organizational diagnostics and the 'heroic organizational doctor come to effect a cure'), I believe this is one of the most apposite statements of one of the principal, and often overlooked, complexities in management of change.

Their term 'mutual creation', describing their view of the complex interactions between people and organizations, reflects their perceptive starting point (and subject-specific terminology) of people as 'actors', i.e. making active choices about their behaviour in organizations and, indeed, elsewhere. It comes from psychology and social psychology, specifically behaviourism, and is a powerful concept in OD interventions and research, and when describing and discussing people in organizations, and organizations and people.

The concept of mutual creation is of some significance in this book, since the work described in it, both as action and as research, got well past the more usual over-simplification of the issues of individuals, groups of individuals, and their various interactions, reactions, and so on. The book thus represents an implicit but clear statement of the iterative nature of work with people in organizations, and organizations and people.

There is in addition the problem of actual language, both in use and in interpretation of the outcomes or results. For example, are understandings of metaphors (journeys, mechanistic, biological and other scientific ones) really 'shared', and sufficiently overlapping to lend real meaning to their use? Second, spatial language ('giving headroom', 'elbow room') and other subcategories of language, e.g. gender-based differences (Gray 1992) and, indeed, non-verbal language (see for instance, Bull 1987; Bull and Frederikson 1995), all count for something when people are interacting. At the very least, they mark our membership of certain group(s) and our difference from others.

An example from a personal, research-based consultancy project illustrates the point. Graphic representations of Handy's four organizational culture types (1985: 188, 190, 193 and 195; see also Handy 1988: 86, 88, 90 and 92; and Pheysey 1993: 46) were used in combination with a brief verbal résumé of the features of each, as a starting point, to assist small syndicate groups of a new organization just being established to define its own, unique organizational cultural needs. At that time, this seemed to fit best their needs as an atypical organization, one of the 'new' organizations in vogue in the literature of the 1990s (see Handy 1989: 70 *et seq.*; Burnes 1992: 71 *et seq.*).

As change agent/researcher, I could not be sure, when evaluating the intervention six months later (without huge additional investments of time from the organization and the researcher), that the meanings of either the pictures or words, or both, were sufficiently congruent. Incongruence may have occurred, at the very least:

- over time;
- between researcher and collaborators;
- between the collaborators themselves; and
- between Handy's original understanding and current interpretation.

Nevertheless, the organization and its members appeared to show a marked agreement on the need for and the effectiveness of the intervention and, indeed, the particular outcome in terms of the specific organizational culture they had identified and developed for themselves. In one sense, if that organizational culture intervention 'worked for them', and the only people who can really judge this are the organization's members, does it matter how or why?

This is, however, an unscientific view, paralleling the Chinese view of their science (if it works, fine, use it), and contrasting with a Western scientific view of 'until we understand how it works, we won't use it'. For instance, Western studies of Chinese acupuncture meridians have failed to find any scientific evidence of their existence. Yet well over a quarter of the world's population (the Chinese) adopt remedies based on a belief in their existence. These remedies have been shown to be as effective/ineffective as Western scientific ones, depending on context (belief in the medicine), rigorous diagnostics (the exact nature of the illness), and so on.

Overall, however, the issue of the intricately linked language, metaphor and meaning is crucial in intervention work. What does a 'democratic and open system of communication' actually mean? Its meaning must vary according to the reception it gets from each individual, which in turn is affected by their past understandings of those words, and other words or phrases like them.

If differing metaphors for organizations and work are in use, should they not be fully explored, again in the opening stages of any intervention? This would ensure understanding by all participants that while meanings were probably not shared fully, they at least overlapped sufficiently to facilitate progress at later stages of the intervention.

IDENTITY

Each person's own 'heritage' in terms of personal and cultural identity, societal and sub-societal group affiliations, etc., must in part determine actions and reactions to any situation:

> People are conceptualized first and foremost as social beings, who derive a sense of who they are, how they should behave and what they should believe on the basis of their group membership. Society, as a collectivity, is comprised of the complex web of intergroup relations which characterize any socio-historical period. (Augoustinos and Walker 1995: 4)

Given that we, as animals, experience the world consciously only through our internal processing of external events and phenomena, which have stimulated one or more of our sensory systems, it would seem that some of these 'core' aspects of the person and identity ('baggage' in training and counselling terms) will predetermine at any rate the limits and range of reactions, if not the specific reactions themselves.

It is also worth pointing out that not everyone agrees with the distinction of 'internal/external'. Ryle (1949) argued that the internal/external distinction is a matter of grammar, that we should describe 'intelligent behaviour' rather than 'intelligence', though as Valentine states (1992: 29):

> This view appears to rule out of court the possibility of any language for describing relations between mental and physical events.

For instance, if I am the sort of individual likely to take a pessimistic view of the world, I am unlikely to take an optimistic view of changes which affect me personally. My reactions (response to the stimulus of the imminent change) will be somewhere within my scale of pessimism, which may or may not overlap with that of another pessimist, or indeed a third affected person's scale of optimism. There is research evidence to back this up:

> For instance, a healthy extrovert with strong self-esteem, a stable marriage, and religious faith will be much more likely to say he is happy than a chronically ill, introverted, and divorced atheist with low self-esteem. (Czikszentmihalyi 1997: 20)

In other words, our starting points in these matters rather predetermine, if not how far we travel (journey metaphor again), then at least to some extent where we do arrive.

The sheer number of factors interceding in just such a reaction to such a stimulus is problematic from the scientific point of view:

- *Personal ones*:
  - headache;
  - good day/bad day?;
  - life stable versus crisis;
  - kids;
  - partner problems;
  - feeling threatened versus engaged/empowered by change;

- age, at the point of engagement with a career, or at the point when beginning to disengage and plan retirement;
- job versus career – not everyone develops a career.

- *Organizational ones*:
  - sector (for-profit, public, non-profit, voluntary) – this can affect the organization, and thus the individuals in it, at the strategic level, e.g. few public sector organizations can simply 'strategize' their way out of low-income-stream businesses, so 'right-sizing' operations can be more or less threatening, actually and psychologically, depending on what type of economic exchange system the organization rests on;
  - culture – so much has been written on this in the management literature, and from a number of perspectives, that it need not be repeated here.

- *Societal ones*:
  - is the country's economy in recession, 'flattening out' or 'on the up' – the search for the 'feel-good factor';
  - is the job, product or service highly or less highly valued than elsewhere or in different times; e.g. three decades ago, teachers in the UK were perceived as having rather higher status than they do now;
  - group identity issues – ethnicity, class, social groupings such as Rotary versus ex-servicemen's or miners' clubs, hobbies; time off to serve as a JP is 'acceptable', but time off to serve as chairman of an ex-servicemen's association may not be;
  - education, skills, aptitudes.

In line with good 'academic' practice, it is fundamental to define another term – what is an organization (see Figure 6.5)? Does it stop at payroll? Does it include stakeholders? Does it include suppliers? Does it even include customers? Boundaries – national, societal, organizational, personal – have all been changing. What effect will this have on analysis and diagnostics, let alone research conclusions, problem solving and solution generation?

Within the new orthodoxy of the 'new organization', hard boundaries are seen as barriers. Conversely, relationship building with suppliers, customers, all potential stakeholders, and even competitors, is seen as both a quality and a survival issue (i.e. clearly strategic). How then does this impact on change management or other organizational development interventions? Does it? Should it?

Organizational culture has entered the practice of OD and seems to provide a useful tool for developing thinking around working practices, style, communication and a number of other areas. Yet there is a certain amount of vagueness of definition in the organizational culture literature as to whether organizations have identity in the form of organizational culture(s), or whether they simply are a certain 'sort of organization'. Harrison (1972), Handy (1985, 1988, 1989) and Pheysey (1993: 23) variously describe organizational culture as the glue that holds the organization together, the symbols, values, rituals, politics, heroes and myths of organizations. Organizational culture is about shared systems and constructs of identity:

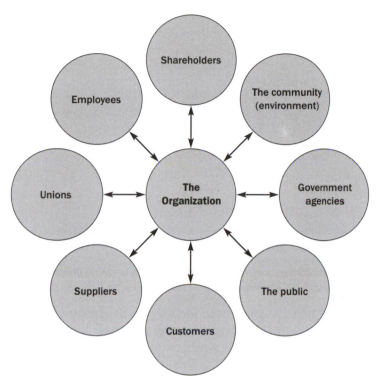

Figure 6.5 Organizational boundaries – where do they stop?

- conventional understandings shared by participants in it (Becker 1960: 305);

- values, heroes, the rites and rituals (Deal and Kennedy 1982: 14–15);

- the rites, customs and values of organizations (Trice and Beyer 1984: 653–669);

- the pattern of basic assumptions that a given group has invented, discovered or developed in learning to cope with its problems of external adaptation and internal integration (Schein 1983: 25);

- the cultural web – rituals and myths, symbols, power structures, organizational structures, control systems, routines (Johnson 1989: 46);

- appropriate behaviour which bonds and motivates individuals, and asserts solutions where there is ambiguity (Hampden-Turner 1990: 11), a rewarder of excellence, a set of affirmations (*ibid*.: 12–13), giving continuity and identity to the group (*ibid*.: 21).

The phenomenon of 'shared meanings' and 'shared understandings' (an analogue for organizational culture) has been described in a variety of ways, from a variety of perspectives:

- scientific communities (Kuhn 1970)

- interpretive communities (Fish 1980)

- cognitive social structures (Krackhardt 1987)

- cognitive communities (Porac *et al.* 1989)
- epistemic communities (Haas 1992)
- autonomous versus espoused values, norms, and beliefs (Heron 1981)
- cognitive groups (Dunbar 1993).

Whether cultures are something organizations have (in which case they can be managed and modified), or whether in fact cultures are something organizations are (in which case management strategies and actions have to fit the culture in order to succeed), seems to revolve around whether or not members of organizations are aware meta-cognitively of their culture(s). Many work groups will declare 'this is the way things are done around here', so implying an awareness of difference, although few may describe this as 'culture'.

This is important because other academic literatures concerning 'culture' also have some difficulty with definition:

> As might be expected, culture is as hard for anthropologists to define operationally (as opposed to theoretically) as intelligence is for psychologists or language is for linguists. (Foley 1991: 15)

Culture is 'modes of behaving and thinking that are passed on from one generation to another by social learning of one kind or another ... couched in symbols' (Fox 1989: 14) and it is 'made up of observable actions and inferable thoughts' (Foley 1991: 15).

Nevertheless:

> Inherent in a common-sense understanding of culture are such characteristics as learning, non-genetic transmission of information between and among generations, high levels of intra- and interpopulation behavioural variability, tool-use and manufacture, and the use of symbolic systems of communication. Beyond this there is some confusion as to whether culture is these observable phenomena or whether it lies in the structure of the mind that makes cultural activities possible. (*ibid.*: 26)

An example might be the Celtic nations who inhabit the UK (Scots, Irish, Welsh, and some would include Cornish and Manx). Among these culturally distinct groups, there is a conscious, one might even say self-conscious, awareness of cultural identity as it distinguishes these people from the rest of the UK, but especially the English. In non-ethnic terms:

> man, in any culture, is faced by a gamut of possibilities: He is the archaic man, the beast of prey, the cannibal, the idolater; but he is also the being with the capacity for reason, for love, for justice. (Fromm: 27)

Mankind is a complex species, and the species' intra-relationships compound this complexity, such that it defies simplistic interpretations and formulae.

People have many identities, each relating to a different cognitive group (Dunbar 1993), but we all start first with a personal one (see Figure 6.6):

> It [basic group identity] is the identity made up of what a person is born with or acquires at birth. It is distinct from all the other multiple and secondary identities people acquire (Glazer and Moynihan 1975: 35)

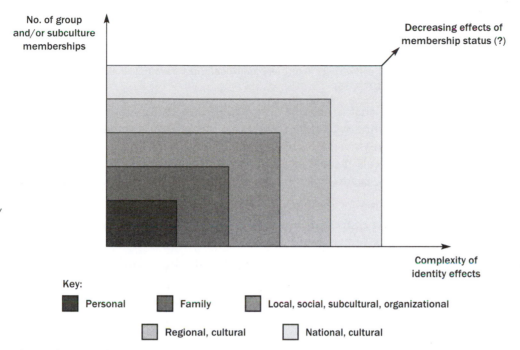

Figure 6.6 Basic and group identities

People then build up layers of identity as they progress through life (Gouldner 1957) – latent social roles and identities, maybe abandoning some, or parts of some, at life-changing events, and while identities evolve and maybe even transform:

> People carry culture with them; when they leave one group setting for another, they do not shed the cultural premises of the first setting. (Becker 1960: 305)

Additional memberships of social and cognitive groups add complexity:

> As a general rule the more people that one chooses to live with, the more complex life becomes: there is a wider choice of possible partners with whom to share food or sex, and each of those partners will have a greater number and more diverse relationships with other members of the group. It is a considerable challenge to keep track of who is friends with whom, who are enemies, and who bear grudges or desires, and then to try to decide with whom to make friends without upsetting your other friends. We have all had some experience of this. In fact we seem to quite enjoy the social manoeuvrings that become paramount as groups enlarge, specially if we are bystanders. (Mithen 1996: 118)

Before starting any intervention, it is perhaps vital to ask the fundamental question: 'what makes a person?', because:

> Administrators have always known that workers' behavior is affected by what they are and who they are away from the job. (Becker 1960: 304)

Following that is the question: to what degree do planned changes affect various aspects and levels of identity? Some of the strictures imposed on the public sector in the last decade have perhaps been seen as adverse because they were perceived to affect adversely one level of identity – that of the professional public servant:

> With this sense of belongingness there goes, all but inseparably, the matter of self-esteem, the supporting measure of self-respect, that every individual must have to live a tolerable existence. (Glazer and Moynihan 1975: 35)

Similarly, if we agree that organizations do have something which for shorthand purposes we can describe as 'culture', whether it is something the organization has and its members 'have', unconsciously or consciously, must also be relevant to OD practice since it too deals at some level with senses of identity.

Within OD there are factors which can be labelled specifically the interactive factors:

■ How 'good' (effective for the purpose in hand) is the manager, trainer, change agent, and all of the above factors in some sort of dynamic, one is tempted to say chaotic, interplay?

■ How 'good' (relevant, appropriate) is the particular intervention (strategy, business plan) to the objective?

■ Is the objective declared, tacit, hidden, mixed, unclear, crystal clear, and to whom?

■ How do we 'interpret' the meaning(s) of all this – strategy, business plan, change intervention, the manager's motives and rewards?

■ So whose is the conclusion, the interpreter's or the players'?

> A first requirement [of science] is that of systematicity. At the very least science must be a coherent body of knowledge. The complexity of psychological matter, notably the diversity and likely interactive nature of relevant variables promises trouble for psychology, a promise that has been amply fulfilled. (Valentine 1992: 4)

The general purport of much OD literature tends to suggest that change must be an accretive process, accumulating complexity en route, but not necessarily in even ways. Some people carry more of their baggage with them longer than others. Some simply do not, or are able more effectively to isolate or compartmentalize these personal issues from the work context and change process some of the time, perhaps differentially in different circumstances, a sort of personal context boundedness.

In the end, no matter how right the downsizing, no matter how many jobs are saved by it, no matter how important this organization's survival is to the local economy, those being made redundant, or floated off as a separate enterprise, or re-focused/retasked into unfamiliar territory, are individuals with multiple identities. All their identities are likely to take some damage or be affected in some way, not just their organizational one(s). This may only be a perception of reality (what else is 'reality' but the 'internal' processing of these 'external' events as to how they affect 'me'?). But it is one which is 'real' to those affected, and they will, more or less, determine their actions on the basis of it:

> Any organizational change that matters strategically will involve winners and losers, and so will involve some managers seeing themselves as potential winners and some as potential losers. (Eden and Ackermann 1998: 10)

For management of change and OD practice and research, the question of identity seems fundamental in that not being aware of it may leave undiscovered barriers to change when identity at some level is threatened. It may also be that the planned changes in some way require modification of one or more identity, identity in part consisting of beliefs. For example, requiring public sector employees, who formerly relied on a public service ethos as a central belief cum building block of identity, to become more entrepreneurial may simply be too radical a transition for them to make. As Hosking and Morley state:

> There is now abundant evidence to suggest that the mind operates according to principles of economy and principles of consistency. (1991: 21)

What this means is that minds are extremely efficient at resisting wholesale or radical changes in beliefs, because of the way in which beliefs are structured in an extensive lateral and hierarchical web. Some change may simply be too much for the individual's available processing power (machine metaphor, but at least a sophisticated and as yet unrivalled information-processing machine).

THE PROBLEM OF SCIENCE

Perhaps this is all to do with the problem of science (see above, Lichtheim 1970). The fields of OD and management of change are such veritable 'minefields' of ambiguity, uncertainty, wider implications, numbers of interplaying factors, that it seems difficult to reconcile the needs of 'science' (replication, rigour, validity, predictive power, etc.) with the needs of organizations and people, and people in organizations ('real life', dynamic, 'live' problems, the need to come to a decision and take action).

In general, then, where much management literature tends towards the classical-scientific, and much organizational behaviour and human resources literature reifies both people and organizations, I would suggest that both management and the management of change should in fact first be about interactions and process, not about recipes. Second, it should be about finding the right questions and asking them persistently. Finally, it should be about determining what can be and has been learned from each part of each aspect of the change process.

That is, I would turn the concepts of change and change management inside out. As long as the literature tends towards a static, entitative language of organizations and people, and people in organizations, we will continue to think of them as things, things that can be manipulated at will. Organic and journey metaphors, for instance, emphasize static events in time: the 'now' state; transition states; the future state. Disregarding the interactive, dynamic and processual aspects will perpetuate these ambiguities in OD and leave the discipline marginalized.

Conversely, tackling these sorts of complexities, starting with our language of organizations and change, may start to change the way we think about them. This can only deepen the analyses we undertake and by their very rigour and appropriateness produce dynamic and more effective solutions. This will make OD more central by improving its visibility on the balance sheet.

There is a 'yen' for simplicity and 'smoothness' in all parts of the management literature which obscures much of the 'richness', bumpiness and complexity of what is going on at any one time. This is so reminiscent of almost all early scientific theory. Compare what is now known as a 'bumpy universe', i.e. a universe in which even the 'blackness' is not even in its blackness, or the 'emptiness' indeed completely empty, with earlier views of an enormous, indeed infinite, void. The universe according to recent findings seems more or less dense in different areas, and somewhat less 'orderly' than sits comfortably with attempts by either change agents or managers at ordering even minute sections of it, i.e. their own domains where they exercise power. Highly topical currently, chaos theory reflects and reiterates this 'bumpy' versus 'smooth universe' view and I think implicitly rejects the utopian and orderly transitions much alluded to under the label 'change management'.

Science is beginning to accept an iterative and accretive body of knowledge which itself reeks of complexity, for instance in whether subatomic particles are particles or waves: this seemingly depends on their behaviour in certain experiments, which in turn depends on whether or not they are being observed at the time (Zukav 1984: 119 *et seq.*) Out of this complexity, a clearer picture of the universe and ourselves in it is appearing.

Like early science, this yearning for simplification, in obscuring the complexities of organizational situations under study, actually makes them less clear and more opaque. Only by acknowledging the complexity of management in action, theories in use, sector value systems, organizational size effects, issues of language, meaning and identity, in situations under diagnosis, analysis or study, can attempts be made at real clarity. This is for the sake of both practical actions, 'in real time', and good research, which lead to more effective and intended outcomes rather than less effective and unintended ones.

The literature of management, organizational behaviour, organizational development and so on needs to take on the challenge of reflecting the complexity of organizations and people, and people in organizations, at almost any level of intervention or study, and for organizations in any sector. This will mature both practice and the literature.

Practitioners can best achieve this by continuing their own personal development. I would commend specifically research skills to add rigour to organizational analysis and diagnosis, and for better contextualisation within the complexities of the subject itself, for instance issues such as sector, size, organizational focus and level. In another direction, interpersonal communications skills, for example neuro-linguistic programming and neuro-associative conditioning among many others, can enhance awareness of issues such as language, meaning and identity.

> Rather, validity in new paradigm research lies in the skills and sensitivities of the researcher, in how he or she uses herself [*sic*] as a knower, as an inquirer. Validity is more personal and interpersonal, rather than methodological. (Reason 1981: 244)

Reason also notes the move from subjectivity to objectivity (science) in order to get away from the dangers of 'naive enquiry' (1988: 12) and argues strongly for a 'participative and dialogical relationship with the world' (*ibid.*: 10), and for 'wholeness' instead of a 'fragmented and theoretical knowledge ... separated from practice and experience' (*ibid.*: 11).

The final 'problem of science', in a sense, is one for academics to resolve. It should only concern practitioners where there is a tendency on the part of a client towards a scientific, linear, cause-and-effect style of language and thinking. This is a highly probable scenario: speak to anyone about their experience of working in an organization and the vast majority will easily provide you with account after account of managers being unreasonable in some way. Their interpretation of 'unreasonable' (in the absence of other data) can most often be laid at the door of their own linear, single-perspective mindset, if not the manager's.

That these experiences remain largely unexplored reflects 'the problem of science' affecting (infecting?) many areas of thought and experience which do not need 'scientific' revelation. Nor indeed, do many of these areas succumb easily to scientific investigation. How many studies exist of the experience of being managed? Studies which adopt a managerialist perspective are incomplete, since they ignore the 'data' (responses) which represent the experience of management action, as a set of stimuli, at the very least.

One component of much OD is organizational learning, that is, if the concept can eventually be shown to exist in businesses other than those dependent on intellectual property. Rigorous analysis and diagnosis followed by appropriate interventions will in all probability enhance organizational learning. This in itself will provide a vehicle for engaging and resolving issues of 'proof' emanating from this specific, one-sided [scientific] organizational interpretative stance.

It should, for instance, elicit accounts of organizational phenomena which reflect multiple perspectives. Where it elicits such widely divergent perspectives that organizational members cannot agree at all (as it should more often than appears the case from the literature), then a good start has been made at resolving differences by admitting them. It is likely that different worldviews and values will be drawn out in such a process. It will take longer, certainly, than the quick-fix recipes more often sought. But it has far more chance of succeeding in developing outcomes that everyone will support, or at least agree not to subvert.

This is a tough agenda for OD practice and research. I recognize that it requires an enormous amount from practitioners and researchers. But it seems to me that if OD is to become a legitimate arm of strategy building, side by side with the hard systems 'number crunchers' of traditional corporate business planning, soft systems OD practitioners have to develop something in terms of practice that is distinctive from the 'trainer toolkit' and the 'navel gazing' or 'touchy-feely' stuff so revered by some. I believe that only reflective practice based on rigorous data gathering and analysis, admitting and exploring complexity and accepting multiple perspectives, will do this.

References

Adler, N.J. (1983), Cross-cultural management research: the ostrich and the trend. *Academy of Management Review*, April, 226–232.

Anthony, P. (1994), *Managing Culture*. Buckingham: Open University Press.

Audit Commission (1991), *The Road to Wigan Pier? Managing Local Authority Museums and Art Galleries*. London: HMSO.

Augoustinos, M. and Walker, I. (1995), *Social Cognition, an Integrated Introduction*. London: Sage.

Becker, H.S. (1960), Latent culture: a note on the theory of latent social roles. *Administrative Science Quarterly*, 5, 304–340.

Bodde, D. (1967), *China's First Unifier, A Study of the Ch'in Dynasty as seen in the Life of Li Ssu*. Hong Kong: Hong Kong University Press.

Bryson, J.M. (1988), *Strategic Planning for Public and Non-profit Organizations*. San Francisco: Jossey-Bass.

Bull, P.E. (1987), *Gesture and Posture*. Oxford: Pergamon.

Bull, P. and Frederikson, L. (1995), Non-verbal communication. In Argyle, M. and Colman, A.M. (eds), *Social Psychology*. London: Longman, pp. 78–98.

Burnes, B. (1992), *Managing Change*. London: Pitman Publishing.

Butler, R.J. and Wilson, D.C. (1990) *Managing Voluntary and Nonprofit Organisations: Strategy and Structure*. London: Routledge.

Clarke, J.J. (1997), *Oriental Enlightenment, The Encounter between Asian and Western Thought*. London: Routledge.

Clarke, M. and Stewart, J. (1990), *General Management in Local Government: Getting the Balance Right*. Harlow: Longman.

Coles, M. (1997), Bosses put the boot into trainers. *The Sunday Times*, 9 February, 7.28.

Costanzo, M. and Archer, D. (1989), Interpreting the expressive behaviour of others: The Interpersonal Perception Task (IPT). *Journal of Non-verbal Behaviour*, 13, 225–245.

Czikszentmihalyi, M. (1997), *Finding Flow, the Psychology of Engagement with Everyday Life*. New York: Basic Books.

Deal, T. and Kennedy, A. (1982), *Corporate Cultures, The Rites and Rituals of Corporate Life*. Harmondsworth: Penguin Books.

Dunbar, R.I.M. (1993), Coevolution of neocortical size, group size and language in humans. *Behavioral and Brain Sciences*, 16, 681–735.

Eden, C. and Ackermann, F. (1998) *Making Strategy: The Journey of Strategic Management*. London: Sage.

Eden, C. and Huxham, C. (1996), Action research for the study of organizations. In Clegg, S., Hardy, C. and Nord W. (eds), *Handbook of Organization Studies*. Beverly Hills, Calif.: Sage, pp. 526–542.

Ekman, P. and Friesen, W.V. (1969), Non-verbal leakage and clues to deception. *Psychiatry*, 32(1), 88–106.

Ekman, P. and Friesen, W.V. (1982), Felt, false and miserable smiles. *Journal of Non-verbal Behavior*, 6, 238–252.

Ekman, P., Friesen, W.V. and Ellsworth, P. (1972), *Emotion in the Human Face: Guidelines for Research and an Integration of Findings*. New York: Pergamon.

Fish, S. (1980), *Is There a Text in this Class? The Authority of Interpretive Communities*. Cambridge, Mass., and London: Harvard University Press.

Flynn, N. (1990), *Public Sector Management*. London: Harvester Wheatsheaf.

Foley, R.A. (ed.) (1991), *The Origins of Human Behaviour*. London: Unwin Hyman.

Fox, R. (1989), *The Search for Society, Quest for a Biosocial Science and Morality*. New Brunswick, NJ: Rutgers University Press.

Fromm, E. (1964), Humanism and psychoanalysis. *Contemporary Psychoanalysis*, 1, 69–79.

Fromm, E, (1998), *On Being Human*. New York: Continuum.

Glazer, N. and Moynihan, D.P. (eds) (1975), *Ethnicity, Theory and Experience*. Cambridge, Mass.: Harvard University Press.

Gleick, J. (1987), *Chaos, Making a New Science*. London: William Heinemann.

Goleman, D. (1996), *Emotional Intelligence, Why It Can Matter More Than IQ*. London: Bloomsbury.

Gouldner, A.W. (1957), Cosmopolitans and locals: toward an analysis of latent social roles – 1. *Administrative Science Quarterly*, 2, 281–306.

Gray, J. (1992), *Men Are From Mars, Women Are From Venus*. New York: HarperCollins.

Haas, P.M. (1992), Introduction: epistemic communities and international policy co-ordination. *International Organization*, 46, 1–35.

Hall, J.A. (1984), *Non-verbal Sex Differences: Communication Accuracy and Expressive Style*. Baltimore, Md.: Johns Hopkins University Press.

Hamlin, B. and Reidy, M. (1996), Effecting changes in the management culture of an executive unit of HM Customs & Excise through visionary leadership and strategically led research-based OD interventions. Conference paper, The Strategic

Direction of Human Resource Management, The Context of Practice: The Lives and Thoughts of HRM/HRD People, Nottingham Business School.

Hampden-Turner, C. (1990), *Corporate Culture: From Vicious to Virtuous Circles*. London: Hutchinson.

Handy, C.B. (1985), *Understanding Organizations*. Harmondsworth: Penguin Business.

Handy, C.B. (1988), *Understanding Voluntary Organizations*. Harmondsworth: Penguin Business.

Handy, C.B. (1989), *The Age of Unreason*. London: Random Century.

Harrison, R. (1972), Understanding your organization's character. *Harvard Business Review*, 50(3) 119–128.

Heron, J. (1981), Philosophical basis for a new paradigm. In Reason, P. and Rowan, J. (eds), *Human Inquiry, A Sourcebook of New Paradigm Research*. New York: John Wiley, pp. 19–36.

Higson, C. J. (1986), *Business Finance*. London: Butterworths.

Hollis, M. (1994) *The Philosophy of Social Science: An introduction*. Cambridge: Cambridge University Press.

Hosking, D.-M. and Morley, I.E. (1991), *A Social Psychology of Organizing – People, Processes and Contexts*. London: Harvester Wheatsheaf.

Johnson, G. (1989) 'Rethinking Incrementalism', 35–56 in Asch, D. and Bowman, C. *Readings in Strategic Management*. London: Macmillan Educational.

Krackhardt, D. (1987), Cognitive social structures. *Social Networks*, 9, 109–134.

Kuhn, T. (1970), *The Structure of Scientific Revolutions*, 2nd edn. Chicago: University of Chicago Press.

Levin, K. (1951) *Field Theory in Social Sciences*. New York: Harper & Row.

Lichtheim, G. (1970), *Lucász*. London: Fontana/Collins.

Lorsch, J. (1986), Managing culture: the invisible barrier to change. *California Management Review*, 28(2), 95–109.

McCarthy, K.D., Hodgkinson, V.A., Sumariwalla, R.D. et al. (1992), *The Non-Profit Sector in the Global Community, Voices from Many Nations*. San Francisco: Jossey-Bass.

McGregor, D. (1960), Theory X and theory Y. In Pugh, D.S. (ed.) (1990), Organization Theory, Selected Readings, Harmondsworth: Penguin Business, pp. 358–374.

McKiernan, P. (1997), Strategy past strategy futures. *Long Range Planning*, 30(5), 790–798.

Mithen, S. (1996), *The Prehistory of the Mind, A Search for the Origins of Art, Religion and Science*. London: Orion Books.

Nye, R.D. (1996), *Three Psychologies, Perspectives from Freud, Skinner, and Rogers,* 5th edn. Pacific Grove, Calif.: Brooks/Cole Publishing Company.

Oswick, C. and Grant, D. (1996), *Organization Development, Metaphorical Explorations*. London: Pitman Publishing.

Pheysey, D.C. (1993), *Organizational Cultures, Types and Transformations.* London: Routledge.

Porac, J.P., Thomas, H. and Baden-Fuller, C. (1989), Competitive groups as cognitive communities: the case of Scottish knitwear manufacturers. *Journal of Management Studies*, 26(4), 397–416.

Radford, J. and Govier, E. (1991), *A Textbook of Psychology,* 2nd edn. London: Routledge.

Reason, P. (1981), Issues of validity in new paradigm research. In Reason, P. and Rowan, J. (eds), *Human Inquiry, A Sourcebook of New Paradigm Research*. New York: John Wiley, pp. 239–250.

Reason, P. (1988), *Human Inquiry, Developments in New Paradigm Research*. London: Sage.

Russell, J.A. (1991), Culture and the categorization of emotions. *Psychological Bulletin*, 110, 450–462.

Ryle, G. (1949) *The Concept of Mind*. London: Hutchinson.

Schein, E. (1983), The role of the founder in creating organizational cultures. *Organizational Dynamics*, 12, 3–29.

Skinner, M. and Muller, B. (1991), Facial asymmetry in emotional expression: a meta-analysis of research. *British Journal of Social Psychology*, 30, 113–124.

Taylor, M. and Lansley, J. (1990) 'Ideological Ambiguities of Welfare', 218–233 in Towards the 21st Century: Challenges for the Voluntary Sector, Vol 2, Proceedings of the 1990 Conference of the Association of Voluntary Action Scholars, 16–18 July 1990. London: Centre for Voluntary Organisations.

Thomas, A.B. (1993), *Controversies in Management*. London: Routledge.

Toffler, A. (1970), *Future Shock*. London: Pan Books.

Trice, H. and Beyer, J. (1984), Studying organizational cultures through rites and ceremonials. *Academy of Management Review*, 9(4), 653–669.

Valentine, E.R. (1992) *Conceptual Issues in Psychology*. London: Routledge.

Waley, A. (1963), *Three Ways of Thought in Ancient China*. London: George Allen & Unwin.

Waley, A. (1964), *The Analects of Confucius*. London: George Allen & Unwin.

Ware, J.R. (1960), *The Sayings of Mencius*. New York: Mentor.

Watson, T.J. (1994), *In Search of Management – Culture, Chaos and Control in Managerial Work*. London: Routledge.

Whittington, R. (1993), *What Is Strategy – and Does It Matter?* London: Routledge.

Wiener, M., Devoe, S., Robinson, S. and Geller, J. (1992), Non-verbal behaviour and non-verbal communication. *Psychological Review*, 79, 185–214.

Wilson, D.C. (1992), *A Strategy of Change, Concepts and Controversies in the Management of Change*. London: Routledge.

Wilson, D.C. and Butler, R.J. (1990), *Managing Voluntary and Non-Profit Organizations, Strategy and Structure*. London: Routledge.

Zukav, G. (1984), *The Dancing Wu Li Masters, An Overview of the New Physics*. London: Fontana.

LEARNING ABOUT CHANGE AGENCY FROM THE 'REFLECTIONS ON PRACTICE' OF OTHER PRACTITIONERS

Introduction to the 'Reflections on Practice' case histories

Bob Hamlin

In the preceding chapters of the book our aim has been to bring to your attention practical insights and perspectives on 'what makes for effective and successful organizational change and development'. We have endeavoured to achieve this in four ways: first, through a critical review and synthesis of context and practice in the field of change management as revealed by the management literature; second, through a personal analysis of the increasing complexities of modern-day organizational life, which challenge the role of managers, trainers and developers as change agents; third, through a pathological perspective on UK managers' experiences of organizational change as revealed through the recent 'Quality of Working Life' research studies conducted by UMIST–Institute of Management and finally through the in-depth reflections of two seasoned OCD practitioners who discuss the practical realities of being a change agent based on their own personal experiences.

In the four chapters that follow, our aim is to help you gain additional practical insights from the 'voices' of other successful managers, trainers and developers who have also helped bring about organizational change, at a strategic or operational level, in organizations in the private, public, voluntary and not-for-profit sectors, respectively. We have invited them to share with you the lessons they have learned by reflecting on their own experience of being an internal or external change agent. In particular, we have asked them to focus upon the process issues of organizational change and development and to reveal not only their successes but also their 'failures', including what they have perceived to be the critical factors. In producing their 'reflections on practice' they were encouraged to write approximately 2500 words on a particular OCD programme with which they had been involved, and to use a common three-part structure for their piece of writing. This structure comprises a brief description of the contextual background of the organizational setting and situation needing to be changed, an outline of the key decisions made in formulating the change strategy and what happened in practice, and most importantly the lessons learned. As a guide, they were provided with a set of questions to bear in mind, though they were asked not to follow these 'slavishly'.

Questions concerning the processes of organization change and development (OCD)

(a) *Background to the organization and setting*

What type of organizational context was it? (e.g. sector, nature of the 'business', products, services, markets, clients, etc.)

(b) *The triggers and drivers of the OCD programme*

What factors were applying that caused the need for change or development?

Was the OCD programme initiated by you or was it a 'given' from above?

How did you become involved either as the change agent or as one of several?

What had to be achieved and why?

To what extent was the desired future organizational state in clear focus to you and the organization, or were you 'taking an exploratory journey into unknown territory'?

(c) *Organizational analysis*

At the outset, how did you go about 'making sense' of the organization through a process of organizational analysis?

What theoretical perspectives, models or conceptual frameworks did you consciously and deliberately intend to use (if any) to help you diagnose the prevailing state of the organization and to describe the desired future state?

What 'complexities' and 'uncertainties' did you perceive to be applying at the time, and how important were these in informing and shaping your thinking about the planned change and/or development processes?

What particular questions about 'process issues' did you pose and answer prior to formulating the OCD strategy?

(d) *The OCD strategy adopted*

What OCD strategies and methods did you adopt in practice? Why these and not others?

What aspects of your organizational and/or cultural diagnosis acted as determinants of the chosen change methods and processes, and why was this?

Did the implementation of the OCD programme go according to plan? What actually happened in practice? Were the OCD initiatives successful and in what way?

What additions or changes in strategy or method did you have to adopt during implementation (if any) and why?

(e) *Evaluation of the OCD programme*

What were the 'critical success factors' applying, whether already existing in the organizational context/setting or deliberately embedded in the OCD processes?

What factors impeded or frustrated the achievement of the objectives of the OCD programme?

Overall, how effective were the originally conceived and, if applicable, the subsequent emergent OCD strategies?

Did 'theory' work out in 'practice', and if not why not?

(f) *Valuable lessons learned for self and other change agents*

In hindsight, what did you do that was most successful?

What should you have done differently to achieve an even more successful outcome?

Which of your original questions concerning the processes of bringing about organizational change and development remain unanswered?

Reflecting upon your own practice, what additional questions should you have asked at the outset of this OCD programme and throughout its implementation?

As a result of your reflective practice as described, what new illuminating insights have you gained about managing OCD and about the role of the change agent?

What particular advice would you give to other change agents operating in other organizations as a result of your own evidence-based practice?

How does your experience as a reflective practitioner challenge 'theory' and the 'received wisdom' on organization change management?

From this set of questions, you will appreciate we were particularly interested that the individuals concerned should reflect deeply upon their personal experiences as change agents; this we considered very important. We wanted them to reveal the way in which they had approached the management of change, and how their change agency practice had been informed and shaped by theory.

Additionally, we were concerned that they should stick to their own natural and preferred styles of writing. The reason for this was that we wanted you, the readers, to recognize immediately these 'reflections' as being real-life personal stories told by practitioners for the benefit of other practitioners. We considered it desirable that, in the main, these stories should be written as first-hand accounts expressed in the actual words of the practitioners themselves, not as second- or third-hand interpretations written for them by other people.

In total, 18 reflections-on-practice case histories are presented in this part of the book. Each of the four chapters focuses upon a particular theme of organizational change and development which appears to be common to all of the 'reflections' comprising that chapter. The four themes have been labelled as 'Reflections on Transformational and Cultural Change'; 'Reflections on Quality Initiatives'; 'Reflections on OD Processes'; and 'Reflections on Training and Development Interventions'. The organizations that provide the settings for these 'reflections' range from large-scale, household-name, national and multinational companies through to small-scale, regionally based organizations which, in some cases, are well known only within their own locality. Most are UK based, but two are drawn from Ireland and the Netherlands. All in their own way give readers a distinctive insight into different facets of change agency in practice, including what has and has not worked. Because of the sensitivities in some of the situations, several of the contributors have necessarily masked the identity of the organizations in which they were operating. A wide spectrum of private sector businesses from industry and commerce are featured. These include companies from the mechanical and electrical engineering industries; from the aerospace, metals and plastics, textile, pharmaceuticals and power-generation industries; and from the banking, financial services and training services sectors. The range of public sector organizations spans central and local government, the National Health Service and the care service sector. A not-for-profit co-operative development agency is also included.

In presenting these reflections-on-practice case histories we have endeavoured to present a rich and diverse range of examples of change agency in practice. We hope they will help to provoke thought, provide useful insights and invoke further personal reflection upon your own practice as a change agent.

Transformational and cultural change

Bob Hamlin (editor)

INTRODUCTION

This chapter focuses on transformational and cultural change in five organizations drawn from both the private and public sectors. Until recently, two of these were part of nationalized industries which have been privatized.

The first reflection on practice relates to the merger in 1996 of two of Britain's largest banks, namely Lloyds and TSB, to create Lloyds TSB, which by 1997 had become one of the largest banks in the world and the third most successful company in the UK. It is written by Paul Turner, HR business director of Lloyds TSB, who at the time was one of the key players involved in successfully bringing about this major programme of organizational change. In writing about the change management process, Paul focuses particularly upon the key role played by the HR function and draws attention to four key learning points regarding the effective management of strategic change.

The second reflection on practice relates to First Engineering, which was formerly BRIS, the branch of British Rail responsible for maintaining the railway infrastructure in Scotland. This new company was set up in 1996 as a management/employee buy-out following the break-up and privatization of the nationalized railway industry in Britain by the then government. The case has been written not by any of the participants in the change process but by Alison Thomas, a professional journalist writing on behalf of the Coverdale Organisation, which had been engaged by the company to help with its transition from 'the security of the public sector to the cut and thrust of the highly competitive and dynamic private sector market place'. The major challenge facing the company was how to achieve the goal of creating a new culture of co-operation and collaboration with a workforce still deeply ingrained with the traditions of a 'railway culture' – a culture characterized by 'a paternalistic environment where sons and daughters followed fathers and mothers into jobs offering security for life, where relationships with management were strained, where strict lines of demarcation were observed, and where a command and control type of structure existed which left little scope for employee initiative'.

The three key players managing this major organizational and cultural change programme, which included an initiative called 'New Horizons', were Primrose McLaughlin, the HR director of First Engineering, Lesley Imrie, who had been appointed as the New Horizons project manager, and Mike De Luca of the Coverdale Organisation, who was acting as the external change management consultant. In this piece of reflective writing, Alison Thomas describes the change management approach adopted by the project team: what worked well; what not so well; and what was still needing to be done at the time of writing. She also highlights for readers the lessons to be learned from the reflections the three key players have made on their own change agency practice.

The third reflection on practice describes the change management approach adopted by Dick Shepherd in bringing about major organizational and cultural change in the Anglia Executive Unit of HM Customs and Excise during his seven years as its executive head from 1991 to 1998. It focuses particularly upon the thinking behind the change strategies he adopted and draws attention to the major internal research programmes he commissioned, which he found 'to be of enormous value in helping to inform, shape and measure the cultural changes'. Margaret Reidy, who was his research officer, has written the case. Based mainly upon the personal reflections of Dick Shepherd, a number of important insights about the effective management of cultural change and the particular value of internal research are presented for readers to consider.

The fourth reflective case history is concerned with transformational change in one part of the electric power generation industry in the Netherlands, following deregulation by the Dutch government in 1995. It tells the story of Professor Jaap Germans, who from 1996 to 1999 was working on a part-time basis as an external OCD consultant with the senior management team (SMT) of the Central Maintenance Department of Electricteitsbedrijf Zuid Holland (EZH), which is one of four regional companies making up the industry. The major challenge facing Jaap and his SMT colleagues was how to quickly effect radical changes in the bureaucratic mindset and working habits of the department. The requirement was that it turn itself into a commercially oriented business unit, serving the needs of external customers as well as its existing 'internal customers' but now in open competition with outside contractors. Jaap reflects candidly not only upon the successful parts of the change strategy but also upon the less successful aspects, which in the early stages resulted in resistance and non-acceptance by the workforce. From these reflections he draws attention to a number of valuable insights regarding change management in general, and also to the importance to trainers, developers and other OD consultants of having at their fingertips a range of 'theoretical and conceptual frameworks' for helping line managers to talk about and critically reflect upon their own change agency practice.

Resistance to organizational change is at the centre of the fifth and last reflection on practice comprising this chapter. The case history concerns a campaign to change the work practices and shift system of workers in the manufacturing plant of a multinational pharmaceutical company situated in Ireland. In the context of

Irish industrial relations, which are normally conducted in an adversarial mode, Peter Shields, the HR director of the company, found himself confronted with the situation of 'a total impasse where change, which [to him] was clearly necessary for [company] survival, was not open for discussion'. The challenge was finding non-adversarial approaches that would lead to a pathway through the impasse. Peter describes in some detail a range of theoretical perspectives that helped illuminate his journey, and in particular the 'real-time change event' method and guidelines he finally adopted and followed, which led to a highly successful outcome for both the company and the workforce. In recommending to other practitioners the approaches he adopted in this instance, he also highlights a number of important insights from his own change agency practice regarding the effective management of change.

REFLECTIONS ON PRACTICE

HR's role in managing change – the case of Lloyds TSB

Paul Turner

The headline said it all. 'TSB says yes to Lloyds after five-year courtship' (*The Times*, 10 October 1995). Two of Britain's largest banks had merged to form a 'banking and insurance giant with assets of £140 billion, 90,000 staff ... pre-tax profits of £2 billion, 3000 branches, 15 million customers and coverage across Britain' (*ibid.*). For Lloyds Bank this was part of an ongoing strategy of growth through acquisition and merger. Cheltenham and Gloucester Building Society was already in the portfolio of companies owned by the bank. TSB had also recognized the potential that could be offered by merger in terms of economies of scale and scope. Lloyds and TSB were ideal partners and, from the end of 1995, set a new strategic agenda for banking and insurance in the UK.

For a start, the merger of Lloyds and TSB created income opportunities from product market strategies that would be enhanced by the sheer scale of the new entity. This was in large part due to the customer profiles of the two banks, which were very complementary. TSB had a different age profile for its customers from Lloyds; Lloyds had a different socio-economic profile (60 per cent in groups A, B, CI). TSB was strong in the north, with 67 per cent of its customers in central England, Yorkshire, Tyne–Tees, the Grampians and Scottish areas; Lloyds had twice as many customers as its new partner in London. The marketing scope was therefore impressive. This was also true of the distribution potential of the merged banks. Lloyds' 2460 ATMs and TSB's 1901 machines together created one of the largest distribution networks in Britain. Together, the banks had nearly 3000 branches and over 10 million card-holders. The strength of Lloyds in the business customer market (375,000 small business customers) completed a marketing profile full of potential.

In addition to marketing opportunities there was scope for cost saving. The *Daily Mail* (12 October 1995) suggested that this factor more than any other would lead to the success of the merger. The paper noted that savings 'could reach £350 million per year by 1999, according to the two banks ... amounting to 10 per cent of current costs. Analysts regarded this as a display of caution. They thought £400m to £450m could well be achieved'. The case for merger in terms of service efficiency and cost savings was a powerful one. The *Full Listing Particulars* (1995) issued by the two banks outlined potential savings as:

■ combining administrative and centralized operations such as head and divisional offices, back office processing and money transmission;

■ rationalizing technology systems;

- merging wholesale banking, including treasury, and certain other units to create more effective businesses; and

- using Cheltenham and Gloucester to manage the mortgage business of the enlarged group.

The scope for marketing enhancement and cost savings were the two key opportunities for the improvement of business performance inherent in the merger and the move was widely acclaimed. In a comprehensive summary of the transformation that was sweeping the financial services sector – of which the Lloyds TSB merger was a prime example – Hamish McRae of *The Independent* (12 October 1995) noted that this was 'proof of the big bank theory'. McRae speculated that the change in the financial services sector was analogous to that which had already happened in manufacturing and retailing. He argued that British financial institutions were potentially threatened by international competition and challenged by consumers who wanted more efficient service and reasonable prices. He welcomed the merger and described it as follows:

> So what we are seeing is the same sort of process that has happened in manufacturing ... the same pressure to drive down costs: and from the customer's point of view, the same homogeneity of service. We clearly want it. We choose the banks (or building societies) that offer the best-perceived service for the lowest price: the cheapest loans, the highest deposit rates. We may regret the loss of the independence of the TSB, just as we bemoan the closure of the corner store or the demise of names such as Austin or Riley. But that is where our actions lead. (*ibid.*)

There was a good deal of support for the merger from the City and within a few days the *Financial Times* could report that 'Lloyds TSB merger terms win enthusiastic reception' (12 October 1995). The external market view of the merger was very favourable and as a result shareholders gained immediate and medium-term benefits from the deal. The TSB share price rose by 79p to 353p on the announcement of the merger – some 29 per cent. Lloyds' share price also rose substantially. Within two years, the share price of the merged companies reached over £10, falling back only when world economic prospects pulled down market prices generally.

This then was the background that preceded several critical tasks associated with implementing the merger. The first of these was to establish a series of strategic objectives that would provide a direction for implementation activity. In February 1996, the retail financial arm of the new venture was ready to launch its aims and objectives. Under the banner of 'A New Beginning' (Lloyds TSB Group 1996: 2) the bank announced that it was looking to build a significant distance between itself and its competitors by

- being a recognized market leader in its own chosen businesses by consistently exceeding customer expectations through superior service and distribution, and by setting new standards of excellence for this industry worldwide;

- utilizing its combined scale to reduce operating costs and so become the lowest-cost producer and distributor measured against any major competitors;

- retaining and developing superior staff with clear accountability for building business.

A prime objective during the early stages of the merger was to ensure that some key principles were communicated which would guide the merger process. The document 'A New Beginning' outlined these (*ibid.*: 5). A summary of the main points is:

■ the overall guiding objective was to create the best possible company;

■ the integration process would be completed as quickly and effectively as possible;

■ staff would be chosen for new positions based on their demonstrable skills, performance record and ability to do the job;

■ business synergies would be aggressively pursued in order to create maximum value for shareholders;

■ there would be a conscious focus on the day-to-day business and its strategic direction during the integration process;

■ targeted cost reductions would be achieved;

■ communications would be frequent, open and honest.

At a very early stage, therefore, top management had laid down some high-level objectives and principles against which the merger could be implemented. These were seen as critical to establishing frameworks within which business units and functions could operate effectively.

The management of the merger process was dealt with at three levels. First, an integration committee was established early on, which would complement the leadership of the executive board. Second, a co-ordination team was put in place that was responsible for planning and tracking the process of implementation. Third, a series of task forces were then set up to deal with the implementation of the merger at functional or business unit level. In approaching the merger in this way, the teams at Lloyds TSB recognized some fundamentals in respect of keeping the day-to-day business running while tackling the strategic demands of the merger. A structured approach was adopted which allowed task achievement to be put in a wider perspective. Communications with all stakeholders was identified as a priority. Finally, the need to ensure fairness in the way staff were dealt with received the attention of all levels from the chairman and chief executive downwards.

Thus by 1996 Lloyds and TSB had merged to become one of the largest financial services organizations in the UK. By 1997, the success of the merger as perceived by shareholders and translated into economic value added had made Lloyds TSB one of the largest banks in the world and the third most successful company in the UK in terms of added economic value. The concept of the mega-merger in banking had been converted into a reality. The immediate success of the merger in the value added to the company and the mid-term successes in terms of cost management had demonstrated scale could be a powerful weapon in the increasingly competitive market of financial services. Within a short time, other financial services organizations in the UK would also follow the Lloyds TSB merger route, and more mergers followed in the USA.

The merger of Lloyds TSB is an example of the effective management of change on a large scale. This change involved setting strategy, 'the direction an organization is headed,' and organization, 'the state it is in' (Mintzburg *et al*. 1998). Both areas were actively managed in the merger process. In tackling such a complex project as the merger of two large organizations into a multi-billion pound leader in many of its chosen markets, a good deal of attention had been paid to four critical elements as outlined in Leavitt's classical model for understanding change (Huczynski and Buchanan 1991: 529). The HR function was instrumental in the success of this change, and the following section looks at some of the actions taken in respect of these four interacting variables, namely:

- people
- tasks
- structure
- technology.

The first of the interacting variables – people – was seen as an absolute priority and the HR function was, naturally, involved from the beginning of the processes associated with it. Two specific aspects were of critical importance in the management of the people element of the merger. These were employee communications and the appointment process.

Communications received a good deal of attention. Under the banner of 'Fit for the Future', a series of briefing documents were issued at regular stages during the merger. The documents were an important part of the commitment to keep everyone informed about the merger as it progressed. It fell to the HR teams to monitor feedback against these outputs and the results were used to modify subsequent communications and determine further actions. This particular aspect of the merger supported the view that this type of attitude survey did have a positive role to play in the process of organizational learning and change (Williams 1998). Inevitably, the feedback contained a broad spectrum of opinion. One particular demand from employees was for a 'road map' of the likely dates of the appointment process and other key events. As a result, a series of time frames were made public and every effort was made to adhere to these.

The appointment process was of utmost interest to all staff. The principles of the process by which appointments would be made were published and included the following guidelines:

- Suitable candidates would be identified and considered on the basis of ability and track record.
- Consistency would be applied to the appointment process, and generic competencies were used in all of the interviews.
- The achievement of equality of opportunity would be a critical objective.
- Interviews would be carried out for all vacancies.
- A 'grandparenting' process would ensure that all appointments would be confirmed by the level above the appointing manager.

This process was undertaken at most levels of the organization, including the appointment of directors.

There were other critical elements in dealing with the people 'variable' as a result of the merger. The human resources activity associated with these was extensive.

- The choice of a single head office from the two in existence required a significant management of the relocation, appointment and departure of staff.
- There were potential difficulties resulting from the anomalies in pay and reward between the two banks. There was a strategic objective to have one workforce and to achieve this presented a significant employee and industrial relations challenge. A way of achieving this objective was to have a harmonized set of terms and conditions. This was implemented within the first year of the merger, for most of the employees, with the resulting clarity of understanding.

At about the same time a new employee relations framework was put in place. To achieve this required extensive and detailed negotiations with two trade unions, each representing large sections of the banks' staffs. An added dimension to this was the need to get agreement to ensure a smooth passage of an Act of Parliament to allow the full merger of the banks. Trade union support for this in Parliament would be critical to success. Eventually, agreement was reached in terms of representation and the Bill was enacted in the summer of 1998.

These, then, were some of the more tangible outcomes of the people activity associated with the merger. However, a significant further challenge was that of trying to create a new culture out of the strengths of both banks. The success of culture change in other companies and industries had proved to be very complex (Harris and Ogbonna 1998). In Lloyds TSB, the different customer bases, technologies and branch networks clearly presented a complex set of cultural variables, so an incremental approach was adopted dealing with operational areas first, such as technology and processing centres. The success of this was very much in line with research findings, which noted that 'a structured and long-term programme of incremental change may prove more efficient in guiding the culture of an organization in a broad direction' (*ibid.*: 90).

The second of the interacting variables was that associated with the 'task' of the organization. This has been defined as 'the reason for the organization's existence' (Huczynski and Buchanan 1991) and was also an area on which considerable focus was placed. The objectives of the organization that were highlighted in an earlier part of this reflection on practice (be a market leader, reduce costs, develop superior staff) were the first indications of the 'task' of the newly merged organization. These were followed up by work in each of the business units and functions to define target markets, cost levels and competitive positions. The overall organization structures were adapted as the strategies were crafted in the light of experience. A particular feature of the definition of the task of the organization was the need to have an inclusive approach. Thus all stakeholders were included in the communication process: customers (through a series of TV advertisements about the fact that the two banks were now 'working together' – the theme of the advertising);

employees, who were informed at each stage of the merger about objectives; and shareholders, who were given a clear understanding of what they may expect for their investment.

Once again the HR function had a role to play in establishing the 'task' variable. In particular, organizational design and development were critical elements of the people factor. Similarly, the training associated with 'working together' at branch level was supported by the HR function. In both regards an inclusive partnership approach was adopted.

The third variable – the structure of the organization – included both the actual organizational structures as embodied in the organograms and the patterns of authority, communications, etc. HR's role in this was supportive: at the highest level working with directors to establish principles of organization design, and then adapting the business operating models to ensure clarity of the people role.

HR's role was less clear in establishing the technology of the organization – the fourth variable and described as 'the tools and techniques that the organization uses in pursuit of its goals' (*ibid.*). The HR function was involved in a facilitative capacity as the debate about which systems and technologies the newly merged banks would adopt. HR was a partner in facilitating the debate that took place.

The role of the HR function in each of these areas was threefold: first, to act as a partner to the business unit or functional director in advising on the human aspects of change; second, to ensure excellence in the administration of personnel and training systems in support of the changes which were taking place; and third, to act as a facilitator of change where issues arose of a cultural or strategic HR nature. The role of HR during the merger of Lloyds and TSB was entirely consistent with the conclusions of Ulrich *et al.* (1998).

These reflections on the merger of Lloyds and TSB provide four key learning points in respect of the role of HR in bringing about strategic organizational change effectively. These are consistent with Cummings and Huse's (1989) findings on the successful approach to change management, as follows:

1 HR had a role to play at the very highest level of the organization and as soon as possible in the process of change. This role embraced both technical expertise (understanding the effect on human resources of the change process) and facilitation in the form of being business partners to line managers. Early involvement of the HR function contributed to successful change management.

2 HR provided an understanding of some of the critical success factors for change. Supporting the top team in developing a clear strategic vision and changing the support systems for the organization (organizational structures, HR systems and information management) were three areas in particular where HR had a significant input. Role clarity was also a contributor to success. HR was able to advise and monitor these areas.

3 It was important to understand employee attitudes towards the challenging objectives set by the merger process and their implementation. HR's role at this time was to act as a barometer of motivation. Responsibility for the staff surveys

at regular periods in the merger resided within the HR function, and the interpretation of responses proved to be of significant added value to the management of the change process.

4 HR had an important role in delivering administrative excellence to ensure the smooth implementation of high-level policy. This can be an underestimated role associated with change. Many of the thousands of transactions of change associated with the merger of Lloyds TSB were administered by the HR function. These included appointment letters, communications, advice on pay, benefits, share-save schemes, profit-related pay, healthcare and so on. Added together, these placed a significant burden of work on the HR function, and dealing with the administration of them efficiently proved to be another success factor. An innovative 'personnel call centre' was set up to ensure a consistent set of replies to telephone queries, and this dealt with up to 1000 calls per day at peak times.

In conclusion, the successful merger of Lloyds and TSB had many contributory factors, and HR played a key part in many of these. Dealing with people issues was obviously one of the roles, but other aspects of communication, organizational design, systems and processes also included significant HR elements. It might be concluded that an early incorporation of HR expertise and partnership in the change process was fundamental to the effective management of change.

References

Cummings, T.G. and Huse, E.F. (1989), *Organisation Development and Change*. St Paul, Minnesota: West.

Full Listing Particulars (1995), Recommended merger of Lloyds Bank Plc and TSB Group Plc.

Harris, L.C. and Ogbonna, E. (1998), Employee responses to culture change efforts. *Human Resource Management Journal*, 8(2).

Huczynski, A. and Buchanan, D. (1991), *Organisational Behaviour*. London: Prentice Hall, p. 529.

Lloyds TSB Group (1996), *Retail Financial Services – A New Beginning*, February.

Mintzberg, H., Ahlstrand, B. and Lampel, J. (1998), *Strategy Safari*. London: Prentice Hall, p. 326.

Ulrich, D. (1998), A new mandate for human resources. *Harvard Business Review*, January–February, 124.

Williams, A. (1998), Organisational learning and the role of attitude surveys. *Human Resource Management Journal*, 80(4), 63.

Transformational change – the case of First Engineering

Alison Thomas

When a nationalized organization leaves the security of the public sector for the cut and thrust of the marketplace, some fundamental issues have to be addressed.

CONTEXT

'The railway culture was in their bones.' This is how management consultant Mike De Luca of the Coverdale Organisation summed up the essence of the problem facing First Engineering when it took its first teetering steps into the private domain. Formerly BRIS, the branch of British Rail responsible for maintaining the railway infrastructure in Scotland, the company was born in February 1996 of a management/employee buy-out with backing from 3i, the Bank of Scotland and the Weir Group.

It was a paternalistic environment where sons followed fathers into a job offering security for life. Relationships between management and the workforce were strained; strict lines of demarcation and a command-and-control type of structure left little scope for employee initiative.

Shifting this deeply ingrained mindset has been a cornerstone of New Horizons, a programme for sustainable change developed in partnership with the Coverdale Organisation. From senior managers to the staff who walk the track, everyone is being encouraged to challenge the traditional way of doing things and ask the question 'why?'

Another key focus has been the development of the skills required to survive in a dynamic marketplace. An organization that had never had to tender for a contract, never considered profitability or customer care, now faced competition from companies much larger than itself with a wealth of commercial experience behind them. 'Our knowledge of the railway and our technical expertise gave us an advantage,' says human resources director Primrose McLaughlin. 'But we knew that in order to harness our potential we had to redefine our direction, get a more contract–delivery focus and encourage teamwork. One of the first things we did was to reorganize the structure of the company. But as the months went by we realized that giving people new job titles wasn't enough. That's why we turned to Coverdale. Unless you manage to carry everyone along with you and radically alter the way things are done – which is how we define culture – you won't get very far.'

As New Horizons' champion on the board of directors, McLaughlin has been instrumental in moving the process forward. The other key player has been Lesley Imrie, New Horizons' project manager and the person who launched the idea. 'Her role has been crucial,' says De Luca. 'It's really important to have someone with her enthusiasm, commitment and ability. Lesley sold it, pushed it, and was eventually given the job of managing it.'

DECISIONS MADE

Before a strategy could be formulated, a clear picture was needed of where the company stood at present (state A) and where it wanted to go (state B). De Luca started by interviewing each director in turn to get individual rather than collective perceptions. This was followed by meetings with a range of managers chosen by Imrie to represent all facets of the business, in terms of not only function but also length of service, an important consideration when evaluating attitudes towards change. The views of the workforce were sought by means of a questionnaire covering every aspect of their working environment. To complete the picture, marketing manager Sandra Ross conducted a gap analysis with clients, which examined the company's effectiveness from both a business and cultural perspective. 'It was a comprehensive procedure,' says Imrie. 'It gave us as clear a profile as you could probably hope to get.'

The decision to include the customer in the consultation process was significant. First Engineering found itself in the unusual position of having one major client, Railtrack, whose experience of operating in a commercial environment was as limited as its own. 'That influenced our thinking,' explains De Luca. 'A key had to be behaviour at the customer interface. How do you interact with a client who may not be ready?' This conundrum was reflected in the feedback, which included comments that were readily accepted as valid and others that were not. All had to be addressed. 'It's a matter of perception,' says Ross. 'Even when we feel the client's comments are ill-founded, we have to close the gap. Maybe they don't understand what we're trying to do. If we don't tell them, they will never know.'

The first move towards determining strategy involved 60 senior managers, who attended two workshops to thrash out the issues. What was the company trying to achieve? How could it become more customer-focused? What would be the most effective way of changing work habits and equipping the business to win through against fierce competition?

Imrie believes that the participation of senior managers at this early stage was a shrewd move. 'One of the outcomes was a request to the directors for a strategy document. This was an important development because it gave a clear focus to what we were trying to achieve. It defined our values, our markets, and our relationship with the client. The fact that it was requested rather than imposed by the board made it all the more powerful.'

De Luca's involvement of senior managers was very deliberate. 'In any change programme, mid-senior managers perceive they have the most to lose and offer the most resistance. They can also seriously impede progress later on. With hindsight I could have done even more work at this level.'

The same principle of fostering widespread commitment lay behind the composition of the steering group, established at the very outset to manage the change process and measure outcomes. Its members represented a cross-section of the business, including two representatives from the unions, which has gone a long way towards softening traditional adversarial relationships. 'The fact that it includes a range of people gives it tremendous credibility,' says Imrie. 'They are really fired up. Whenever we ask if anyone would like to stand down, the answer is always "no!"'

For De Luca, it was also a way of establishing the principle of ownership. For although his role as facilitator was pivotal, he was careful to avoid providing all the answers, much to people's frustration at times. 'It's very important that the company manages the programme itself, addresses the issues, finds solutions. Otherwise when the first problem arises, the immediate response will be "We knew it wouldn't work!" And no matter how much information you give, people only truly begin to understand and develop skills as they go along. A change programme is a learning experience.'

Although commitment from the top coupled with whole-company involvement underpins the New Horizons project, this basic principle was not taken for granted and was the subject of some debate. This was because the company was about to divisionalize its structure, which raised the question of how appropriate it might be to concentrate all efforts on one section at a time. It was agreed, however, that an integrated, holistic approach would be much more effective and add momentum to the change process.

The vehicle chosen was a series of three-day workshops, followed six weeks later by a review day. Already 600 employees have taken part and eventually everyone will attend. Composed of 24 people from different parts of the company, they are designed to provide an opportunity for reflection away from the pressures of the workplace. Participants are expected to analyse work practices and come up with practical ideas for improving efficiency. Known as 'back at work tasks', these can cover anything from equipment design to the storing of data. A sponsor is assigned to each person, and putting the ideas into practice involves collaboration across hierarchical and divisional boundaries. In a further attempt to break down barriers, each workshop is opened and closed by a senior member of staff. Successes are published in the company's bulletin to maintain a high profile.

REFLECTION

If the goal of New Horizons is to create a new culture of co-operation and collaboration in First Engineering, the same principle extends to the client. 'The primary focus must be in customer intimacy' is one of the company's core values, leaving no doubt where priorities lie. The gap analysis will be revisited this year, but in the meantime the relationship with the client has come a long way. A policy board has been set up with representatives from both organizations, Railtrack managers are attending First Engineering workshops, and ways are being sought to work together and develop joint solutions. Strategy and alliance manager Steve Bell explains:

> The approach we have been trying to encourage between ourselves and Railtrack over the last couple of years is one of alliance. The spirit, structure and some of the key objectives have already been agreed, and plans include co-location teams, joint investments and dual initiatives. We are now formalizing the details to clarify how it will operate, how we will measure it and what the decision-making mechanism will be.

The benefits are already apparent – in the renewal of contracts, the extension of markets, and the interest shown in First Engineering by new clients. It is also reflected in turnover, which has risen from around £95 million to £120 million.

As the driver behind the New Horizons programme was the need to empower the company to succeed in a competitive marketplace, this bodes well for the future. There is a danger, however, that the importance of profitability takes precedence over that of behavioural change. 'The cultural element has to be an integral part of everything we do, otherwise it's just seen as a human resources issue, which it isn't,' says McLaughlin. 'One of the hardest things has been to persuade people to tie it into their business plans. We now sit down every month with divisional heads to review their business, including the progress of the change programme. We would have benefited from starting this earlier, but you learn as you go along.'

The sheer practicalities of running a business can also interfere with the change programme, creating a tension between the company's vision for the future and its operational needs today.

When New Horizons was launched, six critical success factors were identified as being crucial to the evolution of a new ethos: commitment from the top; milestones and measures; whole-company input and contribution; communication; the development of skills; and in-house resources. This last involves training coaches and facilitators to ensure that the company is capable of continuing the process and confronting whatever the future holds when Coverdale withdraws in 2001.

Sustainability is also behind the emphasis on skill development. How far the programme has inspired the confidence of the workforce will become clear when the second employee survey is conducted later this year. Some indication is already emerging, however, in the success of the workshops, which are proving effective in streamlining work practices, encouraging accountability and fostering co-operation. 'When someone listens to you it has a tremendous effect on motivation and commitment,' says Imrie. 'It might well be something you had been thinking of for ages and been too embarrassed to pass on.'

This is not to imply that everything has always gone to plan, and various areas of concern have surfaced along the way. One is the need for greater consistency in the quality of support offered by sponsors for the implementation of back at work tasks, something which is now being tackled at senior level through the business review process. Another is the need to track the benefits through, for although potential savings have been estimated at £3.5 million, this has yet to be translated into tangible, proven figures.

Measurement is lagging behind in other areas too, and Imrie has identified several key issues which need to be addressed, such as improving databases to make monitoring more manageable. This is part of a continuous process of review. The three principal change agents constantly confer and feed their findings through to the steering group. 'It's not a straight line,' says De Luca. 'You are forever re-assessing the situation and introducing changes.'

The most recent example arose from a discussion between De Luca and McLaughlin, when they decided on two courses of action in response to current need. The first is a strategy workshop to help managers and directors resolve the conflict that can arise between the business aims of each division and the well-being of the organization as a whole. 'First comes First' is a company motto, meaning that First Engineering must come before all else if it is to achieve its purpose – as defined in the strategy document – of 'providing integrated service solutions'.

The second is a full-scale New Horizons review involving 16 people, including managers, steering group members, employees who have attended workshops and union representatives. The aim is to get direct feedback from right across the organization and reaffirm commitment.

If constant reinforcement is essential to maintain momentum, it is equally important that everyone contributes. This is the thinking behind the steering group, the workshops and the reorganization of management conferences, which are now much more interactive than they used to be. The effects can already be felt. The word 'purpose' has entered everyday vocabulary, barriers are coming down, and the old adversarial approach is dying out. There is concern, however, that at managerial level some individuals have yet to come to terms with the new ways.

De Luca believes that an element of resistance is inevitable in any organization. 'You've got to recognize this at the very outset and decide how you are going to deal with it,' he says. 'That might mean using persuasion, increasing personal development, moving people sideways or even moving them out – there is no one correct answer but you have to decide.' Imrie agrees that the issue needs to be tackled, although she differs slightly in her emphasis. 'A change agent needs tolerance and patience,' she maintains. 'Sometimes the people who take longer to make the transition become the most committed in the end.'

The importance of technical expertise also plays its part in a company noted for the high calibre of its engineering staff. 'When someone with valuable skills can easily find employment elsewhere, it explains why overt pressure to embrace change is not always applied as rigorously as it might be,' says Ross. She also believes that it is all too easy to underestimate the impact the programme has already had, citing as an example an employee who was once disillusioned, demotivated and lethargic. He is now an active participant in the change process and is rapidly becoming a key player.

Hurdles, obstacles, setbacks – no matter how well you plan, they are bound to arise, and the ultimate purpose of a change programme is to empower people to face up to the challenge. 'In times of trouble you can turn and run, or you can work things through together,' says De Luca. 'There are no pat answers.' You must also prepare for a lengthy crusade. When your strategy is to involve as many people as possible, it takes time. The process of learning from experience takes more time. A successful change programme is a long-term project.

Managing organizational and cultural change in the Anglia executive unit of HM Customs & Excise

Margaret Reidy

The organizational setting of this case history is the Anglia executive unit (EU) of HM Customs & Excise, which is a major department of the British civil service. Anglia EU is one of 14 regional EUs comprising the Department of HM Customs & Excise in the UK. The main responsibility or 'business' of the department is to collect and manage VAT, excise duties and insurance premium tax; fight drug trafficking and enforce other import and export prohibitions and restrictions; apply sanctions in support of international peace-keeping; collect customs duties and agricultural levies on behalf of the European Union; and compile trade statistics for and give policy advice to ministers of state in support of these activities. The particular focus of the case history is the change agency practice and approach of Dick Shepherd in bringing about effectively and beneficially strategic organizational and cultural change in 'Anglia' during his time as the executive head from 1991 to 1998.

DICK SHEPHERD'S CHANGE AGENCY IN PRACTICE

When in 1991 Dick Shepherd took up his responsibilities of the then East Anglia Collection, which was subsequently enlarged to become the Anglia executive unit following a global restructuring of HM Customs & Excise, the biggest and most obvious external drivers of change impacting upon his organization were, for example, the introduction of the single market by the European Commission, which held enormous consequences for the department, especially for Customs staff; the UK central government and Treasury 'Next Steps' Initiative which[1] led to the introduction of executive units (EUs) in HM Customs & Excise and the Inland Revenue, and the requirement to operate on 'Next Steps' lines even though they were not autonomous executive agencies; and various HM Customs & Excise HQ-initiated organizational change programmes resulting in major downsizing, delayering and TQM exercises designed to increase efficiency and effectiveness, increase 'value for money', and improve quality of work, outputs and relations with customers while meeting targets and objectives. At the outset, Dick Shepherd recognized a consistent and common thread running throughout all of the change initiatives, namely the need to manage effectively the people issues and the need to bring about change in the organizational culture and management culture.

Although at the time of his appointment he found the Anglia Collection delivering very successfully to the then HM Custom & Excise Board's plan, the organization was being run on very traditional civil service lines. However, with a future that indicated the need for a heavier dependence on people, he believed a lot of internal changes had to be made in order to get to that future state. He was not just thinking about the major externally driven changes being signalled by the board of HM Customs & Excise or the politicians. He felt that the department was somewhat out of kilter with the society in which it existed. This was becoming increasingly noticeable through, for example, the younger people joining HM Custom & Excise, who were coming from very different backgrounds in terms of education and social development, and who brought with them higher expectations in terms of job satisfaction and self-development. On joining the department, these recruits were often coming into contact with civil servants rooted in a generation heavily influenced by military and naval backgrounds stretching back to the post-war years. In addition, some people were joining who were looking for what they perceived to be secure, traditional civil service employment in the department. These members tended to work with diligence but were not always at ease with the more flexible approaches that were now being called for.

Changes were therefore needed to bring about a more flexible organization with a more open management style. Besides achieving a delayered and downsized organization, the department was also looking for sharper accountability and increased professionalism from its people, as reflected in its HM Customs and Excise People Initiative document.[2] Most people in HM Customs & Excise were equipped with good technical knowledge and skills, but these were not always apparent in terms of their overall professionalism. Dick Shepherd felt that staff would need to be trusted and empowered more to support the department's drive for increased professionalism as well as to achieve his aim of increasing people's flexibility in their approach to their work. He believed one of the keys to achieving this shift in culture was to instil courage in his managers by telling them 'it is all right to make mistakes' as they moved from a tall hierarchical bureaucracy to a delayered and more accountable one. He recognized the fact that mistakes in the midst of change are sometimes unavoidable. He also acknowledged that mistakes can actually present learning opportunities to help continuous development and improvement. People responded to this by initiating their own projects and localized change initiatives, which supported the overall change programme within the EU.

He made progress on these through, for example, the implementation of the following carefully considered initiatives:

- He extended the corporate management group (CMG) to include all eleven business heads. Traditionally, the CMG comprised the Head of the EU and his two deputy heads. This move intensified the consultation process, giving all of the key people in the organization a much greater say in the affairs of the unit.

- He empowered his senior managers and business heads as the decision makers within their own units where possible.

- He published a five-year EU strategy plan called 'Painting the Picture' as a consultation document.

- He also made a series of appointments to help with the overall change strategies, such as Communications Officer John Barber to ensure that communications were effective and immediate both internally and in the media; Resettlement Officer Chris Dale to facilitate sideways moves within the EU and also to facilitate changes to the deployment of the workforce brought about by the successive change initiatives, for example, early retirements; and Research Officer Margaret Reidy to conduct internal and comparative research on organizational and cultural change to help inform, shape and measure the planned changes.

The latter appointment was particularly significant. Dick Shepherd wanted a comprehensive overview of the current culture and climates in the various offices of Anglia. He needed this to determine how he could best help his people in meeting change so that stress could be minimized where possible, and everyone had the opportunity to develop the appropriate competencies required for working successfully in the changed organization. To achieve all of this he needed to identify those pockets of resistance to cultural change which could cause potential problems when it came to implementing change initiatives. However, as part of his change strategy he wanted to promote more conducive management/leadership styles as best practice, which meant bringing about changes in the management culture. In the knowledge that some managers were struggling with outdated and inappropriate competencies, he wanted to be in a position to offer them concrete help in the form of research-informed organization development (OD) interventions.

Dick Shepherd was aware that the type of research required to support his strategies for change needed to be extensive and comprehensive, yet timely. Margaret Reidy also felt that to create a reliable framework for the research into the people issues and their inherent cultures would require a social science perspective. This meant wide-ranging and fundamental research to identify the patterns of behaviour in the organization and the impact that the changes had on these. This information was vital in order to create a conceptual framework of cultural and organizational change, since both were considered mutually related. There did not appear to be already in existence a conceptual framework appropriate to the needs of Anglia; those created in private sector organizations did not have a direct fit with the public sector, although there were many change initiatives in common across both sectors. Conceptual frameworks developed by academics for the public sector as reported in the management literature were quite interesting but did not suit the requirements for the initial change strategies that Dick Shepherd proposed for his organization at this particular time.

Hence he commissioned a series of projects, papers and reports relating to change, such as:

1 'A Longitudinal Ethnographic Research Programme on Cultural Change within Anglia' by his research officer, Margaret Reidy. This included the study, identification and measurement of cultural change throughout the organization. The research used various methodologies and methods and was conducted in partnership with Jim Stewart from Nottingham Trent University. This research proved invaluable. It revealed through analysis the emerging patterns of organizational

problems and behaviours, and allowed sufficient time to elapse for the underlying causes of complex problems to emerge, problems of an interrelated nature that existed at different levels of the organization.

2 'The Empirical Research Programme on Managerial Effectiveness' by Margaret Reidy in partnership with Bob Hamlin of the University of Wolverhampton using critical incident and factor analysis techniques. The aim of this study was to identify the criteria of managerial effectiveness and behavioural competencies associated with successful management applying within the changing organizational context and setting of the Anglia EU. The research findings were then used to develop a range of OD/HRD intervention tools designed to bring about further specific changes in the management culture. The power and effectiveness of these research-informed tools rested on the fact that they were derived from the findings of internal research, were expressed in the organization's own language, which 'struck a chord' with people in Anglia, and hence were readily perceived to be directly relevant and fit for the organization.

3 The 'East Anglia Expectations' document (Shepherd 1994) and the 'Anglia Expectations' documents (Shepherd 1995, 1997), which Dick Shepherd used as consultation documents on three-way expectations between the organization, management and staff. For the first time both management and staff were confronted with what was expected of them in terms of attitudes and behaviours. The documents also provided everyone with an acknowledgement of what they could expect from the organization.

4 A 'Review on Communication' from an outside consultancy seeking continuous improvements in communications.

As part of his rolling five-year change strategy, Dick Shepherd also:

- Increased his visits to outlying offices to enable more timely face-to-face communications.

- Held major 'roadshows' as consultation and debating forums throughout the EU when it was undergoing major reviews in the department, such as 'The Fundamental Expenditure Review' in 1997. The 'roadshow' was conducted to allay any fears people might have had by allowing them to ask questions face to face on their immediate concerns.

- Formulated and ran with his own localized concept of a pay and grading experiment primarily on delayering. This experiment was in effect a developmental initiative to enable the further reduction of the management hierarchy, particularly in the senior management group.

- Restructured the EU organization on functional lines to enable more efficient monitoring of resources and operations while furthering corporate cohesiveness through the business heads and their staff.

REFLECTIONS ON PRACTICE

A particular feature of Dick Shepherd's change management approach was to share his vision with his people through a variety of forums from the date of his appointment in 1991 to his retirement in 1998. He had felt that it was important to tackle cultural change on many different fronts. His legacy to his people in Anglia EU has been considerable. They have a fresher and more innovative approach to change, much improved on the attitudes they held before his appointment. The EU survived many turbulent changes and upheavals, but the people were always informed, consulted, supported and led through the changes. He also fostered and nurtured their own change projects, demonstrating the value of empowerment.

Dick Shepherd used the research he had commissioned from Margaret Reidy, Bob Hamlin and Jim Stewart as an essential and integral part of his strategies for change and found it had been successful far beyond his expectations. Although initially it seemed to him an easier option to push through change at the 'hard' systems and processes levels, which historically had been the typical approach adopted in the civil service, he realized increasingly from the research findings that unless the 'soft' people issues were identified and dealt with first, the structural changes would not be implemented successfully. The research convinced him of the critical importance of adopting an integrated approach to strategic change management by giving at least as much time and timely attention to the 'soft' issues as to the 'hard' issues. It taught him that by ensuring that people at the earliest stages understood and were supportive of and comfortable with the organizational changes proposed, the more successful these changes would be. As he says, in driving through his change strategies he could have deluded himself into thinking everybody was OK and that most if not all of his people were on board with the changes. However, he knew that because of his position many people, including some of his managers, would tend in public and in his presence to be 'on their best behaviour', overtly parading support but behind the scenes resisting or even undermining the changes. It was the internal research findings that gave him an accurate picture and measurement of where his Anglia people actually were with regard to the strategic changes being implemented.

The research produced a mass of rich data which told him what people at all levels, including his managers, were actually thinking and feeling. It gave him greater insights into people's attitudes and concerns than were being obtained through his normal channels of management communication. Once he fully realized through this heightened awareness that people had to be made 'happy' about the planned organizational changes, he then gave much more of his personal time, effort and emphasis to the cultural dimensions of his strategic change initiatives. The research findings enabled him to 'hold a mirror up to the organization'. This led to his managers recognizing, accepting and openly admitting ownership in public to both the 'positive' and 'negative' aspects of the existing management culture as expressed in terms of the identified managerial behaviours. The research enabled Dick Shepherd and his managers to target for attention those particular managerial behaviours from the 'old' culture that needed to be held on to and nurtured for the future, and those that had to be discouraged and eliminated.

Despite the potential for interruption and disruption to the work of his executive unit which could have been caused by the various organizational change programmes initiated by Dick Shepherd, he found that by adopting a fully integrated approach to the change management process Anglia's business performance targets and results actually increased consistently year on year.

Since taking over as head of the Anglia EU, Mike Hill has been building successfully on the achievements of Dick Shepherd while also bringing his own new innovative research-informed strategies for change into the organization.

LESSONS TO BE LEARNED FROM PRACTICE

The important lessons and insights for organizational change leaders emerging from the Anglia case history include the following:

■ The need to develop an in-depth understanding of the culture plus the necessary insights to interpret the emerging patterns of behaviour.

■ The need to have ready access to a sufficient amount of reliable data in order to interpret accurately what is actually going on deep inside the organization, particularly the cultural factors, which can cause things either to happen or not to happen.

■ The value of a combination of commissioned ethnographic, longitudinal research and empirical research conducted with 'academic' rigour, which can, as Dick Shepherd says, 'be of enormous value in bringing about cultural change'.

■ The value of the ongoing nature of internal longitudinal research, which delivers a constant stream of valuable data that not only helps sustain the momentum of the change programme but also can trigger additional or new organizational change and development initiatives.

■ The value of OD instruments based on the findings of rigorous and robust internal research, which can be particularly powerful tools for stimulating and bringing about transformational shifts in the management culture of an organization.

■ The recognition that the stronger the foundation of research evidence used to inform, shape and measure organizational change, the greater will be the chances for its long-term survival and success.

■ The need for organizational leaders commissioning research into the culture of organizations to understand the nature of the research process, the importance of rigour and ethical standards such as the issue of confidentiality, and the need to appreciate the significance of the research data and respect its complexity.

Notes

1 The 'Next Steps' programme was launched as a result of the government White Paper (1988) entitled 'The Next Steps' and involved the hiving off of the service delivery functions of government departments to semi-autonomous executive agencies under the direction of chief executives. In the case of HM Customs & Excise and the Inland Revenue, although they were not to become executive

agencies in the full sense of the definition, they have reorganized their activities on 'Next Step' lines as if they were executive agencies.

2   The HM Customs & Excise People Initiative (1991) was launched by Sir Brian Unwin (former chairman of the board of HMCE) and was part of the C&E strategy to foster closer working relationships between management and staff (see Unwin 1991). This required a reassessment by managers of their relationships with and attitudes towards staff.

References

Shepherd, R.C. (1994), *East Anglia Expectations* [an in-house document]. Ipswich: HMCE/East Anglia Collection.

Shepherd, R.C. (1995, 1997), *Anglia Expectations* [in-house documents]. Ipswich: HMCE/Anglia Collection.

Unwin, Sir Brian (1991), *The Customs & Excise People Initiative* [an in-house document]. London: HMCE.

Effecting transformational change in one part of the newly privatized/deregulated power generation industry in the Netherlands

Jaap Germans

This reflection is based on my direct involvement as an external organizational change consultant helping to bring about fundamental transformational change in one part of the Dutch power generation industry.

BACKGROUND TO THE ORGANIZATIONAL CONTEXT AND SETTING

As in other EU countries, the Dutch government is progressively deregulating and privatizing its nationalized utilities and telecommunications industries. For the electricity industry the impact was first felt in 1995. Electricteitsbedrijf Zuid Holland (EZH) was one of four state-owned regional companies comprising the Dutch equivalent of what used to be the Central Electricity Generating Board in Britain. Typical of most nationalized industries, it was highly centralized and bureaucratic, with a large central headquarters which controlled what happened at each of the two large and eight smaller power stations geographically dispersed in the western part of the Netherlands. The challenge facing EZH was the need to transform itself into a lean and fit customer-oriented private sector business capable of surviving in an increasingly competitive market environment. The area of the company's operations particularly affected by the pressures of competition was the Central Maintenance Department, which employed around 300 people. The department was being required to deliver in open competition plant maintenance services, including annual preventive maintenance audits, as well as normal ongoing breakdown maintenance not only to the EZH-owned power stations but also to power stations and industrial plants owned by other electricity companies and companies in other industries (e.g. petrochemicals). It was being targeted to develop and grow its external contract maintenance business within three years from nothing to 40 per cent of the department's annual revenue stream. Faced with the prospect of having to compete for the first time against intense competition from private sector companies specializing in the contract maintenance field, the EZH Central Maintenance Department realized it had to radically redefine its direction, become skilled in tendering for contracts, become contract-delivery focused, and above all more customer focused and profit-oriented. This posed a huge challenge to a management that had never had to tender for contracts, think about customer care or consider the issue of profitability.

As part of an initial HR strategy for the total EZH organization to begin the process of its company-wide organizational transformation, EZH commissioned from the University of Tilburg a major management development programme for all of its senior executives and middle managers. The aim was to educate them into the ways of managing in the commercial world and the private sector. This took the form of a 30-day formal management training programme spread over a 12-month period, and included a series of planned work-based activities and projects that managers were asked to undertake. A total of 60 managers were trained in groups of 20 per programme.

This management development (MD) programme was designed and delivered by myself on behalf of the University of Tilburg in my capacity as director of studies in the field of the management of industries and also acting in my capacity as an independent MD/OD consultant. Having learned about my specialist interest, experience and expertise in the field of organizational change and development while attending the first of the three commissioned MD programmes, two managers from the Central Maintenance Department, supported by three managers from the power stations, asked me in my other capacity as a practising independent MD/OD consultant to help them bring about required organizational changes in their sector of EZH. Specifically, they were seeking to create and put in place a new computerized human resource (manpower) planning system that was deemed an essential information management tool for management to tender for contracts, etc. Past attempts to introduce similar systems had failed. They perceived from my background in manufacturing and commerce, IT, project management, strategic planning and organizational change management that I possessed a combination of experience and expertise that could be of help to them. They had come to realize that in planning to introduce a new 'hard' computerized system the real challenge was the need to change the culture of the Central Maintenance Department itself, to redefine its relationships with other parts of EZH, not least its internal 'customers' – the power stations which now had the freedom to buy maintenance services from outside suppliers if they so wished. An additional need was to find out how to forge effective commercial relationships with its prospective external customers.

THE ORGANIZATIONAL CHANGE AND DEVELOPMENT (OCD) PROGRAMME

It is from this starting point that this 'reflection on practice' begins. I was engaged for a period of three years from 1996 to 1999 to act as an integral member of and as an external adviser to the senior management team (SMT) of the Central Maintenance Department (CMD) concerned specifically with the change process. A significant and critical factor in the equation was the fact that, like myself, Dick Bista, the head of CMD, whose professional background was in electrical engineering, also believed strongly in the need to invest time and effort in the cultural aspects of organizational change. I considered that an early requirement was to identify those specific aspects of the current approach to management, the management culture, style and behaviour that were no longer appropriate for operating successfully in the changed business environment, and to reflect these back to the managers during the early stages of the planning for strategic change process. To do this I made a conscious choice not to carry out a conventional organizational analysis exercise but instead to spend about two months conducting 'action research' in the role of a participant observer and process consultant while also performing as an integral member of the SMT. The reasons for adopting this approach to my change agency practice were strongly informed not only by my past experience as a change management consultant but also by the thinking of Bolhuis and Simons (1999), Zwart (1995), Swieringa and Elmers (1996) and Kets de Vries (1996).

The action research revealed a team of managers who exhibited very high levels of technical expertise and competence, a strong sense of 'ownership' and identification with the EZH power stations and a strong internal client orientation. However, the managers were steeped in the traditional bureaucratic mindset of the Dutch nationalized industries as characterized by an inward focus and by a self-maintaining closed-system, top-down, command-and-control style of management. They experienced very real problems in thinking about and relating to the concept and viewpoint of the 'internal and external customer'. Their outlook was wholly egocentric in that they described everything and planned everything not from the customer's point of view but from their own. For example, when drawing up contracts or tendering for contracts they still engaged in cost-plus and capacity-plus practices, building additional time and costs into the contract to suit them. Hence, during our regular OCD programme planning and decision-making meetings, I reflected back to the SMT what I had observed about their managerial approach and behaviour, as compared with what typically applies in profit-making private sector organizations. I also gave informal briefings at various times on the issue of moving towards an enterprise culture and the implications for themselves.

One of the greatest challenges facing the SMT, besides managing successfully the practical difficulties of introducing the proposed computerized manpower planning system, was deciding how best to, as Todd (1999) puts it, 'lead a critical mass of the existing workforce through a period of intense uncertainty and to do so in such a way that the organization is able to continue operating in its existing internal (and emergent external) markets and relationships whilst learning new behaviours'. My considered view was that the EZH situation required a two-pronged strategy; namely that the CMD should set itself up to operate as if two separate business organizations were running in parallel. The one business would be required to run in the ways of working associated with the existing 'old' structure, systems, staffing and management style, but with managers and staff tasked to discover how to operate this organization successfully in the new climate of the changed internal (and external!) business environment. Although it was anticipated that 'old' day-to-day problems would arise, this did not matter because by investing effort in finding new ways of working, these problems would be taken care of. The other parallel business organization would be a totally 'new' invention, newly created by the SMT and designed such that the organizational structure would be completely in alignment with the highly competitive external commercial environment in which this newly created business had to operate. The main attention of the SMT would need to be focused towards the 'new' organization, with a minimum amount of time being spent on the day-to-day operational issues of the 'old' business. Based on these ideas, the three-year departmental business plan was drawn up, articulating the new vision and mission and incorporating the agreed two-pronged strategy for achieving the department's goals.

IMPLEMENTATION OF THE OCD PROGRAMME

Besides helping to design and test the computerized manpower planning system required for the 'new' organization, I carried out a cultural diagnosis to identify and agree with my SMT colleagues the ideal cultural values required for the new business, including the wanted 'healthy' as opposed to 'unhealthy' aspects of the 'old' culture that ought to be preserved. The implementation strategy adopted a conventional change management approach similar to the 'generic' change management model outlined in Chapter 2 (Figure 2.1), which is set out below for easy reference:

1 Diagnose, explore the present state; identify the required future state.
2 Create a strategic vision.
3 Plan the change strategy.
4 Secure ownership, commitment and involvement.
5 Project-manage the implementation and sustain momentum.
6 Stabilize, integrate and consolidate to ensure perpetuation of the changed state.

However, in applying this model it needs to be pointed out that the SMT was strongly influenced by the 'old' top-down command-and-control management culture. Although from their MD programme studies my SMT colleagues intellectually knew and fully supported the idea of adopting a 'participation and involvement'-based approach to managing the processes of stage 4 of the change management model, in the event they used predominantly an 'information and communication'-based approach typical of the traditional bureaucratic management. Nevertheless, when the various briefings and presentations to the workforce were over it appeared the employees understood the new vision, mission and business plan, and that they were willing to go along with the OCD programme even though this meant exercising more discretion, risk taking and enterprise in the way they did their jobs. However, three months passed by and there was very little take-up of the new ways of working. Although the new three-year departmental business plan was heading for success as measured by the 'hard' numbers-based business performance indicators, it was clearly failing in terms of achieving the desired changes in the 'soft' behaviours, attitudes and values of the workforce. A survey revealed that although the plan was thought to be a good one, employees identified it as belonging solely to the SMT. They did not feel a sense of 'owning' it or of being anywhere near the driving seat. This contributed to their negative reaction, lack of commitment and resistance. Hence the SMT had to go back to the beginning and start again.

This time we decided to hand over (give) to the management and workforce the initiative for implementing the departmental business plan. This meant adopting a change management approach based on involvement, participation and empowerment, though the managers and workers were specifically not told they were being empowered. Rather, their involvement was secured through the process of the SMT again sharing its vision, mission and ideas with the workforce but this time in small groups. Each group comprised from 10 to 20 employees drawn from the existing functional, process and horizontal teams, including representatives from the shop floor. At the close of the 'sharing' sessions people were told that the detail of finding a way to move the change project forward was now in their hands. The only stipulation was that they should summarize their ideas and plans as to what should be done, to commit these in writing for the benefit of the groups of employees they represented, and to submit these to the SMT within a given time. The SMT would not interfere in their proceedings but was available to give help and support as and when required or requested. In contrast to the first attempt at devising and launching the business plan and OCD programme, which were based solely on the thinking of the SMT, this second attempt recognized the fact that the employees themselves were better able to make the necessary connections between the 'old' and the 'new'. It was they who really knew best what had to be held onto from the past and what should be dumped: which ideas proposed for the 'new' organization could or would work and which needed to be modified. Also, they had a better feel for the logistical aspects of the OCD programme and what realistically would be achievable in the time scales proposed.

REFLECTIONS ON PRACTICE

In reflecting on the change agency associated with the three-year business plan and OCD programme outlined above, which, ultimately, were successfully implemented, a number of important lessons for the SMT and for me personally stand out, as follows:

- The SMT has had to learn to deal with the paradox of running a new business invention alongside the existing business and within the constraints imposed by the existing organization structures and culture.

- The SMT has also had to learn how to cope with the paradox of 'top-down' versus 'bottom-up' approaches to managing change.

- The SMT has had to recognize that although in very structured organizations such as EZH change needs to be brought about in a structured way, the process needs to be non-directive. However, the big danger with non-directive approaches is that they can take too long as a result of the difficulties in ensuring that crystal-clear, timely messages are effectively communicated throughout the whole organization. This requires particularly sophisticated methods of communication. With a lack of sustained momentum they risk employees not making the effort to learn the required new ways of working.

■ The SMT has had to learn the hard way the need to take the lead and give sufficient time to explaining and stressing to the workforce the new business realities, and to use the right approaches for securing their ownership of, commitment to and involvement with the change strategy.

My personal observations from this particular experience of change agency within EZH suggest additional lessons as follows:

■ When you recognize that culture is the key issue in a change programme, the temptation is to give more emphasis to this than to the structure and systems. However, you need to give equal attention to both the 'hard' and the 'soft' issues.

■ To help a team of practising managers get to grips with the problems of managing change effectively, you need, as the OCD consultant, a range of theoretical and conceptual frameworks at your fingertips in order for you to give them the language that enables them to talk about and reflect upon their problems and to critically evaluate their own change agency practice.

■ While acting as the OCD consultant in EZH, I came to recognize the risk of my success ultimately leading to failure as a result of my becoming too deeply involved in the management of the organizational change programme. On reflection, my learning and that of my SMT colleagues as we journeyed along our chosen path of change ought to have been guided by an outside person. In hindsight, it would have been better if we had formed ourselves into an action learning set with an independent facilitator.

References

Bolhuis, S.M. and Simons, P.R.-J. (1999), *Lean en Werken*. Kluwer.

Kets de Vries, M.F.R. (1996), *Organisatie Paradoxen*. Academic Service.

Swieringa, J. and Elmers, B. (1996), *In Plaats van Reorganiseren*. Wolters-Noordhoff.

Todd, A. (1999), Managing radical change. *Long Range Planning*, 32(2), 237–244.

Zwart, C. (1995), *De Strategie van de Hoop*. Lemniscaat.

Moving through the impasse – the case of a pharmaceutical manufacturing company in Ireland

Peter Shields

This case concerns a campaign to change the work practices and shift system of workers in a bulk pharmaceutical manufacturing company. From a corporate and managerial perspective there were compelling strategic and economic reasons for change. From the perspective of many of the workers, there were strongly embedded and deeply felt reasons for resisting change.

As the case unfolded it provided me, as HR director, with many opportunities to test and reflect upon theory in practice. In terms of Hinings's (1983) model of factors influencing success in change management, cited in Stewart (1996), the situation presented 'the lowest chance' of a favourable outcome since there was fundamental disagreement on the problem or need for change and upon the solution or change itself. But it did succeed.

The company had been in operation in Ireland for more than 30 years. Its manufacturing facility had developed as a number of relatively small-scale units capable of quick turnaround to produce a wide range of products. This flexibility and stop-gap capability was highly valued by the parent corporation, even though it was expensive. It demanded detailed knowledge of the plant and equipment on the part of staff and high-level practical skills in plant reconfiguration and varied operation on the part of craft workers and plant operators. They were justifiably proud of a long record of successful experience and proven skills.

The manufacturing operations were based on 12-hour shift work covering five weekdays and nights. Weekend working when necessary was undertaken on overtime. The plant was overmanned by industry norms, and work practices which from a managerial perspective were in need of radical rationalization. Small-scale operation and frequent reconfiguration led to very high costs in manufacturing, and the practice of five-day working compounded the inefficient use of plant.

The growing competitiveness of the 1990s led the parent corporation to radically review its global manufacturing network and, as part of this process, to review the role of the Irish plant. While other relatively efficient plants of the corporation were being closed it was decided that the Irish plant should be retained and substantially expanded in its scale of operation, but only if it came into line with competitive standards in terms of work practices, manning levels and seven-day operation.

Prior to this determination by the corporation, management at the plant had, in anticipation of the situation, been attempting to bring about the necessary changes but without success, despite a labour court[1] recommendation that the changes should be implemented in return for pay increases. The considered position of the workforce, as conveyed through union representatives, was that the changes required were 'too much, too soon and for too little money'. Ultimately, the position adopted was that seven-day operation was not open for discussion. Many employees felt that money could not compensate for the encroachment of rostered work on some weekends.

In the context of Irish industrial relations, normally conducted in the adversarial mode (IBEC 1996), robust opposition to change is frequently encountered, but I had never before experienced a situation where change, which to me was clearly necessary for survival, was not open for discussion – a total impasse. Upon reflection this stance is not so surprising. The workforce had succeeded in resisting change despite explanation of the consequence as being closure and despite the authoritative recommendation of the labour court. Employees told themselves believable stories of the success of the plant, of the high profits achieved and of the reliance of the parent corporation upon the facility (Boyce 1996).

Pascale *et al.* (1997) suggest that once the members of an organization begin to believe that they have 'arrived', past successes start to be codified into a winning formula and drift and rigidity are not far behind. The systems, procedures and culture at the plant had become so rooted in high-cost acceptance that the death of the system seemed more likely than reform.[2]

Bardwick (1998) suggests that people and organizations go through four predictable stages as they try to cope with major change. The first stage is denial – coming to acknowledge that reality has changed – is scary. People fear that their knowledge, skills and abilities to cope will be inadequate.

The second stage is to attempt to escape the need for change by doing the old things better, faster and with more people. In the present case, the workforce agreed at one stage that weekend shift crews should be recruited and that established employees should remain on five-day working. Agreement was ultimately withdrawn when it became clear that such an arrangement would substantially reduce overtime. This is consistent with what Bardwick (1995) sees as people's preoccupation with rewards rather than with responsibilities.

Bardwick (1998) calls the third phase 'flailing around'. As she sees it, people have to get past the extremes of their negative emotions of fear, anxiety and depression before they are able to see opportunity and how to do things differently. Such extremes of negative emotions may have been fundamental to the impasse as outlined above.

The final phase of Bardwick's analysis is one of new growth, in which people begin to perceive new opportunities, bringing them into a future which is different from their past. But if they do not succeed in progressing to this phase they face stagnation and death of the system.[3]

Our problem in the present case was how to bring the workforce through the impasse, a problem compounded by the fact that I and my managerial colleagues were viewed as part of the problem within the adversarial system rather than as potentially contributing to the solution. The system had to be moved beyond alienation and adversarialism towards a practical accommodation which the established industrial relations approaches had not and probably would not achieve.

Industrial relations strategies for which there is clear legal precedent could have ranged from reduction or withdrawal of pay,[4] through dismissals for obdurate refusal to comply with change essential to the business,[5] to layoff or announcement of closure to force compliance. While it may be useful in writing for practitioners to point to the availability of these legitimate forcing strategies and their successful legal defence, there is little need to elaborate their potential consequences. Most of us probably have been there and bear the scars.

However, the belief persists that the way to overcome resistance is to overpower it using force of one kind or another, and these forces seldom remove the underlying causes of resistance. For example, force of argument – a good beating with the facts – does not address the emotional foundations of resistance underlying the reasoned arguments that those opposing may present; forcing a deal or throwing money at the problem may provide temporary relief of resistance, but the problem remains to re-emerge (Maurer 1996).

Our journey through the impasse was illuminated by a number of theoretical perspectives adopted, unfaithfully, from the sources acknowledged below. Writing now, in retrospect, about what my colleagues and I were attempting, it all seems very clear, logical and even competent, but the prospect of translating 'soft science' theory into practice in the hard science context of a chemical plant did not imbue me with confidence. Schon (1983) suggests that in such situations science is necessary but in the form of 'action science', which 'would concern itself with situations of uniqueness, uncertainty and instability which do not lend themselves to the application of theories and techniques derived from science in the mode of technical rationality' but that would aim at the development of theories from which, in these sorts of situations, practitioners might construct models and methods of their own (summary based on Thomas 1993).

REFLECTIONS ON THE THEORETICAL MODELS AND METHODS

Though opposition to change is presented as unanimous, there are always tensions between coalitional interests and unity of purpose (Cyert and March 1963). In this case, a dominant coalition vociferously opposed change but the dominance may have been of voice rather than of numbers. Those sitting on the fence needed to be moved (Stewart 1996: 27).

On that hot, humid afternoon when members of the extended family were sitting on the veranda sipping lemonade, nobody in the family wanted to drive to Abilene, Texas, but everybody took up the suggestion to go which had been made out of boredom by one member. Having gone to Abilene they each revealed, on the way home, that none of them really wanted to go there (Harvey 1996). I wondered how many of the people caught in the impasse were passengers on the road to Abilene or, in Irving Janis's (1983) alternative analysis, were trapped in 'groupthink' – a mode of thinking that people engage in when they are deeply involved in 'a cohesive in-group, where the members striving for unanimity override their motivation to realistically appraise other courses of action' (Griffin 1994: 264).

The 'defence mechanisms' described in the literature on groupthink were present in this case:

1 *Illusions of invulnerability* – 'we heard it all before, no way will they close the plant'.

2 *Stereotyping of outsiders* – 'the boss is past his sell-by date'.

3 *Bounded rationality and fethered assumptions* – 'we are right. It is totally unreasonable to expect changes that require weekend working after 30 years of working on weekdays only, we are perfectly justified in opposing'.

4 *Belief in intrinsic morality* – 'Right' as used in 3 above means 'within our rights', but an easy extension of this would be 'we are morally right and the extensive changes required are morally wrong, unjust and outside of any negotiable compensation'. In the subject case the refusal to negotiate had this moral tone and moral duty to oppose.

5 *Self-censorship* – where dissent is weak because it is strongly discouraged within the group.

I concluded that the situation required what Johnson and Scholes (1997: 43, 44) have called a mould-breaking or menu-breaking event in order to expose the 'conspiracy' of groupthink and to move the company on.

The basic theoretical assumption was that since conflict is an almost inevitable corollary of change it must be addressed as normal, legitimate and potentially creative (Waddell and Amrik 1998), rather than repressed as being disloyal and contrary to the 'rationality' paradigm of managerialism (Maurer 1996).

It was Richard Pascale (1990) who reminded management theorists of the dialectic[6] or progress through the resolution of opposing positions. 'While the literature of conflict and its management is abundant no book has explicitly advanced a model that embraces conflict as a source of organisational renewal' (*ibid.*: 277). Pascale presents a model for recognizing vectors of contention and for resolving the dialectic. Essentially, it involves what he calls 'operating from a different paradigm' not attempting to avoid or repress conflict but striving to open up each level of the hierarchy to receive the ideas and initiatives of the ranks below (*ibid.*: 160).

But in the present case there was no mechanism for the ranks to escape from groupthink, to clarify their ideas and to develop initiatives. Members of the organization needed opportunity to examine questions concerning identity – who they were, how they related to the organization, to what extent they valued and were valued by the organization; how it served their interests and how they served or might serve the interests of the organization. In such a detailed analysis it seemed likely that the coalitional interests would be seen for what they were and that a range of conflicting coalitions might be recognized, for example those employees who would welcome closure of the plant in the hope of receiving large redundancy settlements, or those who needed the job and a secure future irrespective of the demands of change. In this way subversion, if it existed, could be disarmed.

It also seemed likely that, since the answers to these questions were based in the history of the organization as well as in its future, many issues of grievance would be aired in the exploration. There would be many opportunities for insights into the causes of the impasse and particularly into the extent to which old grievances and cynicism were blocking the way forward (Anderson 1996).

The adversarial system, to which all parties in this case were subject, forced identity and perceived interest in one of two directions only. It was difficult for either side to legitimize, to any extent, the power and position of the other and particularly since there was a 30-year history of unionized grievances hidden in the ritualized relationships of formalized industrial relations.[7] In this case, employees needed to examine their identity system and experience their power, not just the power of veto leading to impasse and stagnation but also the much more individually challenging power to develop and renew.

Goss *et al.* (1993) advocated assembling a critical mass of stakeholders, doing an organizational audit, discussing the hitherto undiscussable, harnessing contention and creating urgency as necessary steps in reinvention or transformational change. In considering the practicalities of how this might be achieved in this case, I was fortunate to discover a paper by Raymond Cadwell (1995). In his paper, Cadwell described the characteristics of the impasse, which were consonant with our experience. He outlined a method and guidelines for moving through the impasse which he had tested and which seemed entirely in line with what Goss *et al.* (1993) were advocating. Cadwell's theoretical approach was that impasse must be 'normalized' – that everyone affected on both sides must come to recognize that they are all experiencing the feelings of powerlessness, defensiveness, confusion, frustration, distrust, anger and hopelessness. In his consultancy work, Cadwell had experience of using extensive diagnostic interviews at all levels as a basis for producing a report that would mirror to all concerned the feelings on all sides surrounding the issue.

> ... we found that it is most crucial for every member of an organization to get a chance to accept that they are in a situation which feels difficult if not impossible to solve.

His assumptions are that in going through the impasse no one group has a monopoly of expertise. His analogy is that each group and level of the organization has a piece of the jigsaw. He sees the consultant's role as facilitating the jigsaw in coming together.

The diagnostic interviews generate curiosity, which entices people to come and talk, and the full and frank feedback (though not attributed to sources) inspires trust in the process. Building on curiosity, trust and a growing sense of urgency Cadwell invites all members of the organization to participate in a 'real-time strategic change event' – a convocation in which problems with systems, procedures, policies and relationships can be reviewed and directions for change can be agreed.

In the present case, this took the form of a one-day conference involving all employees (except senior management) working in 19 groups of 15 people, each with a facilitator, volunteered from among the non-managerial employees and trained over three days in facilitation. The two-part question posed by Cadwell to the groups was 'What is good about working for this company and how could it be improved?'

The positive form of the question was intended to influence the perspective of the participants and to channel to positive effect the tide of energy, which could have been readily focused on negativism and vitriolic complaint – though there was plenty of both in the air. At the end of a day's very lively debate the facilitators fed back to a plenary session the appreciations and recommendations of the participants. Over 100 recommendations were generated. These were subsequently categorized by the senior management team into those that would be implemented immediately, those that would be implemented within three months, six months, twelve months, those that would receive further consideration and those that would not be adopted.

The real-time change event had a lot of benefits in addition to the list of recommendations. It realized for people that the company was concerned and committed to change and improvement. It put people in touch with their own power in participation and influencing and this was reinforced by publication of the time-scaled list of items to be implemented and further reinforced by the various implementations.

People who had never met before other than to say 'hello' had an opportunity to work together, gain some wider perspectives and overall to review their identity systems, loyalties, attitudes and coalitional interests. There were expressions of amazement by some at the attitudes of others. The recommendations, though each had a positive pole suggesting what should be done, were based on negative poles of what had caused annoyance, grievance, and sense of injustice and alienation.

The real-time change event was a very clear watershed. It opened up the possibility of discussion of change. It enabled management to demonstrate good faith in implementing recommended change and it demonstrated to the workforce that they could exercise power beyond veto. They saw that their power could be exercised in relation to dissident sub-groups and in relation to management. It also re-opened what Pascale et al. (1997) have called 'the contention system', the system by which all parties in an organization can influence the directions of change. Those who had refused to negotiate were urged to do so by many who were not so closely affected by shift work or seven-day working. Those who were affected felt more confident in their power to influence the change.

Within six weeks of the real-time change event formal negotiations had commenced and were successfully concluded within a further ten weeks, which, given the complexity of the issues involved, was a remarkably short period. It was noticeable too that the negotiations were not left just to shop stewards to conclude but that there was a readiness on the part of many who had remained silent in the 'groupthink' situation to take initiatives to express their views and to lead. 'Guerrilla leaders', as Pascale terms them, came out of the woodwork to exercise their influence.

Pascale et al. (ibid.) neatly summarize the theory of this change effort: 'In essence there are three concrete interventions that will restore companies to vital agility and then keep them in good health: incorporating employees fully into the process of dealing with business challenges, leading from a different place so as to sharpen and maintain involvement and constructive stress and instilling mental disciplines that will make them behave differently and then help them to sustain their new behaviour into the future.'

In our efforts to instil mental disciplines, continuing improvement methods were introduced, based on the methodology of Deming (1986). This has enabled employees to enter a learning system and to be actively engaged in ongoing change and development processes.

In recommending these approaches to practitioners I would make the additional suggestion that repeated real-time audit and intervention is necessary to maintain the widest involvement, to debate emerging problems, to test perceptions of the progress being made and to review commitment.

Perhaps I should also comment that since Pascale made his point relating to constructive stress, the literature extensively, and the courts expensively, have convinced us that stress is not constructive. However, my experience has been that as levels of concern over an issue build, so too does the readiness of 'guerrilla leaders' to step in, this providing energy and vision in negotiating the impasse. There are no pearls without grit in the oyster!

Notes

1   An arbitration body set up under the Industrial Relations Act 1946 No. 26.

2   Tichy and Devanna (1986: 44) use the boiled frog analogy for situations like this. A live frog placed in a pan of cold water which is gradually heated will boil to death.

3   Reminiscent of Kubler Ross's stages in *On Death and Dying*.

4   Cresswell v. Board of Inland Revenue (1984), 2 ALL ER713, Chancery, or O'Neill v. Merseyside Plumbing Company Ltd (1973), ICR 96.

5   Woods v. W.M. Car Services Ltd (1982), (ILL 913).

6   For a philosophical discussion of Hegel's dialectic see Desmond (1988).

7   When an organization renews itself it must uncover and alter the underlying assumptions and invisible premises on which decisions and actions are based (Goss *et al.* 1993).

References

Anderson, L.M. (1996), Employee cynicism: an examination using a contract violation framework. *Human Relations*, 49(11).

Bardwick, J.M. (1995), *Danger in the Comfort Zone*. New York: Amacom.

Bardwick, J.M. (1998), Changing Culture. *Executive Excellence*, 15(8), 10. Dublin: Century Management.

Boyce, M.E. (1996), Organisational story and storytelling: a critical review. *Journal of Organisational Change Management*, 9, 5–26.

Cadwell, R. (1995), *Building bridges to the future: getting through the blockages to change*. Bulletin No 13. Dublin: Cadwell Consulting and Training Ltd.

Cresswell v. Board of Inland Revenue (1984), 2 ALL ER713. Chancery Division – refusal to co-operate with change: no work no pay.

Cyert, R.M. and March, G.G. (1963), *A Behavioural Theory of the Firm*. Englewood Cliffs, NJ: Prentice Hall.

Deming, W.E. (1986), *Out of Crisis*. Cambridge: Massachusetts Institute of Technology.

Desmond, W. (ed.) (1988), *Hegel and His Critics: Philosophy in the Aftermath of Hegel*. New York: State University of New York Press.

Goss, T., Pascale, R. and Athos, A. (1993), The reinvention roller coaster: Risking the present for a powerful future. *Harvard Business Review*, 71(6), 97.

Griffin, E.M. (1994), *A First Look at Communication Theory*. New York: McGraw Hill.

Harvey, J.B. (1996), *The Abilene Paradox and Other Meditations on Management*. San Francisco: Jossey Bass.

Hinings, R. (1983), *Planning, Organising and Managing Change*. Luton: Local Government Training Board.

IBEC (1996), *Change and Continuous Improvement, Employee Involvement and Communications*. Dublin: Irish Business and Employees Confederation.

Janis, J. (1983), *Groupthink: Psychological Studies of Policy Decisions and Fiascoes*. Boston: Houghton Mifflin.

Johnson, G. and Scholes, K. (1997), *Exploring Corporate Strategy*. London: Prentice Hall.

Kubler-Ross, E. (1969), *On Death and Dying*. New York: Macmillan.

Maurer, R. (1996). Using resistance to build support for change. *Journal for Quality and Participation*, June, 56–63.

O'Neill v. Merseyside Plumbing Co. Ltd (1973), ICR 96 – refusal to extend skills and change.

Pascale, R. (1990), *Managing on the edge: How successful companies use conflict to stay ahead.*

Pascale, R. Millemann, M. and Gioja, L. (1997), Changing the way we change. *Harvard Business Review*, November/December.

Schon, D. (1983), *The Reflective Practitioner*. London: Temple Smith.

Stewart, J. (1996), *Managing Change through Training and Development*, 2nd edn. London: Kogan Page.

Thomas, A.B. (1993), *Controversies in Management*. London: Routledge.

Tichy, N. and Devanna, M. (1986), *The Transformational Leader*. New York: Wiley.

Waddell, D. and Amrik, S. (1998), Resistance: a constructive tool for change management. *Management Decision*, 36(8), 543–548.

Woods v. W.M. Car Services Ltd (1982), ILL913 – obdurate refusal to co-operate with necessary change.

Quality initiatives

Jane Keep (editor)

INTRODUCTION

This chapter offers you a series of four reflections relating to three public sector organizations and the fourth a manufacturing organization, all based in or around the Midlands. The theme relates to using quality frameworks or qualitative processes to enable or support organizational change. It also echoes some of the cultural change approaches and practices highlighted in Chapter 7.

Graham Smith's reflective case looks at using training and development to support attitudinal, behavioural and cultural changes in the contract services department of a metropolitan borough council. Two quality frameworks, Investors in People and total quality management, were used to implement the changes described while Graham was working as an internal change agent. He charts progress through a very useful 'step change model' which works through periods of diagnosis, development and reflection, highlighting issues around resistance, responsibility and monitoring. Overall, he concludes among other things in his reflections that quality frameworks such as these can sometimes be a substitute for 'developing a true strategic direction' and notes with caution that change is difficult, with underlying tensions such as those where there is a political influence at a local and national level, which is often quite different from the situation where influences are by direct customer contact.

Chris Luty provides an interesting insight into his work as development manager, looking at the relationship between training suppliers and the Training and Enterprise Council (TEC) in the West Midlands, which is in the process of identifying a strategy, and to increase the commercial income of these training organizations and thus reduce their total reliance upon TEC funds. He uses a mixture of data collection methods, including a survey, interviews and the establishing of a joint working group, all of which enable the development of a detailed strategy and action plan. Chris reflects on this work, which gave him the opportunity to use research techniques while he tries to establish academic rigour to support the change process and outcomes. This experience enabled him to assess his own competence as a 'researcher', realizing the importance of testing and piloting data collection tools to enable a more rigorous process. He also suggests that research is difficult in organizations when trying to prove or disprove anything, and that it is often only possible to find indicators or suggestions towards proof.

Julie Knowles gives us a reflection into a charitable organization that provides total care and support to people with learning difficulties in the Midlands. In the particular case outlined she wears many different 'hats', such as role model, mentor, trainer and change agent, and felt that there were too many roles to cover. The organization is implementing *kaizen* in order to recognize the need for continuous improvement, increasing individual and team development, creating empowerment and job satisfaction, and generally improving service quality to the client group. Julie as change agent in her reflective case works alongside her manager, has the realization at the end that there was an earlier need to concentrate on 'fundamentals' such as communication and teamwork, which in the end had slowed down the change process. She also reflects that with hindsight there was a need to carry out some initial diagnoses of the current culture, leadership and management style prior to introducing a new culture which would have enabled a better start point for the whole process.

From a slightly different viewpoint, Prudence Clarke, working as an external consultant, is able to give us a comparative view as her work straddled two plants in one large organization. Each plant was given the same interventions, but the outcomes were different. She also reflects that with hindsight, understanding the different values permeating each of these plants prior to undertaking the interventions would have enabled a smoother change approach, and an emphasis on the cultural aspect of change. This supports Julie Knowle's reflections too.

My role as a change agent in Sandwell MBC Contract Services

Graham Smith

This describes and reflects on my role as an internal change agent in the Contract Services Department of Sandwell Metropolitan Borough Council – principally from 1994 to the end of 1998, a critical time in its history – from a period of being a rather bureaucratic, loss-making organization, through to a time of reasonable financial stability, with the achievement of the Investors in People Award and the adoption of the British Quality Foundation Excellence Model© in preparation for Best Value.

BACKGROUND

In 1989, central government extended compulsory competitive tendering (CCT), which required the control of funding to be a separately managed function from the supplier of that service, thus enabling private sector companies to bid against a council's 'in-house' provider. In response to CCT, Sandwell MBC took the decision to place all operational units (the service providers) into one department of 1700 employees, called Contract Services, which would tender to carry out all the practical activities for the council, ranging from housing repairs to refuse collection and amenity horticulture.

Many client departments, councillors and members of the public were unable to appreciate the new commercial pressures. Goodwill and support declined when unpaid 'extra' work outside the contract specification was no longer carried out. The local press, apparently unable to make the distinction between client and contractor, became increasingly critical of Contract Services and delighted in publishing examples of poor or slow service.

By the mid-1990s, with the combination of reduced spending by client departments and increased competition from private companies, particularly in the building sector, Contract Services began to make losses and risked closure. Initial management action resulted in painful downsizing, limited recruitment, restructuring and reduced terms and conditions of employment, which just about halted the decline. During those difficult years, labour relations were confrontational.

A PROACTIVE RESPONSE TO CHANGE

In 1994, the new director progressively pulled the department together under one strategic management team. That team recognized that in order to secure the longer-term future of Contract Services there was a need to review the whole organization, and then to implement appropriate changes.

The Local Government Management Board (1988) pointed the way forward by stating that 'very positive results can be achieved by linking training and development to policies and the objectives of an organization' and that 'success can only be achieved with the active participation of everyone within it'.

MY INVOLVEMENT WITH THE CHANGE PROCESS

The new management team asked me to focus the role of training and development to support change. I think we all recognized the difficulties that lay ahead. My and their challenge was not simply to change skills and knowledge but also to work towards changing attitude, behaviour and the existing bureaucratic culture.

We in essence chose to follow a five-stage model (see Figure 8.1, the step change plan), though Stewart (1996) points out the need for 'an emphasis upon interrelationships between the different stages that can be distinguished and labelled' and that 'it is simply not possible to systematically carry out a logical series of activities in a linear manner'.

DIAGNOSIS

As French and Bell (1994) considered that 'resistance to change will be less, if the participants have joined in the diagnosis effort leading them to agree on what the basic problem is and to feel its importance', we initially facilitated a series of meetings involving managers, supervisors, trade union officials and representative groups from across the whole department to identify key issues. These were put into two simple lists, under the headings of what we wanted to leave behind and what we wanted to achieve. Essentially, a gap model was created which identified the journey of transition that the organization was now required to make.

Leave behind	Achieve
Top-down management	Shared decision making
Reliance on rules and regulations	Own quality standards
Close supervision	Team-working
Paper-based communication	Visible management
Inequality	Employee development

RESISTANCE

One of the essential issues outlined in our gap model was the need to change the current management style away from being policy- and rule-driven towards individual empowerment, visible management and team activities. This could upset the bureaucratic mindset, where allowing differences at a local level would be seen to be inconsistent with order and planning. Team-working could prove problematic for supervisors, as they currently lacked experience to work in this way, tending to make all the decisions at shop floor level and to discourage participation. The workforce may be confused by leaders who ask for their opinions and conclude that they don't know their job!

To help overcome that resistance, we decided to adopt a total quality Management (TQM) approach and because our business success was highly dependent upon the actions of our workforce, we chose to aim the organization towards the Investors in People (IIP) award. It was felt that this would give direction to the change process and create the milestones needed to help keep it on track. Involvement with IIP would reinforce the idea among employees that change was happening in other organizations in the country, thus removing the potential criticism that change was only a problem for Sandwell. Working towards the achievement of an award would also create interest and enable employees to see that their organization was moving with the times. By becoming involved with a national initiative we found that we gained the support and involvement of the local TEC and the supply of its professionally produced literature.

The use of the IIP process eased the next step, that of allocating responsibility, and the development and implementation of our changes. One of its most powerful attributes was that it provided a vehicle upon which to consider the whole issue of change. It legitimized the discussion so that it was publicly acceptable to discuss change, and thus drew people into the debate who may have felt uncomfortable in being critical of the current management practices. Argyris (1990) referred to this issue of 'when people can't start to talk about it – feeling that counter-rational behaviour is undesirable – as a form of resistance to change – which needs to be addressed and overcome'.

ALLOCATION OF RESPONSIBILITY

This was achieved in two ways: first via the IIP formal commitment; second, the main aims of our change programme were included in the organization's business plan. That plan set out the values and beliefs of the organization, and indicated that each manager was responsible for introducing those desired values and beliefs into their service area. A synopsis of the plan, which stated that they were all responsible for playing their part in supporting the desired change process was circulated to every employee.

DEVELOPING A STRATEGY – THE STEP CHANGE PLANS

The main stages required to implement the change process were based on task, group and individual needs, with teamwork training helping to launch the concept of group needs. The organizational skill development phase involved training programmes being presented for individuals, following a skills audit. Service planning addressed task needs.

In order to achieve the main strategy of the step change plan, I felt there would need to be two supporting strategies, one based on developing service planning within each service group, and the other on developing management and supervisory skills to national standards. These two supporting strategies were thus implemented to coincide with the main strategy, and Figure 8.1 gives an overview of these step change plans headed by the main strategy, supported by the HR development and OD strategy. All three plans are chronological if viewed vertically, so, for example, during the pilot development of the business plan (step 3, main strategy) we also relocated the training unit (step 1, supporting HR development strategy), and immediately commenced the learning to learn process via the health and safety training programme (step 1, supporting OD strategy).

THE BRITISH QUALITY FOUNDATION EXCELLENCE MODEL©

In 1998, to further enhance the organizational development process in readiness for Best Value, Contract Services formally adopted the British Quality Foundation (BQF) Excellence Model. A sample audit of the whole organization was conducted to determine areas for improvement against the model's nationally based standards. This had been developed by myself and 14 managers, including the most senior attending training to become qualified assessors, and the completion of appropriate action plans for inclusion in the team-based business planning process. This has further legitimized the concept of continuous improvement, which I considered to be a key success factor in a local authority keen to embrace effective change.

MONITORING

Managers, together with the chairs of focus groups, met on a regular monthly basis. Their meetings, which proved to be highly effective, were used to provide up-to-date information, check on progress, provide the opportunity to debate change interventions, and help to generate ideas for improvements.

Contract Services has also introduced performance management indicators in all service areas. They are, however, still in the development phase, and it remains to be seen what their true impact will be.

DID WE ACHIEVE EFFECTIVE CHANGE?

Overall, the four-year change programme has been a commercial success. Employee turnover is very low, with virtually all contracts being won against outside competition. Positive news articles regularly appear in the press. By 1996/7, the department returned an annual profit of over £1.0 million. Although four years sounds a long time, in change terms it is not. Consequently, the new culture may not yet be deeply embedded in the organization.

As a change agent, one is constantly aware that without a committed and determined managing director, and the support of senior management, the whole process could fail. Having a member of the strategic management team as lead officer for IIP was a critical success factor.

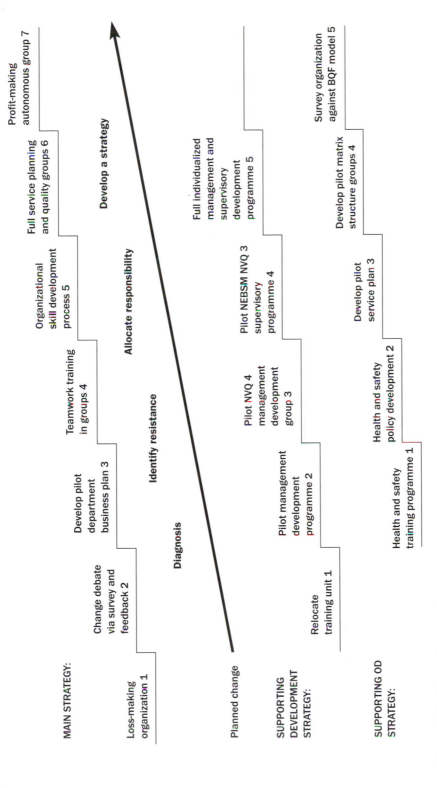

Figure 8.1 Step change plan

I believe we have achieved the concept of employee development linked to business needs. One of our most successful approaches was the methodology of commencing the leadership development process with the middle manager group, then spreading down to supervisory level, laterally to other managers and upward to the senior management group. I believe this proved to be both quicker and more effective than the more conventional top-down or bottom-up approaches.

Team-working has improved, along with increased communication, by the use of team briefings and an in-house magazine. Management is certainly more visible and approachable. By a wider input to service planning, we have achieved a degree of setting our own quality standards. I am less convinced that shared decision making has been possible on important issues, though senior management's decisions benefit from a greater input from all levels in the organization.

Somewhere along the way, I think, some managers and supervisors did lose sight of why we needed to change in the first place, which was to provide a more effective service. The achievement of the IIP award became more than a vehicle for change; in their minds, using the words of Gaddis (1997), it may have become 'a substitute for the demanding task of developing a true strategic direction for the firm – a device for pulling together warring factions within a company around an attractive future prospect'.

I believe the overall organizational development concept inherent in the BQF excellence model, linked to a team-based and informed business planning process, has and will continue to play a more effective role in establishing and regenerating the required strategy than a straightforward reliance upon the IIP methodology. A BQF-style approach will prove to be beneficial as local authorities enter the uncharted waters of Best Value as a replacement for CCT, since it causes an organization to challenge the complex areas of processes, resources, customer satisfaction and business results. It demands attention to the vital areas of policy and strategy as a driver for change. The greatest threat to the BQF model is that the scientific approach, inherent in its method, challenges and will continue to challenge the power and style of any management based on hierarchy.

There are very real signs that participation in change exists at management and supervisory level, although the employees who carry out practical tasks have tended to lack involvement. Involvement of all employees on an equal basis may emerge as more of a reality when legislation surrounding single-status working in local authorities begins to take effect over the next few years.

Perhaps it is unrealistic to expect all employees to simply accept and adapt to the change process. Traditionally, good manual workers have maintained a culture based upon fierce independence and hard work. However, I feel that our front-line workers should and would readily become more involved in providing excellent feedback from our clients and customers, with whom they have regular daily contact. This feedback loop would, as Pascal (1990) suggests, enable us to continuously scan the environment and 'pay attention to small changes, and the weak signals they send, before the organization is swamped by major consequences'.

PERCEPTION AND ITS INFLUENCE ON THE PROCESS OF CHANGE

Despite the claim that a total quality management (TQM) methodology should produce a shared and fully understood vision of the future, my action research in Contract Services indicates that the direction, emphasis and speed of change at Contract Services is driven from several directions (see Figure 8.2), what the advocates of chaos theory would describe as 'attractors', the scale of which are determined by the paradigm of the individual and their perception of the organization. Despite our attempt at planned change, there is still an unresolved cultural tension between those drawn by political influence at a local and national level and those influenced by direct customer contact. It is clear that while some enjoy, and wish to retain, the freedom of decision making based on their perception of power and influence, a number of influential employees are drawn to standards-based methods, by the use of performance indicators, to steer and control the pace of that change.

I do not believe that the effects of these perceptions have been sufficiently well explored within TQM methodology. I believe that changing overt and covert influence of the four attractors outlined in the model will continue to have a profound effect upon both the acceptability and longevity of change programmes, and on change agents working in public sector organizations. If one accepts the argument that 'successful organizations operate in states of bounded instability' (Stacey 1996) then the change agents' interventions designed to constantly identify and rebalance those four attractors, within public sector organizations, may prove to be critical actions in achieving that productive zone.

Given all the challenges that are to come in the politically charged arena of local government and contract service organizations in particular, in which there can be no guarantee of survival, managers and change agents must continue working together to develop and implement proactive change programmes.

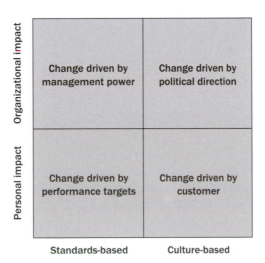

Figure 8.2 The influence of perception on change – own model

References

Argyris, C. (1990), *Overcoming Organisational Defences*. Allyn and Bacon.

British Quality Foundation Assessor Manual (1996). British Quality Foundation and European Foundation for Quality Management.

French, W.L. and Bell, C.H. (1994), *Organisational Development*. London: Prentice Hall.

Gaddis, P. (1997), Strategy under attack. *Journal of Long Range Planning*, 30(1).

Local Government Management Board (1998), *Achieving Success*. LGMB.

Pascal, R. (1990), *Managing on the Edge*. Penguin.

Stacey, R. (1996), *Strategic Management and Organisational Dynamics*. London: Pitman.

Stewart, J. (1996), *Managing Change through Training and Development*. London: Kogan Page.

Facilitating change within a network of training organizations in the West Midlands

Chris Luty

BACKGROUND

Operating in the West Midlands, the Training Suppliers Network is perhaps best described as a consortium of locally based training organizations, each offering a range of, in the main, government-funded training programmes sponsored by the local Training and Enterprise Council (TEC).

The network has existed informally for a number of years, mainly as a forum where training organizations were able to raise pertinent issues with the local TEC. In more recent years, a more formal organization has evolved, particularly in 1994 with the appointment of myself as development manager, supplemented with a further staff member in 1995.

At this stage the relationship that existed between the various training suppliers and their main funding agent, the local TEC, was once described as having 'room for improvement'. A key area of concern for both TEC and suppliers was the virtual total reliance by suppliers on the public funds provided by the TEC. This created a threat not only for suppliers in terms of reduction of available funds and the activity required to access these, but also this in turn had a weakening effect on the overall local TEC supplier base, thus reducing the ability of the TEC to meet its own performance targets.

Therefore, my role was given the primary brief of examining the relationship between training suppliers and the TEC, and identifying a strategy to reduce this total reliance on TEC funds.

RESEARCH METHODOLOGY

The methodology I selected to undertake this particular piece of research could be summarized simply in three distinct stages:

- Initial data collection from training suppliers in relation to their existing portfolio of services, income generated from private and public sources, and general attitude towards developing into more commercially focused organizations.
- Secondary data collection from interviews with selected organizations, key staff members in the local TEC, and any other potentially influential agencies.
- The final stage involved the collection and analysis of data, and the establishment of a joint working group to devise a detailed strategy and action plan to increase the commercial income of local training organizations.

Underpinning this approach was an awareness of the volume and variety of any 'soft data' that may be collected during each stage, and an acute awareness of the 'political' nature and sensitivities that would emerge, should existing values and views be challenged.

As my own personal development had involved a degree of academic research, I was also conscious that any work undertaken would need to have a degree of academic rigour, which could add support to the outcome should the findings be called into question.

In practical terms, the research project resulted in the development of a working group, which, armed with the empirical evidence I had collected, began to look seriously at the implications of the continued erosion of public funding and the longer-term effects on the local training infrastructure. This process in turn created a number of hurdles, both politically and in terms of challenging those existing values, which, although initially considered, proved much more significant than initially anticipated.

REFLECTIONS ON PRACTICE

As with the other examples here, the overall aim of this short paper is to highlight some of my own personal experiences related to this one particular piece of research, the obstacles and barriers encountered and how, if at all, I was able to overcome these.

As I began this particular research intervention, to date my own development had involved a significant degree of academic learning, the path which many of us have followed to develop our consulting skills, understanding the many and varied interactions that exist in organizational relationships and so forth. Armed with my newly found knowledge and an existing understanding of my research subject, I felt fairly confident with the task in hand. All progressed relatively smoothly during the initial stages of the project, with the relatively straightforward steps of initial data collection and analysis. This, of course, led to some initial conclusions being drawn in relation to the existing state of my research subject (the training suppliers) and their attitudes towards potential change.

It was only when I became more deeply involved in the data collection process during the second stage that the flaws in the initial data collection became apparent. As part of the preparation for this data collection, I had devised an extensive questionnaire comprising over 60 questions, examining various aspects of the organizations including both quantitative and qualitative information. Taking this approach, I felt, would ensure a balance in the information collected and therefore create validity in the overall results. However, in practice a significant number of responses proved to be not only very time-consuming but difficult to analyse, particularly where qualitative information was sought. Upon reflection, greater emphasis and testing of the initial questionnaire would have addressed many of these problems and saved not only considerable additional effort but also provided initial results where themes and trends were more easily identifiable.

The second stage of data collection (one-to-one interviews) also provided some interesting results and further insight into my own competence as a researcher.

Armed with the findings from the first stage, I then undertook a series of interviews with senior managers and strategists from a number of training suppliers. The initial problem faced was in the selection of organizations. The initial data gathering, unsurprisingly, had indicated that some organizations had significantly stronger views on the proposed change process than others, and these were the ones chosen to form this key part of the data collection.

However, in a face-to-face situation, it became difficult to distinguish between reality and rhetoric. This meant that clear differences emerged between the initial responses to the questionnaire and those given through, sometimes, quite probing questioning. An example of this would be where an organization made quite extensive claims in terms of commercial business but had difficulty in supporting this through actual evidence.

This clearly 'blurred' my ability to arrive at clear conclusions regarding the current position of suppliers and this in itself, I felt, clouded the overall validity of any results. As a relatively new researcher, I felt that this development in the research programme would somehow affect the academic rigour of the overall findings. There was clearly a case for a degree of concern. As discussed earlier, I believed that any overall findings might at some point be challenged and would therefore need to be sufficiently rigorous in their defence. However, I now realize that possibly through my then inexperience, I was somehow trying to achieve very pure clear research results that would either prove or disprove conclusively my original hypothesis. I have now come to realize that the very nature of my research subject, and arguably ethnographic research in general, can usually only offer an indication or suggestion towards the proof or not of a particular theory, as opposed to giving a decisive concrete answer. My own experience would now suggest that the researcher who rigidly follows a preordained path in search of an absolute answer to their question, thereby discounting any peripheral data they may come across, clearly runs the risk of their work, although being academically sound, offering only very little in the way of solutions to real-life problems.

The logistics of collecting and analysing data from what in real terms was a small number of individuals and organizations proved to be considerably more time-consuming than originally planned. The original questionnaire was relatively extensive, being some 60 questions in length, seeking both qualitative and quantitative data. When originally devised, the questionnaire aimed to look at various key areas of the training suppliers' activity, aiming to identify common themes and concerns. This would then be triangulated against the views and opinions sought from other local agencies such as the TEC and Business Link.

Again during the early research planning stages, on paper at least, it appeared to be a relatively straightforward process, my main concern being whether I would be able to collect sufficient data from a wide enough source to be of use. This proved to be the simplest stage in the overall process as, due to my existing relationship with these organizations, the collection of data and, importantly, access to the decision makers was easily organized.

The initial problem faced was once the data was collected, being able to undertake some objective analysis, and hopefully to arrive at some conclusion. Before distributing the questionnaire to the research group, I had undertaken a small pilot exercise with some organizations to test out the understanding of and possible responses to the questions. This stage also proved valuable as some questions might be considered sensitive, asking as they did for comment on an organization's business strategy and commercial activities. The responses from this enabled me to revise the phrasing of a number of questions, in the hope of greater consistency in the answers that would be provided.

In practice, however, there were still several respondents who had clearly misinterpreted the meaning of certain questions, and the subsequent responses fell outside those initially anticipated. This was potentially a further area of concern in terms of rigour of information, as the overall number of organizations in the research group barely exceeded 30.

In hindsight, further work should have been undertaken on the questionnaire used, as it was a combination of open qualitative questions and more quantitative rating scale-based questions. This possibly confused the respondents, particularly where both methods were used in a single section of questions. When now compiling similar questionnaires, I tend to use either quantitative or qualitative questioning, and limit the combined use of both. This, I feel, not only leads to more consistent questioning of, and responses from, individuals but also simplifies the data analysis.

For this particular research activity, I did not use any form of database to undertake the analysis of the data, as I then believed that analysis of this relatively small sample would not involve a great deal of time. In practice, this was certainly not to be the case. The analysis not only proved to be time-consuming but also became quite confusing at times, with the variety of responses that had been made, particularly to the more qualitative questions asked. It became difficult to identify common themes in the responses, and the deliberate open questioning style in many instances led to equally open responses, which clearly offered little value in the overall analysis. There were several occasions during the many hours of data analysis that I wished I had chosen and stuck to one data collection method.

As the previous paragraphs suggest, the experience of attempting this data analysis led me to a number of conclusions, which now directly influence how I undertake similar exercises:

- It is vital to pilot the questionnaire with as many individuals as possible, listen to their feedback, revise the questions, and pilot again.

- Put yourself in the respondent's place: how would you answer the question 'Will this be of value to you in your research?'

- Make the questionnaire as simple as possible; it may be worthwhile considering two or more shorter questionnaires to cover the same areas.

- Consider at the outset how you will analyse the responses: are you looking for quantitative or qualitative information or a combination of both? How will you disentangle the many and varied answers you may receive?

My own research then moved forward into one-to-one interviews, in an attempt to support or refute any initial conclusions drawn. My experiences of the initial data gathering had left me slightly wary of this stage, and personally greater effort and planning took place before commencing.

Many researchers experience problems with an interview as a means of data collection, and true, a frequent problem is the volume of information that can be provided and the accompanying danger that the discussion may digress into interesting but peripheral areas.

These, along with concerns of how to broach potentially sensitive confidential areas, all formed part of my interview planning process. This led me to devise a series of general questions to be used mainly as an introduction to the interview, and hopefully to steer the discussion in a way that would provide useful information. Overall, this initial planning appeared to assist greatly with the structuring of the interviews and their successful outcome; it is a process that I now include in all preparations for this type of work.

After the data collection, the research continued in earnest with the next and possibly the most complex stage being the application of this information to influence the thinking of the training suppliers towards becoming more commercially focused. This short paper does not allow sufficient space to discuss in detail the various interventions and tactics I adopted in an attempt to influence these organizations. However, any individual who has attempted such a task will, I am confident, agree that thoughtful consideration has to be given about what culture may already exist in the group, and the possible impact of their existing values. In my case, this situation was further compounded by the fact that my research group in fact comprised individual organizations coming together on a voluntary basis for their own mutual benefit.

The negotiations that aimed to develop the overall change strategy took, unsurprisingly, several months and throughout this I realized that my own role was clearly evolving, from that of being initially the consultant, providing the case for change supported by research data, to that of a facilitator, encouraging participation but taking a 'back seat' during discussions.

This personal strategy was in some ways both accidental and contrived. Certainly, I believed that if these organizations were to develop a strategy that was to be both appropriate and emotionally acceptable, involvement and commitment from all was needed. However, to my surprise, in this instance the group 'formed' and 'stormed' relatively quickly and arguably became productive over a short period. Therefore, my involvement rapidly became less necessary.

My reduced involvement in the overall process, I believe, was appropriate in this situation as ownership of the problem was the real issue; however, in a situation where I had been the main change agent, this informality and 'loose' approach may have led to a loss of overall direction. I was fortunate in this situation inasmuch as although the overall aim of the change programme had been agreed, actual real objectives would only emerge through the strategy formulation. Clearly, the situation where a change agent is given a specific set of objectives to achieve from the outset may not be able to afford the same degree of flexibility in approach.

Looking back at my experiences from this stage of the programme, I am able to offer the following conclusions:

■ A balance needs to be struck in research interviews between questions that are highly structured and seek clearly defined responses, and broader, more general questions.

■ Access to the right decision makers is vital but not always guaranteed. Often the political skills of the researcher are put to the test in seeking out key people.

■ Expect your role as the researcher to evolve during the programme, not only from the additional experience gained but also from others' expectations of your function.

■ Try to keep a balanced perspective throughout a possibly extended process. Constantly review and evaluate the changing situation and your contribution towards the final goal.

Implementing *kaizen* in the care sector

Julie Knowles

'*Kaizen*' is one of the most commonly used words in Japan. If it is broken down and translated, '*kai*' means 'change' and '*zen*' means 'good' (or 'for the better'); *kaizen* is therefore more commonly translated as 'continuous improvement'. Writers on the subject agree that it is about ongoing, incremental improvement with the emphasis on process rather than outcomes. In Japan, the lowest common denominator is 'We', whereas in the West it is 'I' (Huda 1992: 4).

In the care sector, generally, the customer is closer to the producer and there is immediate consumption at the moment of delivery, so errors can seldom be rectified. There is also a tendency in the service sector for the point of contact with the customer to be the lowest-paid employees of the organization. The importance of quality in service provision is heightened when the receivers of the service are unable to articulate their needs and desires and remain dependent on others to provide holistic care and support.

The particular service undergoing the change process is a charitable organization that provides total care and support to people with learning difficulties (formerly known as mental handicap). Care is provided in small homes in the community as opposed to the dated method of caring for people in institutions. Each home employs between eight and thirteen care workers, who are not required to have any formal qualifications or experience.

Much is left to the managers' interpretation and skill as to what they should be concentrating on in relation to employee development and customer satisfaction. The organization also relies heavily on the public perception (and misconception) of those in the care sector being caring, dedicated professionals with a vocation to give of their best to those who are in need of care and support.

I set out to implement *kaizen* in the care sector, using both a control group and an experimental group. Both groups were similar in make-up and there was no reason why one was chosen above the other.

In order to ascertain the success of the planned intervention, it was necessary to use questionnaires that measured any changes. The main changes that were hoped for with the implementation of *kaizen* were as follows:

1 To recognize the need for continuous improvement.
2 To increase individual development and team development.
3 To create job satisfaction.
4 To provide empowerment in the job.
5 To generally improve the service given to the client group.

Further criteria were used, such as a person's perception of the work that they were involved in, the commitment given to their work, the attitudes displayed in the team and client group etc. Further measures such as SWOT analysis, Belbin's (1981) team-types, Honey and Mumford's (1986) learning styles and Handy's (1976) culture questionnaire were taken.

The planned intervention was in the form of extensive training and implementation of the concepts of *kaizen* in the workplace. It was identified that the concept needed commitment to time, to process and unquestionably to education and training. It is estimated that in the nine months of the intervention the equivalent of 15 days training was provided. Eight formal training days were given to the experimental group, with extensive literature given out so that each individual could carry out further study in their own time. I worked alongside the manager in order to act as role model, mentor, trainer and change agent – too many roles and too little time!

The initial marketing of the concept received a great shock when the idea was not wholeheartedly accepted. In retrospect, the main reason for this lay in its introduction as '*kaizen*, a Japanese philosophy that will transform the way you work'. This simple statement appeared to shroud the introduction of the concept as employees' minds appeared fixed with preconceived, judgemental perceptions of the Japanese. Imaginations ran riot with predictions of '*tai chi*' being carried out, compliance to management, of longer hours, less pay and of uniform wearing! Following this, it was necessary to hold individual meetings with participants in order to quell their fears and to put the concept into clear language – as should have been done from the outset.

Prior to the intervention, the culture in the workplace was one in which innovation was welcomed and considered the means of achievement. Focus had mainly concentrated on outcomes, and the methods of achieving them had no consequence. The group worked towards overall aims and objectives; however, these were considered as achievable in isolation. That is, improvements might be recognized individually or collectively, but a nominated person or a volunteer would tackle the outcomes/process for solution. 'Teamness', therefore, had not really been encouraged and was misunderstood by the workforce, who viewed it as an individual's ability to get on with others – and to like those that he/she worked with. A blame culture also existed, which was no doubt fostered by the style of the manager but which proved to negate team members' ability to be open, honest and to communicate effectively with each other. This had a knock-on effect, in that no team members had the confidence to challenge the order of doing things or to seek methods for improvement for the people that they were working with. The clients, therefore, had developed few skills and had been denied the chance to experience new opportunities and seek new experiences. This was not due to employees' lack of skill or ability, rather the fear of upsetting the *status quo* in the team. It was important, therefore, to look in depth at the team dynamics and to concentrate time and effort into changing the perceptions and working methodology that had been in force.

The ability of the group to understand the theory and context of *kaizen* was vital for them to implement it in the workplace. It was important for me to constantly relate the theories to the everyday practicalities facing the team so that they could assimilate it into their working day.

At the beginning of each training day, a recap of the previous day took place, as well as an evaluation of the processes of improvement that were being conducted in the team. The importance of this lay in the fact that the majority of the team was not academically minded and had been away from the formal learning process for a number of years.

The training was delivered in a format aimed to enthuse the experimental group so that they recognized that continuous improvement did not mean that they were not delivering an effective service, simply that anything could be improved upon. The catchphrase that quickly started to be used by individuals was, 'that's good, but how could it be done better?' This was exciting to hear as it meant that learning and the change process were not as difficult as they could have been. After the first three days of training, a questionnaire was given to the group so that they could evaluate the learning that was taking place. The group was asked whether they required further training, which thankfully they did, as this was already woven into the fabric of the research methodology!

Revolutionary to the group was the implementation of QC circles. These were set up and used to address such issues as communication within the team, distribution of tasks, etc. Training was given to the team as to the functions of QC circles, which included role-playing quality circles.

It may appear that the group positively received the intervention and change process but, of course, this was not true. A baseline measure was identified as the need to increase empowerment in the group. The group clearly identified that, following the training, they felt able to manage their own QC circles as long as they were given the time to do so. A facilitator for each group was identified by the whole group and I provided further training to allocated facilitators as to how to carry out this role and to guide the QC circle. It soon became apparent that the experimental group did not possess the skills and abilities to go through this process without guidance. It was calculated that four QC circles with four members in each had met for a total of 36 hours and were unable to present the whole group with little more than a quick fix to a problem or an individual's solution. At this point, it became apparent that the manager needed to be a part of the QC circles in order to act as a role model. Team dissatisfaction on a large scale ensued as the team soon reverted to its blame culture – and there was one main saboteur who was instrumental in this process as she had disagreed with the concept from its initial introduction.

At this point, it was necessary to refocus the group and to concentrate on the team and communication elements of _kaizen_. The next training day became quite fraught as the saboteur appeared to have gained supporters and divided the team. It was therefore decided to postpone training days for a while and to form QC circles that were assigned to a particular objective of the organization in order that each QC circle concentrated directly on that objective. I chose and mentored the QC circle members and provided extensive training to the manager. The saboteur was included in a particular group that was made up of team members who were considered strong personalities.

While the above actions were positive for the intervention, there remained a constant obstacle in the form of the team member who refused to acknowledge the progress. In order for the team to continue working with *kaizen* after the research had finished, an extreme measure was taken to remove the person from the team in favour of someone who had ideas that were commensurate with the rest of the team.

While these actions were severe, and its effect on the change process was taken into account, it was felt more important that *kaizen* continued to be used in the group after the trial. It was also recognized that the ongoing, gradual nature of *kaizen* would inevitably mean that the intervention would not be able to measure enormous changes, as this was unfamiliar to *kaizen*. Training days were resumed after two months of instability in the team, whereby aims and objectives were redefined, evaluations took place and the way forward was discussed. The focus on the client group proved successful, as it was difficult for the group to disagree on improvements and change that had a recognized value base – for example, the need for clients to be involved in decision making in their daily life. The fundamental reason as to why objections proved difficult is that those initially chosen not only formed part of the organization's objective but, more importantly, formed the basis of the contractual agreement for the provision of care between the charity and the purchasing bodies (the external customer).

Included in the intervention were training and opportunities for the team which were peripheral to *kaizen* and its concepts. The idea was to increase each person's recognition of the need for continuous learning and hopefully to increase their job satisfaction by doing this alongside *kaizen*. Training in the area of learning difficulties was given and funding provided for employees to attend external courses and gain recognized qualifications, such as short courses with the Open University and the Certificate in Social Care. National Vocational Qualifications were also made available, and several employees took the advantage to take on further study. Despite the above interventions taking place, it appeared that one of the fundamental motivating factors for the team was the fact that myself and the manager conducted training days at weekends (so that the work being done with the clients would be least disrupted). Evening meetings with staff were also arranged. The dedication to *kaizen* also seemed to increase the willingness in the group to learn more than would have been expected.

EVALUATION

There have been some improvements in the experimental group; however, the need to concentrate on fundamentals such as communication and team-working slowed the process down considerably. The manager went through an enormous change process in order to enable the concept to be tested. Much philosophizing has taken place over how overwhelming commitment is sustained as it requires an enormous commitment to time, tenacity and constant enthusiasm from the manager.

It may well be the case with the experimental group that they do it because they are told to do it. At present, the dilemma over the management style and the staff's ability to take on board a radical concept is at the forefront of the change. It is not in question whether there is a lack of belief in whether *kaizen* can be implemented in the care sector; it can be and it should be. It is dependent, rather, on the ability of both management and employees to adapt to a style that is supposedly more empowering, democratic and cross-functional. If I were to carry out the research again, I would determine the culture and management/leadership style before attempting to introduce *kaizen*. A lot of time was spent in this area, which meant that the principles of *kaizen* were not fully implemented.

I still have a great belief that *kaizen* could and should work in the care sector. However, as I was not a working member of the group the enthusiasm soon dwindled after my departure. My role as change agent proved difficult as the manager was unable to sustain motivation without my continuous support and guidance. Perhaps if I had worked much more in depth with the manager before even thinking about implementing *kaizen* it could have been more successful. The manager could, therefore, have taken the role of change agent, with me acting solely as trainer and mentor for him.

Team members were given their own pocket-sized summary of the actions needed in order for the change process to continue, entitled 'In the quest for improvement, you cannot TREK alone':

1 Teamwork – working together with the same aims and values, with honesty, integrity and respect.

2 Responsibility – not 'passing the buck' if you have the ability to do something, only if you do not.

3 Evaluating – how and why we do something is as important as achieving.

4 *Kaizen* – a quest for continuous improvement in self and in the team for the good of the clients.

I hope that every now and again team members take out their card, read it and act upon it.

References

Belbin, R.M. (1981), *Management Teams – Why They Succeed or Fail*. Butterworth-Heinemann.

Handy, C. (1976), *Understanding Organizations*. Penguin Books.

Honey, P. and Mumford, A. (1986), *Learning Styles Questionnaire*. Peter Honey.

Huda, F. (1992), *Kaizen: The Understanding and Application of Continuous Improvement*. Technical Communications (Publishing) Ltd.

Imai, M. (1986), *Kaizen: The Key to Japan's Competitive Success*. McGraw-Hill.

Macdonald, J. (1994), *But We Are Different … Quality for the Service Sector*. Management Books 2000 Ltd.

Robson, M. (1984), *Quality Circles in Action*. Gower Publishing Ltd.

A client–consultant assignment within a precision components manufacturing organization

Prudence Clarke

BACKGROUND AND INTRODUCTION

The subject of this particular case is anonymous to protect the sensitivities of those involved. The case revolves around two separate plants, in different parts of the Midlands (we shall call them Plants 1 and 2), with seemingly similar histories in terms of organizational structure and culture which can be compared when looking at the inputs and outcomes of a period of change. The organization 'enjoyed a reputation for precision production of close tolerance components with a consistently high quality', with a worldwide reputation.

The overall organization this reflection is based upon has been going through continual change whereby two (similar) plants have been acquired and merged by another organization we shall refer to as 'the Group'. The company was aiming to 'gain competitive advantage through service differentiation'; a new managing director had been appointed who, in turn, appointed an executive management team with two operations directors to head up each plant. New management styles emerged (changing from 'command and control' to flexible, flatter organizations with more individual responsibility) and there was much technological investment and change.

The problems encountered to date in the organization revolved around the new style of management, which had been implemented without accounting for the effect the changes would have on individuals. More specifically, those used to 'command and control' were not necessarily equipped to take on extra responsibility for decision making, while mature, relegated managers lost confidence and the discretion to make decisions. Furthermore, the investment in technology did not automatically achieve greater cell manufacture.

This dichotomy and conflict is illustrated in Figure 8.3 (which was developed by Annie Hollings, IPD tutor at Staffordshire University and adapted for this case history).

THE CONSULTANT'S ROLE

My relationship with the client organization began through an approach from the managing director of both plants. He had previous knowledge of a particularly successful project undertaken for a competitor company in the same industry. His request focused on the delivery of a personal development programme and thus my role as the external consultant was fundamentally one to 'develop and deliver a personal development programme for both plants' personal assistants to support the introduction of 'good working practices'. It was felt that this would address some of the fundamental organizational issues and influence the ongoing strategic implementation.

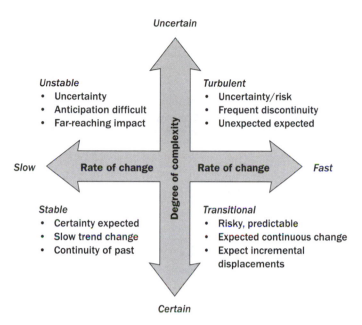

Figure 8.3

THE MAIN INTERVENTION

Intervention at this stage, on reflection, proved to challenge and test my own consultancy skills, although it appeared at that time to be an ideal opportunity to facilitate organizational development through internal change agents, using process consultation principles. The development philosophy I chose to use at the time is outlined in Figure 8.4 and is one I created specifically for the client(s) after undertaking an initial diagnosis. The internal change agents (personal assistants) were to assist their managers in making management choices to bring about 'good working practice' principles in both plants: ultimately to influence, affect and improve strategic and operational management decision making, interpersonal employee relationships, focusing on the Group's expectations of business achievement.

In retrospect, I realized I had conceptually followed McCalman and Paton's (1992) five-step process of planned change, which moves through specific phases as outlined below.

1 *Recognition by senior management that there is a need for change in the organization.* It was accepted by the managing director that the fundamental employment issues were not in place, but not necessarily accepted by the operations director and management team of Plant 1, who viewed the whole exercise as an intrusion into their management authority and on their operational discretion.

2 *Establishment of a change relationship.* The client–consultant relationship was, without a doubt, voluntary and fully accepted by the personal assistants, who

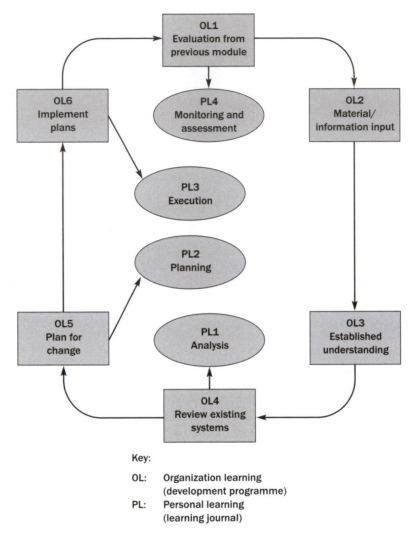

Figure 8.4 Learning cycles

have subsequently been promoted to human resource administrators (HRAs). The relationship between the internal change agents (the HRAs) and the executive management team when working with Plant 2 (EMT2) was more successful in comparison with the lack of cohesiveness in the HRA relationship between Plant 1 and the executive management team (EMT1).

3 *Movement towards the desired change by the organization and its members.* Progress required a continual reinforcement of the same message and values to be gained through the change process – again Plant 2 was far more receptive than Plant 1.

4 *Stabilizing the changes in the organization.* Winning the management and cell leaders over to a more equitable and consistent working pattern and behaviour is now continuously improving, providing a coherent set of employment practice

principles in Plant 2 and an integral part of business operation. Plant 1, however, needed further support.

5 *Allowing the change agent to move on.* The recently promoted HRA in Plant 2 was subsequently promoted to human resource manager (HRM) by gaining considerable credence and recognition. The Plant 1 HRA unfortunately struggled to gain the same recognition and acceptability as an instigator of change.

OTHER INTERVENTIONS

There were a series of further interventions, part of the executive management team's strategy, initiated to bring about a transformational 'change' in operations leading to achievement of the company's mission. These are explained by way of describing the environment, as these interventions could at any one time have impacted upon the outcomes of those highlighted above.

In both Plants 1 and 2 the Investors in People standard was implemented. The organization learned through a series of cross-functional workshops as to what had been gained but also looked forward to setting realistic goals to achieve in the future. Performance appraisal was introduced by another external provider, who initiated this via a two-day programme to develop the skills of line managers, although the delays in ongoing support subsequent to the workshops led to confused priorities in the plants. This system took more than a year to complete its first cycle; and in Plant 1, although the appraisal process was undertaken, no training and development outcomes from this were realized. There was, after this, a general acceptance that the performance appraisal system needed re-evaluating, possible redevelopment and a proper relaunch in order to gain both line management's and employees' understanding of its real purpose and value.

I implemented a personal development programme for the personal assistants, whose learning objectives were to develop best employment practices, improve communication, increase managers' knowledge, control training and development activities, and streamline administrative systems to work towards making a valuable input into the HRM/D strategy. Action learning principles were fundamental to this programme, identifying and taking responsibility for the changes in the workplace, which could be attributed to the personal assistants. One of the outcomes of this was the increased confidence in these personal assistants, and their ability to gain subsequent promotions as a recognition of their effective interventions from this programme.

Kaizen events were set up in Plant 1 and initially developed by on-site Japanese consultants and further developed by internal trainers. The commitment to these events was seen as a business priority, and considerable investment in capital equipment, reorganization of cells, and employee training time were freely given. Effectiveness of training here was seen as the achievement of tangible measures of performance. Having walked around the plants during and after these events, I was impressed with these major changes. The time and financial resources in moving machines around to improve product throughput within time scale was inspirational.

These, among others, were the major interventions; during my consultancy relationship there were many other initiatives in both plants, not least management development training and a world-class manufacturing programme. The impact and results, however, do not appear to have been effective and line managers were known to use innate, or to develop fairly swiftly, creative avoidance skills!

REFLECTION – WHAT WAS GOING WRONG

Overall, the executive and management team's mindsets were still processual rather than humanistic. The managing director spent considerable time with key employees in workshops to identify what they believed was necessary in order to develop continuous improvement concepts in the plant. Such methodology brought about positive results in Plant 2; nonetheless, the managing director continued to complain about the 'blue coat' mentality in Plant 1. This he experienced from key employees (team leaders) who, while at learning forums, were co-operative and positive but, when they returned to their workplace, tended to put on their 'blue jackets' and return to their old comfort zones. Schein's theory on group traditions in leadership style (Schein and Bennis 1965) is particularly interesting when reflecting on these team leaders and raises the question of whether group norms and traditions in an established group are stronger than the will of a new leader. Further, 'as old work groups are disbanded and new ones are formed, individuals find they have to learn not just new tasks but also how to interact with new people and how to deal with new group purpose' (Schein 1988). The drastic and radical change that had taken place appeared to have been taken for granted by the executive management team. There had been considerable investment in developing training programmes, for example for cell team leaders, which had appeared to address the extrinsic elements of development. The programmes had not however addressed their intrinsic needs brought about by the impact of radical change on the elevated team leaders – hence the lack of sustained behavioural change and reversion to 'the blue jacket' mindset. In general terms this could be attributed to the overall lack of behavioural change anticipated from the other programmes.

It seems that initiatives such as the skills training learning objectives tended to focus on how to 'do' rather than how to 'think'. The management development programme thus did not address fundamental human resource management responsibilities. Equally, other problems arose in the appraisal programme, which was not addressing the purpose and value of why the company decided to use an appraisal system; this delayed the system being used as it was not clearly understood, until it became almost valueless.

The Investors in People standard focused on finding the evidence rather than seeking the benefits. An all-pervasive organizational understanding of the objectives behind committing to the Investors in People standard was vital; it was developed initially into a series of workshops in both plants with all line managers and 'cell' team leaders and, as mentioned before, was heavily biased towards their human resource responsibilities. Evaluation of all these events was positive and gave the impetus to go forward with the introduction of changes in operation, primarily based around sharing and understanding the business objectives, communicating the results through different media and methods, such as performance appraisal and resultant training and development activities. Plant 2 in this case carried out its action plan but Plant 1 did not, switching and changing between the different initiatives that made up the overall Investors in People plan, thus losing continuity and commitment.

There was a gap here between the organizational rhetoric and reality. In the Group's annual report, under its 'people' section, it stated 'there are some 7000 people working for Group 'x' in 16 countries … this year's excellent results would have been impossible without their loyalty, diligence and skill … we are deeply grateful to them all and will continue with all our efforts to be good employers.' However, this did not translate effectively within the organization, or fit with their short-term approach to change and policies.

Finally, looking overall at the interventions, there was no doubt that there was an 'initiative saturation' which, for example, in Plant 1 ultimately ran amok. The organization, since merging, had changed from being paternalistic to tough, turbulent and unpredictable. Plant 2's managers were, however, much more receptive to the changes; effective benchmarking against, for example, the Investors in People standard, has subsequently gained them benefits.

In reflecting on my own approaches and the implementation of good working practices with the personal assistants, I worked towards 'helping an organization to do its own diagnosis and to solve its problems' (Schein 1987). Throughout my work, I strived to harness the intelligence in the company, which had not always been recognized or appreciated, rather than be influenced by an imposed set of solutions. The panacea mentality and quick fixes demanded by the company executive management team did not easily 'fit' with my own philosophy, despite having discussed and agreed methodologies during the contracting stage.

Previous mention has been made of action learning principles, that of 'doing the thing' and not relying on 'abstract theories' (Revans 1980). As a method, the learning objectives used in the training programme for the personal assistants were less structured and more empirical, relying upon their 'change process' being feasible (in line with the organization's vision and strategy) and further based upon their own knowledge and understanding of the two plants. This enabled the personal assistants to fully utilize their natural intelligence, unleash their potential and creativity, leading to considerable building of confidence. They were able to use the information input from the external facilitator and in turn reflect upon their 'change' and influencing process in a prepared learning diary completed in partnership with their on-site mentors. In summary, this learning cycle aimed to be time-effective, focused and, most importantly, purposeful. It also took into account the results of Honey and Mumford's learning-style questionnaires (1986) completed by the personal assistants at the initial programme stage. In reviewing my role in this, during the early stages of the personal assistant development programme, we drew up a 'psychological 2 – 1 contract' between the client and myself (the consultant) which was solid and based upon a mutual respect for each other's competence, skills, knowledge and experience. The development process was focused, self-driven and created a high degree of dynamic change in a relatively short period in Plant 2. Plant 1's personal assistant experienced a much rougher ride and required exhaustive on-site and telephone support.

Reflection and learning on this showed a lack of awareness of the difference between Plants 1 and 2. The executive management team, when working with Plant 2 via the newly appointed dynamic and driven operations director, were receptive and willing to commit to the changes, recognized the value and support it would afford them in their management responsibilities and involved themselves fully in the change process. When working with Plant 1, the executive management team saw the intervention as intrusive upon their discretion and autonomy to manage confrontational to *laissez-faire* management styles; to a degree, certain managers felt threatened and did not want practices and procedures and resultant behaviours which might disrupt their established norms. Resistance and lack of co-operation were evident here.

In conclusion, further research should have been undertaken to gain a better understanding of overt and covert governing values permeating Plants 1 and 2. In retrospect, if I had approached the assignment initially with more of an emphasis on addressing 'cultural' change, particularly in Plant 1, then the advice given may have gained validity in the short rather than long term, and conversely certain changes achieved in the short term could have been self- sustaining in the longer term.

Inheriting other consultants' previous mistakes is also not an ideal scenario upon which to build further development and change. For me, the quick-fix mentality, avoiding the questioning of fundamental issues and stop/start of the many interventions, created constant client and consultant frustration. The organization's need for my own intervention dissolved confusingly into the 'expert' and 'doctor–patient' consultancy practices, which further escalated when other consultants were approached with the same organizational problems.

WHAT OF THE FUTURE CLIENT–CONSULTANT RELATIONSHIP?

I feel I can confidently 'exit' the relationship with Plant 2 – particularly as the newly appointed human resource administrator was again promoted to human resource manager. However, what should my next steps be with Plant 1? To continue to force the issue, to take a back seat for a while, to facilitate organizational learning, or to exit the relationship?

References

Honey, P. and Mumford, A. (1986), *Learning Styles Questionnaire: Manual of Learning Styles and Using your Learning Styles*, 2nd edn.

McCalman, J. and Paton, R.A. (1992), *Change Management*. Paul Chapman.

Revans, R.W. (1980), *Action Learning – New Techniques for Management*. Bland and Briggs.

Schein, E.H. (1987), *Process Consultation Volume 1*, OD Series, 2nd edn. Addison-Wesley.

Schein, E.H. (1988), *Organisational Psychology*, 3rd edn.

Schein, E.H. and Bennis, W.G. (1965), *Personal and Organisational Change Through Group Methods*. John Wiley & Sons Inc.

Organizational development processes and interventions

Ken Ash (editor)

INTRODUCTION

The theme of this chapter covers the organizational development (OD) process and interventions. It deals with practical outcomes of 'change' interventions and the required overt and covert and sometimes subtle and unconscious processes used to move organizations forward in their strategic approach to people development.

The first reflection covers the NHS, which, like most organizations, is under pressure to deliver with more and more openness expected for accountability. The NHS has undergone a number of reforms over the years, including the last Conservative government-led 'purchaser–provider' split, which was a large reorganization.

A proposed 'structure reorganization' in a particular NHS trust is the focus of this reflective piece of writing. Jane Keep, who has worked in the health service sector for many years, explains her role as the hired external consultant for this project. From the early stages of the project she realized her role would very much be that of the 'process facilitator'. The OD issues in this case are complex but not uncommon. Her reflections, both professional and personal, are interesting, honest and will be of great benefit to anyone undertaking a similar type of project.

The final outcome has an interesting twist. Jane Keep's reflections on the key issues leading to the final decision would make a well-structured brief by which to work when embarking on such an intervention. Understanding that the task ahead is not going to be easy is worth knowing, and making sense of the situation is the most important aspect of change, even if the outcome of this sense making is that it is all a complete paradox.

The second reflection concerns itself with a 'business leaders programme' (BLP) and how it was used to effect change and development at British Aerospace. Vince McGregor, a member of the HRD team at British Aerospace Aerostructures, Prestwick, gives his experience and reflective views of this programme and the wider more comprehensive business executive skills training initiative, of which the BLP was a part.

The BLP was a senior management training programme which included time spent on the principle that 'by understanding our own individual behaviour this can help us eventually to change others'. The trigger for the OD initiative was British Aerospace Plc deciding to bring all its aerostructures under one umbrella of a single business organization. A change team was set up to move the business toward being world class. Vince McGregor's role was not only within the HRD team, because the project also involved external engineering business consultants and a team made up of a director and two senior managers from the aerostructure business.

Through this reflection readers will be able to further consolidate their understanding of change and pick up on some interesting points regarding interventions, in particular how the risks can be shared. Also, from his experience, this change agent gives an honest comment on where he believes the power of change lies.

The third reflection describes the process and outcome of a change initiative in a manufacturing environment that fostered an established paternalistic management style. The company in question was a privately owned family business, employing approximately 1800 people. Following a two-year management consultancy project driven and carried out by an external team of consultants, I as the company's internal 'trainer' (later to become 'change agent') was tasked to carry forward a large-scale team-working initiative set out by the now outgoing consultants.

This case history covers the questions that should have been asked at the outset but were not, and also through this reflection a clear route has been laid down for others in similar situations to follow, both within the organization and outside. In it I indicate where theory matches practice (and where it does not). I also ask the questions, with reasonable answers, such as if teamworking is seen as a positive approach, why does it on so many occasions and in so many organizations fall into disrepute and lose its value?

The reflection describes the positive factors and the impeding factors which brought about this company's progress to understanding how to sustain the value of team-working. This case study reminds readers that even when managers are aware of the theory and practice of organizational change, to succumb to the temptation of the quick fix or the simple solution may lead only to 'short-termism', with no sustaining foundation.

The next reflection follows an approach whereby management and change theory is eagerly sought to help create a strategy for business development. Chris Newis, one of six development workers, was tasked to determine such a strategy for a not-for-profit organization. His research led him to discover all the stages required, from the importance of a mission statement through to how to evaluate a strategy following implementation. He points out that even if there are weaknesses in the strategy (which may be seen as being unsuccessful) 'there are no failures, only learning'.

This reflection also looks at alternative theory which could have been used. His honest conclusions will help readers to learn from his experience – in particular, when pointing out a fundamental flaw in his approach, which was 'not understanding the complexities of the processes and the nature of change'. Interestingly, this piece of work may lead us to the discovery that all conclusions are transitory in their nature as we struggle to make sense of our organizational lives.

The last reflection in this section of studies looks at a change strategy for an organization after it is 'freed' from being part of a larger corporate entity. It would appear that this change allowed the management to focus on the relevant business issues and in particular the training requirements needed to underpin service to sales, the customer and profitability. Peter Grice explains how the 'broad brush' approach set by 'head office' can divert energies away from the main aim of the business. Basically, it is another example where the blanket approach to training (we are all going to have some of the corporate training whether we need it or not) falls short of being effective or meaningful.

He goes on to emphasize the premise that 'organizations learn through individuals who learn'; there is no guarantee that this will happen, but without the individual learning the organization definitely will not.

Peter's reflection looks at the ideology of the 'learning organization' and pulls out some key lessons to be observed. He also points out a number of approaches that should be avoided, such as 'promoting values before people experience them as this can be counter-productive'. He closes his reflection with the quote that speaks for all the reflections in this section and indeed the book, which is the trite but true comment that 'learning must be seen as a journey and not a destination'.

To restructure or not? Reflections on an NHS healthcare trust

Jane Keep

CONTEXT

The NHS as an 'organization'

The NHS context is one of continuous change. Politically driven, altruistic, service based, having been part of British society for over 50 years, providing healthcare services – 'free at the point of delivery' – known by all, used by many. Being a public service it is under constant scrutiny for higher levels of efficiency, increased effectiveness, continuously improving levels of quality, openness and accountability, with the primary focus on patient care.

Espoused NHS values centre on efficiency and value for (tax-payers') money; fairness and equality not only in service delivery but also in how those providing the services are treated; flexibility to meet patients' needs with flexible employment practices; working in partnership, collaboratively between health and social services, between professions, and within teams; and striving for excellence in service quality.

There are over 42 different professional staff groups, with continued evidence of tribalism between some of them, and nearly one million staff working in the NHS. It is a service that has been faced with many reorganizations of management of the service and how it provides care.

The 'purchaser–provider' split was previously a large reorganizing reform which, under the Conservative government, also attempted to set up more of a leadership focus to the service. This ensured that each healthcare organization, whether a health authority which 'commissions' the services from hospitals and other provider organizations, or a provider organization which would provide patient care via a hospital trust, a community trust or some form of combined healthcare trust, was led by a board consisting of executives and non-executives.

The Labour government has continued with further 'reforms' through a continuous stream of White and Green Papers, directives and guidelines across the UK. The need for effective boards and governance of healthcare organizations has been advocated, in addition to which a search for the 'new managerialism' in the NHS is now in full swing. Unsurprisingly, yet exhaustingly, another round of service-wide reconfigurations and organizational mergers continues, with a view that these will improve services to patients in a cost-effective manner, breaking down the barriers between health and social care.

Healthcare organizations face a constant challenge – to continue to provide a service while reorganizing, refocusing and restructuring in response to the political, technological and societal demands. Leaders of these services are required to be visionaries, strategists, ethical compasses, politicians and organization design specialists. Those 'next in command' are required to be action-focused, task deliverers, efficient, effective, collaborative, innovative, evaluative generalists, with often a specialist string to their bow. Organizational change is one of their consistent tasks – in fact it is the only task they do: plan, manage, review, monitor and if they have time, evaluate change.

Reflections on this particular NHS trust

Each organization has its own unique local context, within the broader context, with its own board dynamic in a mixture of leaders and managers. One particular NHS trust providing community, elderly care and mental health services with over 140 premises and around 4000 staff facing these pressures had a not uncommon additional pressure. It felt it was an open organization, open to suggestions and innovative in aspects of service delivery. It faced all the normal difficulties 'network' organizations face in trying to manage, communicate with and enable staff across this myriad of premises in a wide geographical area.

More specifically, a group of doctors was dissatisfied with the level of involvement they had in managing their service, and in the management and overall direction of the trust. They requested an organizational structural review, placing a lot of internal political pressure on the board for this. They felt disenfranchised and demotivated. They were known to be 'difficult' but the service they delivered was important. The board, led by the chief executive, agreed to a review; as it had been two years since the last organizational restructure it was a particularly good time to look again at this issue.

ENGAGEMENT AND INITIAL CONTRACT

The organization engaged the services of myself, an external organizational development and change facilitator working at the time in an academic unit at a university but with many years experience of working in and around healthcare. After meeting with the chief executive to run through the issues, in addition to undertaking a brief document review (annual report, business plan, organizational structure chart and service objectives) it seemed to me that this would be a tough project, with many stakeholders. Not only were the doctors feeling disenfranchised but so were the other healthcare professionals (physiotherapists, occupational therapists, dieticians, speech therapists). The chief executive was fixated on the idea that the organization required a new structure and would be reporting back to the board on completion of this work with the outcome. He had undertaken a SWOT analysis of the current organizational structure, which was a useful start. He also had views as to the type of structure that could be moved towards.

I contracted with him to undertake the work, clarified the boundaries, stakeholders, my role and the expectations around me, and the project plan/cost for the work. I also asked whether I might face any particular problems from anyone in the trust. It became apparent that one of the directors of the trust felt that this review was his role, and that I would thus need to deal with this sensitive situation with care. At least knowing this from the start meant I was forewarned – and could prepare to be forearmed.

On return from this meeting, having read the documents to check my contextual 'facts' about the organization, I immediately went into the university library to check the literature about organizational structural reviews, particularly healthcare, and project process ideas. I also consulted a professorial colleague who was an organizational psychologist for some further ideas. I felt from this I was able to put together a framework for the process of the work. I realized I was in this case a process facilitator and reminded myself of Edgar Schein's (1987) and French and Bell's (1990) work on process consultation.

PROJECT PROCESS

It occurred to me that I was actually the process facilitator for rather a large and tricky organizational consultation process. This entailed not only gaining the views of those in the organization – particularly from each of the 'disenfranchised' groups – but it also required an element of external stakeholder views too. Thankfully, I was provided with an administrative link in the organization who was able to organize an external stakeholder focus group and a series of internal stakeholder focus groups across the trust during a couple of months.

Prior to commencing these focus groups, the board had set up a project 'steering group' led by the chief executive. This was extremely useful for me as an outside facilitator; not only did this group create many innovative ideas around organization structure and the review itself but also I was able to have an in-built evaluation/ monitoring process through them which enabled me to know at any one point whether I was on track – or indeed whether the overall project was on track. This group were for the most part very supportive. However, one member of the group was also a member of the part of the service that felt disenfranchised. He was quite dominating, moody, self-interested and very difficult at times in the group, providing me with a further 'task' within the project which was to facilitate the group dynamics of the steering group. At times these reached 'fever pitch', as this particular character tested the patience of a saint. He actually got up at one meeting, took his papers and said he wouldn't be returning – slamming the door behind him.

This was certainly challenging behaviour for me to deal with, particularly as I did not actually understand all the underlying dynamics, some of which were fairly historical. I used my professorial colleague back at the university as a sounding board for this, as his organizational psychology came in very useful.

The person who felt the role I was playing was his role was very cold when I was introduced to him briefly, so I arranged to go to see him almost immediately to get the issues out in the open. We talked and were able to understand the positions we were both in. We 'contracted' with one another as to how we would work 'together' throughout this project. This was helpful to do at this stage and reassured me, as I was very nervous about having an irate organization design specialist on my back.

To run the focus groups, the steering group and I developed three potential organizational structures in addition to using the current one as the first point of review. Each of the focus groups was focused on these structures, taking the group members through a range of questions using each of the structures as a trigger, to test their reactions and ascertain their current problems, and understand their hopes for the future.

The internal focus groups were often long and deep, with many therapists, doctors and nurses using them as quasi-counselling sessions to get 'it all off their chest'. There were also some 'difficult' moments where the dynamics were sticky as one or another's personal agenda encroached on the needs of the group as a whole. This was process facilitation with an attitude!

There was also a need for some form of 'evidence base' to the work. These people were from a range of clinical professions working towards clinical excellence, They were predominantly scientists and required 'evidence' for each suggestion rather than taking everything at face value. It meant referring to theoretical frameworks, organizational research and drawing on practice from other similar environments. It constantly meant 'proving' a point or an issue rather than just talking them through it!

The external focus group was different as the external stakeholders had different areas of concern, but provided a large amount of good strong suggestions and advice from their own perspectives as service users, commissioners and providers/suppliers to service deliverers. Written comments were also elicited from external and internal stakeholders.

PROJECT PROGRESS

Overall, during a number of months, views were gained via the consultation process from right across the organization and from external stakeholders. At certain points in the process there was pressure from the board and the project steering group to come to some conclusion as to which of the organizational structures would prove most useful for the organization. At one point, the chief executive, feeling pressured from the board, asked me to undertake a 'vote' from the organization for each of the structures.

From my own perspective, this seemed to be forcing the issue. Something else was happening throughout the consultation, and while in the beginning people were focusing on the structure as being the problem, it was becoming apparent that this may not have been the case, or the solution. I was very aware that pushing the internal stakeholders to vote on a structure was now not going to achieve the outcome the board, chief executive and project steering group were hoping for.

I did, however, call a mass meeting as the last stage of my process facilitation where 60 or so representatives from all aspects of the organization's services and professions were invited to attend – and to vote. The chief executive was waiting by his phone for the outcome. The representatives at this large meeting wouldn't vote – they had seen another 'light' and wanted to do things a different way.

They had realized by working through this intense process that organizational structure was not the issue, and indeed not the answer to their problems. Behaviour and skills were, however. They summarized their views by saying that communication and openness were poor, collaborative working was poor, team-working could be improved, and there were a raft of skills that could be improved to support these issues. They did not want to change the organizational structure. They realized it would only distract them (again) from the behavioural and skills-based issues while they blamed the structure for the inadequacies. This was a revolution.

While I was pleased we had reached this point (and had intuitively known this might be where they were heading), I had to tell the chief executive. He was completely signed up to changing the structure. I telephoned him and he was initially horrified that a new structure was not to be voted for, but that there were other aspects of organization development and change to focus on instead. But he came around, and with the help of the project steering group and the board put together an organizational change and development project as the next phase of this work. As the leader for this – 'head of change' – he appointed the person who had felt it was his place to do my role, and the next project phase commenced.

My role for the time being was complete. However, 12 months later I was asked to go back and undertake a review of progress, using the same focus groups. There was still lots to be done, but things had definitely moved on. The organization had learned from itself and its own resources a very important thing. This in itself had developed the organization and its members. Focus groups and consultations now form a regular process in managing the trust, as does evaluation, and good communication. I had learned a lot from the process too.

REFLECTIONS ON THE WHOLE PROJECT – WHAT HAD I LEARNED?

In my role as an external facilitator – process facilitating as an 'agent of change' – I found I felt very vulnerable. I was glad I had assigned myself a 'mentor' while I was undertaking the work (my professorial colleague). I was also glad to have had access to theoretical frameworks via the university library. Having time to reflect in between various parts of the project was also useful. It gave me time and space to recuperate and also allowed my own intuition to 'kick in', enabling the whole sense-making process to move on gradually for me. I realized I am not a 'quick and dirty' operator but very reflective in the way I work, needing time and space between interventions to make sense of the situation.

Contracting carefully at the outset, checking the internal organizational politics and where I might have difficulties up front, enabled me to prepare myself more than I may have done had there not been any potentially sticky issues.

Sometimes, even though you yourself as a change agent have a solution or know that the thing you are being asked to 'chase' is not the right solution, you need to enable the organization and, more importantly, the critical stakeholders to work their own way through to the conclusions – they need to see things for themselves, their own way, in their own time. This is far more valuable than telling them what they could do. It also enables sustainability when you have completed your work.

Reflecting on the process of the work itself led to both an organizational and a personal realization that involving as many stakeholders as possible is beneficial and possible. This was a form of 'organizational therapy' which turned into 'organizational counselling' and 'self-diagnosis'. The more informed and involved the stakeholders became the more enabled they were. Personal and professional agendas can dominate wider organizational issues, and these need to be uncovered as soon as is possible. 'Discussing the undiscussable' is a necessity, and good process facilitation is required for this. It is possible, it is hairy and scary, but it is worth it. It can move mountains, but debriefing is essential.

Time for involvement and consultation is important, and legitimizing this is even more important. Once the process is legitimized it is enabled to become important, gains clarity and focus – and more key support. Management is normally prescriptive, short-term and action-focused, and it finds enabling time and space to make sense of things and review them properly almost too painful; however, this is an investment as opposed to a short-term change. Investments cost time and money but usually reap more benefits at the end.

Communication needs to be continuous, to all, even the difficult aspects and the turning points. Real listening needs proving. This project gained respect early on as points of view that were given at the start were very quickly and overtly taken on board. Stakeholders could see this and realized that this process was for real.

Perhaps the largest and most profound point everyone learned was that 'moving the furniture around to improve organization effectiveness' was not the only answer to organizational problems. It was all too easy to restructure (again) and move things around, but the difficult issues, of culture and behaviour, remained and still needed tackling. 'Neat structural organizations and good management are not synonymous' (Heller 1996).

Finally, management is a paradox; managers are often managers of 'messes'. They move from one 'mess' to another. Management is prescriptive and action-focused, yet organizations, individuals and society are extremely complex – there are many paradoxes, oxymorons and conflicting issues, and there are often *no* answers to these, least of all recipes for solving everything. Realizing this early on is actually comforting! Life is an iterative process, and while you are undertaking organizational change projects everything continues to move, to iterate, to evolve.

It is tough being an organizational change agent, although I never said or felt it was easy. Being a reflective change agent helps this. Bridging the theory–practice gap with reflection can allow a change agent to move proficiently between the two worlds supporting each with the other. Reflection gives legitimate time to breathe, to intuit, to make sense. Making sense is the most important aspect of change – even if the outcome of the sense making is that it is all a complete paradox!

References

French, W. and Bell, J.R. (1990), *Organisation Development: Behavioural Science Interventions for Organisation Improvement,* 4th edn. New Jersey: Prentice Hall.

Heller, R. (1996), Resist that urge to reorganise. Heller on management. *Management Today,* January.

Schein, E. (1987), Process consultation. *Methodology,* Vol.1. Reading, Mass: Addison-Wesley.

A programme for change within one part of British Aerospace

Vince McGregor

CONTEXT

The organization and proposed change

In January 1995, British Aerospace plc decided to bring together all of its aerostructures work under the umbrella of a single business organization responsible for the work, which would be carried out at sites in Prestwick in Scotland, Chadderton in Manchester and Filton in Bristol. At the Prestwick site, 900 people were involved in this work. However, even with the formation of the aerostructures company and the benefits it would bring through economies of scale, the management at Prestwick recognized that dramatic improvements in performance were required if we were to compete with competition in America and the fast-growing threat from the Japanese, who had already captured large contracts from Boeing.

To achieve the goal of becoming 'a world-class supplier of major aerostructures components', a change team was set up to find solutions which would move the business towards being 'world-class'. The team was formed in March 1995 and included employees from all areas of the business, plus specialists from Price Waterhouse engineering consultants. The consultants brought vast knowledge and practical experience in implementing best-practice and change management techniques based on the Kawasaki production system.

The team's brief included:

- waste analysis reduction;
- review of factory layout to improve manufacturing throughput;
- review of the supplier base and policy;
- provide education, training, and support implementation of best-practice techniques (e.g. *kanban*);
- JIT;
- develop a continuous improvement mentality;
- assist in development of key performance measures;
- define and implement an integrated production team structure, moving away from the functional approach currently utilized.

This was business process re-engineering in reality and it was happening on our doorstep.

HRD INVOLVEMENT

The champions of change

Three people shared the task of championing the change process:

- the managing director of the aerostructures business (who had successfully introduced similar systems in another business),
- the site general manager, and
- a senior manager who was appointed to lead the change team.

All of these people had one thing in common – they recognized that to introduce such a major change successfully not only systems and hard skills had to be covered.

A working partnership

As part of the chosen approach HRD was asked by the change team manager to work with Price Waterhouse to produce a training programme which would cover the *soft* skills required at all levels if we were to effect a positive and permanent change. At a very early stage the crucial role of senior management was recognized. This was that:

- all the presentations to the workforce,
- all of the training on new systems,
- all of the encouragement given to everyone to begin to think differently,

    would be undone if senior management did not alter its own language and behaviours.

This was the beginning of the main push for a senior management training programme, which perhaps by good fortune or by good judgement had begun to be researched by the HRD team six months previously.

PROGRAMME CONTENT AND DESIGN

The Business Leaders programme was designed internally by the HRD function at Prestwick in partnership with the Taylor Clarke Management Consultancy based in Glasgow. It was clear from the outset that something more than traditional management training was required to prepare our managers for the incredible challenges which faced them. It was also clear from the training needs analysis (TNA) that the emphasis of the programme would have to be on the 'softer' people skills so badly needed but so badly lacking.

The programme would be 'process'-based, moving away from the 'injection' training methods which historically offered short-term euphoria but failed to add long-term value to the organization.

It was agreed to offer the programme over one year with initial planning for seven workshops and the option of an eighth covering a topic of the group's choice. Initially, only the first workshop included an overnight stay; however, given the flexibility of time, feedback sessions after dinner and the removal of the participants from the two main areas of stress, i.e. work and home, it was agreed that all workshops would include an optional overnight stay. The workshops were held off-site in a quality hotel.

The learning was action-based using current issues whenever possible (issues were not in short supply) and linked to management competencies. Following the TNA, which showed the importance of stress awareness and stress management, an interview was held with the site occupational health officer. Discussion focused on a number of recent surveys indicating the cost of stress to organizations. *Karoshi*, death from overwork, was officially registered as a fatal illness in Japan in 1989; in 1995, 65 cases were reported.

Given the level of change in our organization it was agreed to include stress management as an integral part of the programme. The management consultant working on programme design and eventually chosen as instructor/facilitator was also a fully qualified stress counsellor. The content of workshops was a mixture of Eastern and Western philosophies, moving from coaching techniques to the right-brain activities of neuro-linguistic programming.

To consolidate learning, coaching took place following workshops, normally on a one-to-one basis at the participants' work area, or where requested on a group basis to apply solution-based techniques to current issues. A model of the programme is given below as Figure 9.1.

Measuring and research instruments used

- Saville and Holdsworth 36 competency model for 360° appraisal (before and after programme);
- Cary Cooper's occupational stress indicator questionnaire;
- trainer's diary notes;
- British Aerospace employee opinion survey;
- external measures such as IIP, EFQM, CBI.

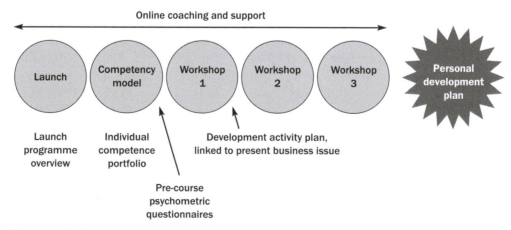

Figure 9.1 The programme model

PROCESS QUESTIONS

'Human relations' concepts necessary in allowing participants to experience Gestalt (another reason for counselling skills within the programme team, as accessing feelings can cause strain) were featured heavily on the programme. Gestalt therapy is based on the belief that a person functions as a total organism. Each person possesses positive and negative characteristics that must be 'owned up to' and permitted expression. 'People get into trouble when they become fragmented, when they do not accept their total selves basically one must come to terms with oneself must stop blocking off awareness authenticity and the like by dysfunctional behaviours' (Burnes 1992).

Gestalt field practitioners seek to help individual members of an organization to change their understanding of themselves and the situation in question, which will lead to a change in behaviour. Burnes (*ibid.*) shows three essential planks of change management:

■ the individual perspective school (of which Gestalt is part),
■ the group dynamic school,
■ the open system school.

The Business Leaders programme concentrated on the individual and recognized the need to use behaviourist theory in tandem with Gestalt; only by understanding yourself can you hope to understand others.

It is a paradox, however, that it required the development of individuals as 'role models' to allow optimum functionality in group dynamics. Burnes (*ibid.*) suggests that the rationale 'is that because people in organisations work in groups, individual behaviour must be seen, modified or changed in the light of prevailing group practices or norms "suggesting that" group behaviour is an intricate set of symbolic interactions and forces which not only affect group structures but also modify group behaviour'.

I would have to pose the question whether group dynamics change the outer self while the inner self remains unaltered. The Business Leaders programme attempted to change the inner self through Gestalt and behaviourism while using group dynamics to help with understanding and acceptance.

The open systems school sees organizations as a number of interconnected subsystems. It follows that any change to one part of the system will impact on others and ultimately the overall performance. People are subsystems in their own right. If people's behaviours change it will eventually change others until effectively the organization will change. The objective of the Business Leaders programme was to act as a catalyst for such a change to take place. Business process re-engineering created the 'hard' systems to allow things to happen, but only the people were able to effect the real change.

REFLECTIONS ON THEORY

The constant in successful change management

During the research process, before, during and after this programme, extensive examination was made of case studies involving changes in large, medium-sized and small organizations. In addition, a project was carried out to support in the first instance the theory that the Investors in People (IIP) model could be seen as one which could act as a catalyst for change in any business. Throughout all of the businesses which introduced change successfully (including some which had attempted to use it for this purpose) there was only one constant factor – a senior member of the organization (senior enough to influence major decisions) who not only had the respect and confidence of his/her peers but also the personality and communication skills to allow everyone in the organization to share his/her vision of the future. To enable everyone to *see* what it would be like, to *hear* how people would be talking about the business, to feel the satisfaction of working in this new organization, this champion of change has to be involved long enough for the change to be accepted as 'the way we do things around here'.

The role of the HRD practitioner

If the observations above are correct, questions must be raised about whether the HRD practitioner could ever be considered to be a change agent. The answer is 'yes' and a further 'yes', which must be qualified. 'Yes' if the practitioner is a senior figure in the organization who possesses the qualities noted, and 'yes' again if the practitioner can influence a senior figure to act as a champion for the proposed change. Even Hammer and Champy (1993) accept that people, not things, affect permanent and positive change.

Theory X/theory Y

McGregor's theory X/theory Y is not as far-fetched as some people make out. The majority of us are happy for things to continue with minimal change. Familiar things are comfortable things; we all have a bit of a lazy streak when we are offered alternatives because we need to expend extra effort (the malaise of British middle management is well documented). We all need someone to follow. Someone to motivate us and excite us about a change. Someone to paint the picture of the future for us because we are either afraid to do it ourselves or we cannot be bothered. We all need someone to intervene on our behalf: our agent in the process of change.

REFLECTIONS ON PROGRAMME OUTCOMES

British Aerospace's values and vision for the future

British Aerospace, as part of its corporate philosophy, focuses on five values which are seen as key to both the current and the future success of the business:

■ *Customers* – 'We will delight all our customers, both internal and external, by understanding and exceeding their expectations.'

- *People* – 'All British Aerospace people will be encouraged to realize their full potential as valued members of the British Aerospace team.'
- *Performance* – 'We will set targets to be the best, continually challenging and improving the way we do things, both as individuals and members of our teams.'
- *Partnerships* – 'We will strive constantly to be our customers' preferred supplier; our suppliers' preferred customer; a respected partner in our industrial alliances; and a source of pride to our Government and our local communities.'
- *Innovation and technology* – 'We will encourage a hunger for new ideas, new technologies, and new ways of working to secure sustained competitive advantage for our Company.'

The outcomes of the Business Leaders programme were measured against each of these values in turn to gauge the extent of the contribution towards the company's vision, quoted below.

> At British Aerospace we are dedicated to working together, and with our partners, to become The Benchmark for our industry, setting the standard for customer satisfaction, technology, financial performance and quality in all that we do.

Outcomes

- *Customers – our highest priority*. Following the programme the internal satisfaction survey showed a rise from 70 to 80 per cent against a range of criteria: e.g. meeting customer demand +32 per cent; belief that the company was oriented to customers +23 per cent. A major £20 million contract seemingly lost before the programme began was regained by utilizing an NLP process of solution-focused problem solving. This problem was used as part of an exercise during the programme and illustrates the benefit of action learning through group dynamics.
- *People – our greatest strength*. People are now buying in to continuous improvement as managers are more encouraging, with new ideas no longer being seen as threatening. Fear has diminished regarding mistakes and the focus has shifted from 'who caused the problem' to 'what can we do to solve it?' The site at Prestwick was the first in British Aerospace to be awarded Investors in People accreditation in November 1994 (reconfirmed at a recent reassessment).
- *Partnerships – our future*. The corporate opinion survey has shown positive trends since 1995. These included a 31 per cent improvement in perceptions of teamworking, 31 per cent improvement in communications and 21 per cent improvement in delegation skills.
- *Performance – our key to winning*. The European Foundation for Quality Management model showed a 150-point improvement in enabling (100 is normally considered exceptional). The CBI 'Probe' survey found the site to be in the UK's upper quartile. Work in progress dropped from £26 million to £17 million. Lead times were reduced by 30 per cent, improvement in late orders was 50–60 per cent, productivity rose by 20 per cent, and the site had a 30 per cent reduction in assembly jigging.

■ *Innovation and technology – our competitive edge.* Innovations in financial systems led to a 35 per cent drop in invoice mismatching. MRP 2, introduced previously with limited success, was reintroduced successfully with a new 'inclusive' pricing system developed.

FURTHER REFLECTIONS ON THE BUSINESS LEADERS PROGRAMME

Peripheral change from the centre

British Aerospace as a company at the time of the Business Leaders programme was over 45,000 strong, with a real need for a corporate change programme which would transform the way the business operated, not by changing systems but by changing the behaviours, language and leadership styles of everyone, irrespective of power or position. This programme would ultimately start with the main board, driven by the then chief executive, now chairman, Sir Richard Evans.

In my opinion, the Business Leaders programme was a substantial part of what the business required (and this is with the added benefit of hindsight) and was in fact one year ahead in delivery of the modular, and admittedly more comprehensive, business executive skills training (BEST) chosen by the company for the 'top 1500'. This would be the programme that would act as the catalyst for the changes noted above and is currently the final stages of evaluation.

Why then could the Business Leaders programme not be included as part of the BEST programme, given the success of attendees? I feel that the answer is rather simple. In any organization of real size, corporate change begins in the centre. It will generally be initiatives developed at the HQ of that business that achieve the necessary support and platform to make a difference *throughout* the organization.

It is at the centre that the power base exists. It is at the centre that the necessary funding exists. It is at the centre that the information so necessary in identification of corporate needs exists. Most importantly, it is at the centre that the individuals with the power and influence (and in some cases the charisma, which tends to grow with power and influence) ply their trade.

Change from the outside in is not only difficult but near impossible. None of the factors noted for successful corporate change exists on the periphery of large organizations. With the Business Leaders programme, success was achieved in no small measure at Prestwick and contributed to the perception throughout the business of the Prestwick site as having a positive approach to the constant changes in our business. It must, however, be recognized that this was successful in *part* of BAe, and even in this smaller scale started in the centre of the Prestwick business supported by sufficient senior people holding the necessary influence.

My reflection follows on not only from my involvement with the Business Leaders programme but also after exposure to BEST and other organizational change programmes (one of which, with the Department of Social Security, was one of the largest computerization programmes in Western Europe at the time). It may be summarized very simply. Change will always begin at the centre. This has been the case in all of the changes I have been involved in and will continue to be so.

EXTENDING THE LEARNING

Partnerships

Change, whether it be through people or systems, is something which is of interest to us all, and strategies or programmes which facilitate change successfully are constant currencies in achievement of business excellence.

When organizations are willing to try new approaches to support positive change, moving employees through the change curve's 'valley of despair' in the shortest possible time, the risk of failure lies firmly within the business. The ever-present consultant may walk away after putting the event down to experience, adding the organization to his brochure list. The hotel may walk away with delegate profits irrespective of programme outcomes. The local enterprise company may, like the consultant, put it down to experience, showing in their report their willingness to support business initiatives in the area.

I feel it is therefore important that all of the 'partners' in ventures such as the Business Leaders programme, which was one of the first to use neuro-linguistic programming, to share the risk as far as possible.

At the beginning of the research for the Business Leaders programme, negotiations took place with various consultants on the basis that our business was prepared to take a substantial risk with a new approach. We felt that this offered a significant learning opportunity for any consultant who wished to be involved and as such they should be prepared to contribute – we asked all the consultants we spoke to if they would work for 50 per cent fees; only one accepted. Luckily, this was a reputable firm with whom we had worked before.

The same approach was taken with the hotel chosen. The venue for the type of training we had in mind was crucial; however, the funding for the pilot programme was limited, and negotiations opened with a hotel manager with whom we had an excellent relationship. A special deal was agreed on the basis that a successful pilot would ensure continuity of the programme and more business for the hotel. This hotel was a genuine partner as it took on some of the risk.

The local enterprise company recognized the importance of our initiative and the potential for Ayrshire businesses. It worked with us from the beginning, contributing not only grant funding but also genuine advice and support.

With this particular programme, British Aerospace at Prestwick still took most of the risk, except that on this occasion there was a genuine sharing between partners who had all contributed to maximize the chance of a successful outcome. The reflection was that in all new programmes there is something for everyone involved, therefore everyone involved should share the risk. In this instance, BAe had the benefit of a positive outcome for its managers, the consultant was able to add an innovative programme to her portfolio, the hotel gained substantial extra business from additional programmes, and the local enterprise company enjoyed the association with a successful programme which could be extended to other Ayrshire companies.

References

Burnes, B. (1992), *Managing Change*. London: Pitman.

Hammer, M. and Champy, J. (1993), *Re-engineering the Corporation*. London: Nicholas Brearley.

The application of team-working in a manufacturing organization

Ken Ash

CONTEXT

The organization

Established in the 1700s, this organization had become the UK's largest independent manufacturer of its product. It was also the largest employer in the town and district in which it was sited. The company occupied two sites in the town of its origin and another site 25 miles away. With an annual turnover of £76 million, its workforce numbered 1500 in the UK, plus another 300 worldwide.

Like most companies in the late 1980s and early 1990s, the company experienced serious economic problems as a result of the recession. Sales suffered as a result, and short-time working became the norm at the factories.

As part of the company's strategy to improve its competitiveness, it undertook a company-wide project lasting over two years. This involved using a consultancy firm to advise the organization and help implement restructuring proposals. The objective of this consultancy project was to sharpen the company's competitiveness against what was identified as worldwide competition. The project team was made up of six members of the company's management and a similar number of external consultants.

This final part of this consultancy project recommended and implemented a number of initiatives and changes. These included a company-wide SWOT analysis, a strategy development process, an organizational restructure, a management development training programme, and the recommendation that in order to remain competitive and a leading manufacturer, a demonstrated commitment to *teamwork* would have to be carried out company-wide.

Organizational analysis

The consultants had carried out a 'hard', impartial and in-depth review of the company through a SWOT analysis and other analytical initiatives, such as management control systems and restructuring opportunities. If a 'softer' internal audit of the company had been taken, the then present state could have been summarized as follows.

The company had celebrated its 200th anniversary. This long history and the associated traditions were the key elements in the company's cultural make-up. The other element was the family ownership of the company. In 1990, almost half of the nine-strong board of directors were family members. This background created an organization with many positive facets. A belief in investment in future projects was well established and must be considered alongside the paternalistic management style, with great emphasis placed on the welfare of employees. In return, the company enjoyed (and still enjoys) great employee loyalty.

However, the culture also exhibited a number of attributes which could be seen to be negative. A hierarchical divisional structure reflected, and in part caused, barriers between departments. This resulted in poor communications and lack of team-working across the company. There was an autocratic management style, which gave no capacity for management decisions to be challenged (a state of affairs perpetrated as much by subordinates as by managers themselves). Overall, there was an arrogant attitude, leading to almost complete lack of commercial orientation.

The company had been a very traditional organization, in terms of structure, management and the use of its human resources. Kanter (1983) refers to two types of organization, segmentalist and integrating. Segmentalist-type businesses have a hierarchical structure with focused areas of authority. Integrating structures have fewer divisions and a wide and downwards-driven sense of authority. The second structure is usually brought about through changing environments, both internally and externally. The company was making the transition towards the latter. The company was moving away from its hierarchical and orthodox structure towards a more flexible system with fewer barriers and boundaries operating between and around the main functions. This development would increase empowerment, the desire and the ability to drive decision making and accountability downwards through the layers of management and onto the shop floor.

THE CHANGE PROGRAMME

The reason for the change and the great shift to embrace team-working was often given as 'to do nothing was not an option'. It was also stated that the company needed to be able to meet its newly formulated core mission, which read:

Our Core Mission is to be the world's leading manufacturer and supplier of its high quality product.

and this would be achieved:

through a commitment to teamwork and continuous improvement.

There is no doubt that the company's reasons for the implementation and further expansion of team-working were credible and logical.

What had to be achieved, although never specifically stated in measurable terms, could be listed as :

- increased employee satisfaction
- improved job commitment
- more appreciation of quality control
- increased individual efforts towards company aims/goals
- motivation through peer pressure rather than a 'big stick' from the top

- reduced management intervention/supervision
- greater productivity
- flexible work practices
- increased employee development.

Team-working as a concept had been wholeheartedly accepted by the company's senior executives as being a sound principle to adopt and operate.

Once the consultants had done their job and were no longer on site the training department, of which I was a member, was left to continue the work of creating the desired future state.

The state of the future was without doubt going to be a journey into the great unknown. The organization had never travelled along this route before, neither had the facilitators in the training department. All that the facilitators had were the words of the consultancy 'friends' echoing in their ears, and under their arms a pile of books spouting enough theory that, if you joined all the words together, would reach from the Earth to the Sun and back again. Practical experience and guidance were about as plentiful as ice-cream salesmen in Antarctica.

The unwritten instruction from higher management was that the blanket approach to team-building/team-working was going to be implemented, whether it was needed or not. Utopia would be reached when everyone was multi-skilled and able to do everyone's job. In the very beginning the strategy was to be almost totally prescriptive, based on the premise that 'you are going to have some of this training whether you need it or not'.

Workshops were planned based on material taken from textbooks and theorists. They included all the well-known (at least to creditable trainers) theories on issues such as the change process in individuals, team roles, ground rule setting, expectation matching, stages of team development, communications, problem solving, interpersonal skills, inter-team development and leadership, etc.

Myself and two other facilitators from the training department were heavily involved in the design and delivery of the company's team-building programme. A series of 'off the job' workshops were planned, which were going to take approximately five to six months to complete the first phase, the format being two- hour workshops at least once a week with the first groups (departments) selected for implementation.

The company's team-working programme was showing a number of features, and although there had been successes in terms of flexibility of labour, openness to management initiatives, closer communications and ownership of tasks, which otherwise may not have been achieved, there were other areas where the team-working value was falling into disrepute through negative attitudes, operatives finding it difficult to fit the concept to their actual job, consequently feeling let down and frustrated. It was when these uncertainties emerged that my doubts about the application of team-working were raised.

The time and costs expended for this team-working programme had been vast, running into tens of thousands of pounds. At this stage, it is reasonable to ask the disturbing question: perhaps the spread of team-building has more to do with team builders and executives and their needs and values, rather than a careful analysis of what is appropriate and necessary for the organization. Critchley and Casey (1991) asked similar questions in their study of top management training.

Process questions

On commencement of the programme, it would appear that not too many questions were asked about how the process was going to be carried out or what the process issues might be. Once the decision had been made to embark down this particular road of change, the focus questions were centred around what the barriers are going to be, how they can be overcome, how they (employees) can be led to the other side, and what role training should play in all this. Whatever the answers were, or the strategy planned to address the above questions, it was only going to be based on theory. Practical experience of this type of exercise on the scale that was proposed was not available from within. This, however, turned out to be the challenge which fired us up, as a group of facilitators, to perform and hopefully achieve.

As the programme continued, one particular issue was impeding the progress, and that was 'why were large numbers of reasonable, open-minded employees, who were prepared to work in this new world of team-working, finding it difficult to put it into practice?' The difficulty manifested itself in the following ways: open resistance, lack of credibility ascribed to team-working and the management of it, also low morale, frustration and a feeling of being let down because they wanted it to work but the job they actually did would not allow it.

There were other issues impacting on the progress and the shaping of the planned change. Although in the early stages I was unaware of how significant or important these issues were, they turned out to be the fundamental pillars in my 'bridge to teamwork' model. These were identified as the 'need requirement', pay and team structure (see Figure 9.2 and Table 9.1).

The basic ownership of situations was also playing its part in the progress/non-progress of the desired change. In areas where managers took ownership through involvement, progress was enhanced. In areas where responsibility for driving these changes was abdicated, team-building was seen as a short-term distraction.

Change requires many things, and this includes getting managers to step outside their 'self-protectionism syndrome' and actively demonstrate that the decisions they make are for the benefit of the company as a whole and not just to meet their own departmental interests. It was obvious that these issues needed to be addressed and overcome. Efforts made to do this took the form of lobbying directors and managers informally, making formal presentations on the state of progress, revisiting the areas where training had been carried out to talk to the individuals and generally trying to stay positive while all this was going on.

The model in Figure 9.2 and the framework described in Table 9.1 is offered as a suggested method of approach to any team-working implementation programme. This study has identified the important issues that must be addressed before, during and after implementation of teams and teamwork.

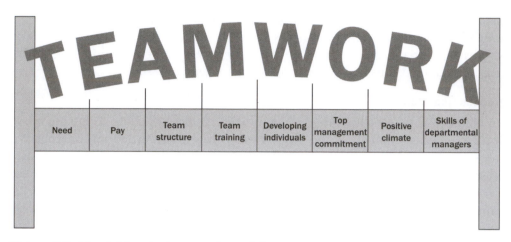

Figure 9.2 The bridge to teamwork model

Table 9.1 Issues to be addressed in support of 'the bridge to teamwork'

Issue	Description
Need	The requirement for teamwork must be identified, otherwise forced teamwork is doomed to failure.
Pay	An acceptable agreed pay structure needs to be in place before the implementation of new working practices, i.e. teamwork.
Team structure	There needs to be a common defined policy on the organization's team structure, i.e. all departments working through either team leaders or supervisors, but not both.
Team training	This needs to be relevant, practical and focused on the real departmental issues concerning teamwork and not a blanket theory approach.
Developed individuals	People selected to lead the teams should be identified from within the team itself. Supported by meaningful, relevant training.
Top management commitment	This needs to be demonstrated on a daily basis by deeds and not words.
Positive climate	A positive climate should be brought about initially by top management, ensuring that the reasons for, and the benefits of, the strategy are communicated and understood. although this alone will not be enough to eradicate resistance barriers.
Skills of departmental managers	Managers must be given the skills and the environment to allow them to 'let go' of items such as information, authority, resources and accountability. In other words, managers need to empower their people and that often requires focused training.

REFLECTION ON THE CHANGE PROGRAMME

As you may have expected, the change programme did not go according to plan in many respects and for many reasons. Increased flexibility/productivity did not automatically result from the company's reorganization and training.

The most significant aspect of the change that did take place was that the team-work training did at least engender a spirit of co-operation among the departmental members even if full flexibility was not achieved.

The issue quoted previously, the *need requirement*, was an area for continuing debate which started about eight months into the programme and lasted through-out the exercise. Disappointingly, I believe, it has still not been fully recognized or understood by 'higher management' how fundamental it is to the approach and success of such an intervention.

There is no doubt that the role of the supervisor within the company has changed and will continue to do so until the complete crossover to team leaders is established. The company's policy on supervisors and team leaders and their role within the pro-duction areas to this day remains ambiguous. Devolution of power to the shop floor in some areas, for example dye processing and engineering, has not carried through, mainly because the role of the supervisor has barely changed, if at all. The supervisor still controls the resource, the information, accountability and authority, which does not allow the most willing of teamworkers to be effective. One of the main reasons why the role of the supervisor has not changed in the areas quoted (dye processing and engineering) relates directly back to one of the 'fundamental pillars' of any future approach – the need requirement. Perhaps because of the way the job process is carried out, there is no 'need' to change the present system of working, so why forcefully change it for an unwarranted theory?

For an organization to change from a traditional classical structure to a team-based one requires changes not only in structure but also in processes, systems, attitudes, leadership philosophy and style and paradigms. When a manufacturing organization takes upon itself to create a teamwork-based culture, it must realize that there are significant issues it needs to address in order to proceed in building such a culture. Awareness of all these issues is of paramount importance for the suc-cessful and effective outcome of the organization's efforts.

This company's team-building approach could be termed as the 'full-blown' approach, whereby exactly the same exercises and depth of training were carried out for all the employees in the selected areas, all together at the same time.

The training was structured through formal workshops by the internal facilita-tors to promote the following principles:

- Openness
- Participation
- Empowerment
- Commitment
- Quality
- Affiliation

with an overall objective to create understanding and commitment to the company's values regarding 'team-working'.

Positive factors

I believe that the 'success' that has been achieved could have been brought about earlier and less painfully if a different approach had been taken. This reflection is based on interim surveys carried out in a number of departments, in addition to the anecdotal evidence collected from group workshops and from individuals in the course of regular visits to these employees in their place of work.

■ On its own, the logic and structure of the team-building training programme would stand up to rigorous examination, with the outcome of at least a merit award. However, other issues were taking their toll on the overall effectiveness of the company's team-building programme.

■ There is no doubt that the required and practical type of team-working is operating very well in a number of areas, noticeably in one production section and the preparatory department. Most of the characteristics required for such a climate are being demonstrated, these being openness, empowerment, participation, concern for quality, commitment to the team goal and not forgetting efficient productivity.

■ Other successes can be listed, one of these being that the company now has a vastly experienced group of people (facilitators and operatives) who can give first-hand advice and guidance to the expansion of the team-working ethos. The advantage now is that the future approach to this subject has been finely tuned, tried and tested, which will give the desired results more quickly, with reduced time, effort and resource being expended. More importantly, all this can be achieved today and in the future less painfully.

Impeding factors

By listing the factors or issues that impeded our original approach, lessons have been learned. Should the company fail in the future it will be because the learning has not been put into practice.

■ The most significant factor which impeded the progress and ultimately the success of the team-working programme was in not recognizing the 'need requirement'; also the blanket approach to the training carried out in the selected areas, whether they needed it or not, was a serious mistake.

■ Not making the structure of the departments uniform and putting off the decision, which will have to be made eventually, impeded progress. Team-working is impeded if you try to work through a supervisor and a team leader. The company operated two systems of leadership within the team-working programme. One was through a staff supervisor *with* a shop-floor team leader and the other was through a shop-floor team leader *without* a staff supervisor. This decision held up the progress of team-working in the areas where there was a supervisor and a team leader, for the following reasons:

- supervisors not wanting to 'let go'
- duplication of duties
- team leaders relying on supervisors
- team leaders testing their authority against supervisors
- shop-floor workers dealing directly with supervisors (because they were there – thus undermining the team leaders).

■ The irrelevance of some of the training was also a factor which held up the progress of success. For example, shop-floor employees found it very difficult to see the relevance of building a tower out of strips of newspaper to their job back in the workplace (even after full explanations about what the points of the exercise were).

The importance of relevant training was never addressed until at least 12 months after the commencement of the programme. Once this was recognized and acted upon, the programme took a giant leap forward.

■ From the outset of this change programme, what would have helped would have been a clear image being given of what type of teams the company was trying to form and operate.

The simple questions like 'what type of team-working is required?' and 'what type of teams do we have?' were never asked until recently, and this is currently helping the organization to move forward to the desired state.

REFLECTIONS ON PRACTICE

For this organization

From my research and involvement in this company's team-working programme, I feel the critical misunderstanding was that senior executives either did not fully recognize the type of team-working they wanted to implement, or if they did, it was misinterpreted by the company's managers and trainers when carrying out that implementation.

First and foremost, this company did have and still has a number of well-motivated, positive, productive teams. These are in areas whereby the work undertaken dictates that they naturally fall into teams. Examples of these are working very well today.

As indicated earlier, the belief is that the reason for their success and effectiveness is the basic 'need requirements' brought about by the type of work that they undertake. The conclusion that the tasks decided upon by these groups are more likely to be accomplished than those assigned by a supervisor is not an isolated finding but a well-documented phenomenon (the Volvo Kalmer plant described in Katz and Kahn (1978) and the Lucas–Japanese joint venture in Marinaccio, (1991) are two examples).

If this company is going to achieve a more forward approach towards an acceptable, reputable team-working strategy, some basic principles need to be understood and accepted. Just as an organization 'cannot be all things to all people' so team-work cannot fulfil all functions at the same time. There is a realization among Ford management that 'an ideal team does not have a hierarchical leader, but a natural leader who emerges when and if the need for co-ordination or representation arises' (Mueller interview, Ford Dagenham, May 1994). The same is true with regard to teams. That is to say, natural teams will emerge and be the most effective. It is these that should be supported and encouraged.

Once these have been identified, the organization should be concentrating its efforts and energies on supporting, developing them and publicizing their effectiveness, which in turn would create this positive climate that I have already identified as one of the main 'pillars' of my 'bridge to teamwork' model.

The most concerning aspect of this research is the realization that the company's attempt at 'full-blown' team-working has been unnecessary and in some cases harmful. This realization is based on the confirmed perceptions of the areas researched within the company, namely a focus group undergoing team-building and team-working, and its involvement in an 'application of teamworking questionnaire' (see Figures 9.3 and 9.4).

On the positive side, there has been a significant shift, in many departments, towards the belief that their overall work efforts are geared to the departmental goal rather than their individual work groups. Without doubt, this has been brought about by the team-building training. This reflection has important implications for the organization's management and its future strategy regarding the expansion of team-working, because team-building interventions are centred on groups who work together in real life rather than a collection of individuals gathered for a training session. As teams are real working groups, an intervention that goes sour can have serious and long-lasting repercussions.

Extending the learning to other organizations

The learning outcomes from this 'change programme' strongly suggest that if an organization can involve its *employees* in identifying its team-building needs, this will bring clarity and ensure the correct focus for any team-building intervention.

For example, to identify the 'need requirement' a short survey should be carried out (application of teambuilding questionnaire) to find how the application of teamwork within that area will 'fit in'. The three key benefits of this exercise would be:

- It allows you to find out how they perceive the situation (team-working in their department).
- This will then allow you to focus on the 'real' areas of concern.
- It also sends out messages that there is a genuine offer to involve them in the process.

Operating a policy of involvement (the application of teamworking questionnaire) reduces the risk of expensive errors and unfulfilled expectations and increases the opportunity to meet the operational needs of the organization.

THE APPLICATION OF TEAMWORKING QUESTIONNAIRE

Please place a ✔ in appropriate box

1. **Who do you consider to be in your immediate Team?**

   ☐ VAT Operatives   ☐ Dye Stuffers   ☐ Dry Preparatory
   ☐ Shift Dyers   ☐ Package Dyeing   ☐ None
   ☐ Other (please state)......................................

2. **Do you think your job allows you to work in a Team?**
   (refer to definitions on the back page)

   ☐ Yes   ☐ No   ☐ Don't Know

3. **How much of your job fits into the following situations?**
   (refer to definitions on the back page)

Working on your own	Co-operation	Working in a Team
%	%	%

4. **Do you think any of the following factors actually prevent you from working in a Team?**

   ☐ Manning Levels
   ☐ Information Flow/Systems
   ☐ Departmental Structure, i.e. Managers, Supervisors
   ☐ Authority Levels of Team Leaders
   ☐ Absenteeism
   ☐ Pay and Reward Systems
   ☐ Your Type of Work
   ☐ The Skill Level Required
   ☐ Leadership
   ☐ Production Targets

   ☐ Others (please state) . . . .

5. **Have you been involved in any of the following Teambuilding Training?**

   ☐ Formal '*Teambuilding*' Workshops
   ☐ Informal Teambuilding Training
   ☐ Neither
   ☐ Other (please state) . . . .

6. **If you have experienced Company Training on Teambuilding/Teamworking, do you think it was relevant?**

Very Much	Not Very Much	Very Little	Not at All

7. **If you have experienced Company Training on Teambuilding/Teamworking, do you think it has helped in any way?**

Very Much	Not Very Much	Very Little	Not at All

8. **Do you feel the following statement is true ?**

   'You need to be trained in teamwork to work in an effective team '

   ☐ Yes   ☐ No

   THANK YOU FOR TAKING THE TIME TO COMPLETE THIS QUESTIONNAIRE

Figure 9.3 The application of teamworking questionnaire

IMPORTANT

In order to create a uniform understanding of some of the terms used in the questionnaire I have defined three situations of 'work'. I would be grateful if you would refer to these definitions when answering the questions.

DEFINITION OF WORKING SITUATIONS

ONE: WORKING ON YOUR OWN

NO NEED FOR HELP TO OPERATE MACHINE.

NO NEED FOR HELP TO CARRY OUT JOB.
(Push truck, Lift bag, Carry package, Find information, Read drawing)

HAS CONFIDENCE/KNOWLEDGE/SKILL TO CARRY OUT JOB.

DECISIONS CAN BE MADE ON YOUR OWN TO CARRY OUT THE JOB.

TWO: CO-OPERATION

SOME HELP NEEDED TO OPERATE MACHINE.

SOME HELP NEEDED TO CARRY OUT JOB.
(Lifting packages, Transporting equipment, Lifting bags, Move machinery)

THE NEED TO PASS ON OR RECEIVE INFORMATION.

DECISIONS ARE MADE WITH THE HELP AND INPUT FROM OTHERS – ON A NEED TO KNOW BASIS.

THE ORGANIZATION AND DISTRIBUTION OF THE WORK WARRANTS NEGOTIATION.

THREE: TEAMWORKING

RELIANCE ON OTHERS TO COMPLETE THE TASKS EFFECTIVELY.

OTHERS ARE RELIANT ON YOU FOR THEM TO DO THEIR TASKS EFFECTIVELY.

THERE IS A **NEED** TO SHARE SKILLS / KNOWLEDGE TO COMPLETE THE TASK.

THERE IS A **NEED** TO CARRY OUT PROBLEM SOLVING/DECISION MAKING AS A TEAM.

Figure 9.4 Definitions of 'work' used in the application of teamworking questionnaire

On reflection, in this programme it was found that teams can be deliberately developed through a series of team-building interventions, but it would be wrong to claim that any collection of individuals (production workers, salespeople, top management group) can be developed into a close and effective team.

My specific reasons for the confidence in this claim is:

- For individuals to embrace working in a team there has to be a 'need requirement'.
- Consideration of the relationship between 'unshared certainty' (Critchley and Casey 1991), when operatives know their job (which is most of the time, approximately 80–90 per cent for this company's workers) and 'shared uncertainty' (which is a rare mode of work), when the operative is uncertain about the task to be carried out. Because this company's production workers operate mostly in the mode of 'unshared certainty', the need for team-building is greatly reduced.

Hence teamwork/team-building may not be applicable.

CONCLUSION

On the face of it, team-working can be seen as a simple process. Yet company after company, including this organization, has found to its cost (both monetary and human reaction) that successful, effective team-working can be as complex and challenging as putting a man on the Moon. The truth about real lasting change is that it is rather more difficult and complex to manage than trainers and managers first imagine. Even when managers are aware of the 'theory and practice' of organizational change, too often they succumb to the temptation of the 'quick fix' or 'simple solution', which can only lead to 'short-termism'.

Organizations usually have only one chance to get it 'right'; failure to do so can lead to unintended and damaging consequences.

As stated previously, the advantage this organization has is that the expertise in the area of effective team-working is now a resource available within the company. Time will tell if the skill and experience gained by the organization will be used wisely and effectively. I therefore conclude that team-working, while widely desirable, is not always needed and that teams are not always positive. A much more cautious and strategic approach would be appropriate, as indicated through some of the reflections given in this study.

References

Critchley, W. and Casey, D. (1984), Teambuilding – at what price and whose cost? *Management Education and Development*, 15, (2).

Kanter, R.M. (1983), *The Change Masters*. London: Unwin.

Katz, D. and Kahn, R.T. (1978), *The Socal Psychology of Organisation*, 2nd edn. New York: Wiley.

Marinaccio, R. (1991) Work and production organisation in a 'Japanese Company'. *Journal of General Management*, 5, (1), Autumn.

Mueller, F. (1994) Teams between hierarachy and commitment: change strategies and the internal environment. *Journal of Management Studies*, 31, (1) May.

Strategy for a restructure in a not-for-profit organization

Chris Newis

CONTEXT

Background to the organization and situation

In 1995, the organization for which I work was faced with what was up to then its most challenging time. The agency in question is Black Country Co-operative Development Agency Ltd – a not-for-profit co-operative business and training organization for ethnic minorities, unemployed people, under-25s and women returners.

At that time, the organization relied for its funding upon four local authorities but in May of that year, due to budget cuts, one authority did not fund the agency. This was closely followed by another authority, which halved its contribution. The agency used the core funding as 'match funding' for the European Social Fund, therefore the cut in funding had a cumulative effect upon the organization's finances.

The organization did not at that time have a management structure or a hierarchy and relied for its management upon six development workers, who undertook management in addition to their business development and training responsibilities. The team decided that I should devote myself to the task of developing a strategic response to the reduction in local authority funding. What follows is an analysis of what turned out to be a continuous journey of discovery for both myself and the organization. The following text breaks down into four interlocking components. The first of these is what happened, in the sense of the changes and the reaction to those changes. The second component is the theoretical basis for the actions. The third component is the new insights that were revealed during the process. The fourth component is my critical reflection upon the actions. These reflections are from my current perception and level of knowledge.

Process questions

For the purposes of scanning the environment in which my organization was working, I used the five external forces model (David 1989). These forces are:

1 Economic

2 Social and cultural

3 Political/legal

4 Technological

5 Competitive.

These external forces impact upon the organization and determine the opportunities and threats which arise from the combination of these factors (see Table 9.2).

Table 9.2 Adaptation of F.R. David's five external forces model

Economic/social/political/legal	Technological/competitive
Local authorities	Enterprise agencies
Government policy	Private consultancy
TECs	Other voluntary agencies
European Commission	Software applications
NVQs	Chambers of commerce
Decline in large organizations	Development of management
Women into business	Training
Women in the workforce	Lobby groups
Working from home	Other CDAs
Growth of small business	
Self-management of housing	
City challenges	
New European initiatives	
Flatter organizations	
Environmental issues	
Employee ownership	

It was also my intention to develop HRD responses in parallel with the development of the business strategy, as described in Rothwell and Kazanas (1989). Changes in demographic composition and distribution, such as the extent to which women were returning to the workforce through self-employment (*Employment Gazette* 1993) and the predictions for growth in the numbers of people working from home (British Telecom 1992) were factors which, in my opinion, would demand a new approach to the design of training products and the adoption of open and flexible learning for those wishing to start their own business.

I became convinced through further reading of Rothwell and Kazanas (1989) that the strategic process must directly include all members of staff – that is, employee development. It should also include other stakeholders and associates – that is, non-employee development. It was considered vital to include the many self-employed trainers whom we subcontracted for business training provision. The organizational strategy issues to be reconciled at corporate level were 'What business are we really in?', 'To be successful what skills and knowledge do we need?' and 'Now can we achieve this success through planned learning?'

Adopting a strategic model

For this purpose, I chose Higgins and Vincze's (1992) objectives, determination and strategy formulation. The rationale for the choice of this model was that such a generic model (see Figure 9.5) appeared to be sufficiently flexible for the purpose of my intervention. The model begins with the mission and values of the organization and facilitates the whole staff being involved in defining mission, vision and values within the agency.

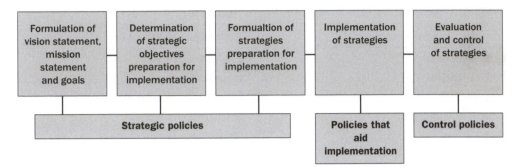

Figure 9.5 Higgins and Vincze's objectives, determination and strategy formulation

The importance of mission is also stressed by Burnes (1992), who recommends nine elements – the first four of which set the conditions for change and the further five are the sequential phases of successful change. The first four are mission, valued outcomes, valued conditions and mid-point goals. Burnes further advocates that strategy be viewed as a series of links in a chain which stretches from the starting point to a vision of the desired future state and that each link is a particular strategy for moving the process forward.

On the other hand, Stewart (1991) recommends a process of planned change, moving from diagnosis to the identification of resistance, to allocating responsibility, the implementation of strategy and finally, the monitoring of change.

The understanding of culture

Edgar Schein (1985) has described culture as 'a pattern of basic assumptions developed by an organization as it learns to cope with its problems of external adaptation and internal integration'. The commitment to minimum hierarchy and equality in the management team of my agency was as strong then as it remains today, although it has been sorely tested in more recent times.

We were therefore building upon the existing culture rather than creating a new one. The task culture, as described by Handy (1989), goes on to say that the problem with the task culture is that it is time-consuming because people are tied up in decision making. 'You would not use this culture to make a wheel', he says.

Vision–mission–values in a 'not for profit' context

In the last three years, more has been written concerning organizational change and strategic development in not-for-profit organizations (Nutt and Backoff 1995) but, at the time of my intervention, authors had only just begun to allude to importance of mission and values in a not-for-profit setting. The features of not-for-profit organizations referred to by Handy (1989) as 'the co-operative psychological contract', plus lack of hierarchy and the identification of task culture, are now interpreted as strengths rather than weaknesses. Drucker (1985) has also pointed out that not-for-profit organizations can and do dynamically out-perform companies driven by the profit motive because 'they start with the performance of their mission'. The ability to focus upon mission and values are seen as key features of organizational culture.

DEFINING THE MISSION STATEMENT

This was an 'inclusive' process involving a number of away-days for staff and management. As facilitator for these sessions I used a set of questions from David (1989) to focus upon what he identifies as the nine components of a mission statement.

1 Who are our customers?

2 What are our products or services?

3 Where do we compete?

4 Is technology a primary concern?

5 Are we committed to economic objectives?

6 What are our basic beliefs, values, aspirations and philosophical priorities?

7 What is our distinctive competence or major competitive advantage?

8 Is public image a major concern for us?

9 What is our attitude towards employees?

This resulted in a new mission for the organization, as follows:

> The company is an ethical business which exists to deliver training, consultancy and business advice to its customers and clients. In order to do this successfully the company relies upon:
>
> ■ the satisfaction of its clients and customers;
> ■ the participation of all employees;
> ■ making profits from its commercial activities.

This was a new mission statement, to which all employees could and did 'sign up to'. I now turned to the implications of adopting that mission.

STRATEGIC IMPLICATIONS

Due to the not-for-profit status of the agency, it was considered inappropriate to become a profit-making organization. I was convinced that any new structure should be a response to the new strategy. This was based upon a review of the literature and particularly upon Chandler's (1963) study of 70 large US corporations, which concluded 'changes in strategy lead to changes in organizational structure', which, Chandler goes on, 'should be designed to facilitate the strategic pursuit of a firm, and therefore follows strategy'.

The structure that I recommended to the staff group was based upon Handy's (1989) shamrock organization (see Table 9.3). Handy had predicted that this model would be adopted by organizations that differentiated between strategic core workers, part-time and flexible staff and subcontractors in order to respond to environmental changes, particularly technology and delayering of organizations.

Table 9.3 The Business Team's adaptation of Charles Handy's shamrock organization

Leaf	Title	Handy's characteristics	Adaptation
1	Professional core	Qualified professionals' own knowledge of the business	Business team managers
2	Contractual fringe	Specialist technology users	Professional associates Outsourcing
3	Flexible labour force	Part-time / flexible employment	CDA staff Placements Secondments Short-term contracts

Our adaptation of the model was based upon the creation of a new leaf – The Business Team Ltd – which would become the profit-making sister company of the agency and would compete in the world of business consultancy and training.

The surpluses would then be passed back to the agency to allow it to become self-financing. Although there were to be two companies, enjoying mutual trading status (see Figure 9.6) it was decided that there was to be only one trading name – The Business Team Ltd. In order to rationalize the relationship between the two companies, I found it useful to view the new organization as a joint venture between two companies, in that it 'exploited the strengths of one partner and mitigates the weaknesses of another' (Higgins and Wincze 1992). The agency's weakness was that it did not have the constitutional means to generate surpluses, but its strength was that it had a great deal of resources and credibility. The synergy of the model was further strengthened by the use of additional flexible resources created by the agency's cohort of professional associates.

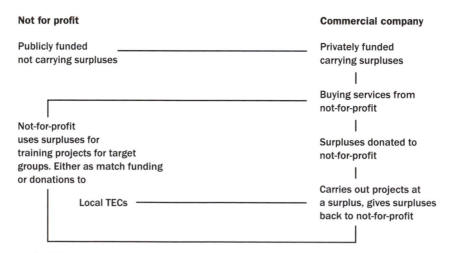

Figure 9.6 Mutual trading status

As I explained to the management team, as a consequence of this model there was the potential to pursue a number of generic linking strategies. We could not have known the difficulties which I as internal consultant would have to overcome in order to implement strategies which had been so easy to put down on paper.

A number of organizational changes were agreed, which led to the creation of an organizational chart (see Figure 9.7). For the first time, management and operations were separated as activities. I argued that without clear leadership we could not change the organization from its grant-receiving culture to a commercial quality organization. This was described by Higgins and Wincze (1992) as transformational leadership, which has three components:

1 Create a vision.
2 Mobilize commitment.
3 Institutionalize change.

PUTTING CHANGE THEORY INTO PRACTICE

In both my internal intervention and my external consultancy work, which was primarily in the public sector, I had been convinced for some time that old methodologies of change consultancy were insufficient for managers wishing to find new ways of managing change. This is particularly the case with the 'planned change' school (e.g. Bullock and Batten 1985 – who state that there are four phases of change).

Similarly, it seemed to me that much of the literature was based upon a theoretical understanding of change, e.g. the life cycle model (Griener 1972), whereas

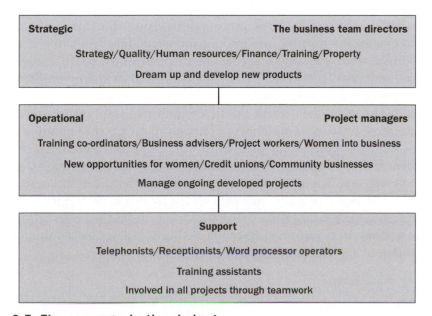

Figure 9.7 The new organizational chart

change seemed to me at this stage to be a process of moving from one state to another – requiring practice as well as theory. Change for me continues to be about how human beings perceive in relation to an organization or work group.

What is necessary is to adopt and adapt methodologies which have been developed in order to facilitate human beings moving from one state to another – which means for me that they have to be based upon psychology. My search for a coherent set of tools had led me to neuro-linguistic programming, which I studied with a practising consultant. The method does not assume that we all share the same view of the external world, but we view the world through our own set of filters (O'Connor and Seymour 1990). The techniques also place importance upon the use of metaphors as a way of sharing understanding.

As facilitator, I found that these techniques proved crucial in allowing the group to reach common conclusions. These were based upon, first, recognition that each of us has our own sensory bias in accepting information – audible, visual and kinetic – and, second, each of us has to take responsibility for the reaction our messages elicit. The techniques also allowed us to contract with each other some profound changes in our behaviour. What is below represents the 'negotiated' background to the intervention I was about to commence. Important among these elements were:

- 'There is no failure – only the opportunity for learning and development'.
- 'We praise in public and feedback in private'.
- 'My view of the world is not necessarily how the world is'.

Since the time of this intervention, the importance of metaphors or 'imaginization' in strategic management (Morgan 1993) has gained, and will continue to gain, wider credibility in organizational change.

It became clear throughout the process of devising this mission that people wanted to change the organization into a commercial business while at the same time retaining what was advantageous about our not-for-profit values, of co-operation, empathy and service. This was expressed as being 'the Marks and Spencer of business advice agencies'.

Alongside the three elements of vision, commitment and institutionalization, the management introduced a number of changes, most notable among which was the increased level of autonomy granted to workers at the operational level. This included control of budgets. A training and development programme was undertaken to ensure that workers could make the most of responsibilities afforded to them. Organizational change became represented by two main factors: first, a large quality assurance project, the objective of which was to gain BSI registration for our products and services; second, a large marketing campaign based upon Porter's product differentiation and adding value (Porter 1985).

Evaluating the strategy

To evaluate the strategy after having operated it for a period of months, I used Rumelt's (1980) four criteria for evaluation of a strategy:

1 *Consistency* – are the goals and objectives of each part of the strategy consistent with each other?

2 *Consonance* – the need for strategists to identify and respond to emergent trends. During the six-month period, new opportunities had arisen in the open learning area and the strategy had proved to be sufficiently flexible to allow us to adapt again to new conditions.

3 *Feasibility* – the strategy must not overtax the resources of the organization. By creating a new layer of project managers the management team had been free to lead the strategic development of the new company.

4 *Advantage* – the strategy should afford the organization an advantage over its rivals. Such an advantage would be expressed in superiority in resources, skills or market position.

The new structure had released resources that had been previously unrealized. Among these were the intellectual resources created by new contracts in quality assurance and human resource development which had been won by the agency. The organization had become a laboratory for the development of new ideas – a learning organization.

Reflecting upon strategic models and conventional wisdom

The conventional wisdom upon which much of strategic management is founded, tells us that if we do certain things, certain results will occur. For example, our organizational goals will be achieved if we:

- *install* the key behavioural attributes which research shows are the causes of excellence;
- *formulate* and select long-term plans using given analytical criteria, implement the plans and monitor progress; and
- *select* appropriate configurations between the various organizational attributes, such as structure, strategy and systems (Stacey 1993).

This makes a number of assumptions which, having gone through the programme of change described above, I consider for the following three reasons to be unfounded. First, it assumes that there are easily identified cause-and-effect links between the organization and its environment. Second, that there is equilibrium, and the elements described above by Rumelt (1980) are present. Third, that there is a stable path that companies may follow which leads to equilibrium.

Wilson (1992) has pointed out that it is extremely difficult to find a link between organizational culture and excellence and that proposed linkages assume 'an unwarranted linear connection'. Wilson has further pointed to a number of ways in which organizations, faced with market change, approach the changes necessary to be successful. Among these approaches is the 'programmed approach'. In this model, the company concentrates upon the 'how' of change rather than the 'what' (*ibid.*).

This is effectively what the Business Team did, through two programmes: first, the quality programme and second the marketing programme. As Wilson points out, such programmes (quality assurance, etc.) set the context in which future change can take place. As Wilson says: 'It is the socio-economic context in which all organizations operate that really sets the strategic agenda'.

REFLECTIONS ON PRACTICE

The nature of change

The writings of excellent management authors lead us to believe that the adoption of such programmes would lead to success. The socio-economic environment, however, intervened to require further adaptations to structure and strategy almost immediately. That is not to say that the strategy was unsuccessful; on the contrary, it created a new dynamic model that led to new horizons for the organization and myself. It was my perception of change, and the interpretation of change that I gave to other employees, which was upon reflection inappropriate.

If as an internal change agent you adopt a pragmatic approach to change, by which I mean if we implement certain actions, there will be a point in time when the programme will cease.

I consider the learning environment we had created at the outset – there is no failure, only learning, etc. – is one I would strongly recommend to internal change agents as being the only insurance policy against failure. Faced with the situation again I would approach the nature of change entirely differently. Below I offer a possible alternative conceptual framework, rather than a model, which internal change agents may wish to consider.

Far from equilibrium

With the benefit of learning undertaken since the original change programme previously described, I realize that the structure we adopted was a 'typical configuration' characterized by a consistency and harmony between the key elements of structure, strategy and systems. This configuration was initially successful and led us to continue with it far beyond its useful life and in defiance of feedback suggesting it should be reformed or abandoned. Stacey (1991) states that success lies in the management of contradictions between 'division and integration; separation and synergy; balancing conservative and radical cultures'. This Stacey describes as being far from equilibrium, when the organization is 'unstable because it is in practice so difficult to design a system that will continually balance diametrically opposed extremes of integration and division'.

In practice, then, organizational structures should be constantly changing, moving between extremes of centralization and decentralization, all in the attempt to chart a far-from-equilibrium course and avoid being sucked towards the stable or unstable equilibrium states. It is the 'saddle' from which the company keeps slipping. This seems to me to give a much more useful appraisal of the nature of change than was present in the traditional strategy texts upon which my intervention was based.

The importance of the above concept of change is, in my opinion, not to be underestimated. This is particularly so of the management skills which are deemed to be necessary for management of far-from-equilibrium organizations. What is necessary is to 'understand the complexities of the processes and the nature of change' (Wilson 1992). This was the fundamental flaw of the change programme undertaken by the Business Team in 1992.

My competencies as a change agent

I have measured my competencies in the process of change undertaken against the clusters of competencies recommended by Buchanan and Boddy (1992). These are:

- *Goals*, that is sensitivity to changes in key personnel, top management perceptions and environment conditions. I would say that I was strong on environment but lacking in the other goal areas.
- *Roles* – team-building abilities, bringing together key stakeholders, delegation of responsibility, networking skills. I would say that my achievements in bringing together a variety of stakeholders – local authorities and individuals – was effective and that my networking in creating new partnerships was also effective. However, I had no facility to delegate responsibility for what was happening at that time.
- *Communication* – to transmit to others, interpersonal skills, personal enthusiasm motivating others. My honest assessment is that my contribution in these areas was not as thorough as it may have been.
- *Negotiation* – selling plans and ideas. I have always been able to raise enthusiasm among partners and employees for ideas and concepts and also to negotiate with others for the release of resources for important projects. I think that proof of this is to be found in our achievement of registration with BSI of our ISO 9001 quality system. The Business Team is the first organization of its kind to achieve this award.
- What the authors call *managing up* – which is political awareness, identifying coalitions, and balancing conflicting goals and perceptions. The Business Team is a political organization with its roots in New Labour interventionism. Similarly to the above, I would estimate my performance in managing the politics of change, particularly among committed stakeholders and non-executive directors, to have been less effective than it could have been.

My indelible impression of the process is that in order to become an internal change agent I had to externalize myself. By this I mean that, even though I was a member of the management team, I had to prove that I knew (or appeared to know) what I was talking about and to gain the respect of project workers all over again.

IN CONCLUSION

The process of reflecting upon the change programme has been useful for me as I anticipate the next piece of research and development in my organization. In addition, my reflections have left me with four conclusions that will guide my thinking in future interventions. These are as follows.

First, that we need new decision-making techniques which allow managers to play out scenarios, using techniques borrowed from psychotherapy and humanistic research. Second, that organizations must be learning environments in which managers are free to roam, seek out knowledge and make decisions in a blame-free environment. Third, that we should elevate human attributes such as intuition and feelings in strategic decision-making processes. Remember that Einstein said, ' I never learned anything using my logical mind'.

The fourth conclusion I have reached is that all conclusions are transitory in their nature as we struggle to make sense of our organizational lives.

References

British Telecom (1992), *A Teleworking Programme*.

Buchanan, D. and Boddy, D. (1992), *The Expertise of the Change Agent*. Prentice Hall.

Bullock, R.J. and Batten, D. (1985) It's just a phase we're going through: a review and synthesis of CD phase analysis. *Group and Organizational Studies*, December.

Burnes, B. (1992), *Managing Change*. Pitman.

Chandler, A. (1963), *Strategy and Structure*. Cambridge Mass.: MIT Press.

David, F.R. (1989), *Concepts in Strategic Management*. Maxwell Macmillan.

Drucker, P. (1985), *Managing for the Future*. BCA.

Griener, L. (1972), Evolution and resolution as organisations grow. *Harvard Business Review*.

Handy, C. (1989), *Managing Voluntary Organisations*. Penguin.

Higgins, J.M. and Vincze, J.W. (1992), *Strategic Management – Texts and Cases*. Dryden.

Morgan, G. (1993), *Imaginisation*. Sage.

Nutt, P.C. and Backoff, R.W. (1991), *Strategic Management of Public and Third Sector Organisations*. Jossey Bass.

O'Connor, J. and Seymour, P. (1990), *An introduction to Neuro Linguistic Programming*. HarperCollins.

Porter, M. (1985), *Competitive Advantage of Nations*. Free Press.

Rothwell, V. and Kazanas, H. (1989), *Strategic Human Resource Development*. Prentice Hall.

Rumelt, R. (1980) The evaluation of business strategy. In Gluek, W.F. (ed.), *Business Policy and Strategic Management*. McGraw-Hill.

Schein, E.H. (1985), *Organisational Culture and Leadership*. San Francisco: Jossey Bass.

Stacey, R.D. (1991), *The Frontiers of Chaos*. Butterworth-Heinemann.

Stacey, R.D. (1993), *Strategic Management and Organisational Dynamics*. Pitman.

Stewart, J. (1991), *Managing Change Through Training and Development*. Kogan Page.

Wilson, D. (1992), *A Strategy of Change*. Routledge.

Creating a learning organization as a strategy for organizational change: 'nature or nurture' in the man-made fibres industry

Peter Grice

CONTEXT

Organizational background

The company was a long-established family business prior to being acquired by Courtaulds in 1986. The Courtaulds Aerospace Performance Materials site in Littleborough, Lancashire, on which the original study was based, was part of the Advanced Materials Division involved in the manufacture of high-performance fabrics and composite materials, which find applications in many markets, including aerospace, medical, defence and electrical industries. The Littleborough business had been acquired with a view to developing a vertically structured composites business operation. At the time of acquisition, the business was diverse in its product range and was finding it difficult to resource this diversity. The purchase brought a focus to the product range and the inevitable rationalization.

Performance Fabrics was formed in 1992 by bringing together two businesses which were located on the same site in Littleborough. Notwithstanding their proximity, the businesses were different in culture and ethos.

The business plan, announced to the workforce and unions at the time of the merger, included proposals for redundancy and identified a number of 'key needs' essential to the future success of the business. These were:

1 To simplify the pay structure and existing terms and conditions.
2 To improve the level of quality and customer service, which it was felt would entail a different approach to how people were to be managed and how a spirit of teamwork was to be developed.
3 To reduce the level of 'lost time' accidents.

THE CHANGE STRATEGY

'An organisation which facilitates the learning of all its members and continuously transforms itself' was an early definition by Pedler *et al.* (1989), and it was this belief which gave rise to the implementation of a change strategy.

The focus was a learner-centred approach using experiential learning for individuals that would lead to organizational learning and subsequently improved business performance. University academics were commissioned into a tripartite partnership to help inform and shape the change process; in addition, they assisted in the critical analysis.

An analysis of this approach identified 'twenty steps to becoming a learning organization', thereby suggesting a template other organizations might wish to consider as they contemplated change strategies (Hendry *et al.* 1994).

The business in Littleborough left Courtaulds ownership in 1994. This provided a significant opportunity to consider the extent to which the principles of the learning organization identified at that time have fared in relation to this change in ownership.

The general principles were revisited with a view to reflecting on how robust and dynamic they were in a period of organizational trauma. To provide a broader dimension to these reflections while further exploring the concepts of organizational change and development, two other manufacturing businesses were considered, both of which have adopted new ways of managing change but which were to some extent exposed to the methods of change at Littleborough. This would allow for some broader perspectives to be established on the nature of organizational change and development and the influence of the interventions. A principal aim was to consider what helps to release and harness the energies which contribute to organizational change, and what significance individual, team and organizational learning had in the processes adopted.

A reflection on these three businesses in the framework of the original analysis ('twenty steps etc.') was made to test the general principles of training and development leading an organizational change process.

LEARNING-CENTRED STRATEGY FOR CHANGE

One of the key strategies adopted, drawing on previous successful experience in other Courtaulds businesses was the formation of a cross-functional team whose brief would be to tackle a business-related project. This team would be encouraged to work in a way which facilitated team-building, developed management awareness of a different way of doing things and had the potential to improve communication across the workforce.

The strategy was based on the belief that an involvement of people at all levels in the change process would challenge the existing view that a high degree of functional specialization and hierarchical control was the only way to run a manufacturing business of this type. Given the declining state of the business and the textile industry at this time, it was felt to be an imperative that new ways of thinking be developed to promote business development and penetrate new markets.

The essential characteristics of this approach were:

> The team would be involved in a personal learning programme which focused on how best to bring about learning in others and which was directly related to their job responsibilities. Their remit was to make learning relevant and predominantly done in-house using company staff.

As part of its own learning processes, the team would consider the question of how they, and adults in general, learn. An outcome of this project would be a programme which stimulated learning in the organization in relation to a key business need.

A pressing health and safety issue provided the focus for the development of a learning programme. The chosen management team took a central role as designers and deliverers of a basic health and safety programme for all site employees.

Previously training, if any, had been unstructured and largely disconnected from business needs, consisting of 'sitting by Nellie' or 'off the job' attendance on short courses. This tended to perpetuate the shop floor/management divide. The company set out to make learning a transforming experience for individuals and the organization. The aim was to have meaningful experiences that would be experienced collectively and create organizational learning and change.

Business benefits were significant – in the first 18 months 'lost time' accidents were reduced from 25 to three. Learning, communication and team-working, coupled with the changes in management style, played a significant part in improving commitment and morale. This led to:

■ absenteeism falling from 3.5 to 1.7 per cent;

■ disciplinary incidents falling from 35 to two per annum;

■ an increase in work flexibility.

The organization retained its BS5790 certification as a consequence of the introduction of standards; the company was awarded Investors In People status in 1994, and for many employees the learning led to nationally recognized qualifications (e.g., NVQs), which in turn increased their self-esteem and personal confidence (indicated in their response to an employee survey).

REFLECTIONS ON PRACTICE

As stated earlier, Courtaulds sold the business in 1994, and despite the removal of the 'corporate superstructure' the management team was left largely intact. This gave an opportunity to test how robust the change process had been. The organization was revisited during 1996–98 to study the developments.

The business displayed a clear focus on success in terms of profitability. Managers were focused on immediate business indicators such as ROS (return on sales). Interestingly, this was perceived as a change (for the better) from the 'Courtaulds days'.

There had been 'run-on' of initiatives but a feeling of relief that the 'corporate diversions' had been removed. This was best displayed in a 'norming' of performance indicators, i.e. there was an increase in 'lost time' accidents which, albeit acceptable to the new management and still good for a textile company, would have been unacceptable for a Courtaulds business.

The business, in refocusing, had rejected the need for external advice and wider business indicators by concentrating on sales performance. However, this may well have been a result of the need to 'swing the pendulum back' as an almost inevitable consequence of the sale and a need to find a new identity.

Learning was not seen to be as important as performance, but the learning started under Courtaulds was based on the Kolb cycle (Kolb 1984). It may be that this state would have been achieved regardless of the ownership issue, because the cycle was due to move into a performance phase.

The evidence was clear that the original values of allowing people to be responsible, make mistakes, work in effective teams and show tolerance to learning times had survived, but the targets had changed. The management made no attempt to develop a new strategy for the new business; a purely market-driven approach was taken. However, some of the values of the previous approach were recognizable.

In summary, many of the principles and values existed but were being displayed differently, perhaps because the challenges were new and the success/failure time scale more immediate and critical.

EVALUATING THE STRATEGY

One lesson learned was that the individuals engaged in the original change process failed to recognize the connection between the process of achieving change and the ultimate goal – profit and sales. From their perspective the steps were in a mist of corporate dogma and generalization, largely chasing corporate targets of indirect value.

The company Novaceta, based in Coventry, is a successful manufacturer of man-made fibre with a good record of cost-based performance achieved by a 'top-down' management approach. In 1994, an employee survey indicated low motivation as well as a poor safety record, even after high investment.

The management was of the opinion that the problem was linked to attitudes and behaviour. It was felt that the organization needed to change in order to provide the framework for effective performance of individuals and less emphasis on the systems and procedures.

Novaceta had access in 1994 to the research done at Littleborough and visited the site. The company decided to adopt the 'Littleborough approach' to effect improvements and change. This approach complemented the existing performance indicators with 'softer' people targets around communication, morale and team-working. A cross-functional team had been established to design and deliver initiatives, and NVQs were used to reward the employees.

The early surveys indicate that employee attitudes have changed and business indicators have been positive. Managers had no previous experience of teaching, and developing a teaching role was a risk. However, there is evidence that it has positively changed the nature of the 'manager/worker' relationship.

It is not possible to attribute the improvements exclusively to the learning initiative, but the climate and culture have improved; this has been confirmed by subsequent employee surveys.

The company Biffa Waste had no contact with the previous two companies but appointed a senior manager who had been exposed to the early development in Courtaulds and used the services of the Man-made Fibres Industry Training Organisation as a catalyst.

above

The need to look at the contribution people make to business success was driven by a serious downturn in profitability and a belief of an individual manager that learning was needed at all levels in the organization. This initiative was done at a local level without corporate pressure or approval and used more external resources in the first phases.

The vision can be characterized as the need to maximize the skills of employees and increase the opportunity to use them. This could be achieved by developing an organization that encouraged innovation and sharing through team-working.

There have been overt business benefits linked to profitability and external recognition by the achievement of ISO 9000, IIP and NVQs. The employee survey has registered an increase in morale and motivation, and labour turnover has fallen. There are a number of clear factors that can be attributed to Biffa successes that can also be observed in the other two companies. These may be considered as the 'critical success factors':

- A degree of local autonomy to promote and carry though the initiative.
- External recognition to reinforce process and success.
- Continued profitability.
- Changes in work practices that embed the change.

There were drawbacks. Not all employees welcomed the changes or their new roles. For example, the maintenance team in Biffa saw the changes as a challenge to its perceived status in the previous method of work.

A PARADIGM SHIFT

In all three companies, it was recognized that the limitations of existing initiatives to change meant that a fresh approach with a different emphasis was required. The early critical mass was never large but was always significant, i.e. management teams (Novaceta), corporate (Littleborough), or an inspired individual (Biffa).

There needed to be early messages sent out regarding successes and benefits gained by both individuals and the business (this was a failing in the original approach at Littleborough that was corrected later on). Individuals at all levels of the organization did not 'buy in' to a programme they considered to be altruistic, or for indirect gain or just an academic exercise. These may be summarized as:

- Capture the hearts and minds of all employees and give them the motivation and opportunity to contribute to their full potential. This success should be externally endorsed and celebrated.
- Develop the principles of teamwork at all levels and in all areas.
- Improve co-operation between the various departments and functions.
- Move away from a negative blame culture to a more proactive and problem-owning culture (learning from mistakes).

- Involve external support, particularly for reinforcing recognition, but always stay in control and be aware of the external agenda.

- Link to business indicators that are meaningful to the individual at their level in the organization.

- Ensure all employees have skills that maximize their contribution to the business.

- Wherever possible, use own staff to do the learning. This reinforces the new culture, embeds the change and ensures the approach continues.

- Involve advisers in the process early to inform and set the strategy; continue this involvement to monitor the process and steer the tactics within the process.

The focus thus moves from the organization to the individual. 'Organisations learn through individuals who learn. Individuals learning does not guarantee organisational *learning*, but without it no organisational learning occurs' (Senge 1990).

This premise was a central principle for each company when it entered the change process. The intention was to move the focus to the individual to achieve the benefits equally in the business. Learning was ultimately seen as an investment.

Individuals often responded to being in the spotlight, and early benefits were achieved in all three companies by this unusual attention to the individual (the Hawthorne effect). However, in all three instances the loop was seen to close with business benefits emerging.

REFLECTIONS ON THE 'LEARNING ORGANIZATION' AS A VEHICLE FOR CHANGE

The term 'learning organization' has been used to define an ideal organization which can cope with continued change and transformation. The strength comes from the individuals acting as a community in a supportive climate – 'communities of practice' (Hendry *et al.* 1994). The original 'Littleborough' research (*ibid.*) concluded 'A learning organization facilitates the learning of employees with a view to continuous improvements and innovation'. This later reflective study revisited the 'twenty steps to becoming a learning organisation', and the key lessons learned are listed in my conclusion.

CONCLUSION

- Learning must be at the centre of the change process, and if the learning is to be maximized it should be learner-centred.

- There must be a business issue to address, where success is achievable and measurable. However, there should be an open and creative reaction to adverse performance data, not a 'blame' culture.

- Engage external support but do not be led from the outside. The energy at Littleborough returned when the Courtaulds corporate pressure was removed, although much had become embedded.

■ Create shared values by working together. One of the characteristics of the learning organization is that it seeks to integrate the efforts of all involved into an effective working community, bound together by shared values and commitments. The development of such a shared value system was significant in all three companies and has allowed them to grow and sustain the change in culture and behavioural style. The trick was to describe the measures in terms relevant to the different groups or individuals.

Creating a learning culture requires values to be linked to business imperatives and operational issues, and to become embedded in behaviour in a variety of ways. However, promoting values before people experience them is likely to be counterproductive. For this reason, avoid using terms such as the 'learning organization' and 'empowerment' unless other people have done so first. The initiatives need to be carried out for the benefit of the business and the individual collectively.

In the case of Littleborough, it was clear that the concepts were transferable and that the cultural norms persist, but as long as the benefits are overt to the business and the individual the principles can be accepted. Also in this way the principles can be sustained in the collective thinking and actions of the community even as the community develops.

One of the central lessons that came from these reflections on change practices was about process. It is not just what you do but how you do it, when you do it and how it fits together with all the other things you are doing. Because this is more likely to result in sustained change. A 'learning organization' is where people continue to learn and adapt and the organization continually refocuses.

The process must contain the reflective part of the learning cycle with equal emphasis on what was achieved and how. The academic influence from Warwick University was particularly useful in Littleborough. The notion of process is crucial and it is important to note here, in conclusion, that becoming a learning organization is a process and that a learning organization is a direction not a prescription – a journey not a destination, in which culture and values develop to reflect the business needs.

References

Hendry, C., Jones, A.M. and Cooper, N.S. (1994), *Creating a Learning Organisation: Strategies for Change.* Sutton Coldfield: Man-made Fibres Industry Training Organisation.

Kolb, D.A. (1984), *Experiential Learning: Experience as a Source of Learning and Development.* Englewood Cliffs, NJ: Prentice Hall.

Pedler, M., Boydell, T. and Burgoyne, J. (1989), *Towards a Learning Company.* Management Education and Development.

Senge, P.M. (1990), *The Fifth Discipline, The Art of Practice of Learning Organisation.* London: Century Business.

Training and development initiatives

Bob Hamlin (editor)

INTRODUCTION

The common theme of reflections in this chapter relates to various training and development initiatives that have been part of wider organizational change and development programmes in both private and public sector organizations. Each reflection on practice is a personalized account, either of the writer's close observations of initiatives taken to bring about change within the training and development function itself, or of their experiences while engaged as a key player in managing change through training and development.

The first reflection looks at attempts to integrate HRD activities in a major high street bank in the UK. It is written by Nick Kemp, who was a member of a training centre of excellence (TCE) set up in 1996 by the bank to co-ordinate the work of its various regional training teams, which traditionally had seen themselves as independent. Nick reflects on the cultural and structural challenges that faced the newly formed TCE team, examines its sources of power and influence and critically evaluates the effectiveness of each of the change approaches that were adopted. He identifies the ambiguities and inconsistencies that arose from 'an organizational imperative based upon cost reduction, and the use of change approaches, which sought to emphasize more palatable, value-oriented messages of partnership and quality'. Nick concludes that these ambiguities, when handled sensitively, can create a powerful catalyst for sharing ownership of change. From the lessons learned from his change agency experience working as a member of the TCE team, he has identified and developed five guiding principles which HRD professionals and other change agents in large-scale organizations may find of interest and value.

The organizational setting for the second reflection on practice is a French-owned manufacturing and consulting organization. From 1990 to 1996 it had positioned itself as a truly multinational business through the progressive acquisition and sometimes aggressive takeover of other international companies operating in the same industrial sector but based in other countries, including Britain and

America. By 1995, the UK part of this French organization comprised five major companies. Each had very different and diverse organizational cultures resulting from their different individual histories and from the differences of original owner-ship, which were French, British or American. These 'original' companies became the constituent parts of a newly formed UK company. Each had a director on the main board of directors, which was led and controlled by a French managing direc-tor. A newly created central human resources team comprising various HR professionals drawn from the 'original' companies was tasked with constructing and implementing a plan 'to develop synergy from the increased scale of opera-tions and diversity of product range, and to create a one-company philosophy'. Peter Mayes, the senior HRD professional in the HR team, was tasked to introduce as part of this one-company philosophy a management development process for all senior managers reporting directly to a main board director. He reflects here on the 'difficulties' he experienced as a trainer and developer working with the directors and senior managers of this newly created multinational matrix organization, including the managing director, whose cultural background was quite different from his own, during this time of tremendous change and upheaval. Although the lessons he reveals are highly personal, they will undoubtedly have a resonance for many readers who have found themselves grappling with the challenge, complexi-ties and politics of helping to bring about change in the 'outfield' parts of their organization from positions based at or near the 'centre'.

The third reflection on practice focuses on the important, complex and difficult issue of race equality in organizations. It features the particular approaches adopted by Jane Hatton, an independent HRD/OD consultant, who was engaged by the Department of Education and Community Services of Sandwell Metropolitan Borough Council, West Midlands. Her consulting task was to explore 'the training implications of developing anti-racist practice' in the department. Jane describes the nature of the organizational analysis she undertook to establish accurately the current situation and to make sense of it, plus the various training initiatives that she selected and the particular training interventions that were implemented. She provides a critical evaluation of the tactics which led to her success and those that were less successful, and describes the factors that helped or hindered the process. Of particular note and interest is the importance and value that Jane places on good-quality 'internal research' being conducted at the outset of a training and development consultancy assignment.

The fourth reflection on practice is offered by Nadine Green, who is an indepen-dent HRD/OD consultant and partner in the Jacques–Bell Partnership (JBP), which she founded in 1997 following a long and successful career as an internal HRD/OD consultant in several National Health Service (NHS) trust hospitals. It focuses on a particular consultancy assignment she and a colleague completed over a six-month period in 1998 for the Southern Derbyshire Management Development Consortium, which comprises four NHS trust hospitals. The assignment was two-fold: first, to provide support to the group of consortium members tasked to develop an Institute of Health Services Management (IHSM) postgraduate certificate in managing health services qualification course. Second, to help improve the group dynamics within the consortium while developing the group as an effective delivery team. The JBP recommendation was to develop a 'management education scheme by open learning (MESOL) model' using action learning as the primary delivery mechanism. This was accepted, but it was agreed that, as part of the course development work, the consortium members themselves would undertake a programme of personal self-development facilitated by Nadine and her consulting colleague through the process of action learning and AL sets. Besides providing interesting insights into her thinking as she moved through the consultancy assignment, Nadine's personal reflections also reveal the very real lessons she learned about the 'theory and practice' of action learning, and about herself in her new role as an external consultant and change agent.

REFLECTIONS ON PRACTICE

Establishing an integrated HRD approach in financial services

Nick Kemp

This reflection looks at attempts to integrate HRD activities in a major high street bank. It reflects on the cultural and structural challenges faced by the 'training centre of excellence' in its co-ordination of training teams that traditionally saw themselves as independent. It also examines the sources of power and influence available to the team and the effectiveness or otherwise of each change approach adopted.

The article identifies the ambiguities and inconsistencies arising from an organizational imperative that was based upon cost reduction and the use of change approaches which sought to emphasize more palatable, value-oriented messages of partnership and quality. It concludes that these ambiguities, when handled sensitively, can create a powerful catalyst for sharing ownership of change.

CONTEXT

This reflection is based upon my work with the HRD department of a major high street bank during 1997. As long ago as 1994, the bank had recognized its need to reduce the cost of its overhead operations. This need was driven by the emergence of smaller, more flexible, niche competitors following deregulation of financial services in 1987. The new competition was not tied by a large network of high street branches and was structurally more able to take advantage of new delivery channels and respond to increasingly sophisticated customer expectations. Improving the cost–income ratio was seen to be an organizational imperative in the face of such competition.

It was not until early 1996 that the bank completed a thorough review of overhead costs. The review established opportunities for cost reduction in a number of areas, one of which was training. It reported that:

1 Training activities were fragmented across the bank's UK operations. Each separate business area had its own training function that addressed only its specific needs. There was no perspective on any common needs across the wider organization. The UK bank had 37 separate training teams, and fragmentation and duplication were estimated to cost the bank between 11 and 19 per cent of its annual training budget – a potential saving of between £3.4 and £6.1 million was available.

2 Training was poorly planned and co-ordinated. There was no central co-ordination of training plans or budgets and therefore no opportunities to determine aggregate demand or co-ordinate supply. In many instances the cost of training, even within the business area, was difficult to assess. In some areas, there was little evidence of the alignment of training plans to organizational plans and priorities.

3 Training carried a very high external consultancy cost. Fragmentation meant that external HR suppliers were identified and selected through over 1000 separate purchasing points, and this lack of co-ordination was exploited by many suppliers, who did not offer the discounts that we might have been entitled to expect. The review forecast annual savings of between £1.5 and £2.8 million against external consultancy spend. The savings were based upon the establishment of a smaller number of 'preferred suppliers' with whom the bank might negotiate preferential rates based upon aggregate volumes of business.

On the back of these conclusions, the review recommended that a training centre of excellence be established to co-ordinate training and development across the bank. The newly formed 'TC of E' was headed by a senior business manager and later staffed by three more managers drawn from both broad business and HRD roles. Our team might have been described as a group of 'poachers turned gamekeepers' – we knew the about the training and business processes and therefore had the technical expertise needed to improve the bank's approaches.

'Central Training', the team responsible for development across the network of high street branches, had been heavily involved in forecasting the potential savings during the overhead review, and HR expertise was seen to be within this team. For this reason, the TC of E was closely linked to Central Training and operated from the same premises.

It also became apparent that we were to be given very little direct authority for the way in which training and development would be resourced, managed or delivered. Instead, the team drew its authority from a newly formed supply management team, which had the backing of the bank's executive and a broader overhead cost reduction mandate. For staff management purposes, we reported through the head of Central Training; in relation to activities and deliverables, we were accountable to the head of supply management, to whom we had a 'dotted' reporting line. In summary, we found ourselves:

1 reporting to the executive of one of the training teams we were responsible for co-ordinating and integrating with others;

2 drawing our legitimate authority and accountabilities from a supply management team, which in turn drew its power from a broad, yet relatively unspecific, business executive mandate;

3 having some but initially a limited expert power base with some members of training teams; and

4 being seen as 'Central Training' by other training teams in the bank. This led to confusion and, in some instances, some hostility from teams who placed strong value on the relationship with their local business and their autonomy. They saw the TC of E as an attempt by the bank to centralize training rather than co-ordinate and integrate approaches.

The next section of this reflection looks at some of the team's activities and their results.

CHALLENGING BUDGETS

Early work by the TC of E was based upon determining the actual financial invest-ment of each of the training teams and identifying opportunities to reduce anticipated costs. This 'budget challenge' involved the bank's central finance func-tion and local business finance directors in what was, in task terms, an information-gathering process.

Training teams universally accepted the challenge of the 1997 budgets. They were used to their budgets being reviewed, and the information was obtained through their own finance directors. For their part, finance directors welcomed a third party with HR expertise providing advice on how they might reduce their costs. However, our ability to challenge budgets was largely dependent upon the extent and the accuracy of the information available to us, much of which was of limited quality.

So the following year we asked people to forecast their 1998 training budgets against a standard template and to produce operating plans that supported their budgets. We also offered workshops and support for the production of these plans. Reaction to these changes was mixed. Most teams were happy to use the template, although the quality and quantity of the information varied. Operating plans also varied in their quality. In the main, those who produced the poorest-quality infor-mation were those who felt that they had no need to attend the planning workshops we offered.

Some areas were clearly cautious about the new direction of the budget chal-lenge. One team suggested that, as their local business area produced large profits, the TC of E had no cause to involve itself in its training budgets – it clearly must be doing things right and should be left to manage its training without our interfer-ence. Despite some hostility, the challenge resulted in estimated savings of £4.7 million against initial 1998 plans.

TARGETING DEMAND

The overhead review team had seen that a 'quick win' cost reduction could be obtained by reducing the number of people attending training courses they did not really need. It felt that savings of around £1.2 million were available from better targeting of training attendance. The project team had recommended that each nominee's request for a training course be tested by challenging it against a series of questions that would determine his/her suitability for the course. These questions were structured into 'decision trees' based upon the content of each training event.

We decided to introduce this 'demand challenge' by asking each training team to establish decision trees for each of their courses. We first wrote to each area's busi-ness executive, who advised us of suitable contact points in their businesses. We then sent a letter to each training team that explained that their executive had endorsed the introduction of decision trees for their courses and gave them a dead-line of around twelve weeks for their introduction. We produced a booklet that outlined the business case for the introduction of trees and provided advice on their development and implementation.

Our approach relied heavily on our authority to introduce these changes with local executive support and, as our approach had been almost entirely 'hands off', we followed up the launch with a review after three months. This showed that little had been done to introduce the changes. A range of reasons for not producing trees were given, most commonly that their existing systems were more effective, their course provision/culture would not support the initiative or that they had more pressing business priorities. Clearly, our authority to introduce changes to operational processes had been rejected. However, we found that the initiative worked well where we spent time actively and personally selling the added value to individual training team heads. For example, more focused demand freed up training delivery time or reduced opportunity costs of attending courses. Where we were able to show the added business value and offer personal support we developed highly vocal and dedicated champions.

In practice, however, decision trees produced very few savings. We found that line managers who were expected to use the trees greeted the nomination challenge with disinterest. They wanted to fit courses to staff needs, not try to 'shoe-horn' staff needs into the course provision. They saw the process as bureaucratic. As the challenge was difficult to enforce, it was heavily dependent upon user perception of value. This resulted in the adoption and use of decision trees being discontinued as a key priority.

CO-ORDINATING SUPPLY

During 1997, as training plans improved, we began to obtain more information on the external consultants that were used for training and development. We built upon this development to introduce a supply management initiative.

The first step in co-ordinating the supply of training was to establish those suppliers used by each training team. All teams were more than willing to contribute this type of information to a supplier list. Indeed, many teams felt that they were providing their favourite suppliers with an opportunity to develop wider business opportunities across the bank. The emphasis we placed on this initiative was one of sharing information.

Supplier co-ordination also allowed us to develop our perceived expertise in relation to the contractual relationship with training suppliers. We developed a number of generic standard contracts for different training and development services and provided advice on the specific content and terms. In this way, we developed a reputation for support and information.

However, despite being able to negotiate improved rates with some of the larger suppliers, we found it difficult to stop training teams using whichever supplier they wanted. Indeed, any such approach was seen to change the basis of our relationship from the provision of advice and support to the establishment and policing of policy.

GROWING THE VALUE OF TRAINING TEAMS

As the TC of E developed from a business review of costs, it is perhaps unsurprising that the activities I have described are centred on reducing demand and supply costs, with clear financial targets. However, we also recognized the opportunity for the TC of E to improve the value of the internal cost of its training teams by ensuring that they worked in the most cost-effective (as opposed to simply the most cost-efficient) way. This led to an initiative to introduce quality and performance standards into the work of each training team. While not expected to produce significant financial savings in the short term, we expected long-term savings that would position the initiative as 'cost neutral'.

This initiative was actively taken forward a few months later than other initiatives, and this allowed us to learn from our earlier experiences. It was clear that our authority to define policies and embed new practices into training teams was limited, so we drew on our perceived value as expert HRD consultants and co-ordinators for common agenda/issues.

We established a working group, which developed a bank training and development standard, which we based upon national standards for training and development. We invited participation from all training teams, and I spent time talking to each group to establish the range of benefits each team or individual might gain from its involvement. Each set of training standards was branded with the local business logo and we established personal learning and development agendas for trainers in selected pilot groups. This was then followed up with an assessment and evaluation of the learning we achieved as a group and how it might be translated into the operating and development processes.

The results were very encouraging – all pilot participants intended to use the standards beyond the pilot process, and the future role of the TC of E was reviewed. This reinforced the view that we were valued for our expertise and co-ordination role. However, despite a very positive experience, participants' views remained mixed in relation to adopting the standards as policy or the TC of E undertaking any central assessment of the extent to which the training teams or individuals were meeting the standards.

WHAT DID I LEARN?

I spent around 15 months working with the bank across each of the initiatives outlined in this reflection. The work gave me first-hand experience of several change approaches and the reactions and outcomes they provoked. I am not suggesting that our approaches were the only ones available to us, or that given a similar brief in a different organization we would obtain the same results. However, across each initiative the structural, political, cultural and personal relationships have remained constant; only our change approaches differed. It therefore allows a fairly reliable basis upon which to make some comparisons and distil learning.

Perhaps the most important thing I learned is that there is no 'right' way of bringing about organizational change. Successful change is based upon developing a 'real' understanding of the factors and issues that exist in the organization and then basing your approach on a clear understanding of the outcomes you want to achieve. Had we applied this basic principle, we may have adopted a very different approach than decision trees to reduce training demand. We were driven by the need to implement decision trees (process) and lost sight of the need to ensure a reduction in poor course nominations (outcome).

As for literature on the subject of organizational change and development, I have found it valuable to read widely, but to look beyond processes and models to the underpinning principles. Principles are more readily transferable to the challenges we face in our jobs. Develop your own models to meet the needs of each change. Using someone else's model is simply using yesterday's solution out of context. I have developed the following principles from my work in the TC of E:

1 Legitimate/structural authority comes from 'the top', but the top is determined by the perspective of those you seek to change. For many, 'the top' is the local finance director, not the chief executive.

2 The most appropriate change approach is determined by the required outcome first and foremost. The type of change and the nature of the audience are secondary issues. Embedding policy in relation to managing supply requires a different approach to developing partnerships in managing supply.

3 Be clear, consistent and open about what you are seeking to achieve. If you want people to change, tell the message, sell the benefits, and where possible centre participation and discussion on implementation issues.

4 Be wary about embarking upon change programmes that do not address the root cause of the problem. In our case, the fundamental problem was that the bank structures were fragmented, and the fragmentation within training was a symptom of a wider malaise.

5 People who commission change often see the battle, but not the war. Even the smallest change does not happen in isolation. It will affect the corporate experience. Where possible, adopt integrated and holistic changes that develop a new corporate experience over time. This supports consistent, effective and cost-effective change interventions.

Creating a 'one-company philosophy' in a French-owned multinational through management development initiatives

Peter Mayes

This reflection on practice is based on my personal experiences when I was employed as one of the senior HRD professionals in the company that is featured in this case history. The reflections are concerned with my professional practice during a time of tremendous organizational change and upheaval and represent the culmination of two years work which required me to learn how to operate on the shadow side of the company and review totally the way I worked with directors and senior managers.

BACKGROUND AND CONTEXT

The company is a French-owned manufacturing and consulting organization that is well known in its industry sector but fairly unknown to the general public. From 1990 till 1996 it had aggressively sought to position itself as a true multinational organization rather than remain and be perceived as a French-owned conglomerate with some subsidiary companies in Britain and other countries. Product and market sectors that were seen as a peripheral to its main activities were being sold off, and this consolidation process enabled the company to focus on what it now considered to be its true markets and areas for future growth.

In 1994, the company pursued an aggressive takeover of an American multinational. This resulted in it achieving a significant market presence in the USA and an expanded product range. In 1995, the UK part of this French-owned multinational now had five major subsidiary companies under its umbrella, and the plan was to create synergy from the increased scale of the business operations and the increased diversity of the product range.

I was part of the UK central human resources team that was tasked with constructing a plan to develop the sought-after synergy and create a one-company philosophy. Each individual company in the UK had very different organizational and management cultures, which had developed through their very different histories and types of original ownership. The diversity of cultures ranged from the French bank-owned 'multinational' with leading-edge technology, to the American-owned service-oriented multinational and the traditional owner-managed British companies.

These separate UK-based constituent parts of this newly created French-owned multinational company were represented on the main board of the new unified UK company, which was led and controlled by a French managing director. The human resources and training and development professionals were perceived very differently by the various directors of each of the subsidiary companies, with some considering them a valuable tool and resource and others regarding them as a waste of the company's scarce resources. This was the context in which I found myself working.

My background had been with the newly acquired and originally American-owned part of the new French-owned company, which some other parts of the wider organization treated with suspicion. My main task was to introduce as a segment of the drive towards the desired one-company philosophy a management development process for senior managers operating one level down from the main board of directors.

THE MANAGEMENT DEVELOPMENT INITIATIVE (AGREEING WHAT WAS NEEDED AND THE DECISIONS MADE)

I undertook a series of one-to-one meetings with each of the directors of all the subsidiary companies to establish their views on how management development initiatives from the centre could assist their business and the ongoing development of their senior people. These meetings were very challenging both in terms of understanding their personal values and for me to remain calm in the face of some strong resistance. On reflection, the majority of these meetings had a productive result in obtaining their commitment to the use of management development as a tool to improve the business. However, with two of the directors the commitment was only superficial in nature. Their subsequent actions demonstrated this in the way they undermined much of the work that was done.

The results of these meetings were summarized, and I was asked to present them to the managing director (MD), of whom I had little prior knowledge. Hence I considered it appropriate first to discuss matters with my line manager, who was the human resources director, so I could gain a better understanding of the best approach to take when discussing this information with the MD. This was necessary as he had a reputation for being very demanding and thorough. An illustration of this was when a particular sales team was required to present to the MD a set of results designed to mask from public view a sales promotion that had failed. The meeting, which was due to last for two hours only, actually went on for seven hours late into the evening. When I asked one of the salesmen how he felt at the end of the meeting, his exact words were: 'about two inches tall'.

At my initial one-to-one meeting with the MD we examined why management development was a necessary component of the required organization development programme. During this discussion it became clear that my understanding of what management development consisted of was very different from his due to cultural differences. Coming as he did from France, where education is strongly valued for its theoretical nature, and where the need to debate and review the thinking behind activities is highly defined, he put a much greater emphasis on those aspects of management development.

We began to examine the needs that were most required in terms of content and subject areas. Change management skills and the need for managers to be more strategic had been identified from the interviews with the directors. The latter was perceived as a prime concern for senior managers to develop. The MD was very keen for his managers to understand how to work within a multinational matrix organization because many of the managers had come from and only had experience of traditional organizational hierarchies.

I wanted to introduce a different form of learning to the managers by using action learning sets as a way of providing additional support to managers, and to create a forum for them to air their concerns and share ideas. This form of learning appeared to be alien to the MD, for I could tell from our discussions that he did not really want to use this type of process.

I also wanted all of the directors, including the MD, to attend the initial pilot workshops. The MD agreed that the other directors should attend but not him. He would review the programme through individual meetings with the providers of the training, which a panel of directors and myself were to select from a short list I had submitted for his approval.

On reflection, this was a flaw in the design of the management development programme. However, to get this far was a substantial move forward and I was keen to make as much capital from this initiative as possible.

The selection panel met the three providers tendering for the business and in the end a well-established management institute was appointed as the deliverer of the programme. My job at this stage was to continue to brief the provider about the company and to give them as much background as possible regarding the culture and style of the organization. It was at this stage that I reintroduced the concept of action learning, and AL sets were built into the design of the overall programme to provide linkages between the series of three-day workshops, which were content-specific.

The pilot workshops were conducted with the directors attending except for one notable sceptic, who, though vocal in his support, never actually attended any of the pilot sessions.

Having obtained a prioritized list of attendees from each director, I then mixed these by location, function and division in order to ensure a consistent mix for each group. These lists were then submitted to the MD for approval. Given his style of management this was a mistake, as he soon started to write new lists of different people from those originally nominated by the directors. This process then repeated itself several times, and I was beginning to wonder if the programme would ever run. Eventually, the names were agreed and the programme, dates, times and other arrangements were established and attendees notified.

The first two groups of managers who attended the pilot programme considered it valuable, and some very encouraging results came out of it. The workshops and the action learning aspects were seen as very positive activities, and a number of the directors also attended the open forum sessions built into the programme. These activities helped to establish for the first time the one-company philosophy, which had been much talked about but little acted upon. One notable exception from the open forum sessions was the sceptical director mentioned earlier.

I decided to see if I could meet this particular director to revisit and understand his views about the programme. After many cancelled meetings, a classic avoidance tactic used wholesale by the organization, I was able to discuss the issues with him. His main point was that all his people were skilled in these areas and didn't need the training and that the other parts of the organization needed to catch up with how his people worked. This situation was further supported in his eyes by the fact that his division ('company') was the most profitable and was continuing to grow. We discussed this at length and I offered the observation that although he had indeed created a highly effective close team, the difference between a close and closed team is very small. I made little impression or progress.

On reflection, the timing of the management development programme should have been delayed as the divisional camps of the old companies were still very strong and the new one-company vision was not shared by many of the senior people. The one-company philosophy meant they might have to give up some of their original power base.

OVERALL REFLECTION ON PRACTICE

On reflection, the main learning points for me from this experience have been as follows:

- Change agents need to speak the language of the business not the language of training.
- Extending an organization along the rubber band of development is fine providing the band does not break.
- Success or failure of a management development programme is not the sole responsibility of the change agent.
- Change agents need patience and persuasion skills.
- Organizational politics is a skill that needs to be learned.
- Training interventions at a senior level are highly political; the change process affects everyone, even directors; compliance does not equal commitment; directors require support too.

During this time of intense pressure for me as the change agent concerned with the management development process, I was able to gain the following:

- Improved skills in negotiating with directors.
- A much higher profile within the organization.
- Recognition for a job that was considered well done.
- An insight into the politics of the organization.
- An appreciation of the values that some directors held and how strong these values were.

- A perception of how strongly people hang on to the past when the future presents a personal threat to them or what they value.

- To be able to stand the pressure that comes with a high-profile job.

WHAT WOULD I HAVE DONE DIFFERENTLY?

The OCD programme would have been more effective if I had:

- Managed to get the attending managers to report back to their nominated directors in terms of their progress and learning as a group.

- Realized earlier than I did that actions speak louder than words.

- Tried to become more aware of the covert disruptive influences of some of the directors and had been more effective in soliciting support.

- Listened more to what directors were not saying rather than what they actually said.

- Put more effort into getting the managing director to attend the pilot sessions and the open forums.

Developing anti-racist practice in Sandwell MBC through training

Jane Hatton

Race equality is an important, complex and difficult issue for organizations to address. There follows a description of the approach one organization took, using the Commission for Racial Equality's (CRE) standard for racial equality (1995) as a framework. The intervention produced interesting reflections, not only about implementing actions to bring about racial equality but also about the role that research-based training can play in a change programme.

The organization concerned is the Department of Education and Community Services at Sandwell Metropolitan Borough Council. The department is a result of the merger of two former departments. The new department employs around 1700 people and is divided into 22 distinct service areas. Sandwell is an urban area which has a racially diverse population with pockets of deprivation.

The department has a Black Workers' Group, which is a focus group to support black and Asian employees and to act as a voice representing their interests. Issues raised at this group are taken to an action group chaired by a member of the directorate. The department operates within a policy framework largely laid down corporately. At the time of the events of this case history, the council had begun to measure itself against the CRE standards and had committed itself to achieving level 5 in all areas by the year 2000. The Department of Education and Community Services decided to go one stage further and not only measure itself as a department but assess each individual service area against the standard.

The standard sets out five levels of achievement, which represent progress on racial equality in five areas – policy and planning, service delivery and customer care, community development, employment, and marketing and corporate image.

The two main drivers for the interventions which took place were issues raised by the Black Workers' Group in terms of the experiences of black employees working for the department, and the desire to achieve level 5 of the CRE standard.

The council has a record of taking equality issues seriously and is seen as 'leading edge' on designing policies aimed to make equality a reality. However, as many writers agree, while there has been no shortage of policy formation, in many areas there is still a large gap between policy and practice (e.g. Ross 1992; Ouseley 1997; Solomos 1989). It was necessary, therefore, to compare policy with effectiveness in practice within this department.

The decision was taken to bring in an external consultant to look at the training implications of developing anti-racist practice. My name was put forward as someone who had worked on equality issues in this, and other, councils. However, the ethics around using a white consultant to explore issues of race are complex. Discussions followed with members of the Black Workers' Group. It was decided the message that anti-racism is an organizational issue, not a 'black' issue, would not be lost by using a white consultant. However, I worked closely with the Black Workers' Group throughout the research and planning stages, and worked with a black co-trainer for some of the implementation.

I stressed that the role of the consultant was not that of 'expert' and that 'off-the-shelf' solutions rarely work in complex areas such as equality. It was agreed, therefore, that some research be carried out within the department to establish the current situation as regards racial equality, and the issues that need to be addressed.

The research was mainly qualitative in nature. Interviews, both individual and group, were carried out with black employees, ensuring as far as possible that the sample chosen was representative in terms of gender, ethnic origin and service area. Interviews were also conducted with white managers, ensuring representation across gender, grade and service area. The information gained from the interviews was supplemented by some desk research on a range of employee statistics.

The desk research produced an employee profile which identified the ethnicity of employees (7 per cent from minority ethnic groups) compared with the ethnicity of the local population (13.3 per cent of the working population are from minority ethnic groups). It also demonstrated that most black employees were concentrated in low-paid and low-status jobs.

Other key areas of concern which were highlighted by the research included the implementation of the employee development scheme, the lack of development opportunities, the department's approach to racist behaviour, the inconsistent levels of awareness of managers and their consequent interpretation of policy in practice and the practice of some front-line staff.

There was also evidence of good practice in the department, and examples of where black employees had been helped to reach their full potential. The overall picture painted by the research was that of inconsistent practice throughout the organization – with good practice not being sufficiently disseminated and bad practice not being sufficiently challenged.

Recommendations were made to the department, encompassing a number of areas. Many of the recommendations were already being looked at, as prompted by action plans arising from the CRE standard audit. The main message of the recommendations flowing from the findings of the research concerned training different levels of managers and employees to embed anti-racist practice into their everyday actions. This was recommended at both strategic and operational levels.

Service area managers were currently developing action plans as a result of the assessment of their own service areas against the CRE standard. The importance of making the link between developing anti-racist practice, best management practice and the CRE standard was stressed for senior managers. A two-day programme for service area managers, delivered jointly by the researcher and a black co-trainer, was recommended to assist service area managers in this task.

It was recommended that all other managers receive training in developing anti-racist practice. This training would aim to facilitate the dissemination of good practice and address the current inconsistencies in approach to equality issues demonstrated by managers.

The important role played by front-line staff in delivering an equitable service would be addressed through training for them. Recommendations were made for a training course to be offered to all front-line staff on the practical implications for service delivery on equality issues (broadened out to include issues of gender, disability and other areas).

Further recommendations included the introduction of positive action training and development activities for black employees (including shadowing, mentoring and work experience), the modification of the content and recruitment criteria for the existing management development programme, training in specific cultural issues, a review of the effectiveness of the employee development scheme, and the need for effective monitoring of any action taken.

Some of these recommendations were already in the process of being addressed. A group is currently looking at the employee development scheme to see where it can be improved. Positive action management training for black employees is also currently being discussed in the department.

The training, which took place as a result of the research intervention, was not completely in accordance with the recommendations. Two strands of training were agreed and commissioned. A two-day programme as recommended was agreed for service area managers. A one-day programme on developing anti-discriminatory practice was agreed for nominated front-line staff. Unfortunately, although some managers attended the training for front-line staff, there was no specific provision for equality training for middle managers.

The first strand of training involved service area managers. It is widely felt that the success of any change programme in implementing anti-racist practice depends largely on the commitment to the programme from those at the top of the organizations (e.g. Anthony 1994; Wilson 1995). The importance of the success of this training was not underestimated, and much time and thought was put into the planning stage. It was decided that the training would be best presented with a team training approach, and I approached Patrick Roach from the Centre for Research in Ethnic Relations at Warwick University, who has done much research in the field of ethnic relations in the public sector. We worked jointly on both the design and delivery of the senior manager training.

Two days was acknowledged as a very short space of time to deal with such a complex subject, and so a method of establishing priorities was required. This was achieved in three ways. Issues had been raised as a result of the initial research described earlier, and these would form the basis of the training. However, within that it was necessary to identify the priorities of two groups of people. The first was the black employees themselves. We attended a number of meetings with a sub-group of the Black Workers' Group to establish the priorities for them in terms of the content of the training. The second was the senior managers. A questionnaire was sent to them some time prior to the training to establish what they saw as priorities for them.

A programme was devised which linked the three strands of anti-discriminatory practice, the CRE standard and best management practice (as illustrated in the EFQM framework) around the themes identified as priorities by the research, black employees and the participants themselves.

The training for front-line staff had different aims from the service area managers' training. There was a requirement to broaden the scope of the training to include other equality issues such as gender and disability. Also, the focus needed to be on operational practice and interpersonal skills rather than strategic issues.

The main focus of the day was on practice, and participants were encouraged to look at their own service area for examples of barriers to equality, and also examples of good practice that could be built on. Case studies were used to promote discussion about application of equality in practice, and then participants formulated individual action plans.

Participants on the training for senior managers appeared to participate fully in the exercises and ensuing discussions. Open debate took place in an environment that was aimed at being challenging without being confrontational. Each manager drew up an action plan for cascading best practice, and communicating actions from the CRE standard action plan throughout their service area.

Following these workshops, I completed a report making further recommendations for future actions which had been raised during the training, including the introduction of a performance management system with appropriate equality performance indicators, the requirement for continued resources and support for managers to implement action plans, a monitoring system that could more easily be used as a management planning tool, and many others. The action plans formulated by delegates were included in an appendix. The completed report was presented to all participants and the directorate. Some of the recommendations arising from this report have already been addressed.

The workshops for front-line staff were well attended. Reactions to the training varied between and within groups, but overall there was a high level of participation. Some early resistance was overcome when the training could be seen to be of a practical nature rather than 'brainwashing', as some participants had feared it might be.

The intervention as a whole entailed far more activities than the training described here, as changes were also made to policy and procedures. It is difficult to isolate the training interventions from other activities when evaluating effectiveness (Brown and Lawton 1991).

In evaluating the training, two 'measures' were taken. One assessed the immediate reactions of participants in terms of how effective they felt the training had enabled them to take action in this area. This was assessed in two ways. First, by looking at the individual action plans they had formulated and assessing whether they had been able to identify relevant achievable actions and at how they intended to monitor and evaluate their actions. Second, by asking participants to complete evaluation forms on completion of the training programme to ask for immediate reactions.

However, these measures would only give an indication of the extent to which the short-term aims of the course had been met (in terms of provoking thought, encouraging people to look at practice and identify practical ways in which it could be improved, etc.); it would not measure the extent to which these actions had been put into practice. The real test of the training would be the extent to which organizational performance improved in the area of equality over a period of time (Wallace 1991). This would require further qualitative research to take place some time after completion of the training in order to form comparisons. This has not yet taken place, due to the time scale required to implement actions before their real effectiveness can be measured. However, reactions of groups of people have been gained since the training, and this gives an indication of the impact that training may have had on the ability of participants to implement their action plans.

In terms of the immediate reactions, senior managers were able to produce some relevant and interesting action plans. These demonstrated the ability to relate the theory of anti-racism to their individual practice areas. Many managers were able to identify creative and realistic actions within their own service areas that had not been 'fed' by the trainers, demonstrating a practical understanding of some of the issues involved.

The evaluation forms completed by senior managers indicated that the practical approach to the training had been well received. Some admitted to feeling uncomfortable, and therefore defensive, about the findings from the initial research, and had been concerned that the training was being offered as a form of 'punishment', but in the event most felt that they had been enabled to take a more positive approach to equality issues.

Front-line staff were able, in the main, to identify appropriate and useful actions they intended to take. Often this was in the form of finding out further information, or practical actions like finding or generating a list of available interpreters in community languages. Others said that they would now challenge racist and sexist humour, not having realized the subtle effect 'humour' can have on the culture of an organization. Many were able to identify subtle, unintentional forms of discriminatory practice, either in themselves or others, or embedded in procedures, which they had not previously recognized and would now challenge. The ability to take the learning and translate it into relevant actions demonstrated that the training had been effective to some extent.

Evaluation forms revealed a varied response. There were some comments on the length and depth of the course (a few feeling it too long and heavy, others feeling it too short and superficial). Most felt that the focus on practice was useful.

The long-term evaluation needs to be cyclical, with results being measured and improved continuously. Not enough time has elapsed at the time of writing to comment with any degree of confidence on the effectiveness of the interventions. However, informal conversations with participants some months after completion of the training have revealed some longer-term reactions. The strong message I have received from senior managers I have since spoken to was that the practical elements of the training were the most useful. In particular, the relationship between equality and quality demonstrated with the EFQM model seems to have been beneficial in helping participants to understand the importance of integrating anti-racist practice into management practice. Some of the actions identified during the training have now taken place, evaluation conducted and corrective action taken.

Informal discussions with front-line staff echoed the value of the practice-related elements of the course. People who had previously attended race relations training said that they had left those courses feeling frustrated, because although they now recognized the problem, they felt powerless to do anything about it. This course, they felt, had helped them focus on practical solutions, which could really make a difference, however small.

An observation made by many participants was that although senior managers and front-line staff had now begun to address the issues, there was a large gap in between which could affect the degree of success of the change programme. Middle managers had featured quite largely in the initial research, in terms of the inconsistent translation of policy into practice, and yet this level of personnel had not been offered training. Many writers suggest that the role of middle managers is crucial in achieving business transformation (e.g. Bird 1997).

The long-term success of this change programme has yet to be properly measured, but some useful reflections can be made on the work carried out so far.

The role of training in a change programme can be reflected upon in the light of this intervention. Most writers agree that training needs to occur in the context of an overall change programme. In this particular case, the training appeared not only to support the change programme but also to contribute towards it. The training undertaken by senior managers enabled their heightened awareness of the issues involved to suggest and promote further changes in areas such as the review of policies and procedures, the introduction of more effective monitoring systems which can act as a valuable management tool, and ensuring that the introduction of performance management and the adoption of the EFQM model will now be based on equality principles.

Another reflection on this piece of practice involves the value of research-based training. Many participants questioned some of my assertions, and I was able to back my observations of the organization with evidence from research carried out in it. Therefore, the training was not based on an outsider's assumptions about what was happening in the organization but on the picture painted by a group of employees. Denial is common on training programmes around equality but was made more difficult as it was based on research.

A personal view is that excluding middle managers from the training may hamper the success of the change programme. Participants on the course expressed a feeling of 'ownership' of the issues, and motivation to address them. However, if middle management does not share this ownership and motivation, then good practice may be difficult to introduce and sustain.

The nature of equality training has moved over the years from an attempt to change attitudes (e.g. Katz 1978) to an attempt to influence behaviour. The practice-related elements of the training involved in this intervention appeared to stimulate participants into thinking about improving practice, and would indicate that a more practical focus is perhaps more likely to produce real change than focusing on attitude.

As ever, the intervention raised more questions than it answered. Although the role that training can play in a change process has been explored, it would be interesting to explore different methods of equality training and compare their effectiveness in similar organizations. It would also be interesting to research whether the conclusions drawn here about equality training could be transferred to other areas of training within a change process.

References

Anthony, P. (1994), *Managing Culture*. Open University Press.

Bird, J. (1997), Human aspects of transformation. *Management Skills and Development*, 1, March.

Brown, C. and Lawton, J. (1991), *Training for Equality. A Study of Race Relations and Equal Opportunities training*. Policy Studies Institute.

Commission for Racial Equality (1995), *Racial Equality Means Quality*. CRE.

Katz, J. (1978), *White Awareness: Handbook for Anti-Racism Training*. University of Oklahoma Press.

Ousley, H. (1997), Must equality issues shout to be heard? *Local Government Chronicle*, 14 March, 14–15.

Ross, K. (1992), Inequality circles. *Local Government Policy Making*, 19(3), 15–19.

Solomos, J. (1989), From equal opportunity to anti-racism. Racial inequality and the limits of reform. *Policy Papers in Ethnic Relations*, Centre for Research in Ethnic Relations.

Wallace, J.B. (1991), *Developing Better Managers*. Kogan Page.

Wilson, D.C. (1995), *A Strategy of Change*. Routledge.

Using action learning to improve the group dynamics of the South Derbyshire Management Development Consortium

Nadine Green

These personal reflections are based upon an organizational change and development pro-gramme carried out in the South Derbyshire Management Development Consortium ('the consortium') by The Jacques Bell Partnership (JBP) during April to September 1999.

The consortium comprises four National Health Service (NHS) trusts in the Derbyshire geographical area. Each is represented by the organizational training and development manager and/or key training department staff. In total, there are eight individuals. The individuals themselves originally established the consortium as a formal professional network several years ago, but its focus evolved to include a joint management development initiative. The consortium gained accreditation to deliver a portfolio of managerial qualifications serving the staff of members' respective organizations. They felt, however, that there was a gap in their portfolio. This gap was the Institute of Health Services Management (IHSM) postgraduate Certificate in Managing Health Services course. This qualification is deemed the preferred qualification for all NHS-based managers as the NHS Training Directorate, the Open University and the IHSM developed it collectively. The qualification currently attracts approximately 35-M (postgraduate level) CATS points and was accompanied by the postgraduate-level Diploma in Health and Social Services Management. Together, the qualifications are known as the Management Education Scheme by Open Learning (MESOL). The NHS executive retains a centralized function dedicated to the promotion of MESOL in the service and offers an annual bursary scheme for NHS and social services based organizations wishing to develop access to the qualification base in their locality.

The consortium identified the 1997/98 bursary scheme as a means of supporting the establishment and development of an IHSM-accredited programme to complement their existing portfolio. It was the aim of the consortium members that they themselves should deliver the twelve-month programme of supporting workshops which consolidate the open learning material, mark the academic scripts and invigilate the examination. This would provide a means of job enrichment and enlargement for all those involved.

The consortium were advised by the executive offices to seek consultancy support from my partnership in developing the project and was successful in its application for bursary money to fund the change initiative. My colleague and I met two representatives from the consortium to discuss organizational context and objectives. The objectives which evolved from the meeting included development of a customized MESOL workshop programme, academic marking skills, assignment design, and administration design and full IHSM accreditation to offer the qualification.

In addition, the consortium wished to be developed as a delivery team. Apparently, the dynamics of the group had suffered during recent years, caused mainly by changes in organizational culture as a result of trust status within the service, changes in consortium membership and now the impending reconfiguration issues (with two of the four trusts merging into one). One of the members was particularly keen on our model of MESOL delivery, based on Reg Revan's model of action learning. She asked if the consortium could be developed as an action learning set as part of our development work with it in order to meet the team development objective. This would serve a dual function in that it would also enable members to contextualize how action learning would work within their own MESOL programmes.

These initial objectives fitted well with our partnership's business philosophy, which was to always endeavour to leave our clients in a confident and self-sufficient state. Our main concern at this point was the time scale, as they wished to be able to commence their programme in line with the start of the new academic year – October 1998. Working backwards from this point (taking recruitment and selection and summer holidays into consideration) this gave us a total of four months in which to achieve the majority of the project. We decided that monthly one-day workshops would be more effective in being able to achieve large chunks of objectives, rather than piecemeal via lots of shorter meetings. This time scale would also enable us to achieve many of the objectives via an action learning model.

We assessed the objectives and analysed them closely, attempting to break them down into specific tasks for each month. Coupled with our delivery of direct knowledge input (as a foundation for the work-based tasks), this model would allow us to meet the objectives while also developing the delivery team.

On a personal level, my initial concerns regarding the programme were not just about the amount of work to be undertaken and the time scale within which to do this but also about the fact that I would be responsible for developing my peers. In professional terms, this group was very much on a par with me – in NHS experience, academic background and managerial responsibility. They were also an established group, with dynamics of their own. The dynamics were also influenced by this professional bias – they were all training and development facilitators – not a shy collection by any means!

I failed to recognize all these strengths at the commencement of the programme, because I was so wrapped up in self-consciousness. I had also completely missed the fact that the power base upon which I had relied for almost all of my work was very different and I therefore had to be aware of this. My power base was based not purely on positional, sapiential and negative power, as it so often is while working as an internal agent of change with perhaps more junior managers. This time, it was almost purely based upon personal and resource power, i.e. my ability to develop rapport with the already established group and my facilitation skills. The consortium members were already established management development practitioners.

I had not considered that in reality these individuals would be far more open and receptive to learning – they had invited us in of their own accord. Why would they be actively looking for faults in my performance? If anything, they had more empathy with and understanding of our position than any other group that I had worked with, because they were practitioners themselves. This also meant that they were able to evaluate my consultancy support more effectively than a layperson – in many ways making constructive feedback even more useful and positive.

Another issue which I had not considered was again that because of their professional backgrounds, the consortium members would be far more interactive, participative, communicative, motivated, skilled in analysis and conceptualization. All of these change agent skills made it so much easier to meet the project objectives. This was true of action learning too. They took to action learning very quickly, especially as one or two of them had experienced being an action learning set member as part of other academic programmes.

A further self-imposed anxiety was regarding the way that our partnership had been introduced to this client. It was the NHS executive arm, experienced in the promotion of MESOL, that recommended us as the programme managers. The fact that the recommendation was from its national office was a huge compliment to our partnership but also could have greatly influenced client-based perception of our ability and scope! I was desperate to ensure that I would not let the national office down in any way, shape or form on what was our first referral. This did place extra pressure on me though, as it was also the flagship project for the newly formed JBP.

Upon reflection, a further learning point for me was around flexibility and willingness to modify existing practice. After I had facilitated the first two action learning set meetings, I realized that the textbook recommendation of a maximum of six set members could be extended – providing the members were in possession of polished interpersonal skills and understanding of process issues. In their evaluation of the process the participants also expressed a desire to modify the structure of the meeting slightly to allow for more spontaneity. I was concerned at this suggestion, as I had modified my existing process several times over a period of years, based upon evaluation of a range of groups, to restrict this element of group process. As already stated, they were a very vocal group and we had a very large agenda to get through at each workshop. I stated my concerns about the proposed change but also recognized that this would be a useful learning exercise for the set members as they would be able to experience the impact of this 'freedom of voice'. This was also bound to be a question that their own future MESOL-based action learning set members would ask! It would have been easy to try to impose my process upon the group, but as a facilitator I had to remember that the set needed to 'own' the process, and effective conclusions can only be drawn from personal experience and reflection.

Although the group very quickly became highly effective within their own consortium-based action learning task, they found it difficult to conceptualize how we used it within MESOL programmes. Again, this was a learning point for me, as I truly believed that their own personal experiences would make this cognitive transfer fairly easy. The only way that I could envisage this learning taking place would be to actually take each member through Kolb's learning cycle, i.e. provide an opportunity for each consortium member to actually observe my colleague and I facilitating a MESOL-based action learning set. Another one of our clients, Mid-Staffordshire General Hospital NHS Trust, agreed access for each of the individual consortium members to their own MESOL programme action learning sets. (With express permission from the individual action learning sets.) These shadowing visits formed the basis of action learning-based presentations from each consortium member.

Part way through the change programme, one of the consortium members was involved in a serious road traffic accident and was absent for the remainder of the programme. This obviously had an impact upon the group dynamics and the allocation of the various action learning-based tasks. There was also concern that the objective of developing a delivery team would be affected. The consortium surprised my colleague and I by becoming even more motivated to ensure that this absence would not hinder the achievement of the objectives and that communication was maintained regarding the development of the project. We also sent flowers from the consortium upon hearing the sad news. Her absence was noticed though, as she had a unique style of participation, sense of humour and approach to tasks. We ensured that her colleague provided an update of her recovery progress at each workshop and that we maintained her clarity of role in the longer-term plans.

I also learned about the power of action learning in challenging traditional roles of trainer and change agent. The catalyst for this learning was the IHSM accreditation panel visit. We had agreed that this part of the process should be approached on a consortium basis – i.e. a team effort, but without the presence of my colleague and myself. We waited in another room while the panel visit was conducted. This proved to be a much more traumatic experience than either of us had anticipated. While waiting, we reflected on why this 'letting go' action felt so different from our MESOL groups, for example, when we send them off into the IHSM examiners' room. Our only conclusion was that the process of action learning and the rapport that we had developed with the group were crucial in the dynamics. We both genuinely felt great angst at not being able to support the consortium during this particularly testing time. I also recognized that this would be a means of evaluating not just the consortium's ability to deliver the programme but also our ability to facilitate their learning and development. This would be an opportunity for the consortium to work as a true team, with a clear vision of what they wanted to achieve. If we had not achieved our objectives, then the panel would find the cracks. The consortium's success was our success.

It was during the first and final action learning set following the successful accreditation panel visit that we shared our reflections with the group. They then became the facilitators in our development, almost allowing us to present as set members, encouraging us to reflect on the fact that every change agent has to 'let go' at some point and that this level of cohesion was indicative of the level of relationship that we had jointly developed. If we had not shared any empathy and anxiety with them during this time, then how could we have been truly giving our commitment to the project? This was the first time that I had ever experienced complete transfusion in an action learning set – which I was supposed to be facilitating!

In conclusion, I can honestly say that this change and development programme has had both short- and long-term benefits at both a personal and organizational level for all of the parties involved. The theory worked, but only with constant tweaking and modification along the way to accommodate the fast-changing environment and individual needs – including my own.

References

Kolb, D. (1984), *Experiential Learning: Experience as the Source of Learning and Development*. Englewood Cliffs, NJ: Prentice-Hall.

Revans, R. (1983), *The ABC of Action Learning*. Bromley: Chartwell-Bratt.

PART

IV

REFLECTIONS ON PRACTITIONER PERSPECTIVES AND REFLECTIONS ON PRACTICE

Towards research-based organizational change and development

11

Bob Hamlin

ANALYSIS

As you will appreciate, the insights embedded in the reflections on change agency practice of the various contributors to Part III of this book are many and varied. One might have expected as much from a diverse range of practitioners who have been involved with such a wide range of OCD programmes operating at different levels in different types of private, public, voluntary and not-for-profit organizations. What is of particular interest is the degree to which many of the insights are the same or similar. This may be surprising to some readers, bearing in mind the fact that most of the contributors are unknown to each other. Of the few that are, most have met or exchanged words only once, and then only at a single meeting convened by the co-editors of this book to discuss the guidelines for writing their respective reflections on practice, which they subsequently produced independently. An analysis of their collective insights reveals several 'lessons', from which a number of generalized insights and conclusions can be drawn concerning effective change agency practice. In general, these lend support to the arguments presented by the authors of Part 1 and Part II of this book and of various authors on change management to be found in the more recent literature. In particular, they help also to illuminate to a greater or lesser extent certain stages of the 'generic model of organizational change management' illustrated in Chapter 2.

The most striking observation from an analysis of the various 'reflections on practice' in Part III is the significance placed by a large majority of the contributors on communicating with all stakeholders for the purpose of securing common ownership, commitment and involvement.

This feature and focus of attention in practice seems to have been deemed of critical importance. Drawing on the reflections of the strategic change leadership team in First Engineering, Alison Thomas highlights the importance given to eliciting the views of 'all stakeholders including customers and clients as well as the workforce' in order to 'get them to understand what is being planned, to establish in their minds the principle of ownership and to foster their commitment'. This aspect of change management is echoed by Paul Turner of Lloyds TSB, who strongly argues that 'people need to be seen as the absolute priority', and that one must 'communicate with all stakeholders'. Based on her change agency experience in the healthcare sector, Jane Keep refers to the need 'to involve as many stakeholders as possible', and to allow them to 'see things for themselves', while Ken Ash in manufacturing strongly advocates the need to involve employees in order to 'identify accurately the need for change', in this case the need for team-working. In the public sector, Graham Smith describes how 'circulating a synopsis of the [change] plan to every employee' of the Contract Services Department of Sandwell MBC had been a key factor in the success of the change process. And Margaret Reidy in HMCE draws attention to the strategic change leadership of the then CEO of the HMCE (Anglia Region), Dick Shepherd, who continuously 'informed, consulted and supported his people through the changes' he initiated.

In the Netherlands, 'using the right approach for securing the active involvement of the workforce in the formulation and ownership of the change strategy, and their individual and collective commitment to its implementation', were seen by Professor Jaap Germans as being significant factors in the ultimate success of the EZH organizational change programme for which he had key responsibilities as a strategic change leader. Whatever approach might be used for securing common ownership, commitment and involvement, Prudence Clarke concludes from her experiences as an OCD consultant working in the metal and plastic components industry that 'employees [can and will] accept and work effectively within constant change as long as they know where change is taking them'.

For many, securing the active commitment, involvement and participation of senior to middle managers was pivotal. For example, in First Engineering Lesley Imrie, the New Horizons project manager, believed the deliberate 'participation of senior managers at [the] early stage was a shrewd move'. In hindsight, Mike De Luca, the outside OCD consultant from the Coverdale Organisation, admits he 'could [and should] have done even more work at this level'. It is interesting to note that in his role as executive head of HM Customs & Excise (Anglia Region) Dick Shepherd took great pains to 'involve his senior and middle managers and to empower them'. Engaged as an outside OD consultant by the Education and Community Services Department of Sandwell MBC to look at the training implications of developing anti-racist practice, Jane Hatton draws attention to how important it was to 'secure the ownership and commitment of everyone, especially middle managers'.

Working as an internal change agent in the Contract Services Department of the same organization, Graham Smith describes the pivotal role of middle managers in 'leading the change and spreading it down, up and laterally'. The damaging consequences of a lack of ownership at the middle management level was all too clear in Ken Ash's reflections. In contrast, as the external facilitator helping a managing director to bring about organizational change in two manufacturing plants of his metal and plastic components company, Prudence Clarke observed the critical factor leading to the greater success of the one plant was the active supportive leadership of the respective management team. Their style of leadership was one of 'developing open and continuous dialogue, following through with positive and constructive feedback, giving praise when due, and learning from past experiences'.

Securing top management commitment and support is also a key focus in the reflections of several contributors. Vince McGregor, reflecting upon the highly successful and widely publicized OCD programme in British Aerospace (Prestwick), which he helped facilitate, argues the success was due in large part to 'senior people at the centre of the organization holding the necessary influence and championing the change'. Having a member of the strategic management team as a lead officer of the IIP change initiative in Sandwell MBC was, as Graham Smith reports, 'a critical success factor' for, as he argues, 'without a committed and determined managing director and the support of senior management the whole process would have failed'. The absence of such commitment caused Peter Mayes to conclude 'you need top management commitment', though Nick Kemp quite rightly reminds us that although 'change is driven by pressures from the top' we need to be clear as to 'who the top is' as perceived in the mind's eye of the respective stakeholders you seek to change.

Nick discovered it is important for trainers and developers to find this out at the earliest stages of a change initiative, particularly if you are employed at the 'centre' of an organization and tasked to help get corporate policies implemented in the various subsidiaries or 'outreach' extremities of the business. Perceptions of 'who the top is' are determined by stakeholders themselves and can be strongly influenced by parochial or internal political perspectives, perhaps also shared with or dictated by their immediate managers. These perceptions can be widely at variance with one's own perceptions.

Jane Hatton is another contributor who found from her experiences in Sandwell MBC and elsewhere that 'the success of change programmes in organizations [in this case implementing anti-racism policies] depend largely on the commitment to the programme from those at the top'.

Securing appropriate top management commitment and support can sometimes be exceedingly difficult, particularly when the preferred and espoused management style of the top manager is incongruent with what 'best practice' calls for. As Julie Knowles discovered when attempting to introduce *kaizen* in the care sector organization where she was employed, the 'autocratic perfectionist' style of the manager impeded the change process, which called out for a more 'supportive and stimulative style' of management. Although there was a belief that *kaizen* could and should be implemented, its success was 'more dependent on the ability of both the management and employees to adapt to a more empowering, democratic and cross functional' management style.

Each of these 'generalized insights' attest to the crucial importance of giving sufficient attention to stage 4 of the 'generic model of organizational change management', namely 'secure ownership, commitment and involvement including top management support'.

The specific overarching lesson to be learned from the reflections in Chapter 7, all of which were concerned with transformational and cultural change programmes, includes 'being clear, consistent and open with regard to what you are seeking to achieve, setting clear strategic objectives and sharing the vision'. For example, Paul Turner of Lloyds TSB discusses the key part played by the 'Fit for the Future' briefing document which was a central plank in the change strategy for bringing about as smoothly, effectively and as painlessly as possible the merger of Lloyds and TSB. As part of his five-year business plan and change strategy for HMCE (Anglia Region), Dick Shepherd communicated extensively with his people, not only by publishing and promulgating his 'Painting the Picture' document and its subsequent updates but also in holding regular 'road shows' around the Anglia region for people to speak out to him face to face.

Peter Grice, commenting on his longitudinal study of three organizations in the man-made fibres industry, stresses the need to 'capture the hearts and minds of all employees and give them the motivation and opportunity to contribute to their full potential; also to endorse this success externally'. Interestingly, Prudence Clarke concluded from her observations in the metal and plastic components company that 'leadership can be seen as the "painters" of the company mission picture to secure the support of all their employees and gain their ownership of the "changing" process'.

These 'lessons' reinforce the importance of stage 2 of the 'generic model', namely the need to 'create a strategic vision' and to promulgate this extensively and effectively throughout the whole organization.

Nine of the contributors saw 'recognizing and addressing the real problems or root causes of problems, including the cultural dimensions' as a key factor in determining the effectiveness of their change agency practice. Jane Keep drew attention to an example where the sponsor of the OCD programme, in her case the CEO of an NHS trust, wanted her to bring about structural change. But her initial OCD initiatives soon revealed 'deficiencies in the managerial behaviours and skills of the managers to be the problem, not the organizational structure'. Similarly, Ken Ash, being tasked to help line managers bring about planned 'top-down' structural change in the manufacturing firm where he was employed as an HRD specialist, identified the real need as that of changing 'the cultural and behavioural issues as reflected in the attitudes, philosophy and style of leadership' in the organization. The need for senior managers to 'change their language and behaviour' was seen by Vince McGregor in British Aerospace as an essential component of the strategic change programme in that company; and in First Engineering the 'cultural element was seen as an integral part of everything' they did.

For Graham Smith in Sandwell MBC the major challenge was that of changing the 'attitudes and behaviours' associated with ' the existing culture', which Jane Keep also found to be 'the difficult issues ' in the healthcare sector. When culture is recognized as the key issue in a change management programme there is, as Professor Jaap Germans observes, a 'temptation to give more emphasis to this than to the structures and systems issues'.

However, the change agent needs to give equal attention to both. Even so, dealing with the 'soft' people and cultural issues before the 'hard' issues may be necessary, as Margaret Reidy observed in HMCE. These 'lessons' clearly illustrate the importance of investing enough time and effort at stage 1 of the 'generic model', which is to 'diagnose/explore the present state and identify the required future state'. They also remind us of the need to diagnose accurately and in sufficient depth the 'beneath the surface' problems, particularly the 'soft' cultural and people-related problems such as people who are very difficult to deal with, who present obstacles, who create impasses, or are likely to be working either overtly or covertly to sabotage the change process. As Jane Keep and others suggest, sometimes it is necessary for the change agent during stage 1 to be prepared to 'discuss the undiscussable' and 'think the unthinkable'.

A common conclusion and generalized insight emerging from the experiences of several of the contributors illuminating stage 5 of the 'generic model', which you will recall is to 'project manage the implementation of the change strategy and sustain momentum', is that of giving enough time for the OCD programme to take root and succeed. Paul Turner of Lloyds TSB concluded that 'a structured and long-term programme of incremental change may prove more effective in guiding the culture of an organization in a broad direction'.

This viewpoint is supported by Mike De Luca: when reflecting on the change programme in First Engineering, he concludes 'You must prepare for a lengthy crusade. When your strategy is to involve as many people as possible, it takes time. The process of learning from experience takes more time. A successful change programme is a long-term project'.

In a similar vein, Jaap Germans observes that one needs to 'give sufficient time to explaining and stressing to the workforce the new business realities, and securing their commitment and sense of ownership for the change strategy'; and Jane Keep concludes that stakeholders need to be allowed 'to work their own way through to a conclusion'.

The contribution that the HR function can make and the strategic role it can play in bringing about transformational change are well illustrated in three of the reflections on practice. In his role as a strategic change leader helping bring about the merger of Lloyds and TSB to form Lloyds TSB, Paul Turner describes how HR 'acted as a partner to the respective business units and functional heads in advising on the human aspects of the change, as change facilitators', and as HR functional specialists 'ensuring excellence in [the associated] administration'. In these roles it provided the top management team with the necessary understanding of the critical success factors for change, carried out the organizational analysis and survey feedback work and supplied the administrative support required during the change process. These roles are similar to the four multiple roles that Ulrich (1997) argues HR professionals should perform as part of the next agenda for adding value and delivering results, namely the roles of 'strategic partner', 'administrative expert', 'employee champion' and 'change agent'. It is undoubtedly the case that Peter Shields performed all these roles in his capacity as HR director of the bulk pharmaceutical manufacturing company in Ireland which is the focus of his reflection on practice. In British Aerospace, Vince McGregor draws particular attention to the fact that the HRD function 'was part of the change team to address the soft skills in the change management process'.

A striking feature that appears common to most of the 'reflections on practice' is the explicit or implicit reference to the role of learning in the change management process and the need for a no-blame culture. Chris Newis, reflecting on his personal experiences in the not-for profit sector, strongly recommends the creation of 'no-failure/only learning' environments, which he considers to be 'the only insurance policy against failure' of change programmes. Nadine Green discusses the value of action learning, while Peter Grice, commenting on his experience as an external change agent and outside observer for the three man-made fibres manufacturing companies featured in his reflection on practice, provides ample evidence of the benefits of investing in learning as part of the change process and of using the concept of the 'learning organization' as a vehicle for change. The 'learner-centred approach using experiential learning for individuals' and 'the moving away from a negative blame culture to a more proactive and problem-owning culture' were considered to be the critical success factors. As he reports, the adopted change strategies led directly to 'organizational learning and subsequent improvements in business performance' in all three companies. However, he argues, 'the process must contain the reflective part of the [Kolb learning] cycle with as much emphasis being placed on it as on the "doing" aspects'.

Being reflective has been considered by many of the contributors to be a very important feature of their respective change agency practice. For example, Jane Keep talks about the need for the various stakeholders 'to have time to reflect and the space for things to make sense'. However, as Jaap Germans points out, the change agent needs 'a range of theoretical and conceptual frameworks at his/her fingertips in order to give managers [in particular] the language that enables them to talk about and reflect' upon the problems within the change situation, and to evaluate critically their own change agency practice.

Chris Newis extols the 'value of honest self-appraisal', though this might require 'assigning to oneself a mentor', which Jane Keep does regularly as part of her professional practice and which, in hindsight, Jaap Germans admits he should have done in EZH.

For me the most significant insight to be gained from the Part III reflections on practice is the emphasis and importance that many of the contributors have placed on the value of conducting internal research as part of their change agency practice. The notion of evidence-based practice, which according to the definition of Bury (1998) is 'the conscientious, explicit and judicious use of current best evidence in making decisions', is well established in the fields of medicine and healthcare. Hence it should not be surprising that Jane Keep, who was working in an NHS trust environment, adopted an 'evidence-based' approach to her change agency practice bearing in mind the existing organizational climate, which 'valued the importance, relevance and significance of good research'. She recognized the need for an in-depth investigation into the deep-seated issues that needed to surface. She then used the findings to form the basis of subsequent OCD interventions. Her long experience as a successful OCD consultant tells us that 'successful change is based upon developing a real understanding of the factors and issues that exist in the organization, and is about basing your approach on a clear understanding of the outcomes you want to achieve'.

A similar approach was adopted by Dick Shepherd, executive head of HMCE (Anglia Region) who commissioned in-depth, academically rigorous, ethnographic, longitudinal and empirical research into the culture of the organization. Its purpose was to provide him with a better understanding of the culture, and to help inform, shape and measure the cultural changes he wanted to bring about. In his own words, he found this research 'to be of enormous value in bringing about cultural change'. Other contributors also refer to the value of internal research.

Vince McGregor used research to reveal the 'soft' issues that needed to be addressed in the British Aerospace strategic change initiative, and Chris Luty also engaged with research to help inform his change agency practice in the context of the Training Suppliers Network in the West Midlands. Jane Hatton talks about the importance of 'research in establishing accurately the current situation and the in-depth issues that need to be addressed' and also of the 'value of research-based training'. As she observes, people often question and challenge the assertions of external trainers or developers. However, when your training interventions 'are not based on your outsider assumptions but on the picture painted by a group of employees [as revealed through your internal research], you can defend more effectively your training decisions. In her area of specialization she tells us that 'denial is common on training programmes, especially in the field of equal opportunities; but denial is made more difficult when faced with the findings of relevant, robust and rigorous internal research'.

This is what Dick Shepherd and Margaret Reidy discovered as part of their change agency experience in the Anglia region of HMCE as illustrated by the following citation from another source:

> Whereas in the past Anglia people had not always responded well to organizational change initia-tives involving external consultants who used external research (to influence change) or adapted off-the-shelf OD instruments that failed to ring true, they were willing to move forward with cultural change through the impact of HRD interventions based on the in-house research initiated by Dick Shepherd. This was because the research findings 'struck a chord', based as they were on the localized experiences of Anglia people expressed in their own words. The findings presented an accurate picture of the actual realities of management practice as experienced and observed within the organization, both the 'good' and the 'bad'. (Hamlin *et al.* 1998)

A research-informed approach was central to the non-adversarial organizational change strategy adopted by Peter Shields as HR director to 'overcome the robust opposition of the workforce' and to 'move through the total impasse' which risked the survival of his company's pharmaceutical manufacturing plant in Ireland. It should be noted that the key 'lesson' learned from his reflections on his company's success in breaking the impasse and subsequently moving quickly to the desired new state was that 'repeated real-time audits [internal research] and interventions are necessary to maintain the widest involvement, to debate emergent problems, to test perceptions of the progress being made, and to review commitment'.

'Further research' is what Prudence Clarke concludes 'should have taken place [for her] to gain a better understanding of the overt and covert governing values permeating through Plants 1 and 2' of the client organization where she was acting as an external OCD consultant for the managing director of the company. As she states, 'In retrospect I should have approached the assignment initially with more of an emphasis on addressing cultural change', which called for a research-based approach.

These examples of research-informed OCD programmes give recognition to the value in adopting an evidence-based approach and lend support to the calls made in Chapters 2, 3 and 5 for a closing of the research–practice gap in the field of organization and management.

DISCUSSION

As can be inferred from the above, and also from Chapters 2 and 5, the task of the change agent is far more complicated than is often supposed. This is due to the fact that modern-day organizations and people are far more complex than is often portrayed in much of the popular management literature. 'Solutions' to organizational change 'problems' are far more difficult to grasp than those offered by many 'experts' and 'gurus' on change management.

In arguing the case for evidence-based management in the field of healthcare, Axelsson (1998) observes that much of the management research of the past two decades has been 'aimed at understanding different aspects of organizational life with little or no ambition (as in the field of medicine) to draw any practical conclusions on the basis of their result'.

From his wide-ranging and historical study of the management research literature, he concludes that:

> Instead, most researchers point out that very few of their results can be generalized from one organization to another. It is difficult to escape a feeling of resignation in this research on organization. The field has been left wide open for consultants and different charlatans to influence managers with their fashionable models of organization and management. The scientific ground for all these models is weak, but they have been widely spread and applied in the management of many different organizations, also in healthcare management. Thus, after nearly a hundred years of research on organization and management, the practical knowledge in the field seems to be back almost on the same scientific level as when the research started. This is a sad development compared with the many other fields where research has been more cumulative and its results are continually enriching and improving practical knowledge.

Around this time, other commentators were also commenting on the lack of a sound and sufficient empirical base in the field of organization and management (see, for example, Hamlin and Stewart 1998), while some were extolling the desirability of evidence-based practice in the field of management (see Stewart 1998).

In light of all the foregoing it is suggested that change agents should become very selective in the theoretical approaches, models and concepts they use to inform and shape their decision-making and change agency practice. They should emulate the model of evidence-based medicine by encouraging and developing a strong research culture and questioning approach, and building into their organizational change and development programmes sufficient time for review and reflection. From such reflection new theoretical insights may be gained as to why particular aspects of managing change either succeed or fail. New ways of approaching the problems of change management may also emerge through the development of new 'theories' informed by the change agent's own professional practice.

To assure maximum effectiveness, research-informed and evidence-based practice ought to become an essential feature of the process of managing organizational change and development, because as Axelsson (1998) reports, 'when Evidence Based Medicine was [first] introduced [into the field of medicine] physicians found very soon that they could improve the quality of their decisions so much that it was well worth the time and effort spent'. In the same way, managers, trainers and developers should find that a research-informed approach leads to an improvement in the practice of management as illustrated by the various contributors to this book. They should be looking for support for their decisions in the empirical evidence from management research and their critical appraisals of it, rather than from the popular management literature. This means basing their decisions on the complex results of good management research rather than the simple 'quick fix' recommendations typical of some consultants and management gurus.

The practical importance of academically rigorous internal/in-company research cannot be over-estimated. Conducting internal research is a process which can help make change occur. It can, when conducted with appropriate rigour, lead to deep-seated fundamental issues concerning the effective functioning of the organization being brought to the surface and being confronted.

For example, such an issue is those aspects of managerial behaviour or management culture which impede or block organizational change and innovation. In-company research which is acknowledged as being rigorous, relevant, robust and ethical, can 'strike a chord' inside organizations, thereby enabling people to admit in public the ineffective as well as the effective features of organizational life, including their own performance or behavioural deficiencies and inadequacies. The particular reflection on practice in Chapter 7 contributed by Margaret Reidy, which briefly describes Dick Shepherd's commissioning and use of internal research as part of his change strategy in the Anglia Region of HM Customs & Excise, fully attests to this assertion (for more details of this internal research programme over time, see Hamlin and Reidy 1997; Hamlin *et al.* 1997, 1998, 1999.) Being able to think and act like an academic researcher gives the change agent, whether a manager, trainer or developer, the additional skills and disciplines required to be a true expert in their own field of change agency practice. This implies having the capability to obtain consistently the results required by the organization rather than getting lost in the processes of organizational change and development.

I advocate strongly that managers, trainers and developers should use sound research to inform and shape their practice as change agents, and to measure their own effectiveness in this role. As Heracleous and DeVoge (1998) claim, research-informed OD can help to 'provide crucial clarity to management on the strategic objectives (of organizational change), on the critical success factors linked with each objective and the actions required to achieve each CSF, which thereby eliminate unrelated and wasteful change initiatives, and lead to more effective and efficient change management'.

However, the question needs to be asked, 'How might this become a commonplace feature of OCD practice, particularly in the area of strategic organizational change?' This brings me to the proposition that OCD collaborations and partnerships between OCD scholars and OCD practitioners can lead to the production of robust and rigorous internal research capable of providing the empirical base necessary to ensure the efficiency and effectiveness of the OCD effort.

In Chapter 2, I referred to various calls for more research-informed approaches in HRD and OCD (see Jacobs and Vyakarnam 1994; Davies 1996; Hamlin and Davies 1996; Quirke 1995; Stewart 1996; Hamlin and Reidy 1996, 1997; Hamlin *et al.* 1997). Based on this experience and the evidence presented in the above reflections on practice, I believe active engagement with internal research by OCD practitioners, preferably in collaboration with OCD scholars to reinforce the academic rigour, is a vital requirement in this field. The key point is that collaborative OCD partnerships between business academics and practitioners, coupled with the support of a top manager, can lead to a strong empirical base of evidence that will enhance significantly the relevance and effectiveness of OCD practice.

As mentioned briefly in Chapter 2, Swanson (1997) in the USA has advocated that HRD professionals should 'advance their professional practice by becoming truly expert practitioners' through what he calls 'backyard research' because, as he claims, 'HRD void of operating principles, theories and good research to guide the HRD effort leads to poor professional practice and undermines the whole credibility of HRD'. Jacobs (1997) has argued that 'the HRD field depends on research being considered an essential counterpart to practice, not an optional activity when convenient nor an extravagance when financially possible', and strongly advocates HRD collaborations between organizations and universities.

However, these should be 'professional partnerships' in which the 'partners' recognize that HRD scholars and HRD practitioners enter such partnerships with their own respective goals, that although these may differ they will complement each other, and that maintaining the integrity of the goals for the common good is important. Thus, in 'HRD professional partnerships', there is a dual goal to advance the HRD field and improve the organization through the findings and application of rigorous internal research. Experience in the UK also suggests HRD professional partnerships can provide the means for closing or bridging the HRD research–practice gap, which, by so doing, increases the chances of improving the 'success rate' of strategic change initiatives (see Hamlin *et al.* 1999).

Building upon the ideas of Jacobs and several tentative ideas generated by a group of OD/HRD academics and practitioners attending the UK-based University Forum for HRD 1997 annual conference, I have devised a 'conceptual framework' to illustrate the connection between 'OCD professional partnerships' and the 'OCD research–practice gap' as shown in Figure 11.1.

The narrow outside 'boxes' to the left and right of the model are there to remind us that the joint research effort is not a 'service contract' but a 'collaborative partnership' in which all partners achieve what they want from the research.

The narrow outside boxes at the top and bottom of the model illustrate the connection between the respective 'stakeholders' who are jointly involved in the active processes of research and consultancy. These need to be relevant, rigorous, robust and ethical if they are to lead to outcomes of maximum value to the interested parties. The large box to the left of centre of the model endeavours to illustrate 'professional partnerships' in which OCD scholars from universities, in collaborative partnership with OCD practitioners, conduct internal organizationally related research to an academic standard. As evidence-based management becomes as firmly established and commonplace as evidence-based medicine, it is envisaged that more and more practitioners will use and/or engage themselves in empirical research as an 'everyday' component of their own professional practice as in the medical profession. Research-informed/evidence-based reflective practitioners in business are likely to become the norm rather than the exception, not least in the

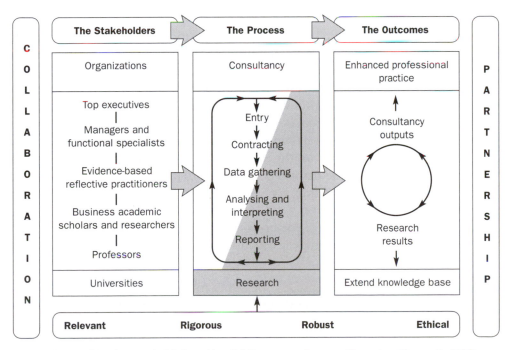

Figure 11.1 Closing or bridging the OCD research–practice gap through OCD professional partnerships

field of managing organizational change and development. The large box at the centre of the model draws attention to the cyclical nature of the processes for conducting internal OCD research and OCD consultancy. These are very similar, if not identical, and follow a 'common' sequence of stages from contracting to reporting. The outcomes from the research/consultancy activities as illustrated in the large box to the right of centre of the model are perceived to be mutually reinforcing. At the outset of a change initiative, 'best evidence' derived from empirical research as reported in the management literature is used to support decisions regarding the initial formulation of the OCD programme. This might mean building an 'internal research' component into the change strategy to obtain additional empirical evidence specifically relating to the particular contextual setting of the organization.

The findings of this internal 'academic' research resulting from the OCD professional partnership is then used to inform, shape and enhance the professional practice of the OCD practitioners, as well as provide research data that can be used to add to the field of knowledge. At the same time, and as a by-product of the OCD consultancy practice, certain outcomes in the form of observations and other data can be used for academic research studies, thereby helping to contribute to advancements in the field of knowledge and of professional OCD practice, but only if both the research and the consultancy practices are sufficiently relevant, robust, rigorous and ethical.

CONCLUSIONS

Several lessons of particular relevance to OCD practitioners and OCD scholars can be drawn from the practitioner 'reflections on practice' as analysed and discussed in this chapter. For example, they suggest that OCD programmes need to be people-focused, strategically led and research-informed if they are to be successful. However, as discussed in Chapter 2, this is unlikely to become commonplace if most trainers and developers remain operationally constrained at the margins of the organization, rather than at its centre. The question is, how might HR people in general become central players on the organizational stage? Certainly, this will not happen unless and until line managers overcome the five OCD 'failings' also discussed in Chapter 2, or until trainers and developers increase significantly their credibility in the eyes of managers.

Herein lies a major challenge for professors and academics in the OCD field, who could and should be making key contributions towards such developments by, for example:

1 Ensuring line managers who study for MBAs fully understand the significance of investing in appropriate HRD effort when managing change. There is a suspicion that insufficient emphasis is given to the 'soft' people issues of organizational change, and that academics from non-HR disciplines tend to undervalue the critical contribution of HRD and HRM professionals. Perhaps greater emphasis should also be placed on helping line managers recognize the

value of becoming reflective evidence-based practitioners who use research to inform their decision making, and who get involved in the research process through professional OCD partnerships.

2 Ensuring that HRD and HRM practitioners develop the necessary skills to operate with competence, confidence and credibility at strategic levels in organizations through the process of continuous professional education and development. This includes helping them develop expertise as internal consultants, change agents, strategic organizational facilitators, and also as research-informed/evidence-based reflective practitioners.

3 Considering doing more applied research focused on enhancing professional OCD practice as well as advancing the OCD field of knowledge.

4 Recognizing the potential of OCD professional partnerships for generating academically rigorous OCD research that is more relevant and of greater interest to managers, trainers and developers than some of the research currently published in the OCD literature.

Finally, more managers, trainers and developers might wish to consider the idea of forming OCD professional partnerships with OCD scholars as a means of enhancing their change agency performance through strategically led, research-informed practice. However, this might mean top managers first recognizing the need to develop in-depth understandings of what is actually going on deep inside their organizations, particularly the cultural factors that cause things either to happen or not to happen. As demonstrated in this chapter and elsewhere, a combination of ethnographic longitudinal research and empirical research can, as Dick Shepherd says, be 'of enormous value in bringing about culture change'. To this end, OCD professional partnerships can make an important contribution.

References

Axelsson, R. (1998), Towards an evidence based health care management. *International Journal of Health Planning and Management*, 13, 307–317.

Bury, T. (1998), Evidence-based healthcare explained. In Bury, T. and Mead, J. (eds), *Evidence-based Healthcare*. Oxford: Butterworth-Heinemann.

Bury, T. and Mead, J. (eds) (1998), *Evidence-based Healthcare*. Oxford: Butterworth-Heinemann.

Davies, G. (1996), Research methods and HRD. In Stewart, J. and McGoldrick, J. (eds), *Human Resource Development: Perspectives, Strategies and Practice*. London: Pitman Publishing.

Hamlin, R.G. and Davies, G. (1996), The trainer as change agent: issues for practice. In Stewart, J. and McGoldrick (eds), *Human Resource Development: Perspectives, Strategies and Practice*. London: Pitman Publishing.

Hamlin, R.G. and Reidy, M. (1996), Effecting changes in the management culture of an executive unit of HM Customs & Excise through visionary leadership and strategically led research-based OD interventions. The 1996 Annual Conference on the Strategic Direction of HRM. Nottingham: Trent University.

Hamlin, R.G. and Reidy, M. (1997), Effecting change in management culture. *Strategic Change Journal*, special edition, December.

Hamlin, R.G. and Stewart, J. (1998), In support of evidence-based human resource development practice. Lancaster–Leeds Collaborative Conference: Emergent Fields in Management-Connecting Learning and Critique. Leeds University.

Hamlin, R.G., Reidy, M. and Stewart, J. (1997), Changing the management culture in one part of the British civil service through visionary leadership and strategically led research-based OD interventions. *Journal of Applied Management Studies*, 6(2), 233–251.

Hamlin, R.G., Reidy, M. and Stewart, J. (1998) Bridging the HRD research-practice gap through professional partnerships: a case study. *Human Resource Development International Journal*, 1(3), 273–290.

Hamlin, R.G., Reidy, M. and Stewart, J. (1999), Effective management culture change through research-based management development; a British case study. *Management Development Forum*, Empire State College, State University of New York, 2(1).

Heracleous, L. and DeVoge, S. (1998), Bridging the gap of relevance: strategic management and organization development. *Long Range Planning*, 31(5), 742–754.

Herriot, P. (1998), *Trust and Transition*: *Managing the Employment Relationship*. Chichester: Wiley.

Jacobs, R.L. (1997), HRD partnerships for integrating HRD research and practice. In Swanson, R. and Holton III, E. (eds), *Human Resource Development Research Handbook*: *Linking Research & Practice*. San Francisco: Berrett-Koehler.

Jacobs, R. and Vyakarnam, S. (1994), The need for a more strategically led research-based approach in management development. BPS Occupational Psychology Conference, Birmingham, UK.

Quirke, W. (1995), *Communicating Change*. Maidenhead: McGraw-Hill.

Stewart, J. (1996), *Managing Change through Training and Development*, 2nd edn. Kogan Page.

Stewart, R. (1998), More art than science. *Health Service Journal*, 26 March.

Stewart, J. and Hamlin, R.G. (1990), The management of change: what contribution can training make? *Training and Development*, August, 11–13.

Swanson, R. (1997), HRD research: Don't go to work without it. In Swanson, R. and Holton III, E. (eds), *Human Resource Development Research Handbook*: *Linking Research and Practice*. San Francisco: Berrett-Hoehler, pp. 3–20.

Ulrich, D. (1997), *Human Resource Champions*: *The Next Agenda for Adding Value and Delivering Results*. Boston: Harvard Business School Press.

Change agency practice – the future

12

Jane Keep and Ken Ash

You will recall that in Chapter 1 we stated our reasons for writing this book, which encompassed some of our frustrations with the world of organization and change management. In particular, these were related to there being far too much literature written by gurus of management for academics or top-flight change agents, and not enough written by and for change practitioners; a lack of realism on the part of academic writers and in the world of change practitioners, narrowing the theory–practice gap; and the difficulty in accessing some of the literature as it seemed too far away from the day-to-day life and practice of change agents. This book has hopefully made an attempt to start to address these issues. This chapter pulls together the learning, insights and key messages gleaned by the offerings and insights of our contributors regarding 'change management' and their 'reflections on practice', and from our own reflections on the whole book.

Bob Hamlin has drawn together many of the key lessons and issues faced by change practitioners in Chapter 11. He links these with theory, and via this and the process and pathway we have trodden in writing this book he has also developed a useful model of reflective practice for change agents.

These messages are intentionally very practical as it is hoped that you, the reader, will be able to relate to and learn from these messages, so that in the future you will be able to bring about organizational change effectively and beneficially, and, from a practitioner's involvement and approach, reflectively.

Taking an overview, it seems that there are a number of key messages and themes regarding organizational change and development that can be grouped together under a number of key topic headings.

REALITY

- Complexity and paradox – organizational life, and indeed everyday life, is full of complexity, paradox, dichotomies and oxymorons. There is reassurance in the realization of this, but this also highlights the need for change agency to function effectively within it: living without simplicity, but designing and delivering change without complexity – this is a paradox in itself! Once past the starting post of this realization, there are a number of key skills and competencies to be learned and developed, including resilience, simplifying complexity, systems thinking, researching and piloting, taking out the jargon and replacing with plain English communication, critical analysis skills, and many more. To some extent these will be specific to your environment and are therefore for you to determine.

- Change is a naturally flowing phenomenon, and too many times we try to push or shove at the wrong points, at the wrong time or at the wrong place. Perhaps we don't look across the whole of the flow of things, perhaps we don't 'bide our time' or remain passive at the most difficult times just because we are used to acting at all times. There is constant pressure for change, and quick fixes, and quick outcomes. To the best of our experience and knowledge this is not the reality, unless you go for quick wins, and 'islands of stability' along the way which offer respite and signing off smaller aspects of larger change problems.

- When appropriate and especially for the survival of busy 'change agents', we need to stay in the 'here and now'. Sometimes when working in change, we should deal with the emotions and issues that are arising then and there, instead of worrying about the future and dwelling on the past, which can be debilitating. Making decisions completely in the here and now is a skill in itself. This also encompasses the need to keep a balanced perspective. Again resilience is called for, calmness, and wisdom.

- It has been cited that 'management' is ill-equipped to work outside 'systems'. Arguably, if you look at the world through a systems-thinking perspective, you can see that organizations and systems have a way of their own and sometimes it *is* the system's fault, and it *is* difficult to change organizations – this is a reality. Recognizing where this is the case is part of this – without 'blaming the system', but rather by working out what exactly you can do to influence or change, and where and when, realizing that some things just can't be changed.

- The rhetoric versus reality of change, we can see demonstrated in many of the case studies in this book, suggests a gap. This gap can be between the perspectives of client and consultant, of leaders and front-line staff, of policy and practice, of espoused and actual. Sometimes just working in that 'gap' is all the organization needs; finding where the gap is, its extent, and why it exists is also important. It seems more often than not to be related to behaviour versus spoken and written word. Dissonance or incongruity management would be key skills here.

UNDERSTANDING CHANGE

- Organizational politics is a key skill area. To use a theatrical metaphor, there is a difference between 'front-stage' working and 'back-stage' working. You need to decide whether you are a 'front-stage' worker or a 'back-stage' worker or whether you feel comfortable working in both worlds. Each area requires different skills and a different perspective. Some change projects require much back-stage prepa-ration prior to front-stage activity. Some projects such as conflict management or mentoring may require only back-stage working, and others such as running team development workshops require front-stage working.

- Knowing where the power of change lies is a fundamental 'tool' when dealing with change. Not only 'appointed' power but 'people power'. Without this knowledge, progress to change can be severely impeded. An example would be a 'hot fire burning' and not knowing exactly what to use to change its nature: water, or wind, or something else? Power and control are big-time players in organizational change and development. Often the role of the change agent suf-fers from the lack of either one or the other or both. Identifying your personal power and control for each project and its stakeholders puts reality into the anticipated outcomes and enables preparation to take place.

- Reflection is an integral part of the change process; without it you lose some-thing. It needs regular capturing, because the longer you leave it the more it changes. A good example is being a witness to a crime. You need to note things down then and there, otherwise the mind has a habit of distorting images before you know it! Process reviews help this, as do habitual critical questions such as how is this going, what have I learned, what could we do better, etc. Reflection is a legitimate part of change agency practice – and needs to be an explicit part of the change process. Reflection also helps players through some of the difficult parts of the change process.

- Change agents also have a responsibility to 'hold a mirror up' to the organization, or to the client. This is part of the process of facilitation and change. Some of our reflective case writers used this technique in their change approaches. While doing this, change agents may need help to hold a mirror up to themselves to reflect on their own practice – with the organization, or from an outsider, to gain balance, and grounding in what are sometimes difficult projects.

- There is a need to elevate human attributes such as intuition and feelings into the 'change' decision-making process, and in understanding and evaluating the outcomes. Although not scientifically based, this approach can be equally good in some circumstances. Because these abilities have come from what we have learned and reflected upon, we should feel able to 'listen' to them. When shared among those we are working with, 'testing out their efficacy', we can learn to use them appropriately.

- Piloting an approach to change helps recognizing the correct ingredients required. Some of our case studies used piloting linked to reflection as a way of evidence-based management of change. Piloting requires evidence and some form of evaluation. It also requires flexibility in the pathway and outcomes as well-evaluated pilots may change what was originally set up. Piloting in bite-sized chunks also enables a more rapid approach to ascertain how to continue and whether it is worth continuing without large-scale change that may need amending part way through.

■ For change to be 'liquid' the creation of a positive climate (or, as suggested by some of our writers, a 'blame-free' environment) needs to be brought about initially by top management, including role modelling. This includes ensuring that the reasons for, and the benefits of, the change are communicated and understood. This alone, however, will not be enough to eradicate resistance behaviours. Gaining top or senior management support was a common theme among our reflective case writers.

THEORY–PRACTICE GAP

■ Evaluation at the outset of any change project enables an understanding of the rhetoric–reality gap. Many of our case history writers wished they had spent more time up front in ascertaining, for example, the present culture as a 'front end' evaluation or analysis, in order to form a stronger foundation upon which to build the change programme and developments.

■ As stated above, recognition of the theory–practice gap is so important. The world of work is a mixture of both of these all the time. For example, if an organization's theory is that team-working would be a sound principle to adopt and operate, how is it that in practice it can quite easily fall into disrepute and end up being devalued? It is understanding that 'gap' that takes theory into practice, and practice makes further theory.

■ The relationships between academia and practitioners requires strengthening. Understanding one another's world is key to all issues of change. The more we can appreciate one another and work together the more we will close the theory–practice gap and enable continuous 'action learning/evidence-based' change management to take place effectively. One cannot exist without the other. Interdependencies should be recognized and built upon.

■ There needs to be more 'practitioner-type/evidence-based' literature compiled by practitioners, as they could now be seen and recognized as the new 'gurus' of 'change management'. The reality of organizational life, such as small organizations undertaking difficult issues, can be shown from a fully rounded, 360° perspective by taking all sides of the fence into consideration.

■ Research into practice requires the translation, and regular linkage between research and practice, practice and research, and, as we have seen from the many reflective cases, and Bob Hamlin's model in Chapter 11, it makes common and commercial sense.

■ The amount of evidence captured regarding 'change' and the increased media to share this information are not being fully utilized. Networks and sharing, both technologically and physically, i.e. face to face, require further development. Elusive journals or books are no longer the only useful medium. Change happens so quickly that there is not time to wait for publication prior to discussing and working with the changing environments and new innovative approaches and ideas.

- Thus more sharing of experiences is required in the change management community. We need to look for more informal and formal learning networks. These networks should cross industries including public, private and not-for-profit, and should cross regional boundaries. Multi-agency and cross-boundary working are common practice in change management and should also be so for change management practitioners. Each change is a learning opportunity.

- The shared experience of change management should be more readily available for small and medium-sized organizations as their needs and challenges could throw up relevant solutions and outcomes for us all to learn from. It is not just the large multinational organizations that undergo change.

- Development in context is also a key aspect. The contextual backdrop of practice is rich in its tapestry and gives a lot to those developing practice and theory. Context is not necessarily about description of the environment but analysis of the difference between environments.

- Practitioners need to find theories or journals that 'talk to them'. Don't try to get into or even follow a theory that is not understandable – not every journal or writer will appeal. But at least spend some time researching, and reading or discussing some aspects of change management or organization development. Not reading, and not keeping up to date, can put change management into disrepute as it should be working towards putting evidence and research into practice and can only do this by drawing from all resources.

MANAGEMENT

- Often management puts the responsibility for change onto the 'change' itself. This may be in the form of a new policy or new initiative, without taking personal responsibility for the effects they have themselves. It is often heard in an organization 'we have a new policy so the problem is solved'. We have a new objective, so we have sorted out this issue. This is only the beginning of change; the questions to ask are 'we have a new policy – so what is my part or role in this? What can I do to enable change?' This in itself can be seen as a 'gap' to be bridged by the practitioner.

- Management by its nature has a controlling aspect. In a 'change' situation it would do well to move into the mode of enabling and facilitating or 'letting go' of control sometimes. It also often forgets the human aspect of change. Content or process without a focus on the human or behavioural elements is potentially destructive. This is also cited in some of the case histories.

- Management must be given the skills and the environment to allow it to 'let go' of items such as information, authority, resources and accountability. In other words, management needs to empower its people and this often requires focused training. This is a dichotomy, as we require management commitment and support for change, but we require those in management to have a light touch in many change management scenarios rather than a heavy 'hands on'. Involving all those affected by the change in the change itself creates more learning, and potentially more sustainability of the change in the future.

CONCLUSIONS

There are many conclusions highlighted above. There are also many key threads running through these case histories. What strikes us in compiling this book is the realization of how much knowledge and expertise practitioners have at their disposal between them and individually. Thus there is a strong case for closer links between theorists and practitioners with regard to organizational development and change.

'Change practitioners' require a newer, clearer identification of their role, or at least the role they ought to play, if influential effective change is to be achieved. This is about the change practitioner being the change practitioner/theorist – the evidence-based or research-based practitioner. This role is far removed from that of being a 'training specialist', responsive only to immediate skill deficits. For the climate of the future it will be more appropriate to understand that developing people must be a dynamic and strategic activity, enabling people to cope with unstable environments. So often OCD people are seen as 'outsiders' or hands-on practitioners without any theoretical frameworks, and this perception does untold damage to progress, implementation and achievement in what otherwise should be straightforward partnership projects.

There is a lot to do for the professional development and professional profile of the change agent, and this requires moving on during the next decade. This includes fundamentally putting reflection into practice, in ways such as that outlined in Bob Hamlin's model.

For the future, it is interesting to note findings put forward by Buchanan *et al.* (1999) in their report on organizational development and change. This report states that in the past theories of change management have so far adopted the standpoint of the management consultants or researchers. It has been these communities that have put forward recipes for effective change or theories to explain the course and/or outcomes of change programmes. They go on to say that it may be instructive to consider the development of change management theory from the standpoint or perspective of the change agent, especially where this is coupled with a greater awareness of the 'lived-in' experience of the change agent's role. Another intriguing element of their findings is the 'poorly understood, poorly defined, poorly recognized, poorly supported and poorly rewarded position of the change agents'. They give two reasons for this: first, the change agent's role tends to be dispersed and de-centred, a 'hybrid' functional role rather than a specialist management position. Second, it is noted that change agency involves a number of potentially distinct, if often overlapping, roles, and it is difficult in most settings to identify 'the' change agent.

However, the perceived lack of clarification, recognition and support is clearly inconsistent with the acknowledged contribution of the change agency role to organizational effectiveness. This creates a paradox in the sense that on the one hand the change agent role is being viewed as critical to success, and yet on the other hand little is being done to develop competency in the role.

Something that is the case now and will continue to be so in the future is that finding business leaders able to initiate specific change projects is not very difficult, while getting theory to match practice is; as has finding support for the development of the practitioner's craft, and the practitioner's ability to successfully see change through in an evidence- and research-based or reflective manner. The time has come to move the profession on to a truly evidence- and theory-based practice. Pragmatism and critical reflective thinking are part of this.

Reference

Buchanan, D., Clayton, T. and Doyle, M. (1999), *Human Resource Management Journal*, 9(2), 33.

Epilogue

Bob Hamlin, Jane Keep and Ken Ash

Our book has attempted to demonstrate the practical value of being reflective as an organizational change agent and of applying theory and research as part of everyday change agency practice. This has been achieved mainly through reflections on change issues as experienced by practitioners, and the practical insights gained as to what helps and hinders in a wide range of settings.

The various chapters comprising Parts I and II of the book make reference to much of the change management literature, describe the role of change agents, offer a range of perspectives on the change practitioner role, and provide many overall reflections and conclusions. These are both theoretical and practical, and provide the 'bread', while the 'meat' in the sandwich is comprised of nuggets and gems gained from insights offered by the various contributors to Part III of the book – and their reflections on practice. They develop theory and give acknowledgement to helpful and unhelpful frameworks and practices.

This has all been part of the continuing development of the OCD field and the need for more support for the continuing development of the profession of change agency. (For example, through more applied research being focused on enhancing both professional OCD practice as well as advancing OCD in the field of knowledge.) Professional partnerships between practitioners and academics are part of this.

We have addressed these issues by pulling together a wealth of knowledge and experience from both academics and seasoned practitioners. By combining these we have offered and given pointers towards some of the 'best evidence' available to help you make decisions on the management of organizational change.

As editors we feel we have fulfilled our intentions in the purpose and outcome of the book. Undoubtedly our own knowledge and understanding has grown. We hope very much that your knowledge and understanding has grown too through the various insights the book provides on the theory and practice of OCD, particularly the insight concerning the use of research to enhance professional practice. The direct use of good research as 'best evidence' to inform practice has become a significant factor in determining success and superior performance in various fields, particularly in the medical and healthcare professions, where evidence-based practice is now common place (see Bury and Mead 1998).

Recently, there have been various calls in the management literature for evidence-based management. For example, Rosemary Stewart (1998), who is ranked among the foremost researchers and writers on management in Britain, argues that although evidence-based medicine draws on more clear-cut scientific research than that available for management, it is still desirable to practice evidence-based management. To her, it is an attitude of mind which:

- thinks in terms of evidence for decisions and about the nature of the evidence;
- asks questions such as: What is happening? How is it happening? Why is it happening? What are the consequences?
- is aware of the potential limitations of the different answers;
- is interested in research to try to find the answers or at least to reduce the ignorance.

She suggests managers need to build a questioning approach into their everyday management practice and encourage the creation of a research culture.

From a broader European perspective, Alexsson (1998) strongly promotes the development of an evidence-based approach to healthcare management in order to improve practice as well as to stimulate research on organization and management. This book fully supports his argument that evidence-based management means that managers should be looking for inspiration and support for their decisions in the empirical evidence from management research instead of being influenced by popular fashion or the simple recommendations of consultants and management gurus. This should lead to increasing demands from managers for organizational research in order to produce empirical evidence upon which practical management can be based. It may also lead to a more applied orientation in organizational research whereby management researchers associate themselves more with the practical problems of management inside different organizations, maintain closer contact with management practice, and communicate their findings in a more easily accessible and useful way.

Just as Bury and Mead (1998) have offered a definition of evidence-based practice in healthcare, including healthcare management, one of us (see Hamlin and Ash 2000; Hamlin 2000/2001) has recently presented the case for evidence-based OCD/HRD and offered the following definition, which is specific to OCD and HRD practice:

> Evidence-based OCD/HRD is the conscientious, explicit and judicious use of current best evidence in making decisions about the management of organizational change including the development of individuals, groups and organizations, integrating individual practitioner expertise with the best available external evidence derived from systematic research.

For evidence-based practice in healthcare, 'best evidence' is based on a combination of three dimensions: research, clinical experience, and patient preferences.

Similarly, Hamlin (2000/2001) suggests that best evidence for OCD/HRD should be derived from a combination of 'good-quality research', the 'consensus of recognised professional experts' and the 'systematic feedback of opinions of client managers/organisations'.

For many managers, trainers and developers, the application of evidence-based OCD/HRD will be an unrealizable goal, for reasons outside their control. However, this does not mean they cannot be research minded and build a 'research orientation' into their professional practice. As has been demonstrated by many of the contributors to this book, they can and many do adopt what Hamlin (*ibid.*) has termed a 'research-informed' approach to HRD practice. His suggested definition for research-informed HRD is as follows:

> **Research-Informed HRD is the conscientious and explicit use of research findings and the research process to inform, shape, measure and evaluate professional practice.**

With this definition in mind, the question that begs to be asked is this: is there a compelling need for either an evidence-based or research-informed approach to HRD practice and OCD practice?

We believe that the key outcomes emerging from this book point towards a resounding 'yes' to that question.

At the outset of our journey in putting together and editing this book it was our intention to demonstrate and prove the usefulness of reflection as a 'tool' for improving OCD practice, and to understand more about the reflective process. Reflecting on our efforts, we found it quite difficult to move the thinking and writing processes of OCD practitioners from being descriptive to reflective. Perhaps this was due to the fact that most change agents are necessarily action-oriented and are not overtly rewarded or encouraged by their own or client organizations to take a step back and to reflect. Our approach in overcoming this barrier to reflection was the development of the set of questions outlined at the beginning of Part III of the book. Just as our various contributors found this framework of questions a valuable tool for reflecting upon their practice in order to critically evaluate and learn from their experiences, we strongly urge you also to try out the framework.

In applying this framework ourselves as an aid to editing the book we have come increasingly to realize that reflection is an essential component of OCD practice, and to recognize the importance of the critical factors for success as summarized in Chapters 11 and 12. Equally, we have come to recognize the critical importance of evidence-based/research-informed practice, which is now firmly established in various fields, and its relevance to organizational change and development.

In conclusion, there are two key messages we would like you to take away from the book: first, that reflection is a legitimate part of change agency practice and needs to be an explicit part of the change process; and second, (but equally important) that HRD practice and OCD practice require if not an evidence-based approach then certainly a research-informed approach. While not suggesting that what we have written and advocated is wholly new, best or the only practice, we believe it heralds the beginning of another dawn – the dawn of the practitioner-led approach to theory building and research.

We would like very much to continue this pursuit and would ask you to reflect on it from your own perspectives and from those of others around you. Input and help from our readers will, we believe, be essential in this continual 'research', and in closing we would ask the following three questions:

- Do our or our contributors' experiences resonate with you?
- What sort of reflections on practice do you have which you could share?
- Would you like to make a contribution to this important area of OCD/HRD development?

If so, let us know by making contract with us via Bob Hamlin at the University of Wolverhampton.

References

Alexsson, R. (1998) Towards evidence based health-care management. *International Journal of Health Planning and Management* 13(4), 307–317.

Bury, T. and Mead, J. (1998) *Evidence-based Healthcare: A Practical Guide for Therapists*. Oxford: Butterworth-Heinemann.

Hamlin, R.G. (2000/2001) Towards evidence-based HRD. In Stewart, J. McGoldrick, J. and Watson, S. (eds), *Researching Human Resource Development: Philosophy, Processes and Practices* London: Routledge (forthcoming).

Hamlin, R.G. and Ash, K. (2000) Towards evidence-based organisational change and development. Paper presented at the NHS-P Research Into Practice Conference. Birmingham, England.

Stewart, R. (1998) More art than science. *Health Service Journal*, 26 March.

INDEX